EMPIRE

The Pioneer Legacy of an American Ranch Family

JEFFERSON GLASS

TWODOT®

ESSEX, CONNECTICUT
HELENA, MONTANA

A · TWODOT® · BOOK

An imprint of Globe Pequot, the trade division of
The Rowman & Littlefield Publishing Group, Inc.
4501 Forbes Blvd., Ste. 200
Lanham, MD 20706
www.rowman.com

Distributed by NATIONAL BOOK NETWORK

British Library Cataloguing in Publication Information available

Library of Congress Cataloging-in-Publication Data available

ISBN 978-1-4930-4836-6 (cloth : alk. paper)
ISBN 978-1-4930-4837-3 (electronic)
ISBN 978-1-4930-7341-2 (paper : alk. paper)

♾™ The paper used in this publication meets the minimum requirements of American National Standard for Information Sciences—Permanence of Paper for Printed Library Materials, ANSI/NISO Z39.48-1992.

Dedicated to
Susan Littlefield Haines.
Her passion for preserving history has brought this dream to life.

CONTENTS

Acknowledgments

It was October 24, 2016. I had an appointment southwest of Casper, Wyoming, to meet Susan Littlefield Haines, owner of the Gothberg Ranch. It was fourteen degrees out and overcast. The roads were dry. As I left Douglas, Wyoming, it was just beginning to spit snow. When I crossed the bridge at the La Prele Creek Road exit, my pickup gave that familiar little wiggle of slightly breaking traction, though the road surface still appeared dry. I had been traveling a little below the speed limit, but slowed a little more anyway. A couple of miles east of the Natrona County line, I slowly overtook a loaded crude oil truck climbing a gradual hill. The low clouds continued to emit an intermittent dusting of tiny flakes, but other than the sporadic miniature whirlwinds of snow escaping around the tires of the semi-truck, temperatures remained in the teens and the road still appeared dry. I gradually moved my pickup into the left-hand lane and eased past the truck just as we topped the hill. I continued at my same pace. As I neared the crest of the next hill, the rear wheels of my pickup broke traction for a second time. I lifted my foot from the accelerator and steered slightly to the right to correct the situation, but too little and too late. The rear of the pickup continued around as the vehicle careened into the median sideways. When the right front tire left the pavement sliding askew, it dug into the soft soil. Almost in slow motion, the pickup rolled onto its top. The downward incline gave it just enough momentum to continue over to its other side, then back upright onto its wheels. I was dazed. My seatbelt kept me behind the wheel, but also held me fast to my seat, whipping my torso across the center console. After an unwanted ambulance ride to the hospital, doctors revealed, as I suspected from the pain, two broken ribs. Thus ended my first day on the project.

Scroll back a few weeks. Susan Littlefield Haines is an avid genealo-gist and an active member of the Daughters of the American Revolu-tion (DAR). At a DAR meeting, she was discussing her ranch's history with another member. In the course of the conversation, Mrs. Haines remarked how she hoped to nominate the ranch for placement on the National Register of Historic Places. The other participant in the dis-cussion was my friend and former colleague at the Cadoma Foundation, Susan Bishop. She suggested that Mrs. Haines contact me, since I had assisted in the research that helped in her family's home being placed on the National Register.

A week after the accident, we finally met and henceforth began my research into Martin John Gothberg and the History of the Goth-berg Ranch. At the onset, Susan Littlefield Haines provided a two-inch binder, a three-inch binder, plus notebooks and folders of material that she had already collected in her research. It included a substantial amount of information on the genealogy of the Gothberg family including infor-mation received from Carol L. Spiers, a genealogist from Fredericksburg, Virginia, who gathered vital information and documents for Susan on the Gothberg family in New Jersey. There likewise were copies of photo-graphs that Susan had received from Martin J. Gothberg's descendants. In addition, she added supporting documentation of restorations that she and her husband, Roy Haines, had performed since acquiring the ranch. The material Susan provided created a wonderful foundation and starting point for my study.

It is with great appreciation that I thank Susan Littlefield Haines. Though I knew some of the history prior to commencing this assign-ment, she truly introduced me to Martin John Gothberg and his ranch. Throughout this mission, Susan has been thrilled with every new discov-ery and thoroughly supportive in every way to reach this end.

I also offer my thanks to Larry K. Brown, fellow author, researcher, historian, and important to this project, volunteer at the Wyoming State Archives. Early on, Larry uncovered essential information at the archives that paved the way for further studies. Of equal importance, Vince Crolla and his staff at the Casper College Western History Center have been extremely helpful locating numerous documents, articles, and photographs used in this volume.

To the reader it will become obvious that a vast amount of information in this text has been obtained from hundreds of newspapers. Many of these publications date back over 150 years. It is with great thanks that I subsequently recognize the following newspaper archives: the Wyoming State Library, Genealogy Bank, and Utah Digital Newspapers.

Certainly not the least of my credits belongs to my loving wife, Debbie. Beginning with nursing me back to health and chauffeuring me around after the accident, she has been there during the course of the entire project. Forever supporting me from proofreading portions of the text as it progressed to taking and editing photographs, she has been there. Ignoring my eccentricities and pointing me past bouts of distraction, she has helped keep me focused. She is incessantly organized, and I would be lost without her.

Though the rocky beginning may have seemed a premonition of a disaster-prone project, the result has proven otherwise.

—JEFFERSON GLASS

Introduction

THE ACCOUNT YOU ARE ABOUT TO READ IS NOT ONLY THE BIOGRAPHY OF a phenomenal entrepreneur, but a history of open range cattle ranches, cowboys, roundups, homesteaders, rustlers, sheepmen, and range wars. Yet, it does not end there. As the Second Industrial Revolution escalated in the late 1800s, so did the demand for petroleum products. What began with a need for beef to feed the hungry cities of the eastern United States fostered the want for wool to clothe them and graduated into the necessity of oil to warm the populous in winter and fuel the mechanized age at the beginning of the twentieth century. All were a part of Wyoming history and Martin J. Gothberg was in the midst of it.

A youth from New Jersey, Gothberg arrived in Wyoming as a teenager in 1880, and learned the livestock business from the back of a cowpony. He rode the open range for cattle barons on the northern plains and experienced a freedom unmatched by anything he had ever experienced before.

A collage of characters shaped the West of the nineteenth century. Large and powerful cattlemen, backed by eastern and European investors, flooded the prairie with herds often numbering fifty to eighty thousand head. They had visions of doubling or tripling their money quickly while their cattle grazed on the free grass of the open range. Others, like Gothberg, wisely invested in the future of the young frontier. Starting with a humble 160-acre homestead in 1885, he continued to expand and develop his modest beginnings into a sprawling cattle and sheep operation, growing into a ranch that spread over thousands of acres of land.

When cattle prices faltered in the 1890s, he added a band of sheep to his ranch. A cautious gambler, Martin Gothberg carefully weighed the risks and returns of this venture and continued to raise cattle; they had been his bread and butter for over a decade.

As towns sprang up around him, Gothberg merged into the mechanical age of the early 1900s, broadening his interests. Being one of the most prominent and honest citizens of central Wyoming, the quiet, often solemn German was both admired and respected by his peers. As his ranch gradually grew, so did other opportunities.

The influx of laborers in the growing petroleum industry created a shortage of housing in the fledgling town of Casper, Wyoming. This condition prompted Martin Gothberg and his friend Walt Blackmore to build the first modern apartment building in Casper. As he continued to prosper, his speculations grew in a variety of directions.

This unobtrusive man ventured into the oil business and excelled. He and a wide range of associates reaped the benefits from some of the most prestigious oil strikes of the era. As Gothberg's business affairs expanded, it required his frequent travel by train to Utah, Texas, and California, prompting him to purchase an airplane for use on many of his business trips. He established a Buick Automobile dealership. Dabbling in real estate, he and Blackmore subdivided a portion of Martin's ranch, establishing Gothmore Park, a retreat for prosperous residents in the foothills above Casper, Wyoming. When the stock market crashed, he worked through it. His investments were in companies whose daily operation he had a hand in, and though they suffered, they remained solvent.

Forever humble, Gothberg consistently understated his affluence and success throughout his life. As he grew older and his health began to decline, he and his wife began to spend their winters in southern California. Though reserved when discussing his personal accomplishments, Martin was very proud of his ranch and the experience he gained as a cowboy in his earliest days in Wyoming. Shortly before his death in 1947, he told friends that he had never achieved much wealth in his real estate or oil ventures, but owed his prosperity to his career in ranching.

Having only a modest education by today's standards, the combination of hard work, intelligence, honesty, and tenacity were the secret ingredients in Martin J. Gothberg's recipe for success. His career in the West spanned from the days of peering from horseback at an eagle soaring against a rich blue morning sky to that of an aircraft streaking across that sky at the speed of sound. He was a pioneer in every way.

CHAPTER 1

Becoming a Range Rider

1880–1884

Martin John Gothberg, circa 1891
COURTESY OF GEORGE EVANS AND LORETTA
BAYOUN, SUSAN LITTLEFIELD HAINES
COLLECTION

PIONEERING FROM THE DAYS OF horse and buggy to the age of fashionably dressed couples relaxed in style on silver-winged passenger airplanes, Martin Gothberg made his mark in central Wyoming. From cowboy to homesteader, rancher to oilman, the Gothberg legacy is extraordinary. Born February 29, 1864, in Lauenburg, Germany, Martin John Gothberg came to America with his parents as a toddler. The family lived in New York City for about four years before moving to Greenville, New Jersey, where he grew to young manhood and acquired a conventional education. There, his father operated a foundry, casting sculptures, architectural features, and chandeliers.[1]

At sixteen, Martin left his comfortable eastern home along with a friend. They headed west in search of adventure. He wanted to see the West, herds of buffalo, and wild Indians. First arriving in Chicago, they hired out on a railroad section gang that took them to Iowa. After reaching there, Gothberg and his travel companion went their separate ways. Fifty-five years later he remembered, "I worked for some time in the brick yards in Manning, Iowa, and for six weeks I was *bull cook* for a railroad gang. Then I went to work for the Union Pacific, which I followed into Ogallala, Nebraska."[2]

Gothberg first laid eyes on Cheyenne, Wyoming Territory in August 1880. The western city was a booming frontier metropolis of nearly 3,500 souls. The Dyer and Inter-Ocean Hotels were elite institutions that hosted an array of guests from cattlemen to United States presidents and dignitaries from around the world. The "Magic City of the Plains," as coined in an 1868 newspaper, became a popular stopover for passengers on the Union Pacific Railroad as well as an operational hub for a multitude of open range cattlemen and ranchers. The Cheyenne Club and Inter-Ocean Hotel were popular gathering places for "resident owners" of many of the largest syndicated ranches in the territory. These institutions sponsored horse races and other events to entertain visitors as well as residents of the city. Cheyenne was nothing like the urban areas of the East where Martin had grown up. The unadulterated wildness of the place was captivating and compelled him to remain, working odd jobs for a year.[3]

September 1881 found young Martin in Denver, Colorado, where he secured employment at Elitch's Restaurant. Working in the kitchen as a helper and cook kept him warm, dry, and well fed through the winter. As weather warmed, however, so did his longing for the outdoors that he had become accustomed to since leaving New Jersey. In April 1882, Martin headed back north to Wyoming Territory.[4]

Reaching Fort Laramie, he gained employment as a herder for the butcher at the post. Fort Laramie was the former trading post of Fort John. The United States Army purchased the installation from the American Fur Company in 1847. For the next several decades, it was the primary military installation to protect migrants for many miles along the Oregon, California, and Mormon Trails. There were several companies of soldiers at the post in that era and without modern refrigeration, a reliable supply of fresh meat was a necessity. Here Martin began to learn the skills of a cowboy on the open range. While working at Fort Laramie, Gothberg lived nearby in one of the abandoned houses at the old adobe trading post of Fort John.[5]

The term *cowboy* came into common use during the heyday of the large open range cattle ranches, the three decades following the Civil War. He rode, roped, branded, doctored, nursed, and herded cattle. A *cowpoke*, or *cowpuncher*, originally referred to a worker in a stockyard who poked or prodded cattle onto railcars bound for eastern packinghouses, or those who rode with the cattle on those railcars and kept them from laying down and becoming trampled while en route. For decades, those cowboys working on the range considered these other terms degrading. Many blame novels and Hollywood for making the titles synonymous. Those graduates from the school-of-hard-knocks in the trade might earn the distinction of *cowhand*. Rex Lewis called them *range riders*, perhaps a more accurate term than many others. Martin Gothberg chose this for his career. Young, virile, and intelligent, he quickly learned the skills of the profession and applied them proficiently.[6]

While living in Cheyenne the prior year, young Gothberg became familiar with many of the region's cattlemen. After working for a time for the post butcher, he went to work for a contractor that supplied beef to the post, Hiram B. "Hi" Kelly, at Chugwater, Wyoming. It is likely that young Martin knew who Kelly was prior to arriving in the area and perhaps had met him in Cheyenne previously. Hi Kelly had been ranching successfully in the vicinity for a number of years when Gothberg came to work for him. In 1879, Kelly expanded his operations by acquiring the Donald McPhee, the LC, the Hamilton, and the North Chug ranches near Chugwater, Wyoming. In addition, he added the Y Ranch at LaGrange and the D Ranch thirty miles north of Cheyenne. At the main ranch at Chugwater, Kelly also operated a store, post office, hotel, and a stage station on the Cheyenne-Deadwood Trail.[7]

For a short time, Gothberg moved on to Alexander Swan's operation near the confluence of Ricker and South Chugwater Creeks thirty miles southwest of Kelly's main ranch. After a stint with the Swan & Frank Livestock Company, the young cowboy rode north to Silas Doty's LL

Ranch. Headquartered on Richard Creek, he spent the winter of 1882 working for the "Double L." It was probably there that Martin Gothberg met Louis Spalding, who became his riding partner and confidant for the next several years. By the following spring, he had augmented his outfit to include both a saddle horse and pack horse, and he and Lou left Mr. Doty's employment in search of greener pastures and greater adventures.[8]

On the wide-open plains of Wyoming, when you left the company of your comrades at the ranch yard, the quiet could be deafening. Beyond the creaking of your saddle and the occasional call of a meadowlark or prairie dog, there often was little to hear. It was common in that era for cowboys to sing to themselves and each other for entertainment. They also sang at times to the cattle that they herded, which sometimes calmed a restless herd at night. Many of the songs were reincarnations of European folk songs with lyrics adapted to life on the open range. Most cowboys would revise the lyrics to fit their current situation. Consequently, many of the songs had dozens of verses and versions. As the boys embarked on their journey, their situation somewhat mirrored that of a popular tune of the time, "Leaving Cheyenne":

> I'm going to Montana, To throw the Hoolihan,
> My foot's in the stirrup, my rein in my hand,
> I ride an Old Paint, A leading old Dan,
> Old Paint's a good pony, he'll run when he can.
> Goodbye Old Paint, I'm leaving Cheyenne,
> Goodbye Old Paint, I'm a leaving Cheyenne,
> I'm leaving Cheyenne, I'm going to Montana,
> Goodbye Old Paint, I'm a leaving Cheyenne.
> They feed in the coulee, they water in the draw,
> Their tails are all matted, And their backs are all raw,
> We ride all day 'till the sun's going down,
> I'm gonna be glad to get out of this town.
> Goodbye Old Paint, I'm leaving Cheyenne,
> Goodbye Old Paint, I'm a leaving Cheyenne,
> I'm leaving Cheyenne, I'm going to Montana,
> Goodbye Old Paint, I'm a leaving Cheyenne.

From the LL Ranch the two boys rode north, probably following the Cheyenne-Deadwood Trail, first along Chugwater Creek, then the Laramie River bringing them to Fort Laramie. Having about fifty miles behind them, they turned west along the well-established Platte River Road. This composite of emigrational trails to Oregon, California, and Utah with its many spurs and cut-offs had already been traveled for over half a century by that time. Eighty miles farther west, their course passed the town of Fort Fetterman, a fledgling community struggling to survive at the abandoned military post of the same name. It was the last point of civilization they expected to see for quite some time. The United States Army abandoned Fort Fetterman in June 1882, and the buildings sold at auction on September 29 were to be removed by the buyers. The land remained a military reservation for six more years. The notorious One Mile Hog Ranch, a saloon and brothel that had operated for years just outside of the military reservation, remained in business. Some of the structures were eventually removed from the post, but many were re-inhabited on the site, as soon as the last guard detail was gone. Almost immediately a raucous and rowdy *Cowtown* was born. Author Owen Wister later used Fort Fetterman as a model for his fictitious city of Drybone in his 1907 novel, *Lin McLean.*[9]

A few months prior to Martin and Lou's arrival in the area, the roundup crew from the Searight brothers' Goose Egg Ranch was celebrating at Altman & Webel's store and saloon at the old fort in midafternoon. They had just concluded gathering a herd of cattle that George P. Searight sold to the CY Ranch. Richard P. "Dick" Elgin was the bookkeeper and paymaster for the Searights. This fine, upstanding man was enjoying a pleasant conversation with friends in the store. J. H. "Arkansas Red" Capps had been drinking heavily at the saloon. Capps roughly grabbed Elgin by the arm demanding money. Elgin smiled and calmly told Red that he had already drawn an advance on his wages and that he should go back to camp and get some rest. When Dick Elgin turned back to his conversation, Red Capps grabbed him again, and giving a violent shove, threatened to kill him if he did not give him more money. At that instant, Capps lost his balance. Stumbling and falling on the uneven floor, his pistol discharged and grazed his hip. Thinking Elgin had shot him, Capps drew his gun and shot Elgin in the chin, killing him instantly.[10]

Arkansas Red fled, grabbing the first horse he came to, which happened to be a spirited mount ridden by Dick Elgin. As Capps swung his leg over the saddle, the horse was already on a run and bucking. Normally the seasoned rider would not have faltered, but the drunken cowboy was soon in the dirt. Red reached the Platte River Bridge on foot and was attempting to procure another mount when cowboy Mike Regan approached on horseback. Red pulled his revolver and hollered at Regan to turn back, saying he had killed George Searight and others and would kill Regan, too. As Regan continued forward, Capps fired, hitting him in the groin.[11]

Newly appointed Albany County Deputy Sheriff Malcom Campbell was not present when the ruckus occurred, but Campbell's brother and another man quickly apprehended Red and brought him back to Fetterman. Deputy Campbell soon had the prisoner locked up in the former guardhouse and placed Tom Walker outside to safeguard Capps. At 11 p.m. a group of masked riders from the Goose Egg overwhelmed Walker and lynched Capps from a protruding log on the outside corner of the guardhouse. The inquest held the next day concluded that Capps met his death by parties unknown. The cowboys of the Goose Egg Ranch held a wake for Elgin and buried both him and Capps in the Fort Fetterman Cemetery. Elgin's grave was meticulously covered with a larger than normal pile of stones to ensure that his rest would not be disturbed by coyotes, wolves, or other scavengers. They buried Capps conversely to the rest of the residents of the cemetery with his feet facing west. "The boys thought that no murderer ought ever to see the sun rise."[12]

Many men in the West of this era were truly bad men, escaping from eastern authorities for a wide variety of crimes in their pasts. J. H. Capps acquired the nickname of "Arkansas Red" presumably because he was from Arkansas, yet he told his employers that he was from Texas and signed the register at the Inter-Ocean Hotel in March 1882 as a resident of St. Louis. Deputy Campbell remembered Capps as "a big, red-headed, happy boy—but whiskey always made him half crazy." Well-known and respected local frontiersman and rancher John Hunton was acquainted with both men. He recorded in his journal, "Dick Elgin killed at Fetterman yesterday. Murderer hung. Nice day."[13]

In a letter to his brother Gilbert A. Searight, George P. Searight outlined the events, concluding that Capps had been in their employ for most of a year and was a good hand. He also mentioned that Capps had kept perfectly sober all summer until this occasion. Dr. J. W. Dysart from Laramie City attended to Mike Regan's wound following the incident and reported to the *Cheyenne Daily Leader* that Capps was cut down and buried the second day after the lynching. They also reported, "Capps was a hard citizen, and declared, before he was lynched, that Elgin was not the first man he had 'downed.' Like Jack Watkins, who once made this country his headquarters, his revolver had no trigger—he pulling the hammer back with his thumb and letting it go."[14]

Riding fifty miles on up the Platte, the two young men stopped at various ranches along the way. It is likely that they paused at Joshua Stroud's ranch on Elkhorn Creek that was growing in reputation for his wife Sarah's culinary skills. She served meals to travelers and the local cowboys to supplement the family's income and seldom had an empty table. A few days after Martin's nineteenth birthday, the boys reached the CY Ranch on the afternoon of March 5, 1883. There were several cowboys there working for the outfit. Among them were Myrian "Mollie" Wolf and Thomas C. "Jerky Bill" Clayton. Jerky Bill, well known throughout the territory as an outstanding broncobuster, later became famous as the best rider in the history of Buffalo Bill's Wild West Show. William P. "Missou" Hines was foreman of the ranch. Hines welcomed the boys and invited them to stay the night, which they did.

The operation headquartered in what had been the adobe trading post at old Fort Casper. The men lived in the building that was about twenty by sixty feet long and divided into three rooms. All of the wooden structures from the old fort had burned down, but the crew had erected a large new log barn. Remnants of plaster clung to the interior walls of their humble abode as the warm, dry quarters soothed the young travelers.[15]

Judge Joseph Maull Carey and R. Davis Carey made up the Carey Brothers Company, owners of the CY Ranch, "C" and "Y" being the first and last letters of their last name. The Carey brothers began ranching on Horse Creek and Bear Creek north of Cheyenne, where they brought in twelve thousand head of longhorn cattle from Austin, Texas. Judge Carey was a Supreme Court Judge in Cheyenne from 1871 to 1876 and a founding member of both the Wyoming Stock Growers and the Cheyenne Club. The brothers expanded their operations northwest to the vicinity of old Fort Casper in 1877. That fall the *Cheyenne Daily Leader* noted, "The Carey brothers will start another herd of 3,000 cattle to their new range beyond the North Platte in a day or two." By 1883, the ranch reportedly ran between fifteen and twenty thousand head of cattle in the Platte River valley. In later years, that grew to forty thousand. The CY branded up to nine thousand calves and sold over one hundred thousand dollars in beef to eastern markets each year.[16]

The next morning, Gothberg and Spalding loaded their outfits on the packhorse, saddled their horses, and continued west. A few miles farther up the river, they came to the nearly completed two-story stone house of the Searight brothers' Goose Egg Ranch, located a short distance from the Platte River crossing later known as Bessemer Bend. There were fourteen men there; six were stonemasons and carpenters building the wellhouse and meat-house and finishing the main house. The stone for the structures was quarried from a bank on the river about a mile downstream, and the mortar burned from limestone mined on the west end of the mountain a few miles to the south. The lumber and other building materials were hauled overland over

Some of the early cowboys on the CY Ranch, from left to right (seated): Charlie Dasch and William "Missou" Hines; (standing) Tom Lamb and John Morton. Photograph taken circa 1880. Ironically, all four men became well-known sheepmen in the 1890s.
COURTESY OF THE NICOLAYSEN FAMILY COLLECTION

one hundred miles from the nearest station on the Union Pacific Railroad at Rock Creek, Wyoming.[17]

James Lane was the general manager of the ranch and hired both Gothberg and Spalding when they arrived. Mr. and Mrs. Lane and a hired woman lived in the large stone house. Mr. Lane immediately put Martin to work helping with the construction. Shortly after the boys' arrival, the workers completed the constructions and left for Cheyenne. The hired woman was Mrs. Renfro, who also had a son employed on the ranch. W. P. Rickerts was the range foreman and John E. Ambuster was a seasoned rider there. Joe and George Lajeunesse, grandsons of famed mountain man Charles "Seminoe" Lajeunesse, rode there also and both were top hands. "Their parents had a ranch on Muddy Creek, east of present day Casper."[18]

Texas cattleman Gilbert Alexander Searight, well established in southeast Wyoming Territory, expanded into the North Platte River valley in 1879. A native of Pennsylvania, Searight joined other pioneer cattle breeders introducing beefier shorthorn cattle into the region to crossbreed with the hardy longhorns brought from Texas. In January, Searight and his brothers purchased five thousand head of shorthorn cattle in Oregon. As he planned the expedition of driving the herd to Wyoming, he recruited the young but experienced cattleman Andy Kerr as his trail boss. Andy gathered a crew of twenty-seven of the best punchers in the territory. They boarded a westbound train for the first leg of their journey to northeastern Oregon on March 4, 1879.[19]

By the time Andy Kerr's crew arrived in Oregon, Searight had increased the trail herd to fifteen thousand head of cattle. While the boys were driving their cattle to Wyoming, Jim Lane was heading up the roundup crew back home on Chugwater and Pole Creeks. The roundup crew loaded fifty-one stock cars at Pine Bluffs with Searight brothers' cattle for eastern markets before heading north with the best brood cows of the Chugwater herd. In the meantime, Gilbert Searight was canvasing Montana and Idaho where he purchased an additional fourteen thousand head of cattle, all delivered to the new Goose Egg Ranch on the North Platte. In a few short months, Gilbert and his brothers had tripled the size of their Wyoming operations. The *Cheyenne Daily Leader* noted,

The Goose Egg Ranch house circa 1900. The well-house and meat-house that were still being completed when Martin and Lou arrived there in 1883 are the two smaller stone buildings pictured to the right. Pictured from the northeast, the home had been vacant for some time when this photograph was taken.
FRANCES SEELY WEBB COLLECTION, CASPER COLLEGE WESTERN HISTORY CENTER

Residents of Bessemer, Wyoming, at the limestone kiln in 1888. Mortar made here was used to construct the Goose Egg Ranch house and other buildings in the vicinity.
COURTESY OF THE BLACKMORE COLLECTION, CASPER COLLEGE WESTERN HISTORY CENTER

"G. A. Searight is apparently trying to break up our grocery houses, judging by the amount of stores he is sending out to his ranches."[20]

Shortly after his arrival at the Goose Egg Ranch, Martin Gothberg helped build barbed wire fences around several hundred acres of natural hay meadows along Poison Spider Creek to keep the range cattle from consuming their planned winter feed. Completing this task, he constructed a three-rail fence with gates around the yard of the main house. He mortised the two lower rails of the fence into the posts and nailed the upper rail into the top of each post, then hewed pickets from pine poles for the gate into the yard.[21]

It was not long before Martin and Lou received their assignment to a new adventure. Each spring the Wyoming Stock Growers Association met at Cheyenne to organize the annual general roundup. Since the ranches were not fenced, the cattle were free to roam wherever they pleased in search of the best grass to graze on and water to drink. When left to their own devices, livestock might drift over one hundred miles during the fall and winter. Each spring the ranchers sent crews to round up the cattle and separate those that had roamed from their home range onto adjoining ranges. Districts were laid out and a foreman appointed for each. Most of Wyoming's newspapers published this information along with start dates for every roundup. The Goose Egg Ranch sent out crews to three of the twenty-two districts established in 1883 not counting the crews sent from other ranches operated by the Searight brothers. The two young men joined the crew led by Bill Crockston early that May. Along with six others, they threw their gear into the roundup wagon that was their mobile headquarters for the next several weeks. The eight men each needed ten horses. They rode from daylight to dark bringing two horses each day to near exhaustion while allowing the balance of the remuda to rest awaiting their next turn out. Crockston's crew met up with crews of a half dozen other ranches northeast of Fort Fetterman, each with a roundup wagon and driving along its own herd of horses. They commenced gathering all of the cattle north of the North Platte River from that point east to the Nebraska state line, including the tributaries: Shawnee Creek, Broom Creek, Rawhide Creek, and north to Hat Creek.[22]

> *"This was quite a sight," Mr. Gothberg recalled. "It looked like an army moving when going from one camp to another, with all the different herds of cattle and horses moving to Hat Creek to make camp for the night. We turned back when the main roundup reached the Nebraska state line, then we trailed the cattle back to the home range, which was north of the Platte river to the Salt Creek country, and west to the Rattlesnake range.*
>
> *"The Hat creek Post office was on the main freight road from Cheyenne, Chugwater, Ft. Laramie to the Black Hills in South Dakota. This round-up district is where we met with another general-round-up working down from the northeast of the state and consisting of about 10 different cattle companies. This made 18 different outfits, with over 200 riders when they pulled into camp on the day set for them to meet."[23]*

Each crew of a roundup district had their own remuda of horses that could number up to 150 head. They also herded the cattle thus far recovered that had strayed from their employer's range.

On cold frosty mornings, the green-broke ponies in the remuda would often do some serious bucking in protest of the work they suspected was coming their way. This might test the mettle of a tired and sore cowboy before he could clear the sleep from his eyes. Most likely, however, the puncher would ride as though his life depended on it. If he lost his seat from the saddle, he would surely suffer jeers and hoo-raws from his peers for many days to come, a far more serious injury to the rider's pride than any bronc would give him if he hit the dirt.

Each morning the crews would head out from camp and gather all of the cattle in an area assigned to them by the roundup foreman. Depending on the number of crews working, they might bring in five thousand head before noon. Each crew brought in four to eight hundred head, kept separate from the other bunches. The crews from each of the ranches then cut out their own cattle from the different groups gathered that morning.

They branded and castrated the calves needing it, then turned them in with their own growing herds.

Within a few days, the two roundup divisions that camped at Hat Creek split up. A group of several wagons, including Gothberg and the wagon of Bill Crockston's crew, went west and joined the two other Goose Egg Ranch roundup crews working to the head of Salt Creek and the south fork of Powder River. Crews from the other outfits dropped out as their roundups reached areas void of their cattle. They would sometimes send one man to continue with the crew from another ranch. He would gather any remaining stray cattle belonging to them they might find later and bring them back to their home range.

While the roundup crews gathered strays, the balance of the Goose Egg outfit stayed on their home range branding calves. The cattle of the Goose Egg grazed on some 1,500 square miles of public land from the Bridger Trail on the west, South Fork of Powder River on the north, Cole Creek on the east, and the Platte River to the south. To Martin Gothberg's recollection, they ran about thirty-five thousand head of cattle on the range and branded about eight thousand calves each year.[24]

In July and August, the boys of the Goose Egg Ranch began gathering beef steers for market. They collected mature steers from across their ranges and began moving them toward the North Platte River near Deer Creek. In years prior to the Fremont, Elkhorn & Missouri Valley Railroad's arrival to Douglas, Wyoming, the nearest shipping point for cattle was on the Union Pacific Railroad at Rock Creek west of Laramie, Wyoming. Once they brought the cattle together at Deer Creek, they made the 120-mile drive through Boxelder Canyon and over the mountains to the stockyards at Rock Creek and sent them by rail to markets in Omaha and Chicago. The Searight brothers normally made two drives of about 3,500 head each season, one in August and one in October.[25]

After shipping cattle in the fall, the ranch cut the crew down to eight men for the winter. They sent two men to a line operation northeast of what later became the Salt Creek oil fields about sixty miles away while the rest stayed at the home ranch until the following spring.[26]

During the winter, Gothberg built a small foundry and blacksmith's shop for the ranch. His experience in his father's foundry made him a knowledgeable metallurgist. While not riding the range, he worked as blacksmith and wagon-wright building and repairing wagons and wheels and most anything else that the ranch might need.[27]

It was common to encounter bands of Indians while riding the vast prairie. Hunting parties could usually leave their reservations periodically on passes to search for wild game to supplement the commodities provided by the government. Even though these hunting parties were not normally aggressive, a lone man might get a bit anxious if he happened on a group unexpectedly. After all, Custer's demise on the Little Big Horn River was less than a decade past. Mr. Gothberg recollected many years later meeting a large band of Indians while riding to Fort Fetterman to get the mail for the ranch.

> *"I saluted them and said, 'How John,' which was the custom," he recalled. "This meeting of an unexpected band of about 250 Indians and squaws, all equipped for traveling, dragging their poles and belongings on ponies, came as a sudden surprise. After I got through them and in the rolling sand hills again, I nudged my horse for a little more speed for a while, glancing back occasionally."[28]*

Chiefs Black Coal and Lone Bear brought their bands from the Shoshone Reservation each year. Chief Lone Bear and his band would visit the ranch to trade blankets for coffee and sugar. He would invite the boys at the ranch to visit his camp and trade horses. They camped on Red Creek at the west end of Casper Mountain while they hunted and tanned hides. These Indians were always well behaved and the riders from the Goose Egg would occasionally visit them at the camp there on a Sunday.

Years later Martin Gothberg reminisced, "Large herds of antelope roamed the range, running in herds from 200 to as many as 500 and 600 head in one bunch on the flats. . . . There were also large herds of elk and numerous deer in the mountains, and occasionally one would see a buffalo. Wolves were plentiful during the fall and winter. . . . The Indians came to this camp for several winters to hunt deer and elk."[29]

The camp consisted of a cluster of government issued canvas tents. The women would be outside their tents on their knees working deer hides into buckskin as the cowboys approached. These women were very adept at using a unique tool made from a piece of elk horn shaped like a seven. They lashed a piece of steel to it and used it like a hoe. Gothberg remembered trying it once. After cutting holes through and ruining a perfectly good hide he decided that he did not have the skill required to use the tool effectively.

Upon seeing the riders approach, the women would disappear into the tents and it would soon appear that men only occupied the camp. Chief Lone Bear always invited the visitors into his tent. They sat in the center among four or five Indians, cross-legged in a circle around a small fire and the smoke floated through a small vent in the roof. The chief would bring out a long pipe with a red pipestone bowl and wild currant bush stem. The pipe was loaded with a mixture of tobacco and willow bark, lit and passed around the circle. Each man ceremoniously took a long draw from the pipe when handed to him. Mr. Gothberg recalled, "The chief could speak fairly good English, but our conversations were not very interesting or exciting."[30]

When encountering a white man, many of the Indians would show their permit to leave the reservation asking the recipient to write that they were being good Indians on the back of the pass. Knowing that the Indian could not read what they wrote and always looking for a practical joke, many cowboys made great fun of writing any sort of derogatory comment. On one occasion, Gothberg recollected meeting a small band of Indians near the ranch. They showed him the permit and then asked him to read the reverse side.

Some cowpuncher had written on the back, "Look out for this highbinder . . . he will steal all he can carry away. If there is anything left he will make another trip after it."

This caused Gothberg to smile and the Indian said, "Heap good. Yes?"

Still smiling he replied, "Yes," but did not recall giving him a better recommendation.[31]

In 1884, the Searight brothers visited their ranches in Texas. In doing so, they discovered catastrophic errors made by the management in their absence. A series of poor real-estate investments made by those left in charge had severely crippled the financial stability of the company. Gilbert and Francis Searight immediately returned with their families to Austin to restore control of the Texas portion of the company. In March, Gilbert fell seriously ill while in New York on business. His daughter Sallie rushed to his aid from Pennsylvania where she was attending school. She managed to nurse him back from the brink of death and successfully brought him by train to their family home in Austin to recuperate.[32]

In June, George P. Searight arrived in Cheyenne from Pennsylvania to spend the summer overseeing the Goose Egg operation. In a drastic effort to rescue the business, the brothers began liquidating large numbers of cattle in Wyoming. Over the next few months, they kept Gothberg, Spalding, and the rest of the crew busy making multiple three-week trips across the mountains, trailing thousands of cattle to the railheads. In August, the Searights shipped thirty-two carloads of cattle from Rock Creek and sold an additional three carloads in Cheyenne a few weeks later. They drove another thirty-five carloads of beef to Rock Creek in October to make the trip by rail to eastern markets.[33]

It was the coming of the end of an era for the Searights in Wyoming. They were a dominating influence on the range in Wyoming for a decade. Now, even the efforts of all the men and the thousands of cattle sold were not enough to save the Searight brothers' Wyoming division. Scarcely a year before, the operation was so successful that the Wyoming & Montana Railroad Company had filed claim on a strip of land from Rawlins, Wyoming, to the Platte River valley in the center of the territory. They intended to build a spur into the heart of the growing cattle country, extending northward from the Union Pacific line, terminating near the flourishing Searight brothers' ranch on the North Platte River. Now the brothers began the process of liquidating the remainder of their Wyoming assets in order to avoid bankruptcy and keep their Texas division afloat.[34]

It was a time of upheaval for Martin Gothberg. For the past three years, he had been living a young man's dream, his dream. Now, it all seemed to be ending. He had found his niche at the Goose Egg Ranch. He enjoyed those men around him, who worked side by side with him. He respected these range riders and all they taught him. Through hard work and open eyes, he earned their respect in return. He enjoyed the freedom of working the range and quickly learned from his peers that hard work, loyalty, and dedication were admirable traits to attain and not taken lightly on the range.

Jim Lane had been the best of bosses. Lane had the capacity to identify the individual talents of each of his men and utilize those skills to the best advantage of the ranch. Consequently, every man had the opportunity to excel, resulting in a feeling of accomplishment not often experienced by the laborers Gothberg was familiar with in the East. The Searights, too, had been friendly when visiting and particularly appreciative of Martin's prowess in the metallurgic arts. It would be disappointing to leave such an admirable employer.[35]

With the handwriting on the wall, Jim Lane began preparing for the spring roundup in 1885. He knew that all of the men that worked for him now would be riding the grub line looking for work at other ranches by the next fall. He did his best to treat his crew honestly and sustain his own integrity during a very difficult time. Martin Gothberg and Louis Spalding had earned the respect of their peers and their employer over these past two years, and Mr. Lane understood that they were the kind of young men that the country needed and that they had the fortitude to see it grow and prosper. With this in mind, he encouraged them to begin their own ranch and file homestead claims. They chose adjoining plots of land nine miles west of the old Fort Casper and five miles east of the Goose Egg Ranch headquarters. They each staked out 160 acres on the meadows surrounding Dobbin Springs near the foot of Casper Mountain. He had journeyed through a lifetime of explorations these past five years, but Martin's greatest adventure was soon to begin.

CHAPTER 2

A New Era Dawns

1885–1892

WHEN JIM LANE TRAVELED BY BUCKBOARD TO CHEYENNE TO MEET with the Wyoming Stock Growers Association and plan the agenda for the spring roundups in 1885, he took Martin and Lou along so that they could visit the land office there and file for homestead patents on the land they had staked out for their ranch. For twenty-one-year-old Martin Gothberg, it was slightly more complicated. He was born in Germany and even though he had lived in America since infancy, he was still not a citizen. On April 4, 1885, Martin J. Gothberg signed a Declaration of Intention to become a Citizen of the United States in Laramie County, Wyoming Territory. The next day he filed his claim at the general land office on a 160-acre desert homestead.[1]

The two young men would not have much time to begin settling in on their own places anytime soon. As the spring roundups began, the Searight brothers began the arduous task of selling off the remainder of their vast herds of cattle in Wyoming and the two young men had their work cut out for them for the next several months. In May of 1885, the Searights sold four thousand cow and calf pairs to the North American Cattle Company on the Little Powder River and the Carey brothers at Fort Casper for a total of $160,000, $3.9 million in today's money. In July, they sold an additional two thousand pairs to the Carey brothers and one thousand more to the North American Cattle Company. They also sold another two thousand pairs to Gothberg's former employer Hiram Kelly and his partner Elias W. Whitcomb, who were then ranging a large herd on the Belle Fourche River in northern Wyoming.[2]

In August, they delivered eight hundred head of cattle to Hugh Jackson near Sundance, Wyoming, followed by thirty-four yearling white-faced bulls to Kent and Bissell on Black Thunder Creek in what was then Crook County the next month.[3]

The Searights' reign as one of the largest cattle operations in Wyoming ended in September 1885. They sold the balance of their Wyoming herd, some twenty-five to thirty thousand head of cattle, to the Carey brothers along with the striking two-story stone house that marked the headquarters of the Goose Egg Ranch for just shy of one million dollars, $24.4 million in today's money. This purchase increased the Carey brothers' herd to seventy-five thousand. James Lane passed through Cheyenne in November with his family on their way to a new home in Texas. He had tallied out and turned over to the purchasers several thousand head of cattle. Though more than half of the range had yet to be worked, Mr. Lane was confident that next year's roundup would complete the contract.[4]

The Goose Egg Ranch pictured from the northwest in 1928 with the North Platte River and Casper Mountain in the background
COURTESY OF THE MOKLER COLLECTION, CASPER COLLEGE WESTERN HISTORY CENTER

Concluding their employment with the Searight brothers in the fall of 1885, Gothberg and Spalding packed their gear and moved the short distance to Dobbin Springs. In addition to their horses and gear, they had purchased a wagon and other helpful tools and supplies during the liquidation of the Searights' ranch. Settling in near the springs, they rolled out their beds and picketed their horses. With visions of grandeur, they laid out plans for a ranch. They had 320 acres between them surrounded by thousands of acres of open range, most of a year's wages saved, and the energy of youth to make it all happen. The meadows had remnants of a corduroy road across the creek, an indication that the military had used the meadows to harvest hay, and a scattering of stumps suggested that either soldiers from the fort or emigrants following the Oregon Trail had harvested a fair number of trees, probably for firewood.[5]

Gothberg and Spalding set out immediately to establish suitable shelter from the soon approaching Wyoming winter. They skidded logs cut from Casper Mountain down CY Canyon and erected two modest ten-by-ten-foot log cabins a short distance apart on each of their respective properties. Due to the very limited amount of time available, the young men may have only constructed one cabin that first fall. They also needed to build some sort of protection from the bitter winter for their horses. This was probably a lean-to or a minimal windbreak that first year. They could have merely hobbled their horses and let them fend for themselves. Though there was little threat of theft by Indians during winter, this is unlikely since the hobbles would give the horses little chance of escape from hungry wolves, mountain lions, or bears. Consequently, they had to hurry to harvest what hay they could from the meadows to feed their horses through the snowstorms of the winter ahead. However hastily prepared, the men fared the first winter in relative comfort. Their menu consisted of bacon, beans, dried fruit, and coffee, heavily supplemented with a lot of wild game at every opportunity.[6]

While Martin and Lou were scrambling to secure food and shelter for winter, Jerky Bill Clayton was wrapping up nearly a year on the road exploiting his immense talents as a bronc-buster and trick-rider among all of the glory and the grandeur of Buffalo Bill's Wild West Show. The tour had kicked off just after Christmas 1884 in New Orleans. Starting in the south, they worked their way north as the weather warmed. In July, the show was in Boston. The *Boston Daily Advertiser* reported, "Tom Clayton attempted to ride the especially difficult horse aptly named Dynamite. In true western fashion, Dynamite tried everything he could to unseat Clayton, even turning somersaults, but Clayton finally subdued the bucking horse. The people of Boston especially enjoyed this feature of the exhibition." After hundreds of shows and countless miles, the performers gave it their all for the grand finale in St. Louis on October 11, 1885. Tired and weary, Jerky Bill could not begin to count the dozens of bucking broncos he had ridden. Soon after the show closed, he packed his gear and headed home across the Mississippi River to Madison, Illinois, where he rested while visiting his family.[7]

When Tom Clayton had recuperated from his tour with the Wild West Show and was idling at his family's home in Illinois, he entertained his family and friends and wooed the ladies of his boyhood with romantic tales of his adventures in the West and on the road. One young lady in particular was entranced by his cavalier stories and laughed at all of his jokes. They were soon in love, and Tom married Allie Young that November. As the weather warmed in the spring, the newlyweds began their journey toward Fort Fetterman. Jerky Bill shared stories with his bride of the remote community and was surprised to discover the new town of Douglas that had sprouted from the prairie in his absence. They continued west and filed a homestead claim on Boxelder Creek at the mouth of the canyon; for a long time Tom had in mind to live in the picturesque valley someday. Six miles northwest of their paradise, another new community called Glen Rock had sprung up around a coal deposit along Deer Creek. Investing much of the nest egg Tom had saved as a performer, they began a cattle and horse ranch.[8]

In the spring, Gothberg traveled to Rock Creek for supplies with a team of horses and wagon. He made the one-hundred-mile trip up Bates Creek and across Shirley Basin in excellent time. At Rock Creek, he picked up his supplies that arrived by rail from Laramie City and began the trek back home. He awoke the first morning of his return trip to a foot of fresh wet spring snow and a mire of mud beneath it. When he reached the Little Medicine Bow River near the thirty-two-mile crossing, the swollen stream appeared impossible to cross. Two men who followed the river from Medicine Bow looking for a place to cross were also there. The three decided to build a raft from some nearby corral posts. Some men from a local ranch who saw what they were doing also enlisted their aid. They spent several days building the raft and crossing their wagons. When they had succeeded, the ranchers tied the raft to the bank and the men continued on their murky way. When they reached Bates Creek, it too was flooded. Gothberg had now been on the road for two weeks, and there was nothing to do but wait for the waters to recede. Five days later, they crossed Bates Creek and Martin arrived home the next day.[9]

When Martin got back home, he went to work for Judge Carey who now had integrated the Searights' Goose Egg Ranch into the Carey Brothers Company. Jerky Bill was still in the East and Missou Hines ram-rodded Mollie Wolf and the rest of the boys on the vast range occupied by the CY and Goose Egg herds. Before long, those thousands of cattle purchased from the Searight brothers wore the CY brand. Martin worked for the Carey brothers intermittently for the next two years as he began building his own ranching operation. In August, the railroad arrived at Douglas, Wyoming. Residents largely abandoned the town of Fort Fetterman, which had been the meeting place and supply point in the area for two decades as the new tent city blossomed on the prairie. Goods now arrived directly by rail, saving the time and expense of freighting from Rock Creek. The birth of the new town cut the travel time for Martin Gothberg's supply runs in half. *Bill Barlow's Budget* moved to Douglas and reported in December, "'Missou' Hines, 'Billy' Jaycox, O. K. Garvey and A. Kennedy, all well-known cowmen, have been with us the past week." The cowhands all wanted to see what entertainment the new city had to offer.[10]

That same fall, Martin Gothberg and Lou Spalding purchased the beginnings of their first herd of cattle and drove them to the meadows at Dobbin Springs. Not long after, Lou was in Douglas: "Louis Spaulding, [*sic*] formerly of the Goose Egg, is building a ranch for himself near the old SE."[11]

— ⁓

In the face of daily life in the wilds of Wyoming, it was not uncommon for Martin to be awakened from a night's sleep by any number of disturbances. The same was not the usual for his siblings in New Jersey. Herman Gothberg raised all of his sons to be mature and responsible young men. By 1887, Martin's thirty-year-old brother Ernst Gothberg oversaw most of the day-to-day operations of the brass works in New Jersey. On the night of April 4, a passerby of the factory owned by the Gothberg family noticed people moving around inside. He ran to the police station, nearly across the street, and reported the situation. With no officers readily available, the sergeant, securing his pistol and nightstick, rushed to assess the situation. After wading through deep mud and water, he found a broken windowpane at the rear of the building, which assured him of a break-in. By then an officer was available and the sergeant sent him to rouse Ernst and bring him to the site. After letting the police into the facility, they discovered only the night watchman. The red-faced sergeant found it difficult to sufficiently apologize for the inconvenience to the young businessman, but Ernst was unoffended and sincerely thanked the men for their concern for his family's property.[12]

— ⁓

That summer of 1887, the Wyoming Improvement Company surveyed and platted the town of Bessemer across the North Platte River from the Goose Egg Ranch headquarters. Crossing the bend in the river became much safer on the new ferry that had gone into business nearby. It was capable of carrying a four-horse team and wagon in relative safety. A year later, a bridge replaced the ferry and further popularized the new town for transportation and commerce prompting the enthusiastic townspeople to call it the "Queen City of the West."[13]

On June 14, 1887, roundup number six poured onto the flat just north of Douglas. Headed by Missou Hines as foreman and Billy Jaycox his assistant, reps from all of the large outfits were accounted for. Certainly,

Martin Gothberg, Lou Spalding, and Mollie Wolf were among the riders in the foray. Martin and Lou still needed an outside income if they expected to grow a sustainable ranch. *Bill Barlow's Budget* reported, "About 150 cowboys were present, with the following outfits and their representatives: Missou Hines, foreman of the CY [Carey Brothers Ranch]; Wm. Jaycox, Hat6 [Carlisle Cattle Company]; Joe Hazen, 9H6 [Benjamin Weaver Company]; Bill Rogers, ObarO [Dumbell Ranch]; Sam Johnson, barll; Ben Morrison, FL; Charley Robertson, OW; Tom King, VR [Frank Wolcott's Deer Creek Ranch]; Pat Woods, 4J; Jim Drummond, 76; Bill Rector, Fiddleback [Fiddleback Ranch], and many others whose names we failed to get." More than likely, an escapee from the remuda of one of the roundup crews, a heavily branded sorrel horse, showed up at Jerky Bill's ranch a few days earlier. Clayton reported the stray to the Wyoming Stock Growers. When riders completed roundup number six in July, Missou immediately headed across to the south side of the North Platte River to complete roundup number five with J. C. Shaw.[14]

At the same time, the Fremont, Elkhorn & Missouri Valley Railroad crews were pushing west from Douglas to the little coal mining settlement of Glen Rock located at the crossing of Deer Creek on the thoroughfare commonly known as the Oregon Trail. After the railroad's arrival, they established a station near the Rock in the Glen just west of the community and soon the new town of Glenrock was established.[15]

~~~

The previous spring, Martin Gothberg became acquainted with Lou Spalding's sister, Adolphena. Their flirtations grew quickly to courting, followed by an engagement before Martin headed out to join the roundup. The months of hard physical exertion and nights sleeping in a bedroll with his saddle as a pillow did not weaken his heart. On October 21, 1887, Martin J. Gothberg and Adolphena Spalding were married at St. Thomas' Rectory in Rawlins, Wyoming Territory. Martin brought his new bride to Dobbin Springs and her new home in their tiny log cabin. After spending the winter in their cozy little bungalow, Martin went to work the spring roundup for a Mormon rancher at the mouth of Cherry Creek in the Big Horn Mountains. Lou Spalding was undoubtedly also working the roundup for any one of several big outfits in the region. Adolphena grew up in the West and was more than likely left to manage their small herd of cattle on her own. Mollie Wolf had gone home to Iowa the previous fall, but springtime found him back working the roundup for Missou and the CY Ranch. When Gothberg returned home after the roundup, he again took work with the Carey brothers at their nearby Goose Egg Ranch.[16]

In May 1888, Walt and Minnie Blackmore, most recently from Ogallala, Nebraska, arrived at Bessemer, Wyoming. Walt was a young pharmacist whose successful business in Ogallala had recently declined in a poor economy. On advice from a friend, an official of the Fremont, Elkhorn & Missouri Valley Railroad, the Blackmores reasoned to relocate to Bessemer. The railroad representative assured them that Bessemer had a bright future and would be the next terminus of the growing rail line, which the company predicted would one day span to the Pacific Ocean. They anticipated the hot springs, a short distance beyond, would develop into a resort destination and the burgeoning new community would grow exponentially. The Blackmores shared a railcar with another friend who also was relocating and packed their entire household, their furniture, and all of the stock and fixtures from their drugstore into the railcar and had the car sent to the "End of Rail," Glenrock, Wyoming.

Arriving ahead of their belongings, Walt and Minnie acquired an unsophisticated log building at the corner of the optimistically named intersection of Fifth Avenue and Broadway. When the freighter with his string team and wagons reached there with their effects, the Blackmores opened a drug and jewelry store. They also carried essentials for local ranchers and businessmen.

The Blackmores advertised:

Walt A. Blackmore
Dealer in
Drugs and Jewelry
Fine Toiletry Soap, Combs, Brushes,
Fancy Articles, etc.

Perfumery in Great Variety
Choice Wines, Liquors and Cigars
Prescriptions Carefully Compounded.
Bessemer, Wyoming

The arrival of the Blackmores to the area was a delight to the Gothbergs. Although Adolphena was wise to western ways and well adapted to life on the high plains, having access to feminine pleasantries and companionship only four miles away must have felt like a breath of fresh air. Minnie grew up on a Michigan farm and the ladies thoroughly enjoyed each other's company. For Martin, Walt must have felt like a kindred spirit. About the same age, they shared a similar degree of eastern education and that entrepreneurial drive to succeed. Unlike Judge Carey and some of the other easterners who frequented the region, Blackmore was more compatible to Gothberg, with similar ideas and goals. They were almost neighbors and the two couples became fast friends.[17]

Walt was not of the personality to sit around waiting for opportunity to come knocking at his door. Soon after their arrival in Bessemer, investors began drilling a new oil well nearby. Due to his profession involving medicines, the workers instantly tagged him with the nickname of "Doc" Blackmore. This initial exposure to the oil business gave Walt an instant attraction to oil exploration and drilling. The knowledge acquired at this early stage of his western experience led the way for many of Walt Blackmore's investments two decades later.

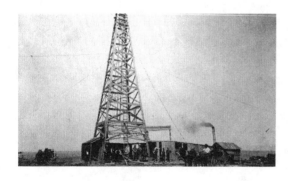

This photograph taken in 1888 near the town of Bessemer, Wyoming, pictures the first oil well in that vicinity. Pictured in the foreground is Walt "Doc" Blackmore driving a visitor to the site in a buggy pulled by a team of mules.
COURTESY OF THE BLACKMORE COLLECTION, CASPER COLLEGE WESTERN HISTORY CENTER

⌐~

While Martin was busy with work that summer at the Careys' ranch, just a few miles to the east the valley was alive with the bustle of people expecting the coming of the Fremont, Elkhorn & Missouri Valley Railroad. Crews were pushing westward from Glenrock, grading the bed and laying the shining new rails of track. Rumor spread that the railroad was planning to proceed west to an area somewhere between the Goose Egg Ranch and Stroud's Station. John Merritt was the first to arrive on horseback with a packhorse and provisions; he camped near the river between Stroud's and the old Fort Casper about the same time the Blackmores reached Bessemer. Charles W. Eads arrived with his wagon on June 7 with his son and daughter, finding Merritt camped near the river. Eads asked Merritt where the new town was as Merritt roasted a rabbit over his campfire on a stick. Merritt replied that he had been here for some time and that Eads was the first person he had seen. He reckoned that this was it and invited the family to join him. The Eadses shared in the meal adding food from their provisions and erected a tent nearby that constituted the first structure in the soon to come town that became Casper, Wyoming. John Johnson and Abe Nelson were next to arrive, followed by a host of others. Before long, dozens were clamoring about and erecting temporary buildings as all were waiting for the railroad to plat the new town.[18]

⌐~

That fall, the ambitious Martin Gothberg purchased more cattle as he and his wife further improved their homestead and developed the property. After a year in the tiny homestead cabin, the newlyweds also began construction of a much more substantial log home at their growing ranch during the winter. The new nine-hundred-square-foot T-shaped home sported higher ceilings and a stone foundation.[19]

Upon completion of the new home in January 1889, many of the Gothbergs' family and friends felt the occasion warranted a celebration. Mrs. Gothberg's mother and Minnie Blackmore began planning the event. Minnie Blackmore, an accomplished pianist who could play most any tune by ear, had a beautiful piano she had received for her tenth

This photograph, taken from the northwest, views Martin and Adolphena Gothberg in front of their new home.
COURTESY OF THE BLACKMORE COLLECTION, CASPER COLLEGE WESTERN HISTORY CENTER

Taken the same day, this photo also includes Martin and Adolphena. It views the home from the south, overlooking the North Platte River valley seen in the background.
COURTESY OF THE BLACKMORE COLLECTION, CASPER COLLEGE WESTERN HISTORY CENTER

birthday and played ever since. They commandeered a group of friends and a wagon and the piano soon graced the parlor in the Gothbergs' new home. A number of guests were invited and soon the day arrived for their gala celebration.

The *Casper Weekly Mail* reported it this way:

One of the most enjoyable events of the season took place at the Dobyn's Springs Ranch on the evening of the 22nd. Mesdames Spalding and Gothberg entertained many of their friends on the happy occasion. The parlor was nicely decorated with flowers and plants, and brilliantly lighted. Piano, violin and piccolo furnished music for the evening, rendered by Messrs. Wm. Matheson and Young, assisted by Mr. Dan Rhoads. The guests began to arrive at four o'clock, continuing to come until a late hour and were received by the hostess and her daughter. The happy guests enjoyed themselves dancing, singing and talking 'till about ten o'clock, when a sumptuous supper was served. The table looked lovely and the good things theron were relished by all, and after supper Mrs. Blackmore played many choice selections on the piano, Mr. White sang several entertaining comic songs, accompanied by Mrs. B. at the piano and Mr. Matheson the violin. Dancing was kept up until 8 o'clock, a.m., when breakfast was announced. All were interested in singing old plantation songs, and closed with several hymns. Among the number present were Mr. and Mrs. Johnson, Mr. and Mrs. Blackmore, Mr. and Mrs. Ford, and Mrs. Peterson from Bessemer. Miss Mamie McDonald, Mr. Frank Berg, Mr. and Mrs. Keith, Mr. Coleman, Miss Atkinson, Mr. and Mrs. Cheney, Messrs. Matheson, Dan. Rhoads, Young, Spalding, Gothberg, Joe Bowie, Prentice, Jake Krouse, John Brennan, White, Schneider and many others. The belles of the evening were Miss McDonald and Miss Keith.[20]

When discussing his mother's piano, R. B. Blackmore recalled:

Several newspaper articles have dealt with it, particularly in connection to country dances, with guests coming sometimes long distances on horseback or by buckboard, bringing box-lunches for midnight snacks,

*putting the younger children to sleep in any available places, danc-
ing until daylight in too-small ranch houses on rough, native lumber
floors; and the gaiety customary at such infrequent social events.*

*It is known as a "square grand" model, of solid rosewood, from
South America, hand carved and originally with a very fine finish to
show the brown wood with darker stripes. After its last trip by wagon
in 1902 it was given a coat of black paint.*[21]

Minnie Blackmore at her McCammon "Full Square Grand" Piano, age 85
PHOTOGRAPH TAKEN IN CASPER, WYOMING, BY **CASPER TRIBUNE-HERALD** PHOTOGRAPHER, JANU-
ARY 1951. COURTESY OF THE WYOMING PIONEER MEMORIAL MUSEUM, DOUGLAS, WYOMING.

The large ranchers in the territory did not look favorably on most home-steaders. Martin Gothberg seems to have been one of the rare exceptions to the rule and not scorned by his wealthier neighbors. Several factors prob-ably contributed to the positive relationship Gothberg had with the major-ity of the Wyoming Stock Growers Association membership. He had lived and worked for these ranchers for several years before he filed for his home-stead, and he was always an honest, hardworking, and reliable employee. Jim Lane, as manager of the Searight brothers, was highly respected among the cattlemen of the area and had himself recommended that Gothberg and Spalding file for their respective homesteads. Gothberg was also far better educated than the majority of the populous in the territory.

Jim Averell and Ella "Cattle Kate" Watson were probably actually married. Regardless, they had homesteads along the Sweetwater River near its confluence with the North Platte. There was much animosity between the pair and several large ranchers in the area, and on July 20, 1889, both were accused of cattle rustling, kidnapped from their home-steads, and eventually hanged by vigilantes later that day.

Having been in the saddle for thousands of miles while riding the range on behalf of several different employers for most of a decade, Martin had become acquainted with a large percentage of central Wyoming's sparse rural population. Jim Averell's road ranch had been in operation for a few years at the time, and Gothberg had probably taken advantage of an occa-sional home cooked meal there when he was in the vicinity, undoubtedly far more palatable fare than what he carried in his saddlebags. Well edu-cated in western ways by that time, the abrupt end of Averell's and Watson's lives must have still been a shock to the twenty-five-year-old easterner. He was only in his second year of marriage when the incident occurred. The permanence of the lynching left him contemplating his relationships with his neighbors and his own mortality.[22] He recalled in later years:

> *I knew well by sight both Jimmy Averell and Cattle Kate. Averell was about six foot tall; of medium complexion with light brown hair. Kate was about 5 feet 4 inches tall, stoutly built dark complexed; withal a very nice looking woman. I don't believe they ever stole any cattle.*[23]

Regardless of the turmoil created by cattle baron verses homesteader politics, Martin Gothberg had a successful year in 1889. His prosperity led to the purchase in 1890 of an additional 160 acres five miles southwest of Dobbin Springs, two miles south of the Goose Egg Ranch headquarters. This property bordered Goose Egg Spring and spanned the North Platte River at the mouth of Bessemer Narrows. It doubled Gothberg's acreage.[24]

A mile north of this land acquisition and about midway to the Goose Egg Ranch headquarters were the remnants of a stone cabin. Perched atop a rocky ridge overlooking the river and Bessemer Bend, the structure was only about nine feet square and not very tall. Built from the surrounding stone, it nearly blended completely into the hillside. Martin first discovered the structure while riding the range for the Searight brothers in April 1883, but made little notice of it at the time. Years later, when reading Charles Griffin Coutant's *History of Wyoming* published in 1899, Gothberg speculated that this might have been the cabin built by Robert Stuart and his party. When returning to St. Louis from Fort Astoria in the Oregon Territory in November 1812, these men constructed a temporary shelter in the vicinity. Subsequently, Martin found the old remains and photographed them. When discovered nearly twenty years earlier there were still remnants of a roof fashioned from scrub juniper branches.[25]

Martin Gothberg sent a copy of this photograph to historian Alfred J. Mokler in 1934 with the following note:

A. J. Mokler Casper Wyo   Nov 30-1934
this is the First House Built in Wyoming
By Robert Stuart and party in Nov 1812
on his Journey from Astoria Oregon-
to St. Louis, with Dispatches to-
John Jacob Astor, at New York-
is Located one mile
South of Goose Egg Ranch House
Look up C G Coutant's History
of Wyo to verify this
First saw House 1883
M. J. Gothberg
Casper Wyo[26]

Old stone cabin near Bessemer Bend, first discovered by Martin Gothberg in 1883. Martin later believed Robert Stuart had built it in 1812.
PHOTOGRAPH TAKEN BY MARTIN J. GOTHBERG, COURTESY OF THE BLACKMORE COLLECTION, CASPER COLLEGE WESTERN HISTORY CENTER.

While Martin planned the management of his growing ranch, his sister Teresa faced personal tragedy back home in New Jersey. On May 29, 1890, her husband, Theodore Frederick Koezly, died in Washington, DC. The cause of his death is unknown, as well as the reason for his presence in the capital city. He was only thirty-four years old. Teresa held a funeral service two days later at her parents' home in Jersey City. The sudden loss was devastating to Teresa and their five-year-old daughter, Doretta.[27]

A year later, Martin's younger sister Lillian traveled by train to vacation in California. Their parents threw a notable *bon voyage* party in her honor. Herman and Sophia held the celebration at their spacious home on Runyon Avenue in Greenville. Live piano and cornet music entertained Lillie and her two sisters as well as a dozen or so guests, mostly young gentlemen eager to impress the young ladies.[28]

The summer of 1891, Martin was again working for the Carey brothers and traveling to Muddy Creek, west of Glenrock, Wyoming, every few days. It is unknown what his duties were there, but the CY was suffering great losses to cattle rustlers in the vicinity at the time, and as a result, Gothberg had been working part time as an extra cowhand in the area. During his tenure there, he was stricken with diphtheria and unable to perform his duties. Gothberg was so ill, he had his wife write a letter to ranch manager Edward T. David for him.[29]

Casper, Natrona Co.
July 2nd 1891
Mr. E. T. David
Dear Sir.
I got a man to stay at Muddy in my place, and hoped to be back there this week, but have been taken sick with 'Dyphtheria,' and may not be able to go down before Monday or Tuesday. I was down Sunday & Wednesday of last week.
Please be kind enough to send by return mail wages up to the 28th. Hoping I may be able to be down soon. I remain yours respectfully.
Martin J. Gothberg
Per A. G.[30]

Two weeks later Martin had recovered enough from his illness to venture from his bed, a feat notable enough to draw comment in the newspaper. By this time, Gothberg's mother-in-law lived next door on her son Lou Spalding's homestead.[31]

On September 4, 1891, Martin J. Gothberg and William "Missou" Hines appeared before the United States Circuit Court Commissioner to make final proof in support of their respective homestead claims. Hines earned the patent on his 440 acres along Dry Muddy Creek, and Gothberg now legally owned his 160 acres at Dobbin Springs. By the time Gothberg filed for his proof, he had erected his log house and a log barn. He had also fenced the entire 160 acres and had forty acres of that cultivated in alfafa.[32] The joy of this success soon diminished, however, when Adolphena's health began to decline. Adolphena and her mother were in Casper on September 15, perhaps to see a doctor. It was about this time that she began to show symptoms of her weakening heart.[33]

On October 28, 1891, Martin and Adolphena Gothberg along with Walt and Minnie Blackmore, Marvin and Lona Bishop, and Bill and Elizabeth Evans attended the wedding of Peter C. Nicolaysen and Clementina Sarah Evans. The ceremony was the first function held in the newly constructed St. Mark's Episcopal Church in Casper. Built by Bill Evans, the father of the bride, Nicolaysen and Evans significantly financed the construction of the new church.[34]

In mid-November, Lou Spalding and his fiancée, Annie Heagney, were best man and bridesmaid for the wedding of their friends Frank Berg and Fannie Eads in Casper. Following the wedding, they boarded the train to Chadron, Nebraska, to visit members of Annie's family there. Martin and Adolphena knew that she could receive much better medical treatment in the East than was available in Casper, Wyoming. It appears that about this time, Martin preceded Adolphena to New Jersey. Encouraged by his family, they leased their property to Adolphena's brother and arranged for an extended stay at Martin's old home of New Jersey.[35]

Adolphena Gothberg witnessed her brother's marriage to Annie Heagney in Casper in early December. On Wednesday, December 9, they and her mother came to Casper in preparation for Adolphena's departure to join Martin in Jersey City. Adolphena came in from the ranch the following day, planning to catch the train east on Friday morning. Mrs. Spalding took a room at the Wentworth Hotel on Thursday, where she and Adolphena spent the night. The following morning, however, Adolphena was too ill with heart trouble to board the train. On Saturday, Adolphena had significantly recovered to begin her journey on the morning train. It seems quite likely that Adolphena's mother may have accompanied her on the journey to New Jersey.[36]

Upon their arrival in New Jersey, Martin soon took over as foreman of the family's foundry. In February, Martin and Adolphena took up residence at 42 Girard Avenue in Jersey City, New Jersey. It was leap year. On Monday, February 29, 1892, Martin could celebrate his twenty-eighth birthday on the actual anniversary date of his birth. Lou and Annie Spalding drove in from their ranch to Casper to celebrate at the Leap Year Ball held a few days earlier.[37]

CASPER, WYOMING, 1891, Second Street, Looking East from Center St. Gros Ventre and Sioux Indian wagons on their way to Montana, as nearly as the picture can be identified.
1 Webel Mercantile Co., general store - replaced by Rialto Theatre. 2 Denecke and Wright Bank - replaced by Rialto
3 Pete Heagney Shoe Shop and residence - replaced by Blackmore Building. 4 Clark Johnson, dray man, residence.
5 Jerry Dain's paint store. 6 Home built by J.J. Hurt, the only one in town with a bathroom.
7 Episcopal Church, moved to east Seventh St. and then to County Fair Grounds for a museum.
8 Barry Harmsmaker home. 9 Methodist Church

Nearby tribes of Native Americans still made annual hunts to secure meat to supplement food allowances through the winter on their reservations. As noted in previous passages, they had made these annual journeys since Martin Gothberg first arrived in the region. In this circa 1894 photograph, bands from the Gros Ventre and Sioux tribes pause with their wagons en route to Montana on Second Street in Casper, Wyoming. Coincidentally, the shoe shop belonging to Annie Heagney's father and their family home are included in the photograph. The Heagneys' business and residence is the third building from the left. In addition, St. Mark's Episcopal Church (constructed in 1891) and the Methodist Episcopal Church (constructed in 1893) are pictured to the right of center.
COURTESY OF THE BLACKMORE COLLECTION, CASPER COLLEGE WESTERN HISTORY CENTER

Shortly after Martin and Adolphena's arrival in New Jersey, the "girls" of the Goth-
berg family posed for this photograph. Perhaps taken around Christmas, 1891.
Back row (L–R): Minerva "Minnie" or "Mina" Gothberg, Teresa "Tank" (Gothberg)
Koezly, Wilhelmina "Minnie" or "Mena" (Lauer) Gothberg, and Lillian "Lily"
Gothberg. Front row (L–R): Sophia Gothberg, Doretta Koezly, Ellen "Nellie"
(Corcoran) Gothberg, and Adolphena (Spalding) Gothberg.
COURTESY OF GEORGE EVANS AND LORETTA BAYOUN, SUSAN LITTLEFIELD HAINES COLLECTION

There is little reference to the time the Gothbergs spent in New Jersey other than that Martin was bored with working in the foundry and
greatly missed their lifestyle in Wyoming. On October 8, 1892, Adolphena
S. Gothberg passed away in their home on Girard Avenue. Family lore
recalls that she passed away in childbirth. Her death certificate gives cause
of death as heart disease, which she had suffered from for about a year. Her
death may have been the result of a combination of the two. Whatever the
cause, Martin was devastated. He continued to work at the foundry, but
his heart was broken, and the tedium of factory work did little to relieve
his sadness. His older sister, herself a widow of only a year and a half, could

37

fully understand his sorrow but could do little to relieve his grief. Within a few months, Martin arranged to return to his ranch in Wyoming. On his return, he stopped for a few days' diversion at the World's Fair in Chicago, but it, too, did little to fill the emptiness he was experiencing.[38]

About the time that the railroad was nearing its final construction to Casper, Gothberg's old friend and former boss at the CY Ranch, Missou Hines, left his employment with the Carey brothers. Like Gothberg and Spalding, he began more earnestly improving his own ranching operation. By 1892, he had also taken on the position of livestock agent for the Fremont, Elkhorn & Missouri Valley Railroad. Among Hines's duties were the tasks of evaluating livestock conditions and contracting ranchers' shipments of cattle, sheep, and wool on his employer's railroad. After canvasing the country north of the Platte River, *Bill Barlow's Budget* reported in March 1892, "He [Missou] believes that 200,000 sheep will be sheared in and about Casper, Douglas and Lusk this season. Cattle have done remarkably well in that section this winter."[39]

In May 1892, Minnie Blackmore was two months pregnant with their first child. The couple made the trip from Bessemer into Casper both in celebration, and to ensure the newly expecting mother an opportunity to shop for items she might need before they could be ordered from Walt's commercial suppliers. Editors of the *Tribune* were seemingly unaware of the reason behind Blackmore's particularly cheerful mood when he stopped by their office: "Walt Blackmore, Bessemer's druggist, was in town last week and made this office a pleasant call."[40]

There were many changes in Martin Gothberg's life over the past seven years. He had grown from a simple range rider for one of the largest ranches in the Wyoming Territory to owning and operating a small ranch of his own. He fell in love, took a wife, and prospered on his beautiful homestead. He purchased additional land, added livestock, and built a larger, more comfortable home at their quaint ranch, a home where they could start a family. He and Adolphena found the best of friends in their almost neighbors, Walt and Minnie Blackmore.

When the future looked the brightest, his soulmate became ill. He returned to the East and a life that he disdained in hopes of finding sufficient medical care for her. It proved inadequate. When he lost Adolphena, Martin Gothberg's world collapsed around him. The drudgery of working in the confinement of the foundry and the claustrophobic crowds of people on the streets compounded his depression. The homeland of his boyhood was no longer his home. Home was his little ranch at Dobbin Springs, in his fledgling state of Wyoming. In Wyoming, he was not stifled, he was inspired. He could breathe, stretch his wings, and reach for the sky. In his absence, however, not all had been sublime. The tensions between cattlemen and homesteaders had continued to grow since the lynching of Watson and Averell. If suppressed anxieties fail to subside, they explode.

CHAPTER 3

Unrest on the Range, Wild West Shenanigans, and Weddings Both East and West

1892–1896

MAJOR FRANK WOLCOTT HAD BEEN A UNION OFFICER IN THE CIVIL War. In 1869, President Ulysses S. Grant appointed him "Receiver of Public Monies, US Land Office," in Cheyenne. Over the next few years, he held numerous appointments in Wyoming's territorial government. None lasted very long. Officials "removed" Wolcott from office as US marshal citing that he was "offensive to the entire populace." They reinstated him, however, when they discovered that his replacement was even more corrupt than he was. During this time, Wolcott founded the VR ranch on Deer Creek, in the heart of the then still active Fort Fetterman Hay Reservation. Though he had practically no cattle and no financial backing in 1871, he was one of the primary founders of the Wyoming Stock Grazers Association, which in 1879 became the Wyoming Stock Growers Association. In 1885, Dr. Amos W. Barber, both a close friend of Major Wolcott and the Philadelphia family physician of aspiring author Owen Wister, arranged a two-month visit at the VR for Wister while he recuperated from nearly a year of continuous suffering from intense headaches. Even Wister, who immensely enjoyed his first visit to Wyoming, noted Wolcott's hatred of the "Nesters," many of whom Wolcott himself had helped file their homestead claims during his tenure at the land office.[1]

For several years, members of the Wyoming Stock Growers had been experiencing substantial losses to suspected cattle rustlers. Only months before he and Adolphena departed for New Jersey, Martin Gothberg had been working east of Casper for the CY Ranch because of promiscuous rustlers butchering CY beef in the area. In 1892, while Gothberg was in New Jersey, the cattlemen renounced efforts by legal authorities to curb the problem. In addition to their regular employees, they imported a number of "regulators," gunmen from Texas, Idaho, Colorado, and elsewhere. Their mission was to enforce their employer's interpretation of the law. In all, they recruited an army of fifty-two men. Former Johnson County sheriff Frank Canton took charge of the Wyoming enforcers with Tom Smith commanding the other gunmen. Major Frank Wolcott, overseeing the entire operation, masterminded the plan and under his direction, they prepared to serve "justice" to over seventy accused rustlers on the association's "black list," in Natrona, Converse, and Johnson Counties, Wyoming. The extermination would begin in Johnson County. In the early hours of April 6, 1892, a secret train stopped east of Casper that unloaded the heavily armed entourage. At the same time, four wagons laden with provisions departed Casper, each pulled by four-horse teams. The well-mounted regulators met up with the wagons northwest of town a short time later and the cavalcade headed north.

One of their first stops was at the KC Ranch on the Middle Fork of Powder River. Shortly after daylight on April 9, they shot and killed Nick Ray from ambush when he left the cabin. Nate Champion held off the gunmen for several hours. Hearing the gunfire, a nearby rancher rode over to investigate. Observing the melee from afar, he rode as fast as he could to Buffalo, Wyoming, to notify Sheriff W. G. "Red" Angus of the affair. He arrived in Buffalo at seven o'clock that evening. At four o'clock that afternoon, the regulators set fire to the cabin and forced Nate out. As he ran from the cabin in his stockinged feet, they mowed him down in a hail of bullets, twenty-eight of which found their target.

As the invasion of the county progressed, the regulators rendezvoused at the headquarters of the TA Ranch, about midway between the KC Ranch and Buffalo. In a remarkably short time, small-scale ranchers, homesteaders, farmers, and a number of citizens of Buffalo, Wyoming, about forty in all, deputized and led by Sheriff Angus of Johnson County, headed to the TA Ranch to arrest the regulators. The gunmen had well-fortified their position at the ranch by the time the first of the posse arrived. The scene soon became a siege. Reinforcements arrived on behalf of Sheriff Angus and soon the regulators were facing a force of over two hundred men. As the standoff progressed, some of the more affluent cattlemen among the regulators managed to send a messenger past the posse with dispatches for the governor at Cheyenne and President Benjamin Harrison in Washington.

Conveniently for Wolcott, the recently appointed temporary governor of Wyoming was none other than his old friend Dr. Amos Barber. Governor Barber sent the National Guard to "protect the citizens of Buffalo, Wyoming," while Colonel Van Horn, commanding three troops of cavalry, left Fort McKinney west of Buffalo to arrest the regulators. On April 13, 1892, escaping the wrath of Sheriff Angus's posse, Major Wolcott surrendered his men to Colonel Van Horn on the condition that they would be protected from the sheriff and his posse. The colonel's men then escorted the regulators to Fort D. A. Russell in Cheyenne, where they were held under house arrest for a short time.

In the end, largely due to the immense political influence of the cattlemen, none of the regulators were held accountable for their actions and all were released. President Benjamin Harrison was so concerned over the volatility of the area that he was prepared to enforce martial law in the county if necessary. In anticipation of the inevitable, he stationed twelve troops of cavalry from two separate posts in Nebraska at a camp between Douglas and Casper, Wyoming, through the summer. Fortunately, the need for their interaction did not arise.[2]

From his many years riding the range for various employers and working many roundups, Martin Gothberg knew dozens of cowboys and range riders from across the state. Many of them, like Missou, Mollie, and Jerky Bill, he considered to be his friends, and some were merely casual acquaintances. He recalled knowing both Nick Ray and Nate Champion. He had ridden roundups with both men. Though he did not consider either of the men dangerous, he failed to comment on their honesty.[3]

Through all of the turmoil in the region, Martin Gothberg's old saddle-mates remained far from the limelight. Mollie Wolf spent much of this time in the Lander area, and Missou Hines was busy from Casper to Douglas to Lusk and Cheyenne securing clients for the railroad. Amidst Hines's constant travel involved in his position with the railroad, he contracted alkali poisoning and for a time it was feared he might lose his eyesight. By October, he had fully recovered.[4]

In the meantime, Jerky Bill's family was growing more rapidly than his ranch, with two toddlers underfoot. He had his own difficulties keeping his livestock in check and others off his hay meadows through the summer. He purchased a wagon in Douglas and enough barbwire to fence his 160 acres. To supplement the family income, Clayton contracted to travel to Denver and "engage in a cowboy's tournament, for sixteen days, $100 in it and all expenses paid."[5]

The two competing Wild West Shows performing at Denver's Athletic Park were not of the caliber of Cody's show, and consequently neither was able to make the profits they expected with their presentations. Both went broke and left many performers stranded without payment for their services. The Laramie *Boomerang* told the story: "The other Wild West show which exhibited at Athletic Park also broke up and some of the parties did not get their pay. All the Wyoming riders, however, secured their pay. . . . 'Jerky Bill,' after following the manager up with a gun, squeezed out $75 of the $100 due him."[6]

In 1890 Casper, Wyoming, had grown in population to 544. Natrona County, formed the same year and comprised primarily of what had been the northern half of Carbon County with Casper as the county seat, had a population of 1,094. That summer, newly arrived brick- and stonemason William T. Evans completed construction of Casper's first town hall on the west side of Center Street between First and Second Streets. Upon completion, Evans immediately began constructing Casper's first schoolhouse. Casper was growing exponentially. With businessmen and public officials nearly waiting in line to contract Evans's services, the Welshman soon moved his family to Casper from Nebraska, their residence of the previous seven years.[7]

By the time Martin Gothberg arrived back in Casper in 1893, William T. Evans had constructed several brick structures in the booming little town. With Gothberg's experience in the Iowa brickyard as a teenager, he recognized that the quality of clay from an area on his ranch was perfect for making brick. By 1894, he struck a deal with Evans and they established a clay mine on the Gothberg Ranch. In a short time, they were hauling the raw material by wagon to Evans's new brick kilns on the northern outskirts of Casper.[8]

One of the premier events of the summer of 1893 was the famous Chadron to Chicago Cowboy Horse Race, in which nine riders with two horses each left Chadron, Nebraska, on June 13, 1893, and followed a pre-determined course to Chicago, Illinois, concluding at the arena of Buffalo Bill's Wild West Show at the World's Fair. John Berry was the first to reach Buffalo Bill's tent on the morning of June 27. Of the eight riders who finished the race, none escaped the scrutiny of the judges and all claims became disputed. There were two purses originally offered to the winner. Buffalo Bill put forward five hundred dollars and the town of Chadron, Nebraska, presented one thousand dollars. After much deliberation by two sets of judges, they declared two different winners and decided to divide the purses among all of the finishers by two separate formulas. Doc Middleton, the reformed outlaw and horse-thief of considerable notoriety from western Nebraska, was the favorite to win until very near to the end. Unable to finish, Middleton brought his injured horse by rail to Chicago. Not implying any sort of victory, he walked the lame horse into the arena well after the leaders' arrival to demonstrate the honor he felt by participating in the contest.[9]

In April 1893, Wild West Show promoters contacted Jerky Bill to display his riding expertise at the World's Fair in Chicago. Other Wyoming riders performed there for Buffalo Bill and other venues. Though not listed on known programs for any of the shows, Tom Clayton may have been there and not highlighted on the flyers. In December, he responded to an invitation from the charismatic desperado Doc Middleton to meet in Chadron, Nebraska. Middleton was planning a Wild West Show of his own. He proposed various possibilities of performing a variety of exhibitions. Though the result would have truly been a *wild* extravaganza, it never materialized.[10]

◆〜〜

While Martin Gothberg was away in New Jersey, the Blackmores added a new member to their family. Their daughter, Marion Leone Blackmore, was born December 21, 1892, in Bessemer, Wyoming. As Casper continued to grow, and urged on by friends there, Walt Blackmore uprooted his drug and jewelry store and moved it to Casper in 1893. There, he enthusiastically joined his fellow businessmen promoting his new home city.[11]

◆〜〜

In June 1893, Martin's brother Ernst Gothberg caught employee Gustave Hermann taking a valuable picture frame from the factory. He pressed charges of larceny against Hermann. Two months later, rumors of poor business and possible financial difficulties for the company brought forth an article in the *Jersey Journal* stating that due to lack of business, the brass works was laying off its workers and possibly closing its doors. In response, Ernst contacted the *Jersey City News*, rival to the *Journal*, who sent a reporter to ascertain the facts. In a rebuttal, published the following day in the *News*, Ernst vehemently denied the *Journal* article. He told the *News* reporter that "no men had been taken off the force but that the old number, [about fifty] was still at work on three-quarter time." The reason for the cut back was not due to lack of business; the company had all the orders that they could handle. Their suppliers, however, had been shut down and sufficient metal could not be procured to work and fulfill the demands. The problem, though, would be ended the following week when the rolling mills were re-opened, and his workers would be back to full time.[12]

To further quench any question of the company's solvency among their employees, Ernst organized the first annual employee picnic and dance held two weeks later. Live music from a Bavarian band kept the festivities hopping, and tables filled with dishes of their favorite foods filled the stomachs of the mostly German workers, their wives and girl-friends, and dozens of children. The gala was held on Saturday afternoon at Gantner's Passaic Garden and lasted well into the evening. Most all of the Gothberg family attended and joined in celebrating with everyone. Perhaps to further smite their rival, the *Jersey City News* reported that the event "was a big success. . . . A large number of Greenville people attended. . . . Dancing was the principal feature."[13]

—◆—

Louis A. Spalding had filed for final proof on his homestead and received his patent on August 14, 1893. Whether unwilling to face his friend and former brother-in-law following his sister's death or some other unknown reason, by the time Martin arrived back in Wyoming, Lou, his wife, and mother had all pulled out and abandoned their ranch. Eventually landing in Montana, they first moved to Denver, Colorado.[14]

Martin Gothberg mourned the loss of his wife and comforted his loneliness and sorrow by working long days on improvements to his ranch. With the addition of Lou's homestead adjoining his own and the homestead he had purchased in 1890 at Goose Egg Spring, he had tripled the size of his original property. As his small herd of cattle gradually grew, Martin grazed them in winter on his own pastures and on nearby open rangeland in summer.

—◆—

Not long after the dust settled from their embarrassment in Johnson County, many of the larger cattlemen focused their antagonism on the sheepmen in the territory, also accusing them of butchering their cattle. John Brognard "J. B." Okie was a notable sheepman who had settled on Badwater Creek, seventy miles west of Casper, a decade earlier. Okie was a "self-made man" with large land holdings. His Big Horn Sheep Company rivaled in size that of many cattle barons of the open range era. He also expanded into freight-ing, road ranches, and the mercantile business. In the days when tensions between sheep and cattlemen were constantly strained, Okie built a sheep empire strong enough to stand up against the cattle barons.[15]

In April 1892, Bryant B. Brooks's V bar V brand was well known among Wyoming's cattlemen. Brooks, a future Wyoming governor, entered the sheep business in partnership with Casper saloon owner Robert White. That spring Brooks and White brought in three thousand sheep to Natrona County from Denver, Colorado. Later that year, White traveled to the East Coast, purchased a band of purebred Vermont Merinos, and shipped them to Brooks's ranch. Brooks was pleased with his new venture until he discovered that the Merinos were infected with scabies. Brooks dissolved the partnership, but through diligent treatment managed to defeat the disease without severe losses. Over the next few years, he became as firmly established in the sheep business as he had been in cattle ranching.[16]

By 1894, the cattlemen established what they called a "dead line," bordering many of their favorite ranges, the implication being that any sheepman that crossed these often unidentified, imaginary lines would be killed. The cattlemen, however, did not feel obligated to honor reciprocal respect when crossing these lines into the sheepmen's territory. Cattlemen and their employees often took positions above grazing herds of sheep and shot as many sheep with rifles as their supply of ammunition would allow. If a herder showed himself, or any resistance, they, too, were targeted. A favorite foray of the cowboys was to gather fifty or one hundred head of steers and stampede them through a grazing flock, resulting immediately in injury or death of dozens of sheep. The sheepmen were on constant alert for cattlemen that crossed the "dead line" into their territory. They painted their tarpaulins black to camouflage their camps at night and were on constant guard to defend their flocks and their outfits. Pioneer sheep rancher Marvin L. Bishop recalled many years later that "it was during that time that I truly learned to shoot!"[17]

By the end of the year 1893, Martin's sister Teresa Koezly was still suffering from the loss of her husband over two years earlier, both emotionally and financially. In September, she petitioned the Hudson County Orphans' Court requesting their aid in resolving the personal estate of her late husband. It was determined that the estate held insufficient assets to pay the debts of the late Mr. Koezly. In December, the court ordered all creditors of the estate to appear before January 26, 1894, to prove their claims, and concluded to sell the family's personal property and real estate in order to fulfill financial obligations. For all practical purposes, in today's terminology, the procedure resulted in personal bankruptcy.[18]

On New Year's Eve 1893, Herman and Sophia Gothberg hosted a large party at their home on Runyon Avenue. Over fifteen guests indulged in dancing, games, and other pastimes, "and everyone present succeeded in having an enjoyable time." Shortly before midnight, the guests adjourned to the dining room to enjoy a splendid supper. As the bells of nearby churches rang out the old year, all drank a toast to the new year and offered each other blessings to their futures. Mister Ariel Martin Childs of New York City was among the guests that evening. He had courted Martin Gothberg's younger sister Lillian for some time and had bid her adieu three years earlier at her farewell party when leaving for California. At twenty-four, Lillie may have been considered somewhat a spinster in that era, but on Valentine's Day the two were married in New York.[19]

In the spring of 1894, Lou Spalding's wife, Annie, spent a month staying with her father, Peter Heagney, and brother John F. Heagney. Pete Heagney ran a prosperous shoe, boot, and harness shop in Casper, and her brother was then the clerk of courts for Natrona County. It is unknown if she visited Martin Gothberg while in Casper, but it was quite likely. They had certainly been well acquainted prior to Martin and Adolphena's departure to New Jersey. Annie returned to her home in Denver, Colorado, in May.[20]

During this time, Walt and Minnie Blackmore happily received a visitor from Michigan when Walt's brother William C. Blackmore visited them in Casper. Bill Blackmore also studied to be a pharmacist and opened a store in Sutherland, Nebraska. Walt and Minnie's store sold everything from stationery to flypaper and fine cigars to bed-bug powder. Minnie taught classes in oil painting, displayed her creations in the store window, and sold the supplies needed for her students to create their own works of art.[21]

On June 13, 1894, Louis Kuhne, Herman Gothberg's old friend from Germany and his first employee in New York City, was violently killed in an industrial accident in the machine shop of Gothberg's factory. Kuhne had been operating a machine when the belt driving it dislodged from the shaft that powered a bank of machinery in the shop. He located a ladder and attempted to re-set the belt on the spinning shaft. After a couple of attempts, he opted to come down and disengage the shaft. When halfway down the ladder, he reconsidered. Not wishing to shut down an entire section of the shop, he resolved to try again. It was a fatal mistake. As he reached the top of the ladder, he momentarily slipped. In regaining his footing, the spinning belt ensnared a piece of his clothing, jerking him to the pulley and whirling him helplessly to death. Ernst immediately shut down the factory and sent everyone home for the day while the coroner removed Louis's body. The incident stunned Herman and terribly shook him. He and Louis considered each other the dearest of friends for many years. Louis had a daughter who lived somewhere in New York City, but authorities were unable to locate her, so with no family found, Herman Gothberg arranged the funeral services and buried his friend in the New York Bay Cemetery.[22]

In the spring of 1895, sheepshearers in central Wyoming united in efforts to receive better pay for the grueling service they performed for the industry. They went on strike. By the end of April, they reached an agreement with wool growers in the area. Among those shearing their sheep at the Casper pens were John B. Okie, five thousand head; then mayor of Casper, Pat Sullivan, thirteen thousand head; and Martin Gothberg's old friend William Hines, seventeen hundred head. By the end of May, it was announced that Hines would bring eighteen thousand head of sheep into the NH Ranch on the Middle Fork of Powder River. "It begins to look as though the Powder River country is destined to be one vast sheep pasture to the great disgust of the small cattlemen who are now running their stock on that range."[23]

Ten years earlier, Frank A. Sanders married Dora Brandt at Dale Creek near Laramie, Wyoming. He was in Glenrock exploring for a new place of residence for his wife and stepchildren in 1889, and soon, he had established a farm near the community of Freeland in Bates Hole ten miles south of Gothberg Ranch. Sanders was growing potatoes successfully and marketing them in Casper by the fall of 1891.[24]

It is almost certain that Martin and Adolphena Gothberg knew the Sanders family prior to their departure for New Jersey in 1891. Adolphena, especially, probably knew who the ladies of the Sanders family were, even though they may not have been friends. In an area so sparsely populated at the time, the women making up a very small percentage of that populace tended to keep track of each other, even if they lived miles apart. The Sanders ladies probably frequented Blackmore's Pharmacy in Bessemer and Adolphena may have met them there. At a minimum, they passed the Gothberg homestead whenever they ventured to Casper. In all likelihood, Martin also passed the Sanders place when tending to his cattle that grazed in the south end of Bates Hole.

Whatever the circumstances, Martin later became acquainted with Mary Enid Brandt, and after a time began courting the young red-haired girl on Bates Creek, who locals teasingly called "Carrot Top." On May 17, 1895, thirty-one-year-old Martin John Gothberg married eighteen-year-old Mary Enid Brandt. The wedding took place at the ranch of Edward L. McGraugh on Big Red Creek in Bates Park near Freeland, Wyoming. Mary Enid was the stepdaughter of Frank Sanders and daughter of Dora Brandt Sanders and Martin Luther Brandt.[25]

Mary Enid (Brandt) Gothberg, circa 1895
COURTESY OF GEORGE EVANS AND LORETTA BAYOUN, SUSAN LITTLEFIELD HAINES COLLECTION

On April 30, 1895, Martin's sister "Miss Minnie Gothberg, a popular Greenville young lady," at twenty-two years old, married Willis Edwin Lund at her parent's home. Her older sister Sophia was her bridesmaid and her young niece Doretta Koezly her maid of honor. A catered supper followed the ceremony, a precursor to guests showering the newlyweds with gifts of congratulations. They departed late that evening to Washington on a honeymoon.[26]

Ernst Gothberg was a prominent businessman and was well known for proudly wearing a large one-and-a-half-carat diamond stud high on his shirt. On July 2, 1895, Ernst took the ferry to New York City on business. When the full ferry approached the dock on the return that evening, everyone crowded to the bow. While the crew secured the boat to the pier, two men pressed against Gothberg. One of the men removed his hat and held it up near Gothberg's chin, causing Ernst to pull his head back to avoid receiving the hat in his face. While being jostled around, the second man unscrewed the diamond from Gothberg's shirt. At home, Ernst noticed the loss and then understood the cause of what had seemed merely a discourteous action by the man with the hat. The next morning, he filed charges against the two men and gave an accurate description of them to Jersey City Police Chief Murphy, but had little hope of recovering his stolen jewelry.[27]

Martin Gothberg's parents, Herman and Sophia, left New Jersey in July on an extended trip to the West. With Martin's second marriage to Mary Enid Brandt following the wedding of his younger sister by only a week, it was impossible for Herman and Sophia to attend. Herman's hard work and diligence had provided a comfortable life in America for his immigrant family. Now just past sixty, the couple could enjoy some of the fruits of their labors. Considering how easily Ernst had so recently been duped by two small-time thieves, Herman questioned entrusting the full control of the company to his eldest son in his absence. Sophia, on the other hand, was not about to miss the opportunity of their long-planned holiday. She reminded Herman that he had raised each of his sons to be worthy businessmen and finally convinced him to have faith in Ernst's abilities.

As weather warmed into the height of summer, they boarded the train west. They vacationed in Chicago and Denver before reaching Wyoming.

On their arrival, Martin and his new bride met them in Casper. After a pleasant meal in the best eatery the town had to offer, they took the nine-mile ride to Gothberg Ranch at a leisurely pace. Along the way, Martin pointed out dozens of novelties and landmarks in the distance, sharing tales of his experiences at each of them. Some of the stories Martin had told them before, but not with the exuberance he demonstrated now that he could actually show them the life and home he loved. Their first visit to Wyoming was both relaxing and invigorating as Herman and Sophia enjoyed the sights and operation of the ranch. Perhaps they did not relish the solitude that drew their son to the region, but now they were able to see it firsthand.[28]

At the time, the Gothbergs' home ranch was still a fledgling cow/calf operation, but Martin and Mary Enid worked hard to build an efficient ranching operation. Structures there consisted of the new log home that Martin built in 1889 and the bunkhouse, situated immediately south of the main house. The bunkhouse was formerly Martin's original homestead cabin. East of the bunkhouse was a thirty-by-thirty-foot log structure that served as a stable, tack room, carriage house, and blacksmith's shop. Farther south was a much larger barn, perhaps sixty by eighty feet, that was razed sometime after 1910. There was a network of corrals, necessary for keeping horses readily available and separating cattle for branding. There was a garden patch near the house to raise a few hearty varieties of vegetables, and some of the cottonwood trees that border the yard around the house today were probably saplings, recently transplanted from along the nearby river.[29]

For the first years of their marriage, the couple spent a large percentage of their time tending their cattle and working on improving their ranch. The Gothbergs' grandson Edwin K. Gothberg recalled a tale that the infamous cattle detective Tom Horn had visited his grandparents.

> *The family also remembers, today, that M. J. said that soon after they built their first cabin that Tom Horn came to the door. Nothing of the visit was remembered except that Mary Enid opened the door while M. J. stood back in a dark corner, ready for any emergency.*[30]

One of Tom Horn's most effective methods of encouraging homesteaders to toe the line was intimidation. It seems likely that he would have made his presence known to a then minor rancher such as Martin Gothberg. Edwin may have confused the time reference, however. Horn was working for the Swan Land and Cattle Company from the Two Bar Ranch at Bates Hole in August through September 1895. If Tom Horn called on the Gothbergs and Mary Enid answered the door, it was likely within this timeframe. Mollie Wolf may have had a similar call at the small ranch he was operating on Squaw Creek, just east of the Gothbergs' place. In 1895, he sold this ranch to J. W. Price for $350 and homesteaded a sheep ranch at the mouth of the Sweetwater River.[31]

Walter A. Blackmore sold his drugstore in Casper in 1894 to Pat Sullivan. He continued to work for Sullivan for a few months and announced his candidacy for the position of Natrona County clerk. He carried the Democratic Primary but lost to Republican Peter O'Malley in the general election by twenty-five votes. In 1895, Walt purchased the Hat-Six Ranch, southeast of Casper. Much diminished in scale by the time of the purchase, the Hat-Six had once been the center of the Carlisle Cattle Company's Wyoming operations. A decade earlier, the Carlisle brothers shipped sixty-four railcar loads of cattle to market for the year from Rock Creek, Wyoming. As beef prices began to drop, the Carlisle brothers began selling off outlying ranches. Their ranching business continued to dwindle, and by 1900 they had sold off their original home ranch in southeastern Utah and gone out of business.[32]

In July 1895, Missou Hines took a carload of horses to Omaha, where he sold them to brokers at a handsome profit. On his return, he stopped in Douglas celebrating Independence Day with old saddle mates and friends. On July 6, he stopped in Casper on his way to Lander to call on customers of the railroad.[33]

In 1895, Martin J. Gothberg joined a team of five meteorological observers around the state for the University of Wyoming Agricultural College. Among his responsibilities was the daily measurement of evaporation levels on his ranch at Dobbin Springs. These interesting studies considered Wyoming's meager annual rainfall, and the results helped validate how critical it was to retain as much moisture as possible in the soil of the region.

"Evaporation from water surface is measured by means of a hook-gauge, measurements being taken every day that the water is not frozen. A tank of galvanized iron holding one cubic meter of water is used. Evaporation cannot be accurately obtained during the winter months, there being only a little over six months of the year that water does not freeze so as to interfere with the record. For six months, from April 17 to October 22, it was 37.020 inches."[34]

When the Gothbergs settled in for winter, Mary Enid was with child. As both their ranch and family began to grow, so did the small ranch of Missou Hines. As Hines continued to oversee livestock shipments for the railroad, he acquired an additional homestead on Muddy Creek and expanded his sheep-raising operation. In December 1895, two of his herders were lost in a blizzard. With his saddlebags filled with food, and bedrolls and blankets strapped behind the cantle, Hines took to the range in search of his missing herders. A day and a half later, he caught up with them, cold and hungry. They soon mustered a fire and disposed of a large percentage of the provisions. With food in their bellies and considerably warmed up, the beleaguered men with their bands of sheep followed Hines back toward their camp wagon shortly thereafter.[35]

The following February, Martin's younger sister Sophia H. Gothberg married Edward Clinton Fuller at her parents' home in Greenville. E. Clinton Fuller was a gold-plater among a throng of jewelers in Attleboro, Massachusetts. After a wedding supper and receiving of gifts, the couple left for Boston on a honeymoon.[36]

Martin's elder sister Teresa Koezly planned a recovery from her emotional and financial losses in July 1896. She took out a mortgage for $2,900 and purchased a building permit to construct a two-story frame house on Claremont Avenue in Jersey City. She expected construction of the home to cost $2,500. Additionally, Teresa's father-in-law, Frederick J. Koezley, passed away on September 22, 1896. Perhaps aiding in relief from her family's financial burden, Mr. Koezly left in his will one-ninth of his estate to his granddaughter, Doretta Koezly. It appears Teresa's plans did not work out as expected, and by 1900 she and Doretta were living with her parents on Runyon Avenue in Jersey City.[37]

≈

In March 1896, Martin Gothberg was again in the employ of the CY Ranch. Bob Devine, foreman of the ranch, was in Johnson County with Martin and a few other CY riders searching for stolen cattle. On March 29, he wrote a letter from D.R. and J.N. Tisdale's TTT ranch to Natrona County Sheriff Hugh Patton describing the situation. He asked Patton to forward the letter to CY Ranch manager E. T. David. With lack of postal service available, Martin Gothberg served as messenger carrying the letters to Casper.

> *Tisdale Ranch*
> *March 29, '96*
> *Mr. H. L. Patton*
> *Casper, Wyo.*
> *My Dear Sir and Friend. I am still here riding. Found all of the calves taken away from the cows. Most every rustler has from 5 to 20 calves penned up and some worked brands. Emanuel [Arminta] came in last night with two worked brands. Those YU cows I have not saw them yet but he says the work is coarse that anybody can tell they are YU cows.*
>
> *I am now after some cows that I hear Keith has worked CY cows into TOY. Emanuel says he can find one or two that the Y is not burnt fresh – burned TO and never touched the Y. We have all been up north fork and all over the range and I am on to all of the men in the business.*
>
> *I will be in Casper about 31 or the 1ˢᵗ of April. Please write E. T. David or send him this letter as I have no way of sending mail from here.*
>
> *We will hold the cows and I will come in to see Mr. David what to do. I think we will bust them up in business as they all are in small bunches watching around. I saw Champion [brother of Nate] and Peterson today. Rode right up on them before they saw us. Champion started for his gun where they had them on a log but I and Sullivan*

stopped him by riding between him and the guns. Will close as Martin is going.[38]

Two weeks later, on April 17, 1896, Martin and Mary Enid were blessed with the arrival of their first child, Edwin George Gothberg. This birth took place at the Gothbergs' home, as was the custom of the time. Mary Enid's mother probably tended to the young mother with her first delivery. A few months later, the Blackmores welcomed their first son, Robert Bruce Blackmore, to the family on November 9, 1896.

It had been a tumultuous four years since Martin lost his beloved Adolphena in New Jersey. He left Wyoming with the lynching of Averell and Watson fresh in his memory and returned in the aftermath of the cattlemen's invasion of Johnson County. Almost as if in retaliation for their misadventure in Johnson County, many cattlemen seemed to begin waging war on sheepmen. This, too, produced few positive results. With beef prices plummeting, raising sheep was becoming more profitable than cattle.

Throughout the time, Martin endured in spite of difficulties. The pleasures he enjoyed working on his small ranch and reuniting with Wyoming friends sped the emotional recovery from his loss. Whether contributing to his recuperation or resulting from it, he fell in love with a spunky, young Wyoming ranch girl and married her. He received a visit from the notorious Tom Horn, yet Horn opted not to leave his calling card. The Blackmores prospered and ventured into ranching as their family was growing, as was the Clayton family near Glenrock. During the same period, three of Gothberg's sisters married in New Jersey and his parents came to visit him and his new bride in Wyoming. He could not help counting the blessings.

As Martin Gothberg weighed in on the prospects of the sheep industry, he was reminded of the wildness of the region he called home. His old saddle pal Jerky Bill still rode half-wild broncos with ease while Missou became a respected livestock agent, though still sprinkled in a few cowboy antics when given the opportunity. It seemed, however, that whenever civilization of the area appeared to be just around the corner, another rattlesnake of the lawless West began feverishly buzzing its tail nearby.

CHAPTER 4

Rough and Tumble Times

1897–1899

WHILE THE LIVESTOCK INDUSTRY CONTINUED TO GROW IN WYOMING, more and more cattlemen transferred their investments from beef to sheep. Missou Hines called on potential clients for the railroad near the Gothberg Ranch on February 24, 1897, when Sheriff Hugh L. Patton recruited him into service. Hines accompanied Sheriff Patton to the 07 Ranch at Bessemer where he assisted the sheriff in capturing, subduing, and arresting a crazy man. After much ado, they delivered the man to Casper: "He was tried before a justice and sent to the insane asylum at Evanston."[1]

❧

Gothberg watched on as his friend Missou Hines's as well as other small operators' ranches continued to grow slightly more rapidly than his own ranch by raising sheep. While Martin contemplated his ranching options, the city of Casper, Wyoming, held its first Memorial Day observation on May 31, 1897. They honored Mary Enid's stepfather, Frank Sanders, among nine surviving veterans of the War Between the States living in Natrona County. Local businesses closed at 2 p.m. and the Odd Fellows held a patriotic program at the hall before a packed house. Leaving there, a procession of attendees filed to the cemetery to decorate the graves of fallen soldiers and erect a memorial in their honor.[2]

Sheep ranching had become so lucrative in the northwest that the Fremont, Elkhorn & Missouri Valley Railroad had built a series of reservoirs to hold water for trailing herds en route to railheads all the way across Wyoming. In July 1897, Hines rode for two weeks round trip to

Soda Springs, Idaho, to check on the progress of a flock of fifty thousand sheep as they made their way from Oregon to his employer's stockyards in western Nebraska. Hines had herders watching two of his own flocks as they spent the summer grazing on lush meadows in the Big Horn Mountains. By September, the Oregon herd had passed through Casper and was resting at one of the railroad's reservoirs northwest of Lusk, Wyoming, as they neared their destination.[3]

Martin Gothberg continued to be cautious and remained raising cattle, which he knew and understood. In August, he applied to lease a 720-acre parcel of land adjoining his original homestead from the State of Wyoming. He made a second trip into Casper near the end of the month, in hopes of receiving news of his application. When Martin made his monthly trip to Casper in September, they had yet to notify him of the results of his lease request. The state eventually did not accept his entire submission, but in November, granted a lease for 640 acres. This acquisition again effectively doubled his land holdings at the time. The convenient proximity and value of this property influenced Gothberg to keep the contract active for the rest of his life. While Martin dealt with land issues in Wyoming, his family in New Jersey suffered another loss when his younger sister Lillian Childs passed away on August 26, at the age of twenty-eight. The circumstances of her death are unknown.[4]

As the evenings began to cool, locals along the North Platte knew that winter was soon approaching. To celebrate one last hoorah before the snow arrived, the town of Glenrock organized a "Cowboy Carnival" commencing on Friday afternoon, October 15, 1897, and proceeding on throughout the day Saturday. The merriment attracted throngs of spectators from both Casper and Douglas. Kicking off the festival was Jerky Bill Clayton, riding one of the roughest broncos that could be found near or far. That exhibition was followed by a free-for-all horse race and cowpony races. The evening concluded with a grand ball on Main Street topped off with a display of fireworks. Saturday was more horseracing and trick riding. It was perhaps during this event that Jerky Bill showed off his fine horsemanship by racing down Main Street at full gallop. Leaning from the saddle, he grabbed a raw egg left lying on the dusty lane. Sliding his mount to a stop a short distance away, he returned to show the cheering crowd the fresh egg held unfractured between his fingers. Throughout the day the celebration continued, brought to a close that afternoon by another display of Jerky Bill's amazing prowess at controlling the wildest of mustangs.[5]

***

Missou Hines spent the last half of November traveling in Fremont County, Wyoming. He called on many of his clients from Wolton and Lost Cabin, along Badwater Creek, to Conant Basin and Lander. On his tour, he contracted one hundred carloads of sheep to ship before year's end from Casper to feed yards in Nebraska. Hines gave a flattering report of conditions on the range, stating that flocks were in excellent shape and early snows were providing plenty of moisture for the herds.

The stockyards buzzed with the frenzy of a hill of ants on December 2, as herders funneled hundreds of Ed Houck's sheep into twelve awaiting railcars while J. B. Okie approached town with another forty carloads in his band of lambs from Lost Cabin, Wyoming. Other ranchers' flocks were already on the trail behind them as the bustle continued, leaving Gothberg further contemplating diversification into the sheep industry.[6]

***

Not long beforehand, Martin Gothberg received a visit from Sheriff Patton calling him to appear on the grand jury for what became the largest murder trial in the history of the county at the time. It all began on the pleasant Sunday morning of May 30, 1897, when twenty-seven-year-old Robert Gordon met his death at Kenneth McRae's sheep camp on Fales Creek, near the western border of Natrona County. McRae brought the body of the young man to Casper on the following Wednesday afternoon. Kenneth McRae told the sheriff that Gordon had come into the camp wagon to eat breakfast on the morning of the accident. He reported to the sheriff that Gordon had spoken a few words with him while he was in bed. As McRae dozed, the noise and concussion of the discharged rifle jolted him. The gun was lying at the foot of the bed. The bullet struck

Gordon in his side at the top of his lungs and exited his other side. Then, Gordon, mortally wounded, jumped from the wagon and cried out, "I am shot! I am shot!" before falling to the ground. McRae went out to where Gordon was lying on the ground and saw the blood running from his side. McRae said that Gordon had worked for him for nearly a year and was a faithful worker and a good young man.[7]

Pete Keith, another herder in McRae's employ, was asleep in his bedroll beneath the supply wagon at the time. Keith sent word to Casper that McRae's story was untrue and urged that authorities should make a thorough investigation into the tragedy. Drs. Garner, Dean, and Leeper made a post-mortem examination of Gordon's body and scheduled a coroner's inquest for the following Saturday afternoon. In the meantime, Sheriff Patton and County Attorney Norton placed McRae under arrest and left him in the custody of Coroner H. A. Lilly. They then departed for Fales Creek to further scrutinize the incident and subpoena potential witnesses.[8]

On June 7, 1897, the coroner held an inquest. Several witnesses testified to their knowledge of the deceased and provided a variety of conflicting accounts that McRae had told them regarding the sequence of events that led up to Robert Gordon's death. Hearing their testimonies, the coroner's jury found significant cause to have McRae bound over for hearing by a grand jury. After numerous delays, the case was brought before the grand jury in November. Future governor Bryant B. Brooks served as the grand jury foreman. The witnesses' testimonies had not significantly changed since the coroner's inquest; the jury was polled and the court issued an indictment for murder on November 15, 1897. A detail of the testimonies from the coroner's inquest is shown in Appendix A, "The Kenneth McRae Murder Trial, 1897."[9]

McRae's trial began January 14, 1898. The jury failed to reach a verdict and the defendant was released on thirty thousand dollars bond. A new trial was immediately called and on February 22, 1898, the defendant was found guilty of murder in the first degree. The court heard the motion for a new trial beginning on April 5. In the meantime, defense attorneys had accused the court of bribery and corruption, which they were called by the judge to show proof thereof or to be held in contempt. The attorneys apologized, claiming that they had been misinformed and consequently were mistaken. The court accepted their apology after issuing a firm reprimand. After two days, the court granted the motion for a new trial and issued a change of venue to move the case to Rawlins, in Carbon County, Wyoming. When the Natrona County sheriff transferred McRae to Carbon County, their sheriff refused to accept the prisoner on the grounds that Natrona County was insolvent and could not pay the upkeep of the man. After several days of banter between the counties, the case eventually proceeded in Carbon County.

There were three attorneys from three separate counties for both the prosecution and the defense. All of the witnesses traveled to Rawlins. The court subpoenaed Martin Gothberg and others who testified to the credibility of several witnesses. The trial began on May 2, 1898, and the jury reached a verdict of not guilty, and "discharged without prejudice" Kenneth McRae on June 2, 1898. The three trials cost Natrona County more than six thousand dollars, or about $165,000 in today's money. Numerous citizens of Casper were outraged with both the cost of the trials and the verdict for a number of years.[10]

As the murder trial of Kenneth McRae progressed, Martin Gothberg was busy improving his hay meadow below Dobbin Springs. In February 1898, he plowed ten acres of his most fertile ground and seeded it in alfalfa. His crop had sprouted and was progressing nicely when on April 14, 1898, the Gothberg family increased by one with the birth of a daughter at their ranch home. Martin and Mary Enid named their baby girl Adolphena Dora Gothberg in honor of Martin's beloved first wife and Mary Enid's mother. Perhaps young Edwin Gothberg had difficulty pronouncing "Adolphena"; whatever the reason the little girl became known as Sis. For both family and friends, the moniker stuck throughout her life.[11]

Much like the previous year, Missou Hines traveled through Idaho soliciting ranchers to use his railroad's services. When he returned to Casper in March, he estimated four hundred thousand sheep from the West would come over the trail that fall for shipment from Casper to feedlots in Nebraska. Following his trip to Idaho, he ventured into the Big Horn Basin, reporting that he had never seen cattle and sheep looking better at that time of year. The country along the Big Horn River was booming. Hines predicted that 150,000 sheep would graze the basin that year. The new town of Thermopolis, Wyoming, boasted a population of nearly four hundred people and growing daily. Business owners were erecting stone and brick structures indicating the permanence of their commitment to the success of the community. They expected the town to draw a large number of visitors to the hot springs, and Missou commented that the town was quiet, orderly, and well governed.[12]

Mollie Wolf had spent most of the winter collecting logs for his new house on the Sweetwater. By this time, the town of Bessemer had constructed their sheepshearing pens, and Mollie was an accomplished shearer. He and the rest of the twelve-man crew began shearing at noon on April 12 and sheared 1,500 sheep per day as ranchers trailed their flocks into the pens for the next five weeks. At nine cents per head, a good shearer could make upwards of ten dollars per day, nearly three hundred dollars in today's money, and far outweighing the prospects of many ranch hands making twenty to thirty dollars per month.[13]

As the shearing crew neared completion at Bessemer, Missou Hines reported that the clip was lighter than in 1897 but was cleaner and of better quality. Within a few days of finishing at Bessemer, the shearing crew packed their gear into wagons and headed north on the Bridger Trail. It took them a couple of weeks to reach Red Lodge, Montana, where they spent the rest of the summer shearing in that area.[14]

After much thought and study, in 1898 Martin Gothberg made the decision to venture into the sheep business on his ranch. Cattle prices had been in a slump for a number of years and many of his friends had rolled their investments over from cattle to sheep. Missou Hines and Mollie Wolf, both seasoned cowmen, had made the transition successfully. Walt Blackmore had purchased the Hat-Six Ranch and with little experience in livestock raising since leaving his family's farm in Michigan, had begun effectively grazing sheep from the get-go. On June 6, Martin journeyed to Laramie. It was time for a change. He launched into sheep ranching by selling a portion of his cattle herd and purchasing a flock of six hundred ewes.[15]

—◦—

At some previous time, Lou Spalding had sold his homestead to Basil M. Spalding. Basil's relationship to Lou is unknown. In mid-June 1898, Martin Gothberg purchased the 160 acres adjoining his original homestead then known locally as the "Spalding Place," from Basil Spalding. Martin later dismantled Lou Spalding's old cabin and added it to his own cabin, doubling the size of what had become his bunkhouse.[16]

—◦—

In June, County Clerk Marion P. Wheeler received thirty thousand brook trout from the state fish hatchery. Crews released fish throughout the county, three thousand into Gothberg's Creek. A few weeks later, Mary Enid's mother came to visit from Bates Creek. While there, the two ladies ventured into Casper to enjoy Saturday shopping in the city. Perhaps they were taking in the huge "slaughter sale" at the Richards & Cunningham store. The company advertised a gigantic sale on summer dress goods and ladies' wraps.[17]

—◦—

As September rolled around, Martin J. Gothberg, Walter A. Blackmore, and William P. "Missou" Hines came together at the Democratic County Convention. Walter Blackmore, delegate for the Muddy Creek precinct, was elected chairman of the convention; Martin Gothberg, delegate for the Bessemer precinct, was appointed to the Permanent Organization Committee; and William Hines, a delegate for the Casper precinct, was appointed to the Platform and Resolution Committee and attended the State Democratic Committee meeting in Cheyenne, securing the convention for Casper.[18]

Of the nominees chosen at the Democratic County Convention, successful candidates for the party in the November election were W. S. Kimball, State Legislator, and Frank Hall, County Treasurer. Martin Gothberg's beloved Democratic Party may not have swept the election, but considering the lesser percentage of voters the party represented in the county, their results were quite optimistic.[19]

Following the convention, Walt and Minnie Blackmore came into Casper from their Hat-Six Ranch, visiting the county attorney candidate and his wife, Mr. and Mrs. Eugene Norton. Walt returned to the ranch while Minnie enjoyed a few extra days in town visiting with Mrs. Norton and other friends. While she was there, Martin Gothberg's younger brother Herman Gothberg Jr. arrived in Casper from his home in New Jersey. Herman planned to stay the winter at the ranch with Martin and Mary Enid.[20]

—◆—

Missou Hines worked for a week in mid-October in Lusk, Wyoming, with engineers from the Fremont, Elkhorn & Missouri Valley Railroad. They were scouting locations for construction of several additional reservoirs in the area near the town. If the railroad collected water for livestock, it would enhance conditions for shearing and shipping operations from the stockyards at that location, producing more opportunities to ship both wool and livestock from that facility. With the system in place, northern ranchers could trail their sheep to Lusk for shearing then trail them back home, rather than hauling the wool in wagons to the railroad, eating into the rancher's profit margins. They planned to ship more wool from Lusk the following year than ever before.[21]

—◆—

In January 1899, Martin made final proof and was awarded his patent on a timber culture consisting of 124 acres of steep mountainside due south of his original homestead. The plot of land, considered unsuitable for grazing, fell under the land patent laws governing timberlands. Although the property may have been less than ideal for most uses, it bordered Gothberg's present acreage and provided direct access for his livestock to the crest of Casper Mountain.[22]

The Bittner Theater Company came to Casper for a weeklong billing at the Casper Opera House. They opened on the evening of January 31 with a performance of *The Galley Slave*. Reviews in the *Wyoming Derrick* praised the performance and excellence of the cast of thespians. The quality of the troupe may not have matched that of the eastern revues

Herman Gothberg Jr. may have been accustomed to, but Mary Enid Gothberg and her brother-in-law enjoyed the presentation: "A local tribe of Indians assisted the Bittner Theatre people in the show the last night. What they lacked in appearance was made up in vocal demonstration."[23]

Mollie Wolf suffered severely when he took a grave fall from a rock at a considerable height at his ranch on the Sweetwater in December 1898. When brought to Casper, he was unable to walk due to the extent of the injuries to his legs. Upon careful examination, Dr. Leeper concluded that his legs were not broken, but intensely bruised. Under Dr. Leeper's care, he remained bedridden for a week and unable to leave his room for several more days.[24]

On Monday, February 13, 1899, a fire destroyed the entire factory belonging to the Gothberg and Sons Manufacturing Company. Amidst a brutal cold snap and amplified by a horrendous blizzard, firefighters battled the blaze that consumed several blocks for hours. Because of the bitter cold weather, a janitor for a nearby school trudged through the snow at a very early hour that morning to ensure the boiler was sufficiently heating the building. Upon his arrival, he discovered the boiler room filled with smoke. A quick search revealed the source: the wooden ceiling above the boiler was afire. He attempted to extinguish the flames but found the water pipes frozen. As the school filled with smoke, the janitor ran from the building as quickly as possible through deep snow to alert the Engine Company No. 13 a block away.

Within minutes of hearing of the fire, the firefighters of No. 13 had the horses hitched and headed out of the station, but high drifts of snow blocked the way, and they were forced to take a circuitous route. Even then, the horses pushed through deep drifts, sometimes to their chests, as they dragged the heavy wagons down the streets. It was 8 a.m. by the time they reached the fire and began hooking their hoses to hydrants, only to find them frozen. With desperate ingenuity, the captain connected the boiler of the engine to the hydrant and forced steam and hot water into the frozen fixture until a passage opened into the water main. By the time the crews had water pumping on the fire, the blaze had grown monumentally. The school was completely engulfed. As the alarm spread across the city, other engine companies began the struggle to reach the neighborhood. Between waves of wind-blown snow falling and a cloud of dark smoke rising, the fire itself was barely visible. Only minutes after the first water reached the building, a gust of wind ominously fanned the blaze, nearly perfectly timed with the fire reaching a new fuel source in the structure. The resulting ball of flame nearly exploded through the smoke, and the heat from the blaze became instantly intensified, turning not only the falling snow, but also much of the deluge of water from the fire hoses, into an ineffective puff of steam. Nearby residents were panicked by the sight and began to grab absolute necessities and evacuate their homes. Few who saw the inferno hesitated.

As the morning progressed, engine Nos. 8, 9, and 15 gradually made their way to the scene and joined the battle, along with truck Nos. 4 and 5. By mid-morning, wind had driven the flames across a vacant lot adjacent to the school and ignited a three-story frame residence. A nearer home upwind from the school burst into flames from the heat radiating from the burning school. Near the school was a two-story brick factory that manufactured photographic equipment, adjoined by the brass works owned by the Gothberg family. Next in line were three frame residences. Just before 10 a.m., Fire Chief Hogan fell unconscious. He was carried to a nearby residence where it was diagnosed that he had suffered a heart attack and smoke inhalation. It was two hours before he regained consciousness and was later transported to his son's home a few blocks away.

At 1 p.m. engine No. 124 finally arrived on the scene, after hours of battling the snow to get there, and the already exhausted crew immediately took their place in fighting the blaze. By late afternoon, the fire was under control, and most of several blocks including the Gothbergs' brass works lay in a smoldering ruin. It is unknown how much of the Gothberg family's financial losses may have been covered by insurance. They were thankful that due to the storm and the hour the fire began, no employees had been injured in the blaze. "The suffering of the firemen was intense. The fine snow, whirling in spirals, sifted down through the smoke and within ten minutes after their work began, every fireman lost all resemblance of humanity. Their breath froze on their mustaches, whiskers and eyebrows, and even their hair, were encased in ice, which had to be broken off from time to time, to permit them to see."[25]

The storm was a terror, even without the fire. The *Jersey Journal* reported in the same issue that the entire Greenville district of the city was storm-bound. "Traffic is entirely suspended. Trolley cars are not running, as the tracks are blocked by fire apparatus sent to the fire at No. 20 School on Danforth Avenue. Trains on the Central Railroad of New Jersey stopped running at noon. Business is at a standstill. The streets are blocked with drifts of snow, many of which are eight feet in height."[26]

As Martin's family endured the brutal weather in New Jersey, so did the sheepmen in Wyoming. The winter of 1898–99 had been devastating for Wyoming sheepmen. The United States Department of Agriculture estimated Wyoming's losses at 236,683 sheep, about 10 percent of the state's total sheep population. It is unknown how Martin fared this first winter of sheep ranching, but many of his contemporaries suffered great losses. Carcasses were stacked on top of each other in shallow draws across the range, where sheep had sought refuge from the driving wind and snow.[27]

Completely recovered from his injuries, Mollie Wolf was anxious to be outdoors and moving. By the first week of April, he joined a twelve-man sheepshearing crew as he had done each season in recent years past. It was labor intensive, but extremely profitable work for a man with the skill and dexterity to do the job quickly. Also on that year's crew were John Brandt and Marvin L. Bishop. Beginning on April 10, 1899, at the Two Bar Ranch and White Brothers Ranch on Bates Creek, they sheared eleven thousand head of sheep. Moving one hundred miles south to Medicine Bow they sheared an additional seventeen thousand head for Walter Highland, E. Vivian, and Charles Coulter. Returning to Casper on Saturday, May 20, the twelve men had shorn twenty-eight thousand sheep in six weeks. Again working at nine cents per head, the men of the crew averaged over thirty-five dollars per week including their two hundred miles of overland travel.[28]

They had excellent weather the entire time, and one member of the crew stated that he had been shearing sheep in Wyoming for eight years and this had been his most profitable season yet. After a quick stop in Casper, they boarded the train for Douglas the following Monday, where they expected to spend the next three weeks shearing the flocks belonging to the Platte Valley Sheep Company.[29]

Having seen the first shearing of his small band of sheep and truly comprehending the value of the dual market potential that sheep provided with both a wool and lamb crop each year, Martin Gothberg traded another small group of cattle for three hundred more ewes. While visiting her family in Bates Park, Mary Enid suffered "a stroke of paralysis." It may have been a case of Bell's palsy or a more serious condition. Regardless, she was very ill and stayed with her mother for several weeks while recuperating.[30]

On the chilly high plains in the wee hours of morning on Friday, June 2, 1899, the band of outlaws later known as the Wild Bunch flagged down the Union Pacific Overland Flyer near Wilcox, Wyoming, between Rock Creek and Medicine Bow. At about two o'clock in the morning, the bandits blew open the strongbox in the express car. An overuse of dynamite destroyed the car, but the robbers made off with the still disputed sum of something between thirty thousand to one hundred thousand dollars in cash and jewelry. Much like the 1969 movie *Butch Cassidy and the Sundance Kid* portrayed, the outlaws split up into small groups and scattered. George "Flat Nose" Curry with Harvey and Lonny Logan headed north.

A posse from Laramie, Wyoming, arrived by special train to the scene of the robbery later that morning before daylight. As soon as dawn shown enough light to see their trail, six members of the posse followed after Curry and the Logans while four others trailed another group of three outlaws also moving north, but by a different route. The entire region had seen heavy rains for several days and the North Platte River filled its banks with a raging torrent of muddy water. As soon as the general direction of escape was determined, railroad detectives notified authorities along the Platte to secure all bridges. Since the river was unfordable in its current condition, the desperados needed to use one of the few bridges to make their escape. A short time later, it began to rain heavily again.

Immediately following receipt of the wire from authorities to be on the lookout for the men, Deputy Sheriff W. E. Tubbs left Casper with six men to secure the bridge at Alcova, Wyoming, a small community nineteen miles southwest of Martin Gothberg's ranch. The Alcova bridge was the nearest point to the robbery where a crossing of the North Platte River could be made. After the twenty-seven-mile ride, these men stood guard in a nearly continuous torrential downpour for thirty-six hours.

As the pursuit of the fugitives focused on central Wyoming, the Union Pacific Railroad dispatched a special train on the Fremont, Elkhorn & Missouri Valley line to Casper. Aboard the train were Sheriff Sheafer of Albany County, former US Marshal T. Jeff Carr, Union Pacific Detective F. Bernard of Cheyenne, Union Pacific Detective A. Vizzard of Omaha, and Converse County Sheriff Josiah (Joe) Hazen. When the men sat down with Sheriff Hiestand in Casper, the group comprised some of the best lawmen in the state of Wyoming. After a few hours' consultation, the special train pulled out returning to Cheyenne. Sheriff Hazen and Detective Vizzard remained in Casper. The group agreed that Detective Vizzard oversaw the operations of the multiple agencies hunting the outlaws.[31]

Sheriff Hiestand hired two men to guard the bridge in Casper on Saturday night. They were on their way there when Detective Vizzard stopped them. He could not dream it necessary to put men at the bridge in Casper, believing the outlaws would not dare to cross a bridge in such a populous place. Maybe not, but the robbers crossed it, and were seen going that way in the night. About 2:30 a.m., George Curry and the Logan brothers rode through Casper in a driving rain, across the bridge at the river and northwest along Casper Creek: "As they were passing one of the saloons someone remarked, 'There's a chance to make a reputation. There go the train robbers,' little thinking that they were really the ones wanted." Thinking nothing of it, no one mentioned the chance sighting until after the posse left town on Sunday in pursuit.[32]

The three robbers had holed up Saturday somewhere in Bates Park waiting until dark. As the rain fell, they cautiously rode through the ranches along Bates Creek, passing by the homesteads of Mary Enid's family, where she was staying at the time, and many of their friends along what is known today as Coal Mountain Road. Reaching the river, they turned east, passing Martin and Mary Enid's home and ranch in the stormy darkness as they approached Casper. Somewhere in Casper, they acquired food and provisions that they lunched on the next day before crossing the river and vanishing into the darkness.

Sunday morning Al Hudspeth was looking for a couple of horses that had strayed in the storm the previous night. When he neared the shack at the five-mile oil derrick, he saw a man standing at the door and rode up to him. He asked the man if some nearby horses might be the ones he was looking for. The man told him gruffly to go see for himself. When Hudspeth started to reply, another man came from the shack with two rifles, tossing one to the man at the door, who quickly threw down on Hudspeth and told him to "hit the road and do it d---d quick," which Hudspeth did. Hudspeth immediately rode to town and advised Sheriffs Hiestand and Hazen of the course of events that morning, adding that the men had three good horses, and the two men he had seen both wore pistols and carried rifles.[33]

Within thirty minutes, Joe Hazen and a posse of a dozen men were mounted and headed out of town toward the shack on Casper Creek.

Sheriff Hazen, as before stated, is a fearless and eminently successful criminal apprehender. He has been highly complimented by the foremost detectives of the land for cases he has handled. He was never known to flinch in time of danger and lawbreakers dread him as they dread no other. He was pressed into the present hunt by the Union Pacific officials, who knew that he would not rest until he had captured his men.[34]

A short distance from the cabin they found the tracks of three well-shod, fast-moving horses. The fresh trail, easily seen in the mud left by last night's rain, headed in a beeline just east of north. The posse followed at a good pace. Sheriff Hiestand had ridden his horse hard two days earlier pursuing another lawbreaker, and the animal had not yet fully recovered. When the posse left Casper, Hiestand rode to the CY Ranch to commandeer a fresh horse and recruit more men for the posse. There he was

Johnny T. Williams and Josiah Hazen, 1886. Photograph is believed to have been taken in Cheyenne, Wyoming, following the 1886 roundup.

remounted and joined by ranch foreman Lee Devine and two other men. Riding four of the finest horses in the valley and loaded for bear, the men followed the trail left by Sheriff Hazen's posse at a gallop.[35]

Two hours after the posse left Casper in pursuit of Curry and the Logans, the six men that had dogged the outlaws from Wilcox two days earlier rode into Casper on spent horses. They had tracked the bandits relentlessly for two days, but sadly had lost their rain-obliterated trail in Bates Park. Hearing that Sheriff Hazen was in chase, they immediately attempted to locate fresh horses to overtake the Casper posse. Finding no replacements, three of the men took their horses to C. K. Bucknum's Star Stable and Livery and sought a place to rest while the others threw a leg over their worn-out mounts and rode out on Hazen's trail.

Shortly after the three departed, the four other posse men from Laramie rode in from Glenrock. They had hunted the other three train robbers, following them north on the Rock Creek to Fort Fetterman Road to within about thirty miles of Douglas. There their query sidetracked toward Laramie Peak, then slipped through LaBonte Canyon. Upon exiting the canyon there too, the rains had obliterated the outlaw's tracks and they subsequently disappeared. These four put their exhausted horses up in Shorty Castle's feed barn and sought food and rest. The next morning the seven men from Laramie, slightly refreshed, saddled their weary mounts and rode in the direction of the last reported whereabouts of the outlaws.

On Sunday afternoon, about twenty-five miles north of Casper and five miles west of the old horse ranch on the road to Salt Creek, Sheriff Hazen and his posse had their first contact with the outlaws. From a rise in the terrain about a half mile away, the robbers fired upon the posse with their Krag-Jorgenson rifles. As about twenty rounds hailed around them, the posse dismounted and desperately tried to locate the source of the rifle fire. Due to the bandits' use of smokeless powder and the distance from which they fired, the posse could not identify their position to return fire. During the assault, no one was injured. E. T. Payton's mount received a moderate wound and Sheriff Hiestand's unfamiliar animal broke free and bolted.

Sheriff Hiestand knew, from his pursuit in the area two days previous, the location of a sheep camp about five miles distant. He made his way on foot in that direction to appropriate a horse from the herder. Sheriff Hazen and the posse kept on the outlaws' trail through the night, mostly on foot. The outlaws led Hazen and his men through the maze of badlands and canyons between Castle and Dugout Creeks. On Monday morning, Sheriff Hazen and Dr. Leeper were afoot tracking the desperados in a ravine along Castle Creek. Hazen beckoned Dr. Leeper, and as he neared Hazen told him they were getting very close. At that instant, a shot rang out from about seventy yards away. The bullet struck Hazen in the stomach and exited his back. He fell immediately. Dr. Leeper dropped to the ground to avoid the hail bullets striking around him. After about ten minutes, the gunfire ceased.

Dr. Leeper did not see the outlaws escape while administering every possible attention under the circumstances to the wounded sheriff. It was several hours before a spring-wagon could be located and the wounded sheriff transported to Casper. Having no available shelter, Dr. Leeper did his best to protect Hazen from the weather as he lay in the open. When two of the men from the posse arrived with Sheriff Joe Hazen in Casper, the authorities intended to bring him to the Natrona House to receive medical attention. Joe asked if there was any way possible to take him home.[36]

Dr. E. P. Rohrbaugh was summoned and made a careful examination, but expressed no opinion of the condition of the wounded sheriff. The train pulled out from Casper about 9:00 and made a quick run to Douglas. Missou Hines and former Sheriff Patton, old friends of Hazen, in company with Dr. Rohrbaugh, escorted him to Douglas and lent valuable assistance to the physician in the care of the patient.

Notwithstanding all was done for the wounded man that medical skill would suggest, he lingered until five o'clock Tuesday evening, remaining conscious until the end. Dr. Barber of Cheyenne had been wired for and left for Douglas at once on a special train but did not arrive until after the patient had passed away.[37]

The posse unrelentingly dogged their trail, but the outlaws continued to elude their pursuers as they continued north. Abandoning their now decrepit horses, in a last-ditch effort the bandits forsook drowning and swam the raging flood waters across Powder River, finally making good their escape.[38]

Led by the Masonic lodges of Douglas and Casper, Wyoming, Sheriff Josiah Hazen's funeral in Douglas, Wyoming, was reportedly the largest in state history at the time. The funeral procession extended several blocks. Governor DeForest Richards and numerous other dignitaries attended the service. The Union Pacific Railroad sent special trains to carry mourners from Casper, Wyoming, and Cheyenne, Wyoming. It is unknown if Martin Gothberg attended the funeral, but there is no question that he knew Hazen. In addition to working together in the past, both men were also active members of their neighboring Masonic lodges.

Not only was Joe Hazen renowned for his prowess as a lawman, he had been a congenial cowboy and ranch and roundup foreman for two

Funeral procession of Converse County Sheriff Josiah Hazen in Douglas, Wyoming, led by the Masonic lodges of Casper and Douglas, Wyoming. George "Flat Nose" Curry, Harvey Logan, and Lonny Logan killed Hazen as he led a posse in their pursuit following the Wilcox Train Robbery, June 1899.
COURTESY OF THE WYOMING PIONEER MEMORIAL MUSEUM, DOUGLAS, WYOMING

decades in central Wyoming prior to his death. Martin Gothberg and all but a few of his peers knew Hazen personally, and it would have been difficult to find many enemies of the warm-hearted cowboy. A vast majority of the populous of Wyoming were outraged by his murder and mourned his loss for quite a long time.[39]

As the dust settled in the aftermath of the foray following the Wilcox train robbery, Martin evaluated the circumstances of his friends and family. They all had been in the midst of what might have become dire conditions, and all had escaped unscathed. Mary Enid, partially paralyzed, convalesced at her mother's home when three treacherous outlaws passed nearly by their door. The two Gothberg children also stayed with their grandmother at the Sanders' homestead while their mother rested. The train robbers had likewise passed closely by the family home at Gothberg Ranch. As a matter of convenience in Mary Enid's absence, Martin often left his younger brother Herman in charge of the ranch headquarters while he took care of business elsewhere around the range. Herman Gothberg had rapidly learned many aspects of Western life, but the situation may have produced dreadful results had he been forced into a confrontation with the three well-armed men. Life in central Wyoming was not yet refined.

A new era was coming to the West as Martin Gothberg and his peers prepared entry into the coming century. In the mechanized world of more populated America, the introduction of the automobile brought many changes. The wave grew and flooded into Middle America. With hard work, judicious investments, and careful management, Martin expanded his herds and properties. At the same time, the industrial centers' demand for petroleum products increased, effecting a growing interest in oil exploration. As industrial areas grew so did the demand for food. Farmers' need for water implemented a national interest in expansion of irrigation systems and constriction of dams to supply and regulate them.

CHAPTER 5

Dawning of the Twentieth Century

1899–1905

JUST A FEW WEEKS AFTER THE INTENSE COMMOTION FOLLOWING THE Wilcox Train Robbery, Minnie Blackmore gave birth to their second son, Floyd Cummings Blackmore, on June 20, 1899. A short time later, Walt contracted future Justice of the Peace Warren Tubbs to construct a new home at the family's Hat-Six Ranch. The *Wyoming Derrick* could not help poking a bit of fun at Tubbs's love of fishing from Hat-Six Creek: "Between the work and fishing, Mr. Tubbs is expected to be gone some time."[1]

Mary Enid Gothberg was slowly beginning to recover from her bout of paralysis and was finally well enough to return home with their children in July. With the excitement of the Wilcox robbery behind them and Mary Enid on the mend, young Herman Gothberg decided it was time to return home to New Jersey. He had initially planned to leave in the spring but managed to continue finding excuses to linger. He glanced over his shoulder as he boarded the train east, knowing the memories of his time in Wyoming would not quickly fade.[2]

As the warm weather of summer continued, so did Mary Enid's recovery. Life at the ranch was pleasant and as her health gradually returned, the rearing of her two small children and the toils of day-to-day life were less demanding. Myrtle Gregg recalled living southwest of Casper, Wyoming, as a young woman: "I loved the ranch life, with lots of horseback riding on the endless range. Besides visiting other ranches, we went to Casper every two months. . . . Martin Gothberg was a rancher

Martin J. Gothberg with two of his prized horses
COURTESY OF MARTY GOTHBERG, SUSAN LITTLEFIELD HAINES COLLECTION

south of the river." The Gothberg Ranch was pleasing to see, nestled near the foothill away from the road. In spite of family illness, train robberies, and a score of other distractions, the Gothbergs had a successful year. Martin shipped a railcar load of sheep on Friday morning, September 29, and half a carload of cattle on Monday to the markets in south Omaha.[3]

The last of Martin Gothberg's siblings officially left the nest when his younger brother Herman Edward married Jennie Gertrude Greville on February 22, 1900, at her parents' home in Jersey City.

The bride was given away by her father. She carried a large bouquet and wore orange blossoms. Miss D. Kosby and Miss Daisy Greville were bridesmaids, and Mr. William Greville, brother of the bride, was best man. Only immediate relatives and close friends of the couple were present at the ceremony. Mr. and Mrs. Gothberg left on a honeymoon tour of Wyoming, where they will make an extended visit to Mr. Gothberg's brother.[4]

77

Herman was much stricken by the same affliction Martin felt nearly twenty years earlier when his feet hit the dirt for the first time in Cheyenne. He so loved his stay in Wyoming after spending nearly a year on his brother's ranch that he returned with his new bride in March 1900. Fully intending on making Wyoming their new home, he and Jennie spent the summer at the ranch honeymooning, learning the livestock business, and working in the fresh mountain air. Minnie Blackmore's parents, Mr. and Mrs. E. B. Cummings of Pontiac, Michigan, also spent the summer with their daughter's family at the Hat-Six.[5]

After Martin filed to prove his timber and stone claim in January 1899, Donald and James Michie contested the entitlement, challenging that they had previously filed a mineral claim on the property. On January 25, 1900, Gothberg visited the land office in Douglas regarding the claim. In April, the county surveyor and a number of other witnesses accompanied the Michie brothers and Martin Gothberg to the Douglas land office for a hearing on the complaint. After hearing Gothberg's first witness, James Michie motioned for a continuance in the case. This being granted, the land office scheduled the hearing to reconvene on June 4. Martin was again at the land office in June with his brother-in-law Arthur Brandt. Presumably, Arthur went to the land office as a witness in the mineral claim case.[6]

Missou Hines reported that shearing that spring brought in over six hundred thousand pounds of wool clipped from flocks at the pens in Casper and the nearby vicinity. Mollie Wolf came to town following the clip for a few days of rest and relaxation before purchasing a wagonload of supplies and returning to his ranch on the Sweetwater. Martin Gothberg kept most of his lambs in order to increase the size of his herd, but Walt Blackmore shipped half a railcar load to market in July.[7]

When the *Natrona County Tribune* announced that the state fish hatchery delivered fifty thousand trout fry to Casper, many young readers were anticipating them being served up for dinner. When it was clarified that baby fish were also called "fry," the youngsters were somewhat disappointed. The young fish were, however, planted in several waterways around the county. Gothberg Creek received five thousand of the little guys to inhabit the stream.[8]

In August, the land office finally made a decision on the Michie brothers' complaint against Martin Gothberg. The judgement was in Gothberg's favor and James Michie immediately filed an appeal to the commissioner of the general land office. In September, the commissioner affirmed the action taken by the local land office in Douglas.[9]

While Martin Gothberg was handling the complaint filed against him by the Michie brothers and watching the new "fry" in the creek, he also planned a new school for his growing children to attend. Unlike the modern public school system, the expense of construction and staffing of rural schools of the time fell on the shoulders of the families that used them. Martin Gothberg, William Misters, and other neighbors held a fundraiser: "A big basket and necktie dance is to be given at the home of Wm. Misters Friday evening September, 21, to aid in the fund. Everybody is invited, and it is to be hoped that a large crowd will be in attendance as the cause is a most worthy one." Martin also sold half a railcar load of cattle in October. Ironically, he had to share the car with the Michie brothers, but after all, business was business.[10]

January 1901 found Missou Hines in Salt Lake City, Utah, conducting business for the railroad. A widespread influenza epidemic known at the time by the French term *La Grippe*, reached Wyoming: "La Grippe is epidemic, not only through the length and breadth of America, but in every country in Europe. The whole world is in the grasp of the grippe germ and there are thousands of fatalities."[11] Martin Gothberg contracted the illness, and fearing infecting his seven-month pregnant wife with the extremely contagious disease, called for a physician to come to the ranch and help him combat the virus.[12]

Mary Enid's mother, Dora Sanders, and children had been staying with the Gothbergs at the time helping her expectant daughter and nursing her ailing son-in-law, while Mary Enid's younger half-sister also received treatment for a broken ankle in Casper. With her daughter's ankle on the mend and Martin's condition improving, Dora felt that Mary Enid could manage the situation and opted to return home.[13]

As the weeks passed, Martin's disorder improved and Mary Enid's condition continued to mature. On March 17, 1901, Walter Arthur Gothberg came into the world a healthy baby boy, most likely named for longtime family friend Walter A. Blackmore. Beyond the new arrival, the next few months passed peacefully and without struggle. By 1900, the E. H. Gothberg & Sons Manufacturing Company was back in full operation following the devastating fire of 1899. Martin's brother-in-law Willis Lund was working there at the time. By 1901, the business was presumably flourishing, as Martin's sister Minnie Lund was comfortable leasing a summer cottage for the season that July at Narragansett Pier, Rhode Island. The condition of the region in central Wyoming was so tranquil that when Walt Blackmore presented the staff of the *Tribune* with a half dozen fresh trout he caught on his ranch, the editors were inclined to note the occasion on their front page.[14]

That fall, Tom Clayton purchased a team of draft horses he put to work on his Boxelder Creek Ranch and Ed Rice lost six hundred sheep in a snowstorm. After several weeks of searching, Rice had nearly lost all hope of ever recovering the flock when Walt Blackmore's herders discovered them among his Hat-Six herd. In the end, they had traveled several days' distance from where they were last accounted for, and Rice recovered all but two animals: "Mr. Rice considers himself about the luckiest man on the range."[15]

Martin Gothberg was a founding member and a key player in the Natrona County Wool Growers Association. As the organization gained influence, so did their membership. When they met in Casper on November 28, 1901, the combined membership owned over 250,000 sheep. An assessment of five dollars for every one thousand sheep was made of the members, of which they paid six hundred dollars at the time of the meeting. They agreed to pay $108 of that money to the National Livestock Association toward the salary of their attorney to represent the wool growers' interests in Washington, DC.

The members resolved to support livestock inspectors in the performance of their duties in efforts to control the spreading of infectious diseases on the public range. The membership favored the formation of a Wyoming Wool Growers Association and communication with other associations within Wyoming to set a wage standard for herders and shearers. They appointed delegates to attend the upcoming National Livestock Convention in Chicago and requested the executive committee to solicit to non-member sheepmen in the county by explaining the advantages of belonging to the association. In conclusion, they scheduled the next annual meeting of the association for February 21, 1902.[16]

When the Natrona County Wool Growers gathered for their annual meeting in February, Martin Gothberg was again in the center of the proceedings. The first course of business was the election of delegates to attend the state convention at Cheyenne on February 27. The largest worry of the ranchers was the matter of eradicating scabies and the quarantine of scabby sheep. They believed the spreading of this disease was due to foreign outfits coming through the country with diseased sheep and spreading among the bands of local sheep owners. They nominated Steve Tobin to be appointed by the state board as sheep inspector for Natrona County. They recommended that all disputes between members be resolved by the association in lieu of the court system, and still of key concern was establishing a uniform pay scale for herders and shearers statewide.[17]

A con man targeted the Gothberg family's brass works in April 1902. A man using the name S. A. Vendig and claiming to be a private detective from Brooklyn contacted the factory declaring he had uncovered a ring of thieves stealing brass fittings from the company. Mr. Vendig told Ernst Gothberg via telephone that if he was interested in pursuing the matter, he was available for hire. Ernst made an appointment to meet with Vendig at the plant a few days later. Ernst Gothberg was not nearly as naïve as he had been seven years earlier when he lost his expensive diamond stud on the ferry. Thinking it unlikely that his employees were stealing inventory from the factory, Ernst soon verified that if any pilferage was occurring it was insignificant. Reassured, he contacted Captain Nugent and Detective Bennet at the Fifth Precinct across the street from the factory. Armed with the inside scoop, the three devised a plan to put a sting of their own on Mr. Vendig.

On the day of the appointment, Detective Bennet, disguised as a mechanic in the factory, positioned himself to overhear the conversation between the proprietor and the con man. When Vendig arrived at the office, Ernst ushered him out into the factory, suggesting those clerks who were probably doctoring the paperwork to cover the thefts should not overhear them. Positioning themselves near Detective Bennet who feigned to be repairing an idle machine, Ernst began the interview. Ernst made himself appear totally taken in as Vendig related the fabricated story of how he uncovered the alleged ring of thieves while working another case. As Vendig continued, he itemized the fees necessary to pursue his investigation. As he concluded his proposal to Gothberg, Vendig added, "You must not say anything to those wise guys across the street . . . they are a jealous bunch and would endeavor to hinder our operations."

With that, Detective Bennet stepped out, and showing Mr. Vendig his badge, suggested they go talk to the "wise guys" across the street. When questioned by Captain Nugent, with both Ernst Gothberg and Detective Bennett as witnesses, S. A. Vendig confessed to the scheme.[18]

In May 1902, Owen Wister's phenomenal Western novel *The Virginian* hit the streets. By the end of August, it had already sold one hundred thousand copies. The people of Wyoming were well aware that Mr. Wister based many of his characters on personalities he met in his travels. Wister portrayed some characters almost exactly as the people he met along the trail, and others were composites. A few years later, in his 1907 novel, *Lin McLean,* Wister used Fort Fetterman as the basis for his fictional town of Drybone. In his story, he moved the geography around to suit his plot. Boxelder Canyon was between Douglas and Drybone instead of its actual location, which was west of both. There is no question that he modeled Dr. Barker after Dr. Amos Barber, former doctor for the military post of Fort Fetterman then later for the town. Barber, the one-time governor of

Wyoming, was an acquaintance of Wister and close friend to his family's physician in Philadelphia. In the same way, he loosely based his character Jerky Bill on Gothberg's old saddle mate of many open range roundups, the gifted horseman Jerky Bill Clayton. Mr. Wister obviously admired the setting of Jerky Bill's ranch at the mouth of Boxelder Canyon and used the site as the home of his title character, Lin McLean.

There was much dispute among the old-timers of Wyoming about who certain characters represented in the new novel. "The Virginian" himself was obviously a composite, but it is difficult to miss the similarities between Martin Gothberg's friends and old saddle pals and characters from the book. The story is set on the Skunk Creek Ranch belonging to Judge Henry some two hundred miles from Medicine Bow, Wyoming. The Virginian was a cowhand who became the foreman of that ranch. Wister's description of the ranch house and yard would place the story in real life at the Goose Egg Ranch after Judge Joseph Carey's CY Ranch absorbed that operation. Wister, however, sets the Goose Egg Ranch elsewhere in his story, and the Skunk Creek Ranch seems to be closer to Buffalo, Wyoming. Missou Hines was the foreman of the CY Ranch at the time of one of Mr. Wister's visits. The story of switching the babies at a ranch party there was well known long before the novel reached the printing presses. Hines, who hosted the real-life party, took credit for instigating the mischief.

A cowboy from Lander, Wyoming, James Dollard, received credit as the man behind the dubious character of Trampas. Therefore, it appears that just like in *Lin McLean*, Wister probably juggled the scenery and the characters of *The Virginian* to suit his purpose. The novel obtained worldwide acclaim and still receives praise by many as the best Western novel ever written. It obviously brought much attention to Wyoming. When people like Martin Gothberg read the story, they mused that they knew about this or that bit of lore that Wister weaved into his tale.[19]

When confronted in a letter nearly twenty years later, requesting that the author settle a dispute between readers of where certain events in the story took place, Wister replied:

Dear Boys:–
When I wrote The Virginian, *I was writing Fiction and not Geography.*

Very truly yours,
Owen Wister[20]

In May 1902, proponents of erecting a telephone line from Casper to Bessemer and Bates Park held a meeting at the ranch of Jake Crouse in Bates Park to discuss the project. After considerable discussion as to the best plan, they decided to erect the line by private subscription. Each man that contracted to have an instrument placed in his house would erect thirty poles along the route and pay forty dollars for placing the instrument and stretching the wire. Martin Gothberg, Robert Carey, Daniel Speas, Rollin and Daniel Clark, Edward McGraugh, Jake Crouse, and a dozen of other interested parties along the suggested line agreed to the proposal.[21]

By August, the Rocky Mountain Bell Telephone Company had erected a long-distance line to Casper. The company suggested that every post office and many ranchmen in central Wyoming would soon have "telephonic communication" with Casper and adjacent towns: "The Bates Hole Telephone company now has a line under construction sixty-eight miles long. At present, it has twenty-six subscribers or stockholders, each of whom is constructing his share of the line as far as poles and setting is concerned. At a meeting held at the Freeland schoolhouse a few days ago, they decided to incorporate and elect officers. In the meantime, they are going ahead with the work of construction."[22]

It is normal for Wyoming to be plentiful with grasshoppers through the summer months. A late hard frost will often kill off enough of the young insects to lessen their effect, but that was not the case in 1902. In July, the *Wyoming Derrick* published Gothberg's observations.

Martin Gothberg reports an unusual number of grasshoppers along the east end of the mountain and in the glades this year. They have taken everything green in one of his pastures, and are attacking all native grasses. Ravages of the insects are also reported from the eastern portion of the county.[23]

Depredations of the grasshoppers did not interfere with the effects of other insects on the ranchers' livestock. In late August, Martin Gothberg and Bill Ford combined forces and ran both of their bands through the dip tanks at the Platte River sheep pens. Even with the double crew, the job took most of the week.[24]

Walt Blackmore's wife, Minnie, was suffering from a serious and lingering illness, and they came to a decision that living in town would be much better for her health than on their Hat-Six Ranch. With that in mind, they purchased two lots in July in the new Park Addition. Before construction had hardly begun, however, Minnie's condition worsened. The Blackmores journeyed to their family home in Michigan where the children stayed with relatives while Walt accompanied his wife to Chicago for treatment. After multiple surgeries at the Chicago hospital, Minnie began a rapid recovery from her long illness. By September, her doctors considered her to be in sufficient health to leave the hospital, and she returned to Michigan to sojourn with family as she recuperated. In the meantime, Walt returned to Casper to oversee his ranching operation and the construction of their new home.[25]

Nearly as soon as Walt Blackmore's feet hit the platform at the Casper train station, the court called him to jury duty along with Martin Gothberg on the murder trial of Edwin S. Murphy. Murphy had killed one of his former sheepherders and wounded another, resulting in the loss of the herder's arm after the disgruntled men threatened to kill Murphy for shorting their pay.[26]

In 1902, Martin J. Gothberg renewed his water use permit with the State of Wyoming for the creek from Dobbin Springs to three quarters of a mile downstream toward the Platte River. At the same time, he received another permit for a quarter mile of the stream in Gothberg Draw, paralleling Jackson Canyon to the southwest.[27]

That fall, Gothberg sold a railcar load of cattle to buyers in the Omaha stockyards. He purchased two thousand purebred ewes imported from Oregon for five dollars per head from Judge J. W. Blake and his son Jay. He then founded the Lone Tree Sheep Company, ranging the herd in the very southern end of Bates Park, in Carbon County, on Lone Tree and Stinking Creeks and on the steep slopes of Shirley Rim. In November, he hired Ned Sanchez, an experienced and knowledgeable herder from Lost Cabin, Wyoming, as foreman of the Lone Tree operation.[28]

While Martin Gothberg shipped cattle to Omaha, his brother underwent surgery in New Jersey. For several years, Ernst Gothberg suffered from a growth on his back, often aggravated by any number of circumstances. On October 13, Dr. G. R. Dickinson successfully removed the tumor. The surgeon performed the procedure at the patient's home, a common practice of the time, and Ernst fully recovered.[29]

As the year-end neared, F. C. Hoepner completed stringing wires and installing instruments for the Freeland Telephone Company. Just before Christmas 1902, Martin Gothberg and many of his fellow ranchers and homesteaders southwest of Casper linked to the telephone system. Completion of the system resulted in an instant connection to friends, law-enforcement, and medical aid as opposed to a lengthy horseback or buggy ride, perhaps of several hours.[30]

His heart taken by storm by the handsome widow Mrs. Martha Northington, Missou Hines asked for her hand in marriage and she accepted. In

November, Hines purchased the home of Dan McKenzie on Wolcott Street and the couple prepared to move into the home succeeding their wedding. They were married in a grand ceremony in Casper on December 10, 1902. The newlyweds rang in the New Year with ten of their friends celebrating over dinner at the Warner House.[31]

—❦—

Walt Blackmore reassessed his business interests and finances in 1903. He sold his property in the Park Addition to D. D. Crum and opened a new meat and vegetable market in Casper. When Ned Sanchez came into town to resupply the herders at Gothberg's Lone Tree Sheep Company in January, Blackmore was advertising in the *Natrona County Tribune*:

> *W. A. Blackmore*
> *Dealer in*
> *Fresh, Salt and Smoked MEATS*
> *Vegetables, Oysters and Fish*
> *Telephone No. 28 b*
> *Casper, Wyoming*[32]

—❦—

While Ernst Gothberg recuperated from his surgery, he visited an automobile show in Jersey City. After working on and around machinery since childhood, these mechanical wonders fascinated Ernst. The automobile bug had soon bitten and infected him with the desire to have one of the mechanized creatures for his own. It was all he could think about, until finally he succumbed and ordered a brand-new one. When notified that his motorized buggy would arrive on Friday, the thirteenth day of March, the representative asked if he would like to postpone the delivery until Saturday to avoid the curse of the evil day. Not realizing that he was soon to become the talk of the town, Ernst reassured the man that he did not fall victim to such nonsense and accepted delivery of his new automobile on Friday.

When the machine arrived, Ernst fired up the engine, jumped in the seat, and guided it down the side path of his yard with the finesse of a seasoned motorist. He turned the corner and swept down the boulevard, demonstrating the grace of the vehicle with ease. He jaunted up and down the boulevard showing off his new toy and proudly exclaiming, "Why this is as easy as running a sewing machine!" as the engine chug-chugged down the street. Soon tiring of the scenery, Ernst pulled back the lever and urged the machine to higher speed as he prepared for a spin down the Old Bergen Road. Before long, a friend spotted Ernst, hollered, and waved as Ernst approached. Ernst smiled and not wishing to appear rude released the steering stick to wave in return. At that critical moment, one of the front wheels struck a stone and the vehicle instantly veered in a semi-circle. Mounting the curb, the rogue contraption narrowly missed an electric pole. Bumping a picket fence, the contrivance re-entered the roadway and performed a perfect figure eight before jumping onto the far sidewalk for a fifty-foot sprint. The automobile had just begun to vigorously show Ernst what it was able to do when, with supreme effort, Gothberg managed to regain control of the steering apparatus.

Returning to the roadway, he motored away. After checking himself to make sure that he was still in one piece, Ernst breathed a sigh of relief. Too embarrassed to look behind him for witnesses, he sported a different route home. As he entered the carriageway beside his house, Ernst placed the contraption in a lower gear and headed toward the barn. Just as he reassured himself that all was well, the confounded machine again displayed its superiority. As he rounded the corner, the rear wheel clipped the house. After removing two lengths of siding, a corner molding, and a length of rain gutter, the feral machine reared on its hind legs like a wild mustang and attempted to climb the rear wall of the abode when the engine finally stalled.

Exhausted and exasperated, Gothberg extricated himself from the seat. After managing to dislodge the vehicle from its perch, Ernst found a rope and dragged it into the barn. He tied the wheels to the floor, then closed and locked the door, thus allowing his captive to contemplate its mischievous conduct in darkness. As he crossed the yard to the backdoor of his home, he anticipated how nice a hot bath was going to feel.

Ernst evaluated the damage to his beautiful toy. The dashboard displayed a split from top to bottom and the brass lamps were dented and askew: "When the carpenters and tinsmiths came the next day they glanced knowingly at the place where the automobile was stored, smiled significantly and then went to work."[33]

Ned Sanchez journeyed into Casper in April from Gothberg's sheep range. Mollie Wolf was also in town from his ranch on the Sweetwater, and Walt Blackmore had purchased a lot on Beech Street and was constructing a new home in anticipation of his family's return from Michigan. Minnie and the children arrived on the train on the evening of the thirtieth and resided at the Warner House for a time. Martin Gothberg had recently filed for final proof on forty acres at the mouth of Gothberg Draw.[34]

This beautifully restored 1903 Curved Dash Oldsmobile is similar to the one purchased by Ernst Gothberg. It is on display at the Texas Transportation Museum in San Antonio, Texas.
COURTESY OF THE TEXAS TRANSPORTATION MUSEUM, SAN ANTONIO

For several years, Jake Ervay, John Landon, and Boney Earnest had been negotiating with European investors over several thousand acres of land potentially rich in oil reserves. Much of this oil land was west of Casper in the Rattlesnake Basin. It also included property south of Alcova, Wyoming. Details of any agreements made are uncertain, but it seems that the men each received somewhere near one hundred thousand dollars in cash and stock early in 1903, equal to about $2.8 million today. During this time, Boney Earnest became the vice president of the Natrona Improvement Company, holding some four thousand acres of prime oil land in Natrona County. By June 1903, this company was transporting oil well drilling machinery from the railyard in Casper to the Alcova Oil Field on the land south of the town to begin exploration.[35]

When July rolled around, the second murder trial of Ed Murphy finally reached the docket to be heard. The first attempt had ended in a hung jury, nine for acquittal and three for conviction. As the court prepared final jury selection, they interviewed the pool of jurors. "M. J. Gothberg had formed an opinion based on newspaper talk, but would give the defendant a fair and impartial trial," reported the *Wyoming Derrick*, " and had the appearance of making a good juryman." Gothberg was impaneled on the jury; Walt Blackmore was excused. After several days in session and much deliberation on the case, the trial again ended in a hung jury with eleven in favor of conviction and one for acquittal. The court scheduled another trial for January. Before the third trial date arrived, Murphy filed an affidavit that he was bankrupt and destitute; he had no money, no property, and no credit. He was unable to secure another attorney for his defense and requested the court appoint an attorney for him. The county had already accrued some twelve thousand dollars in court expenses on the case. Considering the financial burden on the county treasury, the commissioners adopted a resolution requesting Prosecuting Attorney J. M. Hench dismiss the case before the county also became bankrupt. The court honored the resolution and Murphy was released. Without further ado, Edwin S. Murphy disposed of his few remaining belongings and returned to his former home in the East.[36]

While Martin Gothberg was on jury duty, William Hines, Senator Patrick Sullivan, H. A. Duncan, and Judge John S. Warner incorporated the Casper Livestock Commission Company. They began with capital of fifty thousand dollars, being dealers in horses, cattle, and sheep throughout the West and Midwest. Officers were Pat Sullivan, president, and William Hines, secretary, with the business office in the home of Judge Warner in Casper.[37]

Things were bustling in Casper, and Ernst Gothberg had tamed the beast in his barn sufficiently enough to occasionally convince his wife, Minnie, to ride with him. On Independence Day, Ernst and Minnie joined two other couples in their own motorcars on a jaunt to New Haven, Connecticut. A journey of less than two hours today took the group about ten hours that day. They began the spree with exuberance, leaving an occasional cloud of dust as they sped down the road. Within a few miles, however, they chose to slacken their pace significantly. The roads beyond the outskirts of the city were much more suitable for a leisurely speed. Maneuvering through deep ruts left by wagons and carriages during wetter seasons gave way to steep hills that slowed their gait. When the road smoothed enough for higher speed, the choking dust engulfed all but the first vehicle making traveling in a convoy nearly impossible. With the slower pace, the journey became more enjoyable for all of the participants. At four o'clock that afternoon, the three automobiles wheeled into New Haven. After securing lodging, the jocular motorists bathed and enjoyed a pleasant supper while taking in the local celebration of the holiday. With an early departure the next morning, the group expected to arrive home in midafternoon. The machines stood the test well, but their operators failed to take into account their fuel supply on Sunday. After running out of gasoline and a two-hour hunt for a source of replenishment, the three couples arrived back home at five o'clock that evening.

After the excursion, Ernst stated that he certainly learned that Connecticut roads were not in nearly as good condition as those of New Jersey. With that, the *Journal* reported, "Mr. Gothberg is enjoying a trip to Long Branch and [will] return today."[38]

Since the McRae murder trial five years earlier, John Landon had fairly well managed to stay out of the limelight. He had supported himself for years with his modest ranch west of Casper, and having acquired some knowledge of mining from a brief residency in the Black Hills of Wyoming and South Dakota twenty years earlier, he often dabbled in prospecting for minerals. He achieved slight success with a partnership in a mine, the Virginia, at the Grand Encampment in southern Wyoming, but had never accumulated much serious capital prior to his venture into oil properties. After several years of careful management, he had acquired a substantial amount of what he felt was valuable oil land. A man of impeccable character, known around the state as "Honest John," he never attained significant success until he, Boney Earnest, and Jake Ervay closed their big land deal.[39]

John Landon came into town from his small ranch near Ervay suffering with a fever on August 9. Dr. Rohrbaugh checked him in at the Grand Central Hotel. As the week progressed, his condition worsened. Under the watchful eye of the doctor, his body continued to weaken, and all the while his fever did not. Within a few days, he succumbed to an unknown illness at the age of forty-nine. The land deal of a short time ago did not feel nearly as sweet when Boney and Jake bore their old friend in his casket to the grave.[40]

Government engineers were exploring various sites in Wyoming along the Platte and Sweetwater Rivers for possible irrigation and flood control projects for some time. In August 1903, their sights were set on the Grand Canyon of the Platte, now known as Fremont Canyon. Casper's *Wyoming Derrick* newspaper reported the beginning of preliminary excavations and testing:

> *The government drillers are now engaged in clearing the bed of the Platte river in the Grand Canyon, a few miles above Alcova, preparatory to drilling to determine the depth of bedrock. The river through*

the canyon is strewn with big boulders and rocks and men are drilling holes in the largest rocks so that they can be blown to pieces. It will then be possible to get boats up the river in the canyon to place the machinery where the drilling is to take place.

A hand drill was used at Devil's Gate, but this outfit was taken to the railroad at Rawlins and shipped to Arizona, and the drilling machinery at the Grand Canyon above Alcova will be run by steam. An engine was taken out from Casper for that purpose last week.

The drilling outfit put down four holes at the proposed site of the Devil's Gate dam last year. A row of three, was also put down this year, and the drillers had the first hole part way down on the third row when B. A. Fowler and A. P. Davis, the government experts, arrived on the ground, and the latter gentlemen immediately ordered them to pull up the machinery and commence operation above Alcova.

When the preliminary work is completed at that place, the preliminary work will be done in the smaller canyon at Alcova, from which place the ditch will in all probability be taken out.

The Grand Canyon is about eight miles up the river from Alcova, and is from eight to ten miles in length. The walls are quite high, the highest point being 1,550 feet. The extent of the basin or reservoir is based on a dam to be built in the Grand Canyon 220 feet in height. It is estimated that the lake thus formed will be twelve to fifteen miles in width, and will cover most of the ranches on the Sweetwater river. The water will probably back up the Platte river to Seminoe mountain, a distance of at least 20 miles.

Among the ranches that would be covered by this immense area of water would be the Weaver ranch and Boney Earnest's Pick ranch on Sand Creek, Earnest's Canyon creek ranch, and the following ranches on the Sweetwater river: Julian's home ranch, Mollie Wolf, Frank Julian, C. F. Baker, Conway, W. B. Bohanan, and the water will come within a short distance of the buildings on Bothwell's ranch.

The Grand Canyon is pronounced the second best site for a reservoir in the United States, the best being in California. It is expected that the first work will be done in the Grand Canyon of the Platte.[41]

Martin Gothberg and many of his friends and associates would be greatly affected if the Platte River were dammed above Casper as proposed. Thousands of acres of fertile grazing would be submerged; friends and fellow sheep ranchers, like Mollie Wolf, Marvin Bishop, and many others, would lose their ranches entirely to the waters of the coming reservoir. On the contrary, hundreds might reap the benefits of extensive irrigation canals winding their way for miles across vast expanses, bringing life-giving water to the wide and arid Wyoming prairie.

The small community of Alcova struggled to survive near a series of hot springs flowing from the walls of a smaller canyon below the Grand Canyon of the Platte. An eastern resort syndicate planned a health resort here in 1891 and named it for the coves in the canyon wall near the springs. After discovering that most of the people of Wyoming only bathed once a week on Saturday if they needed it, the disheartened investors abandoned the project. Now little more than a rustic general store and post office, Alcova was a gathering place for local ranchers in the vicinity.[42]

A correspondent from the *Wyoming Derrick* visited Alcova in search of a scoop on the government's exploration project in the canyon. He found Boney Earnest, who invited the journalist to partake of his recently completed "buggy road," and come to visit his ranch, adding satirically that he best not wait too long or he might need to come by boat. Mr. and Mrs. Bohanan also stopped to retrieve their mail and for Mrs. Bohanan to pick up some sewing needles. They, too, invited the columnist to visit their ranch. Before long, Mollie Wolf drove in with his buggy, avoiding the discomfort of riding astride whenever convenient due to his injuries five years earlier. Mollie visited the post office twice each week since beginning a courtship with his neighbor Frank Julian's younger sister, Wilda. Mollie was nearing final proof on his homestead on the Sweetwater River. Without knowing if all of his hard work may have been wasted, he continued making improvements on his ranch as time and finances allowed. All anyone could do was wait to see what engineers and geologists discovered, and ponder what might develop as the result.[43]

Amid a wide assortment of circumstances throughout the year, Martin Gothberg's operations were successful. His purchase of the purebred ewes from Oregon had been prosperous as well as the development of his grazing operations with the Lone Tree Sheep Company. In May 1903, Fremont, Elkhorn & Missouri Valley Railroad re-established passenger train service from Chadron, Nebraska, to Casper, Wyoming. Shortly thereafter, the company was reorganized to form the Chicago & Northwestern Railway. On September 20, 1903, five railcar loads of Gothberg sheep left the Northwestern railyards in Casper en route to market at the stockyards in south Omaha, Nebraska. The loading of Gothberg's sheep and twelve other carloads belonging to Dave Schoening and George McClellan did not go without incident. So exasperated was Missou Hines with the interference of children in the railyard that it prompted him to post a notice in the newspaper the following week:

> Wm. Hines, stock agent of the Chicago & Northwestern railway, desires the Tribune to say that parents must keep their children away from the stock yards while stock is being loaded. Twice during the past week children have come close to being killed or maimed by the train by their carelessness, and besides the danger of being hurt, the children are continually disturbing the stock that is being loaded into the cars. Mr. Hines says he dislikes to drive the children away, but if the parents do not keep them away from the yards he will be compelled to do so.[44]

Martin Gothberg accompanied his shipment of sheep to Omaha and perhaps on to Chicago. Taking advantage of already covering half of the journey, he continued east to visit his family in New Jersey. It is unknown if Mary Enid joined Martin on this trip, but he stayed for several days in the Greenville district of Jersey City at the home of his sister and brother-in-law, Minnie and Willis Lund.[45]

Under a combination of circumstances, Boney Earnest was making changes in his business profile late in 1903. His oil company was busy drilling the first of several wells south of Alcova, and despite occasional breakdowns and lack of access to parts, equipment, and machinery at the remote location, they had reached a depth of 1,320 feet. In expectation of losing his ranch to the depths of an enormous reservoir, and at the same time anticipating the success of his oil investments nearby, he began erecting a new store building at Alcova. The manager of drilling procedures for the oil company, J. C. Hollebaugh, also conducted negotiations for a new business building there. The little community was bustling, with many of the oil workers living in a tent camp near the drilling operation with their families. Several new residences were built, and a number of families had moved into Alcova for the winter.[46]

A few days before Christmas, Martin and Mary Enid purchased 160 acres near Freeland in Bates Park from Mary Enid's stepfather, Frank Sanders. Two weeks later, Gothberg filed for a cash sale timber and stone claim on another forty acres four miles southeast of the home ranch on Casper Mountain.[47]

Through the holidays, the Gothbergs celebrated their success in recent years. Mary Enid had fully recovered, and their family and ranch continued to grow. Many of their friends prospered as well. Martin's brother Herman loved Wyoming nearly as much as Martin did, but his new bride, Jennie, was less enthusiastic, and they returned to New Jersey. His brother Ernst also fully recovered from his surgery and the family business also thrived.

Martin Gothberg looked optimistically ahead to the coming year. His sheep herds had grown to something over ten thousand head, and with enthusiasm he anticipated a good profit from his next wool crop. Though Casper was rapidly growing, much of the outlaw element of the old culture still lingered on the fringes of local society. It was not long before the Gothberg family again was exposed to the wilder ways of the recent past.

CHAPTER 6

Camelot on the Plains

1904–1906

EXCEPTIONALLY MILD WEATHER PROMPTED MID-WINTER REPORTS OF remarkably productive range conditions. The *Wyoming Tribune* reported, "One thing that is very gratifying is that sheep are unusually healthy, there being much less scab and other diseases to which they are subject than usual. Stockmen as a rule are in good shape and are feeling easy over the outlook." Rumor that government tests at the Grand Canyon of the Platte had proven the rock was of sufficient stability to form the foundation of a substantial dam flourished. The *Tribune* went on to say, "Residents of Natrona County feel jubilant over the announcement that the government is figuring on putting about $2,000,000 into that section for irrigating purposes." All felt if the prediction of that venture carried through, the Platte River valley would become one of the richest agricultural regions of the state.[1]

With the growing euphoria of Casper becoming a yet-to-be-realized Camelot of the plains, rumors abounded among the residents based upon visions of grandeur. Since obtaining statehood a decade earlier, Wyoming had yet to proclaim a permanent state capital. With so much optimism surrounding future irrigation, residents pushed hard for the city of Casper to receive that honor. Perhaps more realistically, banker and business-man C. H. King, accompanied by William Hines, traveled to Chicago to meet with officials of the Chicago & Northwestern Railway. Extension of the railroad beyond Casper to Lander was the subject of discussion. Upon their return, Mr. and Mrs. Hines attended a party at the home of then State Senator and Mrs. Patrick Sullivan. Since their marriage, the

Hineses had become quite popular in the inner circles of Casper's upper class. Missou's knowledge of regional matters and gregarious personality made him a popular guest at these events, but increased business travels for the railroad were contributing to more and more absences from his new wife.[2]

— —

Tom O'Day had once been a member of George Curry's Hole-in-the-Wall gang. Following their bank robbery at Belle Fourche, South Dakota, he was captured and escaped jail in Deadwood, South Dakota. He had been in and out of jail for numerous offenses over many years. Tom O'Day, notorious cattle rustler and horse thief, was caught by surprise in the Big Horn Mountains with twenty-three horses stolen from the CY Ranch and others in Converse and Natrona Counties in November 1903. When apprehended, he initially hesitated to raise his hands until Sheriff Frank Webb threatened to shoot him. "Good God, Webb," O'Day exclaimed, "don't kill me!"[3]

At his first trial in February 1904, the jury, to no one's surprise, could not reach a verdict. Six men were for conviction and six for acquittal. Tom O'Day was well known throughout the state and had many friends on the other side of the law that might cause trouble for the jurors who convicted him. The court selected a new jury and a second trial immediately followed. This jury also failed to reach agreement; eleven were for conviction and one for acquittal. This gave the prosecution some hope that they might still attain a conviction. A third jury was drawn. Martin Gothberg served on the jury for this trial, which proceeded without much mishap. The testimony was heard again. Before sending the jury to deliberation, Judge Craig instructed them that O'Day was not being tried for any misadventures in his sordid past nor for his reputation, but only the crime for which they had heard evidence. Possible retribution meted out by O'Day's confederates did not intimidate this third jury. It was not long before Martin and his fellow jurors reached a verdict, finding Tom O'Day guilty as charged. When he heard the finding, O'Day was incredulous. Despite his obvious guilt for the theft, he simply could not believe the jury would convict him, and he did not attempt to disguise his contempt for the sheriff, the prosecuting attorney, the court, and the jury.

Prior to sentencing, Judge Craig made his position clear to O'Day, "In the early days of Wyoming," he said, "it used to be the custom to rustle stock, and if a list could be compiled of all the men who had gotten a start in life by this method, it would make quite a large catalogue. But those days are past, and Tom, you ought to have quit when the rest of the boys did. If I were to sentence you for all the crimes you have committed, you would go to the penitentiary for the remainder of your life, but your sentence shall be only for the crime upon which you have been convicted." With that and the ring of his gavel, he sentenced Tom O'Day to six years of hard labor at the Wyoming State Penitentiary.[4]

While Martin Gothberg was on jury duty, Pat Sullivan and Missou Hines were in Lander, Wyoming, soliciting business for their Casper Livestock Commission Company. While there, Senator Sullivan never missed an opportunity to lobby for the proposed relocation of the state capital to Casper. Walt Blackmore purchased property on South Center Street and contracted construction of a new meat and produce market at that location. As Pat and Missou returned to Casper, pleased with their successful marketing venture, Walt was receiving a shipment of ironwork necessary for the completion of his new brick building. Workers had been stalled awaiting the arrival of the steel and now could push forward toward completion of the structure. Boney Earnest also purchased the lot east of M. N. "Shorty" Castle's Silver Dollar Livery on West Second Street in anticipation of future oil business expansion.[5]

In April, B. B. Brooks, Pat Sullivan, and Missou Hines represented the wool growers of Natrona County at the annual meeting of the State Board of Sheep Commissioners. A primary concern discussed at the convention was the spread of scabies. The highly contagious disease continued to threaten Wyoming flocks. Preventing its introduction and managing quarantines of infected herds while they were being treated was of critical importance.[6]

In May, Mollie Wolf came to Casper for supplies while Missou Hines escorted a client of his Casper Livestock Commission to Lander. At Logan Gulch, the prospective buyer inspected the sheep belonging to the estate of Phillip Weisser. At the same time, Tom Clayton guided prominent Denver stockman J. C. Munn to Boney Earnest's Pick Ranch. In expectation of the loss of Earnest's land, Munn negotiated the purchase of nearly all of Boney's livestock.[7]

When he returned from Lander, Missou took his wife on a short getaway to Douglas. Arriving home, the Northwestern Railroad presented a fine new carriage to Missou, a reward for his outstanding service.[8]

The first week of June, Martin Gothberg began shearing his flock of sheep. His shearers performed the majority of the task at the home ranch before Martin sent the herds to summer rangelands.[9]

On June 14, 1904, the Chicago & Northwestern Railway general manager George P. Bidwell and Superintendent Hughes arrived in Casper in a private car. There, Mr. Bidwell held a conference with several of the most prominent residents of the area. He showed the businessmen maps of proposed areas that would be subject to irrigation if three large dams were built along the North Platte River above Casper, the first dam being eight miles above Alcova. In all, Wyoming could expect to irrigate 1,380,000 acres as a result of the project of which 207,000 acres were in Natrona County. With the information Mr. Bidwell petitioned, the townspeople heartily approved the project. The railroad men presented the same proposal at Douglas, prompting an identical result from the citizens there. With the verbal support of dozens of central Wyoming's key figures, Mr. Bidwell headed to Washington, DC, where he easily convinced a sufficient number of legislative delegates of the project's importance, and they immediately appropriated one million dollars toward the construction of the first dam.[10]

Back in New Jersey, Martin Gothberg's sister Sophia Fuller visited their sister Minnie Lund in Jersey City. Sophia and her six-year-old son Clint traveled from their home in Attleboro, Massachusetts, to celebrate the Fourth of July with the Gothberg family.[11]

❧

Much to the surprise of many friends, Mollie Wolf married Luwilda Julian on July 12, 1904. Wilda was the daughter of Thomas H. and Sarah C. "Kate" Julian, and sister of Mollie Wolf's close friend and neighbor Frank Julian. Wilda's family then resided near Ferris, Wyoming, between Alcova and Rawlins. The family of the bride attended the unpretentious wedding, held in Casper at the home of Justice of the Peace Frank Jameson.[12]

❧

In 1904, the *Natrona County Tribune* visited Walt Blackmore's Hat-Six Ranch while chronicling the exploits of neighbor and gubernatorial candidate Bryant B. Brooks. "As you round the extremity of Casper Mountain you see, nestling between that acclivity and the 'hog back,' the house of the old Hat-Six company—the Carlisle Cattle Co. that flourished in the palmy days of the cattle industry. Here a gentleman named Blackmore has succeeded the above company, though in a somewhat more modest way."[13]

A month earlier, William Kreinbuehl, father-in-law of Warren G. Miller, pled guilty to forging a voucher on Blackmore's Hat-Six Sheep Company and awaited sentencing to the state penitentiary. The crime most likely quite embarrassed Mr. Miller, a prominent sheep and lumberman in the region, whose ranch and timberlands bordered Blackmore's ranch.[14]

While Martin Gothberg and his fellow ranchers began shipping livestock to market that year, Missou Hines once again faced the continual problem of young boys playing around the railyard as cattle and sheep were loaded. This year, posting handbills in addition to newspaper posts, Hines pleaded with parents to cooperate with railroad officials in keeping the youngsters away from this dangerous working environment.[15]

Promoters held the fourth annual Wyoming Industrial Convention in Casper in September 1904. Martin Gothberg submitted mineral samples from around his ranch and Mary Enid brought in a vast array of vegetables from her bountiful garden. The convention was a huge success and attracted participants and visitors from around the state. Rumors were rampant that this established festival would preempt the proposed state fair that still had not materialized after two years of planning. The State Fair Commissioners were even unable to confirm a permanent home for the celebration as numerous cities vied for the venue.[16]

As his health began to decline, Frank Sanders, Mary Enid's aging stepfather, applied for a Civil War pension. Congressman Frank Wheeler Mondell presented Mr. Sanders's case to the bureau of pensions. The board approved the application after two months for the very paltry sum of eight dollars per month, about $225 in today's money. After a long battle, Mr. Sanders finally received a 50 percent increase to his pension in 1908, thanks to the efforts of Congressman Mondell. In October, Mr. Sanders became very ill. Mrs. Sanders twice called Dr. Rohrbaugh to make the trip to Freeland from Casper to administer to her husband.[17]

While Martin Gothberg's sister and brother-in-law, Minnie and Willis Lund, entertained city officials and prominent citizens in Jersey City for Sunday dinner, Martin was arrested for perjury in Casper. On January 17, 1905:

Martin Gothberg, one of Natrona county's well known citizens, was on Tuesday morning served with information, charging him with perjury, the information being sworn out by Prosecuting Attorney Butler. Gothberg was summoned as a juror to serve on the regular panel, and on Monday morning when he was being examined as to his qualifications, it is alleged that he declared he was not a citizen of the United States and he said he had not taken out his second papers, and thereupon he was excused from jury duty by the court. His trial will be had during the latter part of the term.[18]

The circumstances behind Gothberg's arrest and any confusion regarding his citizenship seems unrecorded by any of the newspapers at the time. At minimum, Prosecuting Attorney Alex T. Butler and Martin J. Gothberg most certainly were acquainted prior to the incident. Gothberg had served on multiple juries in past cases, which Butler had prosecuted. On the thirtieth, Judge Charles E. Carpenter dismissed the case.

On Monday morning the case against Martin Gothberg, against whom information was filed in the district court, charging him with perjury was dismissed by Judge Carpenter, on account of there being no grounds for action. As will be remembered, the charge was made against Mr. Gothberg on account of some misunderstanding concerning his citizenship when he was being examined as to his qualifications to serve on the regular jury panel. In dismissing the case, the court said the whole matter came up before him, and it was wholly a misunderstanding by the court as well as by Mr. Gothberg, and the matter had been fully explained to the court before the information was filed. Mr. Gothberg is one of Natrona county's well-to-do and highly respected citizens and never before has he been accused of violating the laws of our country, and upon this charge he has been wholly exonerated and held entirely blameless.[19]

Martin Gothberg seems to have been a relatively quiet man. Having a substantial education by the standards of the time, he served on numerous juries. Being of above average intelligence, he probably held back a bit of a smirk when the prosecuting attorney excused him from the jury panel. That smirk most likely grew to a controlled belly laugh after hearing the lambasting Judge Carpenter meted out to Prosecuting Attorney Alex T. Butler following Gothberg's dismissal. Carpenter's exact words are unknown, but the *Cheyenne Daily Leader* reported it this way: "Prosecuting Attorney Butler was roasted to a brown turn by Judge Carpenter for causing Gothberg's arrest."[20]

In February 1905, construction began on the diversion tunnel that would be necessary to carry the flow of the North Platte River, enabling crews to build the Pathfinder Dam at the head of the Grand Canyon of the Platte. Surveyor, explorer, and bearer of a half dozen other titles, John C. Fremont became known as "The Pathfinder," for which the dam is named. Robert Stuart's Astorians originally named the canyon "The Fiery Narrows" on return from the Pacific Ocean in 1812. Fremont and a few adventurous members of his 1842 expedition floated the rapids of the treacherous canyon on their return from the West. The endeavor can only be called a success since no one was killed, but they lost or damaged a considerable amount of equipment when their boat capsized and left the crew swimming literally for their dear lives in the rapids. Most often called the Grand Canyon of the Platte, about this time it received its official present name, Fremont Canyon.[21]

Investors drilled the first oil well in the area three miles northwest of Casper in 1888. By 1889, a number of additional wells were completed, and numerous oil claims were being located around the county. The progress and success of these explorations continued over the next several years. In the spring of 1895, the Pennsylvania Oil & Gas Company fired up the first refinery in Casper and began successfully manufacturing lubricating oils immediately. The petroleum industry continued to grow and by 1905 contributed to a generous percentage of the region's economy. In 1903, the Belgo-American Company purchased all of the Pennsylvania Oil & Gas Company's holdings in Wyoming. The six hundred thousand dollar price tag included the refinery, fourteen producing oil wells, and 105,000 acres of oil land in the Salt Creek field. The new company boasted of huge expansion plans, including construction of a large new refinery and a railroad from Orin, Wyoming, to Lander. Casper, Lander, and Orin were all vying for the chance to host the new refinery for nearly a year, which promised to bring hundreds of related workers and immense prosperity to whatever site they chose.[22]

Casper's economy was teeming with opportunity as local financial leaders chomped on cigars while calculating where their investments would prove most profitable. Walt Blackmore purchased the property east of the Webel Mercantile Company on Second Street in January and razed the former *Casper Tribune* office on the site to make room for a brand-new grocery and meat market. Charles C. P. Webel, owner of the twenty-five-foot lot between their previous facility and Blackmore's property, collaborated with him on construction of the new two-story, fifty-by-one-hundred-foot brick structure. A solid brick wall separated the two businesses and the architect designed the front to complement Webel's original building. The finished structure achieved a seventy-five-foot frontage on the southeast corner of Second and Center Streets, the first fifty feet from the corner belonging to the Webel Mercantile Company and twenty-five feet to W. A. Blackmore's Meat and Produce Market.[23]

Many of Walt Blackmore's associates doubted the sensibility of his large investment in the new store, but Walt went ahead with his plan, hiring the experienced and capable James King of Chadron, Nebraska, as the butcher for the new market. He leased his old building to B. H. Aronson & Company, wholesale and retail liquor dealers from Fremont, Nebraska. Aronson's partner, L. P. Larson, had been in the wholesale liquor business in Nebraska for several years. He also owned a portion of the Fremont Brewing Company that prepared to join Aronson in the Blackmore building. The Fremont Brewing Company was one of the largest breweries in the Midwestern states, and held a substantial portion of the beer market in Wyoming. As soon as the building was available, Aronson worked at a frantic pace refitting and preparing it for his trade. Boney Earnest had also applied for a liquor license for his store in Alcova. Earnest and Aronson's licenses were both approved just days before Aronson's planned opening. On April 20, 1905, he unfastened his doors and opened up for business.[24]

After the Belgo-American Company abandoned their plans to build the railroad from Orin to Lander, the Chicago & Northwestern Railway obtained their surveys and began plans to extend their service to Lander, Wyoming. Shortly following the purchase, Missou Hines headed out to call on his many clients in that area. "Missou Hines returned home last Friday night from a two weeks' trip through the Lander Valley, where he was soliciting stock shipments for the Chicago & Northwestern railroad."[25]

When construction work began on the extension of the Chicago & Northwestern tracks from Casper on May 2, 1905, Marvin L. Bishop was already planning a sheepshearing operation along the route. His second eldest daughter, Katherine, filed a homestead twelve miles northwest of Casper on a predominantly level expanse of greasewood and sagebrush the local natives called Cadoma, meaning "to hide." The tract spanned the coming railroad tracks; it was the perfect location for shearing pens.[26]

Every day, Martin Gothberg saw the evidence as the economy of the region grew so rapidly it seemed it could burst. A growing number of men and equipment had moved past his ranch going to and from the developing oil field south of Alcova for two years. Though most transportation for the excavation of the diversion tunnel for the coming dam used the emigrant trail north of the river, the flow of traffic on the road before him became a continuous stream. By the time actual construction of the dam began, there would be five hundred men and eight hundred horses employed to create the reservoir.[27]

—◦—

At about five o'clock in the afternoon on Friday, May 12, 1905, three criminals escaped from the Natrona County Jail in Casper. The inmates were Lee Clubb, also known as Ed Lee, a former deputy awaiting trial for horse stealing; Bill Wardlaw, a forger recently extradited from Joplin, Missouri; and sixteen-year-old Marty Trout, also extradited from Missouri for cattle rustling. While Sheriff Frank K. Webb was gone to Wolton, Wyoming, to bring in notorious badman Black Mike Smith after he shot up the town and wounded four men in the process, the trio contrived their breakout. When the sheriff's nephew, young Deputy C. F. Webb, brought them their dinner, Trout and Clubb overpowered him. They bound and gagged him and placed him in their cell. Taking the deputy's keys and revolver, they also released Wardlaw from his cell.

The sheriff's wife was in the kitchen. They subdued her, then also tied and gagged her. Knowing his way around the office, Lee Clubb quickly procured all of the guns and ammunition there. Placing Mrs. Webb in the jail, Clubb removed the handkerchief from her mouth and apologized if he had hurt her. Grabbing what food they could put in their pockets, the three locked up the jail and slipped out the side door. They separated there and all made their way toward Casper Mountain, meeting up again at the Northwestern roundhouse. As they entered the pasture of the CY Ranch, they met L. W. Bailey and Ralph Galbraith on horseback. Bailey hollered at the men to come back before they got into worse trouble, but they ignored him. Ralph came to town and sounded the alarm as Bailey, unarmed, followed the men toward the mountain. When Lee Clubb fired a couple of shots in his direction, Bailey returned to town.

On his way, Bailey met Casper Marshal Sheffner and a posse consisting of Shorty Castle, Abe Greenlaw, Blake Horn, and a number of others in pursuit. Being afoot, the fugitives made quick time crossing multiple fences as they fled, easily outdistancing the posse. After the men crossed the first hill from town, Lee Clubb lay down in a ravine and waited for darkness. Bill Warlaw told authorities after his capture that after crossing the second hill, Marty Trout caught a grazing horse. He fashioned a bridle from his suspenders around the horse's lower jaw, and bareback, headed southeast and was not seen since.[28] Wardlaw continued southwest. At one point, Blake Horn exchanged shots with a man in the brush near Garden Creek, probably Clubb, but none took effect. The posse followed their trail until dark. When they were unable to see their tracks any longer, they returned to town. The marshal placed guards at all of the bridges along the Platte River and main roads leaving the area.

Sheriff Webb arrived in Casper with his prisoner overnight and left with a posse in pursuit at first light in the morning. Webb thought he found tracks of two men returning to Casper. Unable to locate any further trace, the posse returned to town. Men watching the Platte Bridge in Casper thought they saw a man approaching in the dark on Friday night, but after seeing the guards, he fled. On Saturday evening, the guards being out of sight, Lee Clubb approached the Platte Bridge at Bessemer. When hollered to halt, he turned and ran. Clubb had made a dry camp on Gothberg Ranch near the west end of Casper Mountain on both Friday and Saturday nights. For two days, the outlaw remained unseen nearly outside the Gothbergs' back door.

On Sunday night, a herder saw one or two suspicious men, probably Bill Wardlaw and Marty Trout, near Gothberg's Lone Tree Sheep

Company camp on Stinking Creek, forty miles south of Casper. That same night, Lee Clubb stole a horse and saddle from Martin Gothberg's neighbor, Bill Misters. On Monday morning, Sheriff Webb telephoned from Jake Crouse's ranch that Clubb was in the vicinity and he needed assistance. By four o'clock that afternoon, Webb was back in Casper, having tracked Clubb to within two miles of town, still mounted on Mr. Misters's horse. Monday, a man saw Trout and Wardlaw on Bert Cheney's ranch on Corral Creek. On Tuesday morning, Bill Wardlaw came into Tom McDonald's sheep camp on Red Creek nearly starving for food. McDonald took custody of Wardlaw and sent word to the Two Bar Ranch to call for the sheriff. In the sheriff's absence, Justice Tubbs deputized Marshal Sheffner, who rode out and took custody of the man.

Sheriff Webb left early that morning to Big Muddy Station west of Glenrock, Wyoming. From there he telephoned at about noon requesting help and saying he knew exactly where Clubb was. What happened as a result is unknown, but Lee Clubb, using the alias Ed Lee, succeeded again in eluding the sheriff and Frank K. Webb did not take it lightly. Webb actively pursued Clubb and Trout for quite some time. Webb eventually apprehended Lee Clubb in Rock Springs, Wyoming, in February 1910. Marty Trout, jailed in California later that year, never returned to Wyoming for trial. For additional information on this story, see Appendix B, "The Jailbreak, 1905."[29]

In 1905, the stone building at Gothberg's home ranch was constructed. It seems logical that Martin Gothberg may have contracted Bill Evans to construct the building. He and Evans had worked together for several years mining clay for Evans's brick manufacturing. Evans was not only a brick mason, but an accomplished stonemason and plasterer as well. However, there may also have been numerous stone workers arriving in the area in anticipation of the coming massive dam building project. With that employment prospect yet to begin, Gothberg could have temporarily hired stonemasons available in the area at that time who were anxious to get to work.[30]

Before the dust settled from the escaped prisoners running around on the ranch, Martin and Mary Enid welcomed the arrival of their daughter, Emma Loretta Gothberg, into their family on May 14, 1905. At the time, Martin was dealing with the land office in Douglas on the final patent for an additional forty acres of land southeast of the home ranch that adjoined his other property on Casper Mountain. If the recovery from giving birth to Emma, taking care of the household and the other children, raising a garden, chickens, and a host of daily duties typical of every ranch wife, plus watching for fugitives, were not enough to keep Mary Enid busy, she also hosted her half-sister's wedding two weeks later on May 28, 1905: "On Sunday afternoon at the residence of Martin Gothberg, Miss Ada Sanders of Freeland and Mr. Frank Johnson of the VR were united in marriage, Rev. J. L. Craig officiating."[31]

In 1905, the city of Portland, Oregon, organized a celebration for the one hundredth anniversary of Lewis and Clark's arrival to the Pacific coast. Promoters planned the Lewis & Clark Exposition to rival the grandeur of a World's Fair while focusing on exhibits surrounding the settling of the American West. Wyoming may not yet have officially acquired the nickname of the "Cowboy State," but there was little question that the residents took great pride in their "boots and chaps" heritage. With that in mind, the *Wyoming Tribune* in Cheyenne sponsored a statewide "cowboy contest," in which the favorite riders in each of the seven regions of the state would win a trip to the exposition. The late nomination into the race did not deter Tom C. "Jerky Bill" Clayton. He joined the contest to represent Natrona-Converse Counties in May, with all of the vibrato and gusto his friends expected of him, nearly six thousand votes behind the leader. "There are now forty-three men in the contest from various parts of the state. T. C. Clayton, familiarly called Jerky Bill enters the contest today from Converse County with 100 votes."[32]

With the flurry of activity surrounding the Pathfinder Dam project, the *Wyoming Tribune* in Cheyenne sent a reporter to Casper to write a story on the development of the venture. He described the landscape and the ranchmen that inhabited the region. The correspondent interviewed eight of those ranchers being displaced beneath the reservoir's twenty-two-thousand-acre surface. Some, like Boney Earnest, had been there for a quarter century. All of his 1,200 acres of deeded land would be submerged, and most of the rangeland he used surrounding it. As the correspondent worked his way toward Casper, he visited many of the ranchers along the route.

> *Mr. M. J. Gothberg filed on his land twenty years ago. It is a pretty place close up against the foot of the mountain. When Mr. Gothberg first filed on his land, he worked out summers for cow outfits and improved his ranch during the winter months. This he did for about eight years, when he married and since then has remained permanently on his ranch. He has 600 acres, all fenced and forty acres under cultivation, besides much natural meadow. He owns over 100 head of cattle and of course, some horses.*[33]

As was his nature, Martin Gothberg modestly understated his assets. He never boasted of his success or wealth. He had, in fact, pieced together over nine hundred acres of deeded land and leased another 640 acres in Natrona County. He had also acquired land in Carbon and Albany Counties by purchasing smaller ranches, and grazed many of his sheep there and on the surrounding rangeland. At the time, he owned no less than three thousand sheep and probably doubled that number. Never leaving the cattle business, his herd was sufficient enough that he shipped a railcar load of market beef to buyers in the East that fall, without diminishing his herd.[34]

In June, school superintendent Miss Effie Cumming spent several days visiting the Gothberg and Clarkson schools. "Miss Cumming has now made an official visit to every school in the county since she took the office of superintendent the first of the year, and she is very much pleased with the progress and the bright prospects for the several districts." Armed with the favorable report from Miss Cumming, Martin Gothberg and Bill Misters began planning a new schoolhouse for their children. The Misters' homestead was two miles east of Dobbin Springs. A school located on the eastern border of the section Gothberg leased from the state would split the travel distance for the Gothberg and Misters children.[35]

Walt Blackmore pledged to enter a float for Blackmore's Meat Market into Casper's "Monster Fourth of July Parade." As promotors solicited merchants to enter floats into their jubilee, Tom Clayton leaped forward in the cowboy contest, securing over five thousand votes in just a few weeks. "In the Natrona-Converse contest T. C. Clayton, or 'Jerky Bill' as he is sometimes called by his friends, gets a big bunch of votes and goes up to second place." Martin Gothberg's sister Minnie and her two children spent the Fourth with their sister Sophia's family in Attleboro, Massachusetts.[36]

With the bustle from the oil business in Alcova centered several miles south of the community and the construction of the diversion tunnel several miles to the west, the little village slipped into the drowsy, mundane dogdays of summer. The *Natrona County Tribune* reported, "The only excitement we have had here lately was a fishing match between Boney Earnest and James Finley, the winner to have the fish and dress them. Boney's catch was twenty-seven and Finley's one." While Boney was enjoying his fishing, Mrs. Earnest hosted Mr. and Mrs. D. Hammer, who visited from Detroit, Michigan, in search of real estate prospects.[37]

In July, Martin Gothberg filed an application for an injunction against the Kimball Livestock Company. Details of the case made by Gothberg are unknown, but the court denied the application and the demurrer of the defendant sustained. Martin Gothberg, Donald Michie, and four witnesses for both sides of Michie's land contest case all traveled on the train together to testify at the land office in Douglas. Tom Clayton boarded the train in Glenrock, also visiting Douglas on other business. Clayton did not hesitate to campaign for votes in the cowboy contest while he was in town.[38]

In August, the tracks of the Chicago & Northwestern Railway reached Cadoma, Wyoming. In anticipation of losing his home ranch to the waters of the coming reservoir, Marvin L. Bishop had already begun constructing corrals for shipping livestock in the fall and to serve as shearing pens in the spring. Here the railroad created their first station west of Casper and established train service to Cadoma as track laying crews continued on west. The village of Cadoma consisted of a small railway station, a couple of houses, stock pens, and a post office where Marvin's wife, Lona, was postmaster. Many area ranchers were anxious to take advantage of the convenience of postal service being available twelve miles closer than Casper.[39]

When Walt Blackmore's younger sister Ella arrived in Casper from Michigan for an extended visit, the buzz around town was all about the *Wyoming Tribune's* big cowboy popularity contest. Locals argued about who best would represent Converse and Natrona Counties when attending the Lewis and Clark Exposition in Portland, Oregon. The townsfolk looked for a civilized candidate that would cast a refined image of the people of Wyoming. Those who plied the trade of "cowboy" themselves wanted the roughest, toughest wrangler the country had to offer.

Tom Kearns from Casper led the competition from the beginning and Lee Moore from Douglas had followed in second place. As the end of the cowboy contest drew near, Jerky Bill surpassed Moore and closed to within one thousand votes of Kearns for the two counties. In the final weeks of the contest, the three men exchanged the lead in the heated race for the counties numerous times. In the last days Lee Moore surged ahead and held on to win the trip to Portland with 28,200 votes. Tom Clayton came in second place with nineteen thousand votes and Tom Kearns followed with 13,700 votes.[40]

On August 26, 1905, Rasmus Lee hauled logs cut earlier for firewood from Gothberg's property on Casper Mountain to his home ranch. As he brought the cargo down the mountain that morning, the wagon pitched, spilling it over and throwing Mr. Lee to the ground below as the entire load of logs rolled over him. The violence of the crash dislocated Rasmus's right shoulder and the blows received from the logs left him badly bruised throughout his body with terrible cuts and bruises to his face and head. Fearful for his life, Martin brought him to town as quickly and carefully as possible. Gothberg delivered Mr. Lee to Dr. T. A. Dean who immediately attended to his injuries. Dr. Dean reset his shoulder and dressed Rasmus's wounds. After fully assessing the injuries, Dr. Dean found nothing life threatening. Though badly beaten, Dr. Dean expected Mr. Lee to make a full recovery. A week later, his cuts, bruises, and sprains were well on the mend.[41]

As the newspaper tallied the votes in Cheyenne for the cowboy contest, Boney Earnest loaded six railcars of his cattle, perhaps the last of them on the train in Casper. He and his wife accompanied the herd to south Omaha where they oversaw the delivery at the stockyards. He contemplated that perhaps he had been too quick to dispose of them. He had been in the cattle business for a long time. He owned his own ranch for over thirty years. The new Pathfinder Dam would not be completed for quite some time. Nonetheless, he did not want to wait too long. The market was strong and he already had investments in the oil business that occupied the majority of his time. They arrived back in Casper on September 22, 1905. Spending the night there, they returned home the next day. For the Earnests, it was the end of one era and the beginning of another.[42]

Along with Boney Earnest's cattle, Martin Gothberg shipped three railcar loads of sheep to south Omaha. He also planned to ship cattle soon, but had not yet sorted his herd.[43]

In early October, Martin Gothberg and William Misters entertained bids for sixty logs, peeled and delivered to a point midway between their ranches. In addition, they needed eighteen poles for rafters and hoped to have a new sixteen-by-eighteen-foot schoolhouse constructed for District No. 14 on the site before winter.[44]

By the middle of the month, Gothberg loaded a railcar of cattle in Casper with beeves from his ranch. As the twenty-two-car cattle train departed for Omaha markets on the fifteenth, Gothberg's neighbor Daniel Clark and his son Frank inspected their flocks grazing on Salt Creek.

Fresh from a summer feeding on the meadows of the Big Horn Mountains, Clark planned to ship a large portion of his sheep to market from the new station at Cadoma on November 9.[45]

Mary Enid Gothberg and the children journeyed to Bates Park in November to visit with friends and Mary Enid's family. With winter just around the corner, visiting later in the year was unlikely, if not impossible. With that thought in mind, Martin brought his flocks down to lower elevations from their summer grazing range. In December, he herded fifty of his bucks in from Bear Creek to winter at the home ranch on Dobbin Springs.[46]

The case of Martin J. Gothberg vs. Kimball Livestock Company from the previous July appeared again on the district court docket in January. Nothing else regarding the case made mention in the *Tribune*.[47]

By 1905, Martin's brother-in-law Willis Lund had entered into the business of wholesale distribution of brass fixtures. In March of 1906, Willis was in California on an extended business trip when, in her husband's absence, Minnie Lund traveled with their two children to visit her sister Sophia Fuller in Attleboro, Massachusetts.[48]

In April, Martin's twenty-one-year-old niece Doretta Koezly sold a lot on Claremont Avenue in Jersey City to William Peckham. Two weeks later, Ernst Gothberg purchased two lots on Bartholdi Avenue from Otto, Gustav, and Henry Lembeck for $1,500, then sold a lot at the corner of Lembeck and Romar Avenues to Margaretha Albrect for one hundred dollars. Ernst then contracted Muller & Lauer Construction Company to build two frame houses on the Bartholdi Avenue property for $2,338. The contract did not include the foundations or basements, which Ernst paid mason H. Donough $1,200 to construct.[49]

Willis Lund returned to California in May, accompanied by his wife, Minnie. The trip may have included business calls, but primarily it centered on the Shriners' delegation visiting the city of Riverside. When a local reporter interviewed Willis and Minnie, they exclaimed that the area resembled "the Garden of Eden!" Remarking on their recent automobile tour, they added, "The drives are simply charming."[50]

CAMELOT ON THE PLAINS

Also in May, William Hines traveled to Lander, Wyoming, to locate a site for the railroad to build stockyards west of town and solicit livestock and wool shipments from that location. Upon his return to Casper, he received word of the death of his friend and supervisor, Mr. G. O. Dennis, division freight agent for the Chicago & Northwestern Railway. Mr. Dennis shot himself at Deadwood, South Dakota. Hines left immediately for Blair, Nebraska, where the funeral and internment took place.[51]

In June, Martin Gothberg's father and brothers incorporated their brass works. The H & E Gothberg Manufacturing Company filed their articles of incorporation with a capital stock of sixty thousand dollars, about $1.6 million today. They listed the nature of the business as manufacturer of bronze and brass ornaments and fixtures. The *Journal* listed the incorporators as Edwin H. Gothberg, Martin's father; Ernst Gothberg, his eldest brother; F. W. Gothberg, who seems to have been Martin's elder brother Bernard; and Herman E. Gothberg, his younger brother.[52]

In 1906, Gothberg sheared thirty thousand pounds of wool from his flock. In June, he sold his clip to the Silberman Brothers Company for $6,750, equivalent to about two hundred thousand dollars today. It was about this time that Martin obtained Charles "Pancake Charley" Stevens's ranch along Stinking Creek in northern Carbon County, Wyoming. Revenue from Gothberg's sale of his wool probably made the purchase possible. The ranch consisted of about 640 deeded acres. There also were at least 1,200 sheep included with the land. Family lore tells the story of the purchase price being two thousand dollars. Pancake Charley insisted on payment in cash, so Martin loaded sixty pounds of silver on a packhorse to deliver the money. The value of silver at the time would suggest closer to two hundred pounds, making the need for a packhorse more likely.[53]

The end of July found Mollie Wolf helping his brother-in-law Frank Julian put up hay on his neighboring ranch along the Sweetwater River. His wife, Wilda, helped her sister-in-law Anna with dinner while their two-year-old son, Leslie, played on the floor. Leslie discovered a wooden box under the bed and opened it, finding a tin can inside. Inside the can were small white chunks that might have looked similar to candy. Just then, his mother saw him and took the box away from him. In an instant, she saw the label on the can, "Strychnine." She hoped that the boy had not sampled the contents, but soon it was obvious that he had eaten some of them. Every remedy the ladies could think of was tried as the men were urgently beckoned in from the field. Dr. Lathrop was summoned from the nearby community of Pathfinder and arrived very quickly, but the poison had taken effect on the child rapidly and he succumbed before further aid could be administered.[54]

As Mollie and Wilda tried to absorb the shock of the death of their only child, Martin Gothberg's parents, Herman and Sophia Gothberg, and younger sister Sophia Fuller arrived in Casper for an extended visit with the family. This being Martin's parents' second visit to Wyoming, they were wonderfully surprised by the growth of the young city of Casper, barely a cow town during their previous stay eleven years earlier. There were many new businesses, some even sporting concrete sidewalks. Martin's parents were overjoyed to see Mary Enid and their growing family. Four delightful children, whom their grandparents had never met, were bursting with excitement to show them everything they could around their country home. Edwin and Walter, ages ten and six, anxiously worked to impress upon their grandfather what mature young men they were. Eight-year-old Sis was excited to learn from Aunt Sophia what it was like to live in a city, and, of course, Grandma could not get enough of little Emma.[55]

Their visit with Martin, Mary Enid, and the children was splendid. They enjoyed the fresh, clean air of the Wyoming plains and fishing from Bates Creek, not far from the farm belonging to Mary Enid's parents. They enjoyed walks and horseback rides in the foothills of Casper Mountain, but mostly relished spending time with their beloved family. They had spent perhaps the most pleasant few weeks of weather available in the Northern Rockies, but frosty, clear mornings warned of the coming snows of winter. In early September, Mr. and Mrs. Gothberg and daughter Sophia bid their tearful goodbyes. Both those leaving and staying promised not to allow so much time to pass before their next visit. As Martin, Mary Enid, and the children waved their final farewells, the train left the station with their loved ones bound for their respective homes in New Jersey and Massachusetts.[56]

In October, Martin bought one thousand Oregon ewes from Tom Kinney, a prosperous businessman and rancher from Rock Springs, Wyoming. He and Mary Enid, then joined by Harry E. Parsons, formed the Dobbin Springs Sheep Company and acquired an additional 160 acres of land in the six-mile draw eight miles northwest of his home ranch. They also established the Gothberg-Lindsey Sheep Company in partnership with Noah Lindsey, obtaining another 160 acres of land in northern Carbon County. The Gothbergs invested a total of twenty thousand dollars in the two companies, equivalent to approximately $560,000 today. They held two-thirds ownership of both companies.[57]

As county commissioners approved Martin Gothberg's brands for another year, his friend Walt Blackmore advertised on the front page of the *Natrona County Tribune* that Blackmore's Market carried everything needed for a holiday feast. "Make your stomach glad by ordering a good Christmas dinner . . . 200 turkeys–300 chickens, ducks and geese . . ." and a wide array of fresh fish, meats, and produce were all to be on hand for Christmas and New Year's celebrations.[58]

As another year came to a close, Martin Gothberg assessed his family's prosperity. In spite of brushes with outlaws, and friends preparing to lose their ranches beneath the depths of the impending Pathfinder Reservoir, the entire regional economy was bursting at the seams. The Gothbergs had a working telephone in their home at the ranch. Martin had taken his profits from a record wool crop and reinvested much of those funds into more land and livestock. With moneys earned from the sale of lambs, he and Mary Enid formed two new companies to further expand the growth of the Gothberg Ranch. Most certainly, all were looking forward to, as their friend Walt Blackmore advertised, a holiday feast. The fare may have included delicacies from Walt's market, beef or lamb from the family larder, or fresh venison from the foothills of Casper Mountain. Whatever the case, no one left the table wishing for more.

CHAPTER 7

Grand Larceny in the Red-light District

1907–1909

WHILE THE GOTHBERG RANCH CONTINUED TO GROW OVER THE COM-
ing years, the Northwestern Railway planned to cross South Pass and
proceed westward. Martin treated Mary Enid to a holiday at a first-class
hotel in Chicago and he was again called to jury duty on a most unusual
case. None of this materialized, though, before a springtime blizzard paralyzed the North Platte River valley.

———～———

In February, the one-and-a-half-year-old case of M. J. Gothberg vs. Kimball Livestock Company was again continued, and again, there was no
explanation in the *Tribune* beyond "demurrer sustained."[1]

———～———

Martha Hines purchased a stock of millinery goods and fixtures from
Mrs. R. D. Jones in Casper in January. By March, she set herself up and
opened a brand-new millinery and dress making shop complete with fit-
ting and changing rooms. All the ladies of the area, most certainly including Mary Enid Gothberg and Minnie Blackmore, were delighted with
the new enterprise. Her shop represented a growing culture in their frontier town.[2]

———～———

In April, Martin Gothberg leased 280 acres three miles south of the home
ranch in Gothberg Draw from the State of Wyoming. He also applied

for water rights for 113 acres of his land bordering Lone Tree Creek. As Martin's flocks continued to grow, water usage became more and more critical in the arid sage-covered hills and canyons of southern Natrona and northern Carbon Counties.[3]

Sunday, May 12, 1907, was a beautiful spring day in Casper, Wyoming. Pleasant temperatures brought dozens of folks from their homes to bask in the sun at their favorite fishing hole or picnic spot. Lo and behold, a violent springtime blizzard loomed out of sight in the west. At noon, the sleeping monster began to rouse, bringing a scattering of light rain showers. By midafternoon the tempest fully awakened, the wind rose to a gale, the mercury plummeted, and a dispersed sleet turned to a driving snow. In moments, the prairie wore a blanket of three inches of heavy, wet snow.

Many younger residents scoffed at the squall, thinking it would not last. Early pioneers prepared to dig in for the siege. Six teens were picnicking near Garden Creek at the foot of Casper Mountain. They dashed to their horses and made a record run to town, but not before becoming soaked to the skin in ice water. A. J. Mokler and S. W. Conwell were fishing near Hat-Six Ranch and drove their buggy hurriedly back to town, soaking wet, but still laughing at the price they paid for a couple of nice strings of fish. The ferocious storm was not yet finished. It dumped a foot and a half of snow on the Platte River valley before nightfall.

A couple traveled ten miles west of town to a sheep camp. Their horses balked in the storm, prompting them to stay the night. On Monday, their team played out halfway home in the heavy mire, forcing them afoot in the snow, slush, and mud. Three companions caught at Walt Blackmore's ranch chose to stay the night. After fighting very deep mud on their drive to town the next morning, they were uncertain that they had made the right choice. When they assessed the damages a few days later, they decided that no one was seriously injured and should add the experience to their banks of wisdom.[4]

On May 25, Martin Gothberg received land patents on two homesteads. One was a forty-one-acre tract in Gothberg Draw with Frank Deuel, and the other was forty acres eight miles southeast of his home ranch on the divide between Casper and Muddy Mountains with Jim Silver. The Gothberg Ranch continued to grow in land and livestock. At this point, Gothberg had amassed not less than two thousand acres of deeded land plus leases of several hundred more acres. Additionally, his sheep herd had grown to over eleven thousand head, and his sheep and cattle still grazed on thousands of acres of open rangeland whenever possible.[5]

Walt Blackmore now operated two meat markets in Casper. Business was thriving, but the grueling pace of operating both stores was taking its toll on him. In June, he announced that neither store would be open on Sundays any longer. He advertised politely, asking his customers to plan on Saturday to make their purchases last until Monday. He received strong ridicule from his clientele, many complaining that lacking an icebox, they had no means of keeping their meat fresh for two days, especially in summer.[6]

On June 12, the president of the Chicago & Northwestern Railway and an entourage of other high-ranking officials of the company arrived by special train in Lander, Wyoming. Local interests promoted an array of resources in the vicinity. To the chagrin of area stockmen, the president and other leading representatives were most interested in the oil industry of the area and mining on South Pass. Two months later, Missou Hines, on behalf of the railroad, escorted another group of journalists and other businessmen to the area, including a demonstration at the oil field known as the Henderson Oil Wells. All of the wells were capped, but representatives claimed the thirteen wells would each produce fifty barrels of oil per day when put into production.[7]

In September, Missou Hines guided a team of six railway surveyors for the Chicago & Northwestern from Lander across South Pass to Pinedale, Wyoming. A few weeks prior, he had taken F. A. Haines, chief engineer for the company, over the route. The *Pinedale Roundup* surmised that Mr. Haines had selected the preferred route on that trip and the surveyors were there to lay out the grade. To add to the rumors, Haines brought his family to Brooks Lake, ninety miles northwest of Lander, on a fishing trip while the surveyors worked their way to Pinedale. Missou Hines could, of course, show the crew where Haines designated the line to run. The *Roundup* concluded that soon the Chicago & Northwestern Railway would extend on westward to the Pacific coast. Their optimism seemed plausible at the time, but the vision never materialized.[8]

—◆—

Shortly after Missou Hines and the survey crew left Lander for South Pass and Pinedale, one of Martin Gothberg's sheepherders died in the bunkhouse at the home ranch. Gothberg had only employed Alonso Bosler for less than a week, when another herder, Harry Starks, awoke in the bunkhouse to find Bosler lying across the foot of his and Bosler's beds. When Starks could not rouse Bosler, he called Gothberg. When Gothberg came to the bunkhouse, he found Bosler dead and called coroner Henry A. Lilly to the ranch. Lilly took the body to Casper and held an inquest. The jury found Bosler's death the result of heart failure. His younger brother had worked in the vicinity for quite some time, but Bosler had arrived from Kansas only a few days earlier. He was only thirty years old but had suffered from dropsy (edema) for some time and a severe case of typhoid fever a year earlier. Most recently, he recovered and came to Wyoming for work. He had a five hundred dollar life insurance policy payable to an aunt in Missouri in his possession, but no recent receipts, and Alonso's brother believed it had lapsed. They buried him at Highland Park Cemetery.[9]

In October, Martin and Mary Enid teamed up with John Harris, founding the Gothberg-Harris Sheep Company. The Gothbergs contributed two-thirds of the twenty thousand dollar capital investment, about $342,000 in today's money, to form the company. The business purchased another 120 acres on Lone Tree Creek in far southern Natrona County and made that the center of operations for the new company.[10]

—◆—

In November, the Chicago & Northwestern Railway furloughed Missou Hines and C. W. Cook, both long-term employees of the company. The *Douglas Enterprise* did not pull any punches expressing their displeasure with the act when giving their report of the dismissal:

> *With a view of retrenchment the Northwestern railway management last week suspended Missou Hines, who has been stock solicitor for that road for twenty years and abolished the office of general passenger and freight agent of the Wyoming & Northwestern division, which position has been filled acceptably by C. W. Cook since the completion of the road, and who had been in the employ of the Northwestern system for over twenty years. Not a very keen appreciation of a life time's service by faithful employees, when they are laid off in the manner these gentlemen were. Douglas Enterprise.*[11]

Missou did not laze around for long. With his typical resiliency, he was back working in short order. Days after his discharge from the railroad, he accepted the position of regional inspector with the State Board of Sheep Commissioners. He reported to Commission President Wilson in Douglas, Wyoming, on December 10, 1907. Two weeks later, he was on the job in Lusk, Wyoming, issuing a quarantine on a band of sheep exposed to scabies.[12]

A week before Christmas, Martin and Mary Enid Gothberg were in Chicago, Illinois. The nature of their visit is unknown, but they stayed at the prestigious Briggs House on the corner of Randolph and Wells Streets. The hotel's clientele often had business at the courthouse just east of the accommodations or were there attending a performance at the famous McVicker's Theater just down the street. The 80-by-180-foot, five-story Italianate building, while not the most luxurious hotel in Chicago, was very well outfitted. The Briggs "has always been celebrated for the comfort, neatness, quiet, and admirable order of its appointments, and also for the excellence of its table and the general hospitality of its proprietors." The celebrated hotel dining room served the finest seventeenth century–style French gourmet cuisine in the city. They were famous for a variety of elegant dishes that graced their menu. Meals began with oyster or terrapin soup, followed by fish. Next, came the main entrée, perhaps rabbit or veal, and finally, dinner was finished off with a decadent dessert on the order of chocolate mousse or crème brûlée, possibly.[13]

The Gothberg Ranch again increased its size. With the final proof on a homestead in Carbon County, Mary Enid Gothberg added another 160 acres of deeded land to the ranch in January 1908. The property adjoined Pancake Charley's ranch, which Martin purchased two years earlier. March 7, 1908, Mary Enid secured a lease for eighty acres from the State of Wyoming. This parcel on Stinking Creek in Carbon County was three miles south of Charley's ranch. At the same time, she leased another forty acres, twelve miles west of the home ranch. This property spanned the Oregon Trail and centered around an area the Gothbergs used as winter range for a portion of their sheep.[14]

On February 1, 1908, Walt and Minnie Blackmore formed a partnership with Edward Gue from Newcastle, Wyoming. Gue, the highly regarded operator of a meat market in Newcastle for most of a decade, was well qualified in the business. The company incorporated with twenty thousand dollars in capital, the Blackmores holding two-thirds of stock. The Blackmore and Gue Company continued operation of Blackmore's Meat Market and planned to expand into the livestock business in the future.[15]

Not all was as promising for the Blackmores at their ranch. On January 31, Missou Hines visited his supervisor in Douglas regarding a flock of sheep he thought had scabies. On February 4, 1908, he issued a notice of quarantine. The infected herd consisted of eight bucks and 252 ewes on the Hat-Six Ranch. Blackmore recently purchased the presumed healthy animals from a Mr. Davis, who imported them from another state. The quarantine area included Blackmore's entire ranch and portions of his grazing range.[16]

In April, Martha Hines advertised a "new gasoline range for sale cheap" and a special Easter sale at her shop on Saturday the eighteenth. She offered substantial discounts on all Easter hats and suits. While Martha contemplated her dress sale, Missou pondered the infected flock at the Hat-Six Ranch. An issued order only weeks ago by Governor Bryant B. Brooks demanded that infectious and communicable diseases afflicting all species of livestock be eradicated using every reasonable means. Blackmore's sheep were not responding to normal treatments for scabies, a condition normally cured without difficulty. Missou called in Dr. Pflaeging, the state veterinarian, to assess the problem.[17]

On May 9, Missou accompanied the state veterinarian to the ranch. The diagnosis and result were devastating.

On Saturday State Veterinarian Pflaeging and state Sheep Inspector Hines destroyed 220 head of sheep belonging to W. A. Blackmore because they were suffering from an incurable and filthy disease. These sheep were quarantined last winter and were supposed to be suffering from scab, but it now turns out that the venereal disease was the cause of their condition.

There was no cure. Euthanasia was the only known manner of preventing the disease from spreading. Governor Brooks's proclamation struck home with a shocking blow.[18]

Following the sickening task of killing hundreds of ailing sheep, Missou traveled to Cheyenne where he represented Natrona County at the Democratic State Convention. While Walt Blackmore attempted to absorb the numbing shock of both the physical and financial loss of his sheep, his brother came to Casper for a weeklong visit from Sutherland, Nebraska. Bill Blackmore had not been in the area since 1894. Casper's growth pleasantly surprised him, not to mention the growth of his brother's business interests since his previous visit. In 1894, Walt and Minnie operated a fledgling pharmacy and variety shop. Now they owned two prosperous meat and produce markets, a small ranch, and one of the more significant business buildings in Casper.[19]

On June 28, 1908, Mary Enid Gothberg's half-sister Villa I. Sanders married Albert L. Shapley at Freeland, Wyoming. Al previously resided near Wheatland, Wyoming, and the couple planned to live near Freeland. The wedding took place at the home of Justice William H. Cheney. Jess Shapley acted as best man and Nellie Cheney as bridesmaid. The bride's sister, Ada Johnson, and her husband, Frank, hosted a reception afterward.[20]

About the same time, Martin Gothberg filed charges against Frank Hill for stealing eight to ten sheep from the Gothberg Livestock Company. Hill received a preliminary trial before Justice of the Peace Warren E. Tubbs and furnished a bond, placed at one thousand dollars. Frank Hill, a fairly well-known ranch hand, had made the newspapers around Wyoming after becoming lost in a blizzard north of Cheyenne in March 1906. After two days and nights of aimless wandering, he rode in at a ranch twenty-five miles away suffering a severe case of exhaustion and frostbite.[21]

Unable to stand the embarrassment of the label of sheep-rustler, the lowest of lows for any respectable cowhand, Hill accused Gothberg of being a horse thief. He pressed charges against Martin Gothberg for branding Hill's horse with the intention of theft. Sheriff J. A. Sheffner rode to the ranch and applied the warrant for Gothberg's arrest. In Casper, everyone was fully aware of the circumstances of the case, but one and all, including Gothberg, went through the motions to ensure that each person followed the full letter of the law. Justice Tubbs held a preliminary hearing and bound the case over for trial. Tubbs set the bond at one thousand dollars, which Gothberg paid and he returned home.[22]

Frank Hill may have missed the short bit of notoriety following his experience in the blizzard, or perhaps the incident left him physically unable to perform the work of a ranch hand. Whatever the reason, he seems not to have seriously pursued an honest career afterward. Before either case made it to district court, Hill found himself again arrested. This time, along with two others, for robbing a Union Pacific employee of his paycheck, forging his signature, and cashing the check in a Rawlins,

Wyoming saloon. District Court Judge Carpenter dismissed the charges against Martin Gothberg in January 1909. In June, a cashier at the Casper National Bank discovered a check written on the account of J. W. Longshore to Frank Hill for eighteen dollars. Mr. Longshore's signature was a forgery, and when questioned, he did not know anyone named Frank Hill. It is not known who cashed the check. That is the last known record of Mr. Hill's crime spree. It is unknown if Frank Hill ever received punishment for any of the wrongdoings he was accused of.[23]

In July 1908, the town of Casper adopted a resolution that local businesses replace the wooden boardwalks in front of their establishments with concrete sidewalks. The requirement resulted in Walt Blackmore's construction of a twelve-by-sixty-foot sidewalk in front of his market on Second Street. While Walt contemplated his sidewalk project, the Wyoming State Fish Hatchery in Laramie planted thirty-five thousand young trout in Hat-Six Creek on his ranch. On the same shipment, they delivered five thousand trout to Dobbin Springs Creek on Gothberg Ranch. In all, they planted sixty thousand fish in Natrona County streams, and residents requested an additional sixty thousand fish for other tributaries to the Platte.[24]

~~~

As Missou Hines spent more and more time away from home, his marriage suffered. Martha Hines sold her dress shop and opened an eatery and boarding house just down the street from Walt's market. She advertised in the *Natrona County Tribune:*

> *The WESTERN INN*
> *MRS. HINES, PROPRIETOR*
> *THE BEST OF EVERYTHING IN SEASON*
> *Best Meals in Town for 35c*
> *Good Rooms in Connection*
> *Second Street in Wood's Building Casper, Wyoming.* [25]

In the same issue, she posted a firm but pleasant notice to debtors: "Having disposed of my stock of goods I would respectfully request all those who are indebted to me, to call and settle at their earliest convenience. M. E. B. HINES"[26]

After being open for less than a month, Martha Hines closed her Western Inn, citing that she could not find reliable help. The *Tribune* reported, "She conducted a first class restaurant, and many of her patrons regret that she was compelled to close." With their marriage awash, Martha Hines moved to Thermopolis, Wyoming.[27]

While this all transpired, Martin Gothberg applied for a land patent on 160 acres in Emigrant Gap, seven miles northwest of the home ranch. A month later, he purchased a lot on South Wolcott Street in Casper. The *Natrona County Tribune* reported that he would "soon build a nice cottage in Park Addition and will move to town with his family." The home he would build was a bit more than a cottage. As the Gothberg family grew, Martin and Mary Enid wanted their older children to attend a larger school than the one-room schoolhouse near the ranch. Martin felt that his Eastern education had been of great advantage in many aspects of his life, both personally and in business. Consequently, he wished the same or better for his own children. The family's financial status had greatly improved in recent years. Martin Gothberg had the respect of nearly every resident and was considered one of the most prominent citizens of the county. The Blackmores and other prosperous friends of the city were anxious to see the Gothbergs welcomed into the social calendars of local society. In September, the town council approved building permits for State Senator Patrick Sullivan and his future neighbor, Martin J. Gothberg.[28]

As plans for the construction of the new home on Tenth and South Wolcott Streets matured, Martin focused on his ranch. Within a few weeks, he made final proof on two other adjoining forty-acre parcels of land there. These were joint homestead claims with William Shelton and Grandeson Dorsey. Amid the busy land transactions, he managed to gather the livestock he planned to sell that fall. On September 19, 1908, Martin Gothberg shipped two railcar loads of cattle and three railcar loads of sheep to market.[29]

In November, the State of Wyoming approved several appropriations of water for the Gothbergs. The Gothberg-Harris Sheep Company received approval for Lone Tree Creek and Stinking Creek in southern Natrona and northern Carbon Counties. Mary Enid also obtained appropriations on Stinking Creek. The state granted appropriations to Martin on Sheep Creek, east of Bates Creek, and on Dobbin Springs and Dobbin Springs Reservoir.[30]

In October, the *Casper Press* noted the Gothbergs' new home under construction on South Wolcott Street. A bit more than the cottage originally announced, the ten-room, three-thousand-square-foot brick home was taking shape. The *Press* described, "Mr. Gothberg's house will be one of the largest and most attractive looking residences in the city."[31]

As construction progressed on the luxurious new Park Addition, residents of Casper were taking notice. This neighborhood is now on the National Register of Historic Places and presently known as the Historic Wolcott District. In 1908, the *Casper Press* told the story of its birth.

A building boom is on for sure in Park Addition and one who passes that way can stand on one corner and looking about see at least $200,000 worth of new homes in course of construction. Masons and

View of Dobbin Springs Reservoir in the foreground of the Gothberg Ranch at the base of Casper Mountain. Circa 1920.
COURTESY OF THE WESTERN HISTORY COLLECTION, CASPER COLLEGE WESTERN HISTORY CENTER

carpenters have been at work for some time in the Park Addition ter-
ritory and stakes were set Saturday for the foundation of a $6,000
house just south of F. O. Wilmarth's $6,000 new home and Contractor
Shaffer is planning a fashionable house to go up on the Evans lot pro-
vided Mr. Evans will sell the lot for $1,000. Evans gave $150 for the
lot 18 months ago. Mr. Butler refused $500 last week for the vacant
lot just north of the Chapman residence on Durbin Street. Oliver G.
Johnson is building a handsome bungalow just north of the residence
of Mr. Hummel and Martin Gothberg is also building a fine home
and this is about completed and will be ready for occupancy this season.
Hon. P. Sullivan is building a new home which when completed: will
be one of the most sightly homes in, the state. Roderick Gordon has
just moved into his new $6,000 house being one of the most attrac-
tive homes in this part of the state. The H. O. Smith home is a palace
and is modern in every respect and adds to the appearance of that
part of Casper. The A. J. Cunningham; mansion shows up from; the
west with: a grandeur that only money, design and location can give
a home. M. N. Castle has about closed negotiations for the James Hart
lot and expects to have his home well under way before New Years.
There are dozens of other beautiful homes, there also. Park Addition
is the new part of town and is making a greater showing than a like
amount of territory in any town in the west.[32]

Before the year ended, Gothberg purchased sixty-five acres of land from the State of Wyoming adjoining his home ranch. He expanded his ranch by over five hundred acres in the past year, and Gothberg Ranch now spread over four thousand deeded acres and not less than one thousand acres of land leased from the state. In addition, Gothberg still utilized several thousand acres of open rangeland on which his cattle and sheep grazed. A large, new home in the most sumptuous neighborhood of Casper neared completion, yet as always, the new home was quite modest in comparison to the palaces and mansions built around him.[33]

As construction of the new Gothberg home on South Wolcott Street progressed, many evidences indicated the prosperity of the family. When all seemed to be going well, an inspection on January 2, 1909, of three thousand head of Gothberg's ewes found them infected with scabies. The inspector quarantined the herd and seventy-five square miles, forty-eight thousand acres of winter rangeland north of Casper that Gothberg's sheep occupied as well as herds belonging to other area ranchers. Two weeks later the deputy state veterinarian found an additional five thousand head of rams belonging to Gothberg, Davis, and La Rue infected at Gothberg's home ranch and added them and their pastures, another 1,400 acres, to the quarantine. A mite that burrows beneath the sheep's skin and lays its eggs causes scabies. When shorn, the sheep are dipped in a tank or trough of insecticide that usually eliminates the vermin. In midwinter, however, this is not usually an option. Treating a band of sheep of this size in freezing temperatures is extremely difficult. Gothberg believed a band of out-of-state sheep herded through his rangeland the previous fall infected his herd.[34]

Martin Gothberg was not alone. There were over eighteen thousand head of sheep quarantined in Natrona County. The infestation was nearly epidemic. In February, the State Board of Sheep Commissioners held a special meeting with area sheepmen at the Grand Central Hotel in Casper. Two commissioners and several inspectors were present. The *Natrona County Tribune* reported:

> *The sheep, they said, were yielding nicely to the treatment, and conditions were much improved over a month ago, but they advised strict quarantine for at least a month, and possibly longer. It was agreed that the quarantine would be maintained and the owners of the diseased sheep must pay all the expenses incident to the cleaning up of their bands, such as dip, labor, publication of quarantine notices, etc. They are determined to stamp out the disease, and although it will be expensive for some, it will be much better for all in the end.*[35]

It was expensive, but not as expensive as the loss of livestock if the condition was not eradicated. It was essential to eliminate the disease before the flocks were moved to summer range.

While Martin dealt with the quarantine, his brother-in-law Willis Lund checked in at the Westminster Hotel in Los Angeles, California. As the economy of southern California boomed, so did Willis's wholesale brass products business. The flood of orders required him to spend more and more time in California. Minnie loved the climate when she visited in 1906 and thus the Lund family chose to relocate to the area. By 1910, they were living in Berkley, California. The United States Census that year listed Willis as a gas fixture dealer, on his own account.[36]

If the state quarantine was not enough turmoil in his life for the moment, the district court called Martin Gothberg to serve on the jury of a grand larceny case. Then again, the unique circumstances of the charges may have provided an amusing diversion, perhaps even a controlled chuckle. It appears that Mrs. Elizabeth Robinson was the proprietor of a "gentlemen's resort" on David Street in Casper. Mrs. Gertrude Gardner, a female resident employee of the establishment, found her sealskin coat missing from her room on the night of March 10, 1908. On April 8, 1908, she discovered Mrs. Robinson wearing the coat. Mrs. Gardner notified the authorities, who had Mrs. Robinson arrested and charged with grand larceny. After a preliminary hearing, the judge bound the case over for trial and released Mrs. Robinson on bond. Mrs. Gardner left the establishment and embarked to employment elsewhere.

When the case came to trial in January 1909, Martin Gothberg and his fellow jurors concluded that the sealskin coat was worth fifty dollars and determined that the value warranted a charge of grand larceny. Resolving whether the accused was innocent or guilty was less easily decided. After hearing final testimonies on Friday, the jury deliberated throughout the night, not reaching a verdict until 11:30 a.m. Saturday morning, finding her guilty as charged. Upon receiving the verdict, Judge Carpenter ordered Mrs. Robinson be taken into custody and placed in the county jail to await sentencing. Her attorney, Judge M. C. Brown of Laramie, requested her release on bond, but Judge Carpenter held fast, stating that since being tried and found guilty, the bond no longer applied. Mr. Brown made a motion for a new trial and said that he would "endeavor to keep the woman from going to the penitentiary until her case can be viewed by the supreme court."[37]

Martin Gothberg fulfilled his duty as juror in Elizabeth Robinson's grand larceny case, but the story did not end there. Conveniently and almost assuredly not a coincidence, the Wyoming State Legislature enacted Section 136 of the 1909 session laws, nearly immediately following the conviction. The tidbit that slipped through nearly unnoticed amended the statute and now allowed bond for all bailable felonies except second-degree murder after conviction, while pending appeal of the verdict. Within days, Judge Carpenter was forced to set bond for Elizabeth Robinson. Friends of Mrs. Robinson paid the $1,200 bond, and very soon after she departed for California, an act totally contrary to the conditions of her bond. The *Natrona County Tribune* released a scathing report on the atrocity concluding, "It would appear that the enactment of this law is a practical doing away with penitentiary imprisonment for any and all persons who have either money or friends enough to furnish bonds, especially in the light of the small bond required in the case, for very few criminals but would gladly forfeit $300 a year to avoid the state's prison."[38]

When Judge C. H. Parmalee opened a short session for the July term of district court in Judge Carpenter's absence, Mrs. Robinson did not appear before the court and Judge Parmalee revoked her bond. Before Mrs. Robinson arrived on the afternoon train, Judge Parmalee had already left town and the paperwork filed. When Judge Carpenter held the August session, he set aside the bond forfeiture imposed by Judge Parmalee. Following a severe lecturing to Mrs. Robinson not to leave the state, he again set the bond at $1,200, which she posted.[39]

When Mrs. Robinson appeared before the Supreme Court in Cheyenne in November, the *Wyoming Tribune* reported, "Mrs. Elisabeth [*sic*] Robinson, a resident of Casper, is said to be quite wealthy, and has never been in urgent need of a cloak, such as she is accused of stealing from Mrs. Gardner, also of Casper." In January, the court handed down their decision to revert the case back to Natrona County District Court for a re-trial, noting that one of the most important witnesses in the case, presumably Gertrude Gardner, was no longer in the area. Mr. Brown then applied to the district court for a change of venue, which they granted, and the trial moved to Converse County. In August 1910, two and a half years after the alleged crime, the case again made it to the docket. After thousands of dollars spent in court costs, with few witnesses available to the prosecution, the judge dismissed the case. Unlike the earlier reporter from Cheyenne, the *Natrona County Tribune* spoke more plainly when they wrote that Elizabeth Robinson would return to "her house of ill-fame."[40]

In May 1909, Walt Blackmore and his partner, Ed Gue, advertised that they purchased a railcar load of grain-fed steers and were selling the choice cuts of beef from these animals at the same low prices they had been selling lesser quality beef previously. Only a week later, they sold their butcher shop and fixtures to Mr. A. J. Huskey for $2,500. Blackmore still owned the building and leased it to Mr. Huskey. Upon the sale, Blackmore conveyed that he intended to concentrate on the business of his Hat-Six Ranch through the summer. Mr. Gue announced that he would leave Casper, but was undecided of a particular destination.[41]

Blackmore and Gue published the following notice:

> *Having sold our business to Mr. A. J. Huskey, we are anxious to close up our accounts and earnestly request all knowing themselves indebted to us to please call "at the old stand" and settle same, and all those holding accounts against us will please present them for payment. Thanking the public for their liberal patronage, we remain, Your[s] truly, Blackmore & Gue Co.*[42]

Later that month, the State Board of Sheep Commissioners met in Cheyenne and a number of ranchers from Casper and Douglas attended to protest dipping order number 27. This order required the dipping of all sheep for certain parasites prior to July 15, and a vast number of sheep were presently grazing in areas far from any available facility to perform the process. The commissioners recognized the difficulty of complying within the timeframe and extended the date for compliance to September 1, 1909, which was satisfactory to the sheepmen. Missou Hines's appointment as inspector for the region was nearly expired and the ranchers asked for his retention to the position. The commissioners turned down this request. "This action is regretted by the wool growers of this part of the state who know his peculiar fitness for the office and the great good accomplished through his efforts during the recent fight against scabies."[43]

Upon his departure from the Board of Sheep Commissioners, Missou Hines became the regional representative for Foster Burns & Company of Chicago, Illinois. Among other products, Burns manufactured B & C cresol dip, regarded as a highly concentrated, high quality pesticide for dipping sheep and other livestock. They advertised locally under the heading "Sheepmen Attention":

> B & C Cresol Dip is in a class by itself. It has many imitators but no equals. Refuse substitutes. Ask for the genuine with the red, white and blue label. Sole manufacturers, Foster Burns & Company, Chicago, Illinois. Richards & Cunningham Co. Casper agents, or see Missou Hines.[44]

And:

> Beware of imitators. Don't accept anything "just as good." Buy the original B & C Cresol Dip, 1 to 141. Look for the red, white and blue label. Sole manufacturers, Foster Burns & Company, Chicago, Illinois. Richards and Cunningham Co. Casper agents, or see Missou Hines.[45]

In June, Walt Blackmore and Ed Gue left Casper on a business trip to the Isle of Pines in the Caribbean Sea. The island, governed by Cuba, is located off the coast, south of Havana. The area, promoted as a tropical paradise, attracted the businessmen's attention. Both experienced in the retail sales of fruit and vegetables, the island sparked their interest with possibilities of entering into the wholesale growing and marketing of these products. If favorably impressed with the conditions, they would invest in real estate and move their families there.[46]

Returning home on July 5, 1909, Walt Blackmore may have missed the local celebrations of Independence Day but professed his patriotism enthusiastically with his joy to be home. As advertised, both the Island of Pines and Cuba shared agreeable climate for the growing of a variety of tropical fruits. Organizers presented them with oranges, limes, lemons, pineapples, and an array of other locally grown fruits for their sampling. Most common vegetables had never been successfully grown there. There also were problems with reliable transportation and the availability of ice or refrigeration. Blackmore could not help noticing cases upon cases of pineapples rotting on the docks awaiting a ship to carry them to American or European markets.

Had these disorders not been sufficient to deter him, the political and justice systems of the Cuban-governed island were completely unacceptable. He soon learned why most expats who invested there kept their families in the States. When Walt discovered that Americans, especially white Americans, had absolutely no rights to defend themselves or their families from assault or murder, he could hardly believe it. Accustomed to American ideals, the judicial process left him stymied. If a Cuban national assaulted or killed a member of his family and he injured or killed that person in defending himself or that family member, a black officer of the law would arrest him. A black judge would try him without the opportunity of hiring an attorney or even being able to appear in court and find him guilty. They would imprison or execute him without any opportunity of recourse. Walter Blackmore was truly grateful to be an American and back on American soil.[47]

—•—

While Walt and Ed cruised to an awakening in the Caribbean, Missou Hines took a position selling stocks for Wyoming Consolidated Asbestos Company operating on Casper Mountain. Unaware in that era of any hazards involving the handling of the unique mineral, Mayor W. S. Kimball concocted a distinctive method of promoting Casper by endorsing the product. He fluffed a small bunch of long asbestos fibers at one end creating a small white artificial flower. The flower sewn to a purple ribbon imprinted "Casper Asbestos" became a miniature corsage or boutonniere when pinned appropriately and worn by Casper boosters at Cheyenne and Lander Fourth of July celebrations. The company ordered six hundred of the little badges and distributed them accordingly. In the meantime, company representatives Missou Hines and S. E. Colyer of Denver sold stocks in the company to investors all over the United States and Canada.[48]

In late July, Missou escorted several investors to the asbestos mines on Smith Creek owned by his employer. Accompanied by Mr. A. A. Patterson of the *Cheyenne Tribune*, the gentlemen were able to observe the mine in operation. Missou found this portion of his duties with the mining company very similar to showing clients and representatives of the railroad to various remote locations during his two decades representing them.[49]

―⁓―

As Missou Hines showed the asbestos mine to potential stockholders, Martin Gothberg nursed a sore hand. The flying hooves of a horse caught Gothberg's hand while he was holding a log at his ranch. The shoes of the horse did not sever his fingers when trapped against the log, but pinched them cruelly enough to break two of them and brutally smash the others.[50]

The previous spring, the Gothberg family moved into their newly constructed home on South Wolcott Street. Homer F. and W. F. Shaffer were both successful building contractors and electricians in Casper. Homer also managed the telephone company there. A month earlier, they each purchased lots in the Park Addition near the Gothberg residence. As Martin's hand began to mend, the Shaffer brothers prepared to construct two of their own new homes in the neighborhood.[51]

―⁓―

In 1903, Walt Blackmore leased 160 acres from John Cosgrove on the northern outskirts of Casper. Cosgrove, a longtime resident of the area, retired to Omaha wishing to be closer to family in his declining years. When Cosgrove's brother passed away shortly thereafter, he inherited the adjacent eighty acres. Blackmore eventually gained ownership of a percentage in both properties. With its convenient proximity, Walt Blackmore used the property to pasture and hold livestock pending slaughter for his meat market. Since selling the meat market, he no longer required full

The Gothberg home on South Wolcott Street in Casper, 2019
PHOTOGRAPH BY DEBORA GLASS.

use of the small ranch. After his return from the Isle of Pines, Blackmore advertised that he would "pasture a few milch cows at the Cosgrove place."[52]

Walt Blackmore was a very active man. Feeling somewhat restless without the meat market to occupy a majority of his time, he treated his family to a vacation in Denver. In their absence, Ed Gue and his wife welcomed the arrival of a new baby at their home in Casper. Both mother and child were healthy and happy.

The interior of the Gothbergs' "town" home still contains many of the home's original embellishments, 2019
PHOTOGRAPH BY DEBORA GLASS

Since their disappointment in prospects on the Isle of Pines, Mr. and Mrs. Gue had also been idle. With their new addition, the young family began planning their next segment in life. Eventually they chose to return to Newcastle, Wyoming, where Ed Gue purchased an interest in the A. M. Nichols Meat Market and Supply Company.[53]

In August, Martin Gothberg filed a contest against the homestead entry of Owen Downey on Lone Tree Creek. The claim adjoined property belonging to Gothberg in far southern Natrona County. Gothberg alleged that Downey had neither established residence nor cultivated or improved the tract of land as required by the Homestead Act. The land office in Douglas, Wyoming, reviewed the contest and found Mr. Downey's claim invalid by requirements of the law. As a result, the land returned to federal jurisdiction and Mary Enid Gothberg filed a homestead claim on the parcel.[54]

Missou Hines returned from the Wool Growers meeting in Rawlins and reported that the sessions were very worthwhile. Hines left a few days later for Lander, Wyoming, with Dr. Scott W. Peck. Dr. Peck previously held the position of state veterinarian and later state sheep inspector; both were positions from which he resigned. Upon their arrival, the *Wyoming State Journal* noted that Dr. Peck would remain in the area for several days.[55]

While Missou was in Lander, Martin Gothberg advertised the sale of four hundred buck sheep from his ranch at Dobbin Springs. The halfbreed Leisters were young and healthy at one to three years old. Walt Blackmore brought in a basket of beautiful Yellow Transparent apples grown on his Hat-Six Ranch. Walt showed off his bounty in the window of Wilson Kimball's drug and jewelry store. Not long afterward, Walt and Minnie received approval for water appropriations on 207 acres of their ranch along the Clear Fork of Muddy Creek.[56]

Blackmore's respite was short-lived. He soon left on a series of business trips promoting a land deal with the Chicago, Burlington & Quincy Railroad as they approached Casper with a new line. The CB&Q

proposed building their depot, switchyard, machine shops, roundhouse, and warehouses on the outskirts of Casper. Walt lobbied the Cosgrove Ranch to the railroad as the ideal location for the operation. He left Casper on October 23, 1909, headed for Omaha. There he met with John Cosgrove where they put together a plan to sell the ranch to the railroad. The two men then traveled to Chicago where they pitched their land to the CB&Q. Feeling confident, they returned to Omaha and soon after Walt returned to Casper, arriving on November 12.[57]

Ten days later, Walt was in Cheyenne taking care of other details necessary to the plan. In December, the CB&Q sent E. M. Westervelt, a real estate agent for the Burlington, to Casper to negotiate with the land-owners for the necessary property to construct their facilities. The railroad laid out their own plan, which included eighty acres belonging to William F. Dunn, Eugene McCarthy, and Patrick Sullivan; forty acres to James F. Stanley; and twenty-seven acres to Walt Blackmore and John Cosgrove.

Dunn, McCarthy, and Sullivan asked $250 per acre for their eighty acres, but the railroad was only willing to pay $100 per acre. The trio argued that if the property were subdivided the lots would be worth $100 each, far more than the $250 per acre they asked for. Mr. Westervelt reasoned that they were not negotiating city lots and that the balance of their real estate would be worth far more with the railroad in place than without. Sullivan and McCarthy agreed that the benefit of the railroad to Casper outweighed their own profits, but Dunn refused to accept less than $150 per acre for his share of the acreage. The parties left the table without an agreement.

Blackmore and Cosgrove reached an agreement for their twenty-seven acres with Mr. Westervelt. So did James Stanley, but prices were not disclosed. The Casper Industrial Club, made up of most of Casper's most prominent citizens, tried to reason with Dunn, but he refused to budge. They finally agreed to raise the additional $1,333.33 by subscription and pay that money directly to Mr. Dunn. The Industrial Club then contacted Mr. Westervelt, whose office was in Lincoln, Nebraska, who agreed to the terms.[58]

As the end of the year neared, Mollie Wolf sold his ranch on Bates Creek to George M. Rhoades. Mollie purchased the ranch from the Blattenberg brothers when crews were constructing the Pathfinder Dam, which eventually resulted in the flooding of his Sweetwater Ranch. They scheduled the transfer of possession for May 1910. Mollie expected to sell his cattle in the spring and move farther west with Wilda, perhaps Lander, Wyoming. Rhoades planned to incorporate the ranch into his Bates Creek Livestock Company and use it as a hub for summer range operations.[59]

Martin Gothberg ended his year purchasing from George Madison forty acres southeast of the home ranch adjoining his other property on Casper Mountain. Looking back, he had had a good year. He had a beautiful new home in town, where his children could attend a conventional school; he managed to limit his losses with a scabies infestation at the worst time of year. If he thought of his friend Walt Blackmore and his scheme of moving to the Caribbean, he probably smiled and told himself, "Well, if he had moved his family down there, at least they would all be warm right now."[60]

As for himself, Gothberg was fatigued. At forty-five, his body already ached from all of the bumps, bruises, and beatings he had given it, taken in stride during his youth. How many times had a green bronc put him in the dirt during the roundups or a rope jerked from his hand by a wild steer? His crushed hand was healing remarkably well, though the recent cooler weather reminded him of the injury and a few older ones every morning. On December 12, 1909, Martin and Mary Enid boarded the train "for the south where the gentleman will endeavor to improve his health, which has not been the best of late. They expect to be gone a month at least." Their exact destination was unspecified. If California, they probably visited his sister Minnie and her family while they vacationed there.[61]

CHAPTER 8

Behind Every Great Man . . .

1910–1911

WHILE MARTIN GOTHBERG WORKED HARD AND WORKED SMART TO expand his growing ranch and provide for his family, he did not work alone. Mary Enid Gothberg labored side by side performing the many duties required in running a successful ranch. In addition to her physical efforts involving a ranch wife's daily life, like her husband, she was highly intelligent. Most of the decisions made in the ranch's operation were made jointly. Legal and business documents show her continued involvement in many aspects of both the financial and tangible management of the ranch. All this while rearing children, managing the family household, and nursing herself and her family through ailments and injuries.

Walt Blackmore seemed unable to remain out of the meat business for more than a few months. In January 1910, he purchased the furnishings and opened a meat market in the previous location of Harry G. Duhling's Market. The business had operated from one of Blackmore's former facilities in a building next door to the Adsit Hotel, but had moved to a new location on the north side of the hotel on Center Street. The *Casper Press* reported that Blackmore had recently purchased the building. When Blackmore built his new meat market on Second Street in 1905, he leased the other building to B. H. Aronson and Company, a wholesale liquor distributor. He advertised his new market under the heading "Blackmore is Back."[1]

While Walt began reestablishing relationships with old customers at his market, Martin Gothberg and the Kimball Livestock Company finally settled their ongoing dispute of nearly five years. Details of their agreement remained undisclosed, but in the end the district court dismissed the case. A few months later, Gothberg continued to expand his ranching operation. In June, he purchased 160 acres from Bob Weston just west of the home ranch.[2]

Missou Hines traveled to Cheyenne representing both the Wyoming Consolidated and the North American Asbestos Companies in January. It was not long, however, before he found a new line of work. In February 1910, Mr. William Fitzhugh and Mr. William Henshaw of the California Oil Syndicate, also known as the California Company, brought four oil well drilling rigs into the Salt Creek Oil Field north of Casper. They hired Hines to oversee the transportation of the steam-powered machinery over forty miles from the railroad in Casper to the field. It was quite an undertaking to move this much equipment overland in that era, especially considering its extraordinary weight. The steam engines alone often weighed over ten tons and might require as many as thirty horses or mules to pull the heavy load over the prairie to their destination.[3]

When April rolled around, Missou visited Casper from the Salt Creek field. He told the *Tribune* that the California Company had four drilling rigs operating in the field, employing forty men. They had more machinery coming in and expected to have one hundred men working there within the next two months.[4]

Within a few months, Missou's responsibilities with the oil company evolved into a security position in which he led a group of armed former cowboys whose job it was to prevent trespassers, vandals, and competitors from entering company property. As animosity grew between the California Company and a primary rival over a productive quarter section of oil land that both companies claimed ownership to, the occupation became strategic. For details of the events, see Appendix C, "The Salt Creek Oil Field War, 1910."[5]

In the midst of a hot, dry summer, railroad-grading crews for the Burlington line toiled in the sun as they worked their way west toward Wolton, Wyoming. A camp of over one hundred men consumed a substantial volume of food. Cooks and camp-tenders slaughtered cattle daily at the camp to feed the hungry men. The railroad purchased cattle from a variety of stockmen, but many area ranchers became suspicious that the ownership of some cattle were unverified. Specific laws regulating inspection of hides from slaughtered cattle were ignored at the remote location of the operation.

Natrona County Sheriff J. A. Sheffner received numerous complaints by area stockmen of violations of both state law and county resolutions on the matter. In mid-July, he appointed Mollie Wolf as deputy sheriff to work in conjunction with the Fremont and Johnson Counties' sheriff's departments to see that the law was enforced. Mollie spent about a week inspecting hides from the livestock in question and arranged a system for continued inspections. All parties concerned with the problem satisfactorily agreed on the solution and resolved to cooperate in complying with the statutes. As a result, Mollie became a part-time employee of all three sheriff's departments, though it seems he sometimes had trouble collecting his salary from Fremont County.[6]

For those of a superstitious nature, Monday, June 13, was a very unlucky day for several Casper residents. A thunderstorm arose quickly in the late afternoon that stunned several parties in the downtown area. It seemed to many that the clouds were peculiarly close to the ground. Druggist W. B. Millett stood in front of his store leaning against an iron support for the awning, when a bolt of lightning struck and threw him to the sidewalk. Mr. Millet said that there were little sparks of electricity dancing about on the sidewalk after the bolt hit. He sustained several burns on his back from the bolt and it singed his shirt and suspenders. His mother and Mary Enid Gothberg were walking home after shopping at the time. About half-way there, the bolt lit upon them. The ladies were severely stunned by the jar, but both kept their feet. The bolt also tossed Don Lobdell to the floor of his store. It drove two employees of the electric plant to the ground and burned their hands. Since these incidents all occurred in close proximity, it is unknown if there were several simultaneous strikes or perhaps just one. In final assessment, the events did not cause any fatalities or set any buildings afire. Injuries seemed relatively minor.[7]

At the age of thirty-three, Mary Enid Gothberg had paid her dues. She grew up in an area where ranching, farming, and gardening were the lifestyle. Hard work earned food for the table. Large families represented more hands to share in the work, and the little hands of small children became trained at an early age to the tasks and chores that they were able to perform. She had married Martin Gothberg, owner of a fledgling cattle ranch. She had worked diligently, side by side with Martin on the ranch, bearing him four children along the way. She was the kind of woman that Bill Kittredge summed up nicely in his musing many years later:

This country fosters a kind of woman who never seems to bother about who she is supposed to be, mainly because there is always work, and getting it done in a level-eyed way is what counts most. Getting the work done, on horseback or not, and dicing their troubles in jokes. These women wind up looking fifty when they are thirty-seven and fifty-three when they are seventy. It's as though they wear down to what counts and just last there, fine and staring the devil in the eye every morning.[8]

The ranch was succeeding only because of the shared intelligence and hard work of the young couple.

After living in Casper for over a year, Mary Enid Gothberg became quite comfortable with the ease and the slight bit of luxury accompanying life in the small city. Though she still visited her family at Freeland and helped at the ranch on a regular basis, she often mingled with the ladies in their neighborhood, and perhaps even lost a little bit of that weathering that accompanies the handsome, dignified look that ranch wives almost always receive after years of long days, working outdoors alongside their husbands. It was bittersweet news when her friend Minnie Blackmore told Mary Enid that her family was spending the winter in Pomona, California. To avoid upsetting the Blackmore children's school year, Minnie and the children were leaving in late August to a home located near that of Walt's brother. Mary Enid would miss the company of her friend but could not help in sharing her joy through prospects of her protracted visit, filled with the warm, sunny days of southern California in winter.

In July, Walt Blackmore hired Gus Barlitt who moved from Ohio to operate his meat market on Center Street. In August, he leased the market to Gus and his brother, W. C. Barlitt, who owned a meat market in Lander. Transfer of possession of the market to the Barlitt brothers took place on September 1, and Walt prepared to wrap up business dealings with his various investments in Casper to allow for joining his family for an extended stay in California.[9]

A near-record number of railcars of livestock left from the various stockyards in central Wyoming during the first week of September. One hundred twenty-three carloads of sheep were loaded at Casper, Cadoma, Bucknam, Natrona, and Wolton, Wyoming. One hundred thirty-four railcars of cattle left from the same facilities. At the same time, forty-nine carloads of sheep were loaded at Moneta, Shoshoni, and Hudson, Wyoming. Among the many ranchers marketing livestock at the time, Gothberg sold seven railcars of sheep and one railcar of cattle.[10]

Later that month, Martin Gothberg showed final proof with Benjamin F. Scott and John D. Scott on forty acres between Lone Tree Creek and Bates Creek in far southern Natrona County. He also leased 160 acres of state land that bordered his property on Casper Mountain and an additional 160 acres next to the 640 acres he already had at the home ranch. At the same time, Mary Enid renewed her lease on the forty acres from the state adjoining their property twelve miles west of the home ranch. She also leased eighty more acres bordering the Scott holdings, twenty-five miles south of the home ranch.[11]

In mid-November, Martin Gothberg brought his breeding bucks into the home ranch from their summer range. Reassessing his herd, he optioned to sell a number of them. He advertised in the *Natrona County Tribune* that he had three hundred quality Leicester-cross bucks for sale. The one- and two-year-olds were available at Gothberg Ranch, nine miles southwest of Casper. As the weather cooled, he again felt the pains of old wounds. On December 10, 1910, Martin left for Hot Springs, Arkansas, where he hoped the therapeutic waters of the famous health resort would heal his body. He planned to stay a month. He had not spent Christmas away from Mary Enid since their courtship began.[12]

⌒

Mollie Wolf continued inspecting hides and overseeing the cattle butchered at the Burlington Railroad grading camp as the crews inched west through the winter. As it began, Natrona and Johnson Counties continued to pay their share of his salary, and Fremont County continued not to pay their share. By this time, Fremont County owed Mollie over two hundred dollars in back salary, about five thousand dollars in today's money.[13]

⌒

Gothberg home ranch in winter, circa 1910
COURTESY OF MARTY GOTHBERG, SUSAN LITTLEFIELD HAINES COLLECTION

In March, Walt Blackmore was back in town. In November, Will Creel had purchased A. J. Huskey's Meat Market in Blackmore's building on Second Street as well as Huskey's home and other properties in Casper. Through a progression of telegrams and special delivery envelopes, Walt managed to avoid returning to Casper to handle his end of the paperwork with Mr. Creel. Now he was busy tying up loose ends of business transactions that accumulated in his absence. One such project was moving the warehouse of Fremont Brewing Company, part of A. B. Aronson's operation, from its location west of the Adsit Hotel on Midwest Avenue to a lot Blackmore purchased south of the Chicago & Northwestern tracks. He also had his old butcher shop next door to the warehouse that he moved to a lot north of the Burlington tracks. Both these buildings occupied part of the Adsit Hotel lot, which Walt sold and had to give possession of the grounds on March 15.[14]

In May, Walt purchased the home of George L. Moffatt in the Park Addition for $2,700. He already owned the adjacent lot north of the Moffatt's household. Soon thereafter, Minnie and the children returned to Casper from California and set up housekeeping in their new home. A few weeks later, Casper's town council approved a measure requiring downtown businesses to remove the old boardwalks in front of their institutions and construct concrete sidewalks adjacent to their establishments. Walt Blackmore was heartily in favor of the project. When he received the order for improvements on two of his properties comprising 120 feet of five-foot-wide sidewalk, he anxiously complied.[15]

—◦—

While driving her buggy on June 19, an unknown distraction spooked Mary Enid Gothberg's team of horses and they bolted. Though a capable horsewoman, without the benefit of brakes on the light buggy, Mary Enid was unable to regain their control. Fearing serious injury as the team raced wildly away, she selected what appeared a likely location for a relatively smooth landing and bailed off the speeding vehicle. As she leapt from the buggy, however, the lines became entangled around one of her feet. When her body reached the end of the slackened reins, they instantly cinched tightly around her foot, and with a jerk, as if the full weight of her body reached the end of a cracking whip, the leather umbilical cord snapped her ankle instantly. Yet, the horror was not over. What was left of her severely broken ankle, what tendons, skin, and muscle tissue managed to remain attached, held her fast to the frantic team as they tried to flee in terror from the monstrous predator they imagined had attacked them, dragging her behind, bouncing like a rag doll across the prairie.

Eventually, by some miracle, the tether loosened or broke, releasing her as the team and her buggy sped away in a cloud of dust. What took place in an instant seemed a long time. In partial consciousness, everything became quiet. Someone gathered up the bruised, battered, broken, and bleeding woman and carried her back to town. The doctors did their best to set the shattered ankle. They likely administered laudanum or other opiates commonly used at the time to deaden the pain. A nurse or maid would watch over her and care for her children as she lay in bed for weeks, barely able to move. It must have been monumental when she finally recovered enough to hobble on crutches.[16]

While Mary Enid convalesced, Martin Gothberg tried to stay close by. As she began to mend, he was able to focus more of his attention to affairs at the ranch. John King was a pleasant young man who worked for Gothberg for several years as a camp mover. John held a good reputation among his many friends and acquaintances, though he suffered from an incessant inability to hang onto his money. On August 9, King left his employment at the ranch. Martin wrote him a check for ninety-two dollars, all of the wages due, and the young man departed, apparently on good terms by all accounts.

When John King got to Casper, he felt the need to celebrate his recently acquired freedom and commenced to have a "good time" at the Diamond Bar. As the day progressed into evening, he noticed that his finances were dwindling and produced a second check for $120 bearing Gothberg's signature that J. P. Callahan, the proprietor, knowing Martin Gothberg was obviously good for the amount, cashed. King continued to socialize for a while longer before retiring for the night.

The next day, the bank returned the check for $120 to the bar with the note, "signature not correct." Callahan rode out to the Gothberg Ranch taking the returned check with him. After meeting with Gothberg, he learned that the check for ninety-two dollars was payment in full for John King's services to date and that the check for $120 was a forgery. When Callahan returned to town, he made a search for King, but as he suspected, the young man was nowhere to be found.[17]

The story made it to several newspapers around the state, but evidently, the people around Manville, Wyoming, were unaware of the crime. In short order, John King found employment with rancher Addison A. Spaugh of that vicinity. King's pleasant personality gained him acceptance there and he apparently performed his duties efficiently. It was not long, however, until he again discovered his expenditures exceeding his income. The apparent success of his previous ruse gained him confidence and endeared him to repeat the swindle. In this instance, though, everyone in the town of Manville knew A. A. Spaugh's signature. The forgery was recognized immediately, the check was not cashed, and John King found himself arrested and in jail before he could jump the next train out of town. When brought before the judge, King pled guilty to forging Spaugh's signature, and the court sentenced him to twelve to fourteen months in the state penitentiary. Had he not repeated his crime, he may have escaped from the law for some time. It does not appear that he ever faced punishment for the forgery in Casper, but his freedom only lasted another month before justice was served.[18]

Only days after John King's departure from Gothberg Ranch, Scott Marks, a camp mover for Gothberg, rode urgently into the ranch yard at about midday. When looking for a shepherd on Casper Mountain, Marks discovered the man dead beneath a tree apparently struck by lightning. Marks saddled a fresh horse at the ranch and returned immediately to the site to begin collecting the flock that had scattered since the storm. Gothberg called the coroner and prepared to join him in the investigation. That afternoon, Gothberg and the coroner arrived at the camp. The carcasses of 175 sheep surrounded the herder's body lying face down beneath a splintered tree, and his deceased dog lay nearby.

A thunderstorm struck the mountain in the afternoon a week earlier. It appeared that the herder, a man named Renner or Rannell, took shelter from the rain with his dog beneath the tree. The sheep may have already gathered in the shade of the trees seeking shelter from the hot afternoon sun when the storm hit. The herder was unknown in the area. Gothberg had hired him only the day before the storm struck.[19]

Ernst Gothberg was sixty-four years old. He had worked hard in the brass works since an early age, beginning as an apprentice mold maker before the age of fourteen. In recent years, he had attained a comfortable lifestyle for himself and his wife. The previous year he retired from the brass works leaving the operation of the company to his brothers Benjamin and Herman. He did not consider himself wealthy, but though he and Minnie had no children, they enjoyed their leisure time in a variety of ways, most often together. In his retirement from the factory, Ernst dabbled in real estate and other investments. Shortly after retiring, he loaned Max Konigsberg $4,750 on a three-year mortgage at 6 percent interest.[20]

Ernst Gothberg loved automobiles and was more than pleased on August 10 to go along for a ride in the open air. It was a pleasant summer day when his good friend Dr. Finn invited him on a trip to Farmingdale, New Jersey, to visit an old patient. As they hurried home in Dr. Finn's machine the following day, they took the road leading to Freehold, New Jersey. Midway between the towns, they came upon a farmer's wagon unexpectedly and in avoiding a collision, Dr. Finn turned the wheel too quickly. The car skidded and slid down an embankment, crashing into a tree. Both men were thrown several feet from the vehicle and were at first presumed dead by the driver of the wagon. When the farmer discovered they were unconscious, but still alive, he beckoned help and loaded them in his wagon, carrying them back to Farmingdale. There, a local doctor met them. He had the two men taken to Our House, the hotel in Farmingdale, where doctors and nurses administered to them for several days.[21]

A week later, Dr. Finn had sufficiently recovered from his injuries to return home. Ernst's more serious injuries, however, were complicated by his being bedridden for a month. Ernst had suffered from kidney trouble for years, perhaps a development from the tumor removed from his back in 1905, and the confinement following the accident brought on a condition that resulted in his death. Ernst Gothberg was one of the best-known men and prominently socially connected in the Greenville district of Jersey City. Perhaps unintentionally, Ernst's obituary failed to mention his brother Martin.[22]

In September, Martin Gothberg purchased forty-two acres of land two miles west of his home ranch from William I. Ogburn. Bill Ogburn had homesteaded the land a number of years earlier. The property spanned the North Platte River and adjoined state and federal land to the west. With its river access and close proximity to the main ranch, the tract was a valuable asset for either cropland or winter pastureland. Though small in acreage, the parcel added another piece to the growing Gothberg empire.[23]

When construction of the Burlington line between Powder River, Wyoming, and Boysen Dam halted, Mollie Wolf's duties as a deputy sheriff also ended. After a stint of jury duty in July, Mollie went to work for the Franco-Wyoming Oil Company in the Salt Creek field. It is unknown in what capacity Mollie was hired, but his experience in law enforcement suggests that he became one of Franco's "line riders." Mollie's old boss on the CY range, Missou Hines still led a similar force of riders for the rival faction, which by then had merged into the Midwest Oil Company.[24]

As the Gothberg family celebrated a relatively quiet Christmas at their home on South Wolcott Street, Missou Hines and Mollie Wolf, who had ridden the range together for many dusty miles, came to town over the Christmas holiday. Though employed by competing oil companies, in the spirit of the season, the two men were not against respectfully sharing a drink together.[25]

Mary Enid Gothberg's ankle had not mended properly following her accident. Her immobility making socializing difficult, the family did not venture far and consequently declined invitations to many local holiday festivities. The Blackmores remained in Casper this season. The close proximity of the families' residences allowed shared celebrations on a smaller scale. It had been a difficult year, but the Gothbergs persevered. The family counted their blessings that Mary Enid had recuperated from most of the injuries from her accident, while mourning the loss of Martin's brother. There was a new year ahead and they looked forward with anticipation to whatever it might bring.[26]

When investors around them began reaping big profits in the oil business, Martin Gothberg and Walt Blackmore weighed the possibilities. Walt jumped into the game forming the Blackmore Oil Company, but Martin hesitated. After William Hjorth struck it big with a gusher oil well on Blackmore Oil Company leases, prospects began to change rapidly.

CHAPTER 9

There's Gold Under Them Hills
...Black Gold

1912–1913

As the Chicago, Burlington & Quincy Railroad progressed, they established primary distribution points along the line through Wyoming. They built a large reservoir for water supply at Bonneville, Wyoming, for a freight distribution center. The company designated Casper and Greybull as primary passenger depots of the new line and Casper as the regional headquarters for the system between Billings and Denver. They already had acquired a number of acres of land within the city limits beginning with their initial investment in 1909. On March 4, 1912, the CB&Q made a deal with Walt Blackmore and Pat O'Connor for the purchase of twenty-four additional acres for one hundred dollars per acre.[1]

Mary Enid's injured ankle may still have restricted her mobility, but it could not keep her from attending her eldest son's eighth-grade graduation ceremony at Central School. Martin and Mary Enid watched on as their son Edwin Gothberg, one of twenty-six pupils of Central School, received his diploma. As part of the exercise, the students received transfers to Natrona County High School to attend their first year there in the fall. Edwin just turned sixteen a month earlier, the same age as Martin had been when he left New Jersey after graduating high school thirty-two years earlier. That Edwin was older than other students in his class had nothing to do with his intelligence. He was a fine student. His setback in education was purely a result of inaccessibility to quality instruction, the very reason Martin moved his family into town.[2]

⌐◦⌐

The federal court summoned Martin Gothberg and Chester Bryan to Cheyenne as petit jurors in May 1912. They left Casper by the train on May 13, and Gothberg checked in at the Inter-Ocean Hotel when they arrived. They may have shared the room or Bryan may have stayed elsewhere, but his name escaped the register of the six primary hotels of Cheyenne at the time. The city was full of delegates attending the state Democratic Convention. There were many areas of interest to Wyoming's ranchers on the table. Of particular attention was the prospect of significant changes in federal land laws. Specifically, troublesome to many stockmen were proposed revisions to homestead and open range laws.[3]

The length of their stay is unknown, but in June Gothberg filed a claim for damages with Natrona County for one thousand dollars. County workers altered the road across two sections of his home ranch resulting in considerable loss of pasture. The county appointed an appraiser to assess the damage sustained. Having received the appraiser's report, in their July meeting, the county commissioners allowed the sum of $175 to be paid to Martin Gothberg for alteration of the road across his property, and directed the clerk to issue a certificate for that amount to Mr. Gothberg. Gothberg filed a civil suit against the county in district court. Eventually settling the case in 1914, "Martin J. Gothberg vs. Board of County Commissioners. By agreement of parties, the case was dismissed. Plaintiff having given a deed to the county for certain lands for road uses at cost of plaintiff." It remains unknown if he received additional payment from the county.[4]

⌐◦⌐

In the meantime, back in New Jersey, Martin's widowed sister-in-law Minnie Gothberg was having similar legal difficulties. Her late husband's debtors seemed likewise to ignore their obligations to Ernst Gothberg's estate. Ernst had loaned Jacob and Rebecca Lauton an unknown sum on a mortgage in November 1909. Following his death, they had failed to continue making payments on the contract, forcing Minnie to foreclose on the property in June 1912.[5]

At the age of seventy-nine, Martin Gothberg's father was becoming frail in body, but his mind remained sharp. After a lifetime working in manufacturing, his lungs were no longer capable of enduring the poor air quality generated by the factories of the industrial age. Nine years earlier, he retired to South Orange, New Jersey, away from some of the pollution of Jersey City. He still returned, however, to conduct business. Unaffected by his children's difficulty collecting payments, the following February he loaned Henry Eisenberg five thousand dollars on a mortgage on two adjoining properties on Armstrong Avenue. The rate was 6 percent for three years.[6]

On the other hand, the H & E Gothberg Manufacturing Company was expanding their business nationally. In California, Willis Lund was making a big impression on architects and designers when marketing lighting fixtures produced by the Gothberg family in New Jersey. When units became available in a new luxury apartment building in San Francisco, the owners advertised among the amenities, "individually selected fixtures in the Gothberg style, something new and attractive not found in any other apartment house in the city."[7]

Animosities between the Franco and Midwest Companies had lessened to a point that both companies dissolved their security squads. Mollie Wolf left his position with Franco-Wyoming. He and Wilda left Casper in September for an extended stay with Mollie's family in Snipes, Colorado. Missou Hines became head wrangler for the Midwest Company. In that era, the company had not adopted the use of trucks to transport oil and machinery. Hines was in charge of the vast herd of draft horses that the company maintained.[8]

Early in 1912, Walt Blackmore, in partnership with seven other local businessmen, received oil leases on twelve locations outside the "segregated area" of the Salt Creek Oil Field established by geologists of the

Franco and Midwest Companies. William Hjorth, millionaire capitalist of Jamestown, New York, liked their proposal and contracted to drill an oil well on their location with a contingency to drill twelve more wells on their other locations. Hjorth Oil Company began drilling their first well in August. On October 6, 1912, they struck oil at 1,775 feet. The gusher was the largest well in the region, far exceeding the best wells that the Franco and Midwest Companies located within the established field. The success of the well ensured a promise of future prosperity for the Casper entrepreneurs.[9]

In addition, that year Walt Blackmore ran unopposed in the Natrona County Democratic Primary for state senator. In the general election, Walt lost to the popular Republican incumbent and former business associate, Pat Sullivan. Both men ran an honest campaign and Blackmore was pleased with a respectable showing of 40 percent of the vote in his second entry into politics. He was also quite proud that neither he nor his opponent spent a single penny campaigning.[10]

The Hjorth Oil Company gusher struck October 6, 1912. It was just outside of the Salt Creek Oil Field and became the largest oil well in the region at the time.
COURTESY OF THE BLACKMORE COLLECTION, CASPER COLLEGE WESTERN HISTORY CENTER

After suffering for over a year, Mary Enid Gothberg boarded the train on Election Day for Rochester, Minnesota. There, she would visit the famous Mayo brothers' medical clinic. She made the long trip at the insistence of her husband and in hopes that pending an examination, they could perform reconstructive surgery and repair her shattered ankle. The results of her trip to Minnesota are unknown, but further mention of her injury has not been found. Presumably, the famous doctors successfully restored her damaged limb and she resumed a normal life.[11]

At the end of November, Walt Blackmore and several partners incorporated the Blackmore Oil Company. Patrick J. O'Connor and James P. Smith, partners in the Hjorth Well, were among the investors. They established the company with visions of dealing in every phase of the petroleum industry, from real estate to refining. They capitalized with one hundred thousand dollars, of which Walt was the majority stockholder. Perhaps not surprisingly, Martin Gothberg was not a shareholder, though he probably carefully examined the prospectus. Walt Blackmore was president of the company. George Rhoades, R. D. Richards, T. J. Metz, and Pat O'Connor made up the board of directors.[12]

In December, Martin J. Gothberg purchased another 160 acres from Bob Weston. This parcel bordered the forty-two acres along the North Platte that Martin purchased in 1911 from Bill Ogburn. Pleased with the Ogburn property, Martin was eager to expand into the adjacent prime bottomland along the Platte. The property's proximity to Gothberg's home ranch made the arrangement even that much sweeter.[13]

A few weeks prior to Mary Enid's departure for Minnesota, Martin Gothberg received a telephone call from the Albany County sheriff. The Albany County officials upon suspicion arrested Ade (or Adie) Irwin when he passed through Laramie, Wyoming. Based on Irwin's actions, they suspected he had stolen the horse that he rode. When the sheriff telephoned officials in Casper to tell of Irwin's arrest, the authorities knew nothing of the theft. Based on the description of the animal, they referred the sheriff to Martin Gothberg. Martin owned dozens of horses and he did not know that this horse was missing until the Laramie sheriff described the animal Irwin was riding. Sheriff Sheffner traveled from Casper, returning with Ade to stand trial for the theft.[14]

In 1908, authorities arrested the then twenty-two-year-old Ade Irwin for burning down the Association's Shearing pens a mile west of Casper. Ade confessed to the arson, telling officials that Marvin L. Bishop, prominent sheep rancher and owner of his own shearing pens at Cadoma, Wyoming, had paid him fifty dollars to do so. Ade's younger brother Dallas Irwin corroborated the story saying that Bishop had offered him the fifty dollars earlier, but he refused. Bishop flatly denied ever discussing anything even remotely resembling their story to anyone. Months of trial revealed the true account. In conversation with a friend, Bishop had grumbled that he wished a bolt of lightning would strike his competitor's pens. Ade overheard the conversation and felt he was helping Bishop by his actions. When caught, Irwin attempted to turn the blame on Bishop.[15]

Ade Irwin was "considered of unsound mind." Throughout the ordeal, it became obvious that younger brother Dallas was willing do nearly anything to protect Ade from punishment. While Ade Irwin and Frank Seese, both charged with arson, awaited trial, they escaped the county jail. They made their getaway by sawing the bars from the window of their cell and prying several rocks from the outside wall. "It is thought they had friends on the outside that aided them." Two months later the White County sheriff captured the men in Ely, Nevada. Natrona County offered a reward of $250 for Irwin and fifty dollars for Seese, which the Nevada sheriff received.[16]

The court eventually exonerated Bishop of any wrongdoing. Convicted of arson, Ade received a sentence of eighteen months in the state penitentiary. Edward M. Irwin, Ade's father, later applied for a pardon based on his son's mental condition, which it seems the court granted. After his arrest for stealing Martin Gothberg's horse, the *Natrona County Tribune* did not sound very accepting of Ade's cognitive deficiencies: "Irwin has served a term in the penitentiary for arson and has been mixed in several horse stealing cases before but because of being considered of unsound mind, he has escaped a penitentiary sentence."[17]

In late December, Judge Charles E. Carpenter died from complications of Bright's disease. Judge Carpenter presided over the district court for many years and had been in Casper only a few weeks earlier. When district court convened in January, Judge V. Jean Tidball presided. Clerk of the Court Fred E. Place presented Judge Tidball with a full docket of important civil and criminal cases. In the case of the State vs. Ade (Adie) Irwin, for stealing Martin Gothberg's horse, the trial came up on Saturday, February 1, 1913. Judge Tidball did not vacillate. When the first jury failed to reach a verdict, he immediately impaneled another. They soon brought in a judgement of guilty, but recommended a light sentence, considering the defendant's mental condition. Judge Tidball studied Ade Irwin's past record and saw a long list of offenses with few convictions before reaching his decision. He disagreed with the jury's recommendation. Judge Tidball felt that Ade Irwin had failed to learn the error of his many crimes, large or small. He sentenced him to three years of hard labor in the state penitentiary.[18]

In March, Mollie Wolf was back in Casper working as a deputy to Sheriff Sheffner. On March 6, John Williston and Frank Connors burglarized the store and post office at Moneta, Wyoming, in Fremont County and made off with some revolvers and ammunition. In the wee hours of March 11, they broke into the store and post office at Powder River, Wyoming, in Natrona County and blew up the safe with nitroglycerin. The resulting explosion destroyed the front of the building. The thieves made off with ammunition and $115 in cash. Sheriff Sheffner and Deputy Wolf rode the train to Powder River that morning and from there pursued the outlaws on horseback. The criminals eluded the sheriff and deputy for two days, but rancher Henry Johnson and two of his hired men apprehended them three miles west of Bucknum, Wyoming. Sheffner and Wolf brought the two men to Casper and transferred them to Cheyenne on federal charges. Henry Johnson received a reward of four hundred dollars per man from the federal court.[19]

Though not immediately convinced of the viability of investments in the oil industry, Martin Gothberg fully understood that the natural resource was plentiful in central Wyoming. From his earliest days in Wyoming, he remembered seeing oil seeps as he rode the range. When camped near Salt Creek during a roundup for the Searight brothers in 1883, there was an oil seep nearby. The oil formed a thick film on the water and the men of the crew used it to soften the leather of their saddles and gear. Martin recalled, "In later years, before the town of Casper was built, I would go to the north end of Oil Mountain, where there was also an oil spring, to get oil to use for my mowing machine."[20]

After mulling it over in his mind through the Christmas holidays, Martin decided to take advantage of Walt Blackmore's offer and purchased stock in Blackmore Oil Company. Much sooner than he expected, his investment proved a wise choice. On March 16, 1913, at 3 a.m., Blackmore Well No. 1 came in with a vengeance at 1,520 feet. Located about a half mile south of the Hjorth Well, the Blackmore gusher came in with even more force than the predecessor did, and engineers estimated its production at several hundred barrels per day. Expecting a strike for a number of days, an oil-saving device was ready, so the drillers were able to withdraw their tools and cap the well with only insignificant losses of oil. The second successful well outside the proven field verified that contrary to the opinion of the geologists, the wildcatters had guessed correctly, and a stratum of oil-bearing sands lay under the sagebrush there.[21]

Blackmore Oil invested a large percentage of the original capital in their own drilling rig. Where Hjorth Oil Company left only 12.5 percent of the profits to be shared between the lease holders, the stockholders in Blackmore Oil Company realized 100 percent of the yield. Martin Gothberg and his cohorts did not become instant millionaires because of their investments in the company, but Blackmore Well No. 1 provided an excellent start toward that outcome. At the next shareholder's meeting, they voted unanimously to continue explorations. The company's drilling rig began work on Blackmore Well No. 2 as soon possible.[22]

Blackmore Oil Company's drilling rig was working on Well No. 2, about five miles north of Well No. 1. On June 8, it seemed as if everything was proceeding perfectly for the drillers when the flame from the nearby forge lighted gases escaping from the well, and within seconds an inferno engulfed the entire operation. It is fortunate that members of the crew were not immediately by the well when the fire ignited. It is unknown how much damage the machinery sustained beyond the obvious loss of the wooden derrick and other flammable materials. Regardless, the company suffered damage of at least a few thousand dollars in equipment, a setback but not a catastrophe. Fortunately, no one was killed or seriously injured.[23]

Two weeks later, Martin Gothberg traveled to Cheyenne, Wyoming. He stayed at the Inter-Ocean Hotel for two consecutive weeks and perhaps he again served jury duty. Martin also was in the midst of foreclosing on a creditor and he may have been in the capital regarding that process. The previous December, Gothberg loaned Frederick F. Price of Freeland one hundred dollars on a chattel mortgage, with two horses and a foal as collateral. In June, he had yet to receive any payment on the loan. Casper Attorney A. H. Conn filed the foreclosure in Casper on the mortgage on July 3. The present debt with accrued interest totaled $107.20 plus legal fees. The clerk scheduled the auction of collateral on the courthouse steps at ten o'clock on the morning of July 24, if the creditor did not pay Martin J. Gothberg the sum of $190.00 plus legal fees and interest accrued by that time.[24]

By November, Walt Blackmore was looking at other financial opportunities. He and Pat O'Connor along with their wives formed the Casper Land and Investment Company. The company began somewhat modestly with ten thousand dollars in capital stock. They began subdividing and selling a couple of additions to the city of Casper over a somewhat short period and made reasonable returns on their investments.[25]

Some perhaps considered Martin Gothberg's good friend Walt Blackmore a schemer, but more truthfully, he was an addicted investor. He was always excited about some new idea he had every time the two men got together. During these visits, they would brainstorm new ideas. Martin was the calculated thinker of the two, and between them they usually managed to take into consideration all of the necessary steps needed to bring a project to completion. While Walt often took financial risks that Martin found unworthy, when the two men agreed on a business proposal, it was usually destined to succeed. Such was the case of the Ideal Apartments in Casper, Wyoming.

Both men were very aware that with the rapid population growth in the area associated with the petroleum industry, Casper was suffering a shortage of both temporary and permanent lodging. They also had each spent enough time in urban areas to understand the advantages that apartment living provided for many families and individuals. They hired A. M. Garbutt and Charles I. Weidner as architects to design a multi-story, 40-by-130-foot structure to accommodate the Ideal Apartments. The building offered a variety of quarters from studio apartments with kitchenettes and Murphy beds, all the way up to modestly luxurious multi-room suites.

Casper had never had an apartment house and the influx of businessmen and laborers connected with the oil fields often surpassed the capacity of hotels and rooming houses. Gothberg and Blackmore's new facility would greatly relieve that congestion with its fourteen studios and twenty-one larger apartments. On Sunday, February 1, 1914, Gothberg and Blackmore boarded the train for Omaha. In their absence, the *Casper Press* announced their plan.[26]

Martin and Walt kept the location of their new enterprise a secret until they finalized a deal for the property. Walt Blackmore and John Cosgrove worked together on land sold to the railroad a decade earlier. It appears by the trip to Omaha that Cosgrove still held an interest in the location chosen for the apartment building. When excavations on Center Street began for the basement of the apartment building the first week of March, locals quickly deduced the purpose. The site was on the southeast corner of Center Street and Fourth Avenue, at the time a block south of the Natrona County Courthouse erected in 1908.[27]

On April 28, with the foundation and basement completed, Gothberg and Blackmore contracted L. Larsen and Karl R. Jorgensen to construct their stone and brick building. They bid $19,664 for the structure, heating and plumbing excluded. The cost of the building was equivalent to nearly a half million dollars in today's economy. Work commenced immediately.[28]

As construction of the Ideal Apartments continued, Martin contemplated the purchase of his first automobile. Charlie Webel had purchased a new Cartercar early that spring and was dissatisfied with it. Cartercars were equipped with a unique gearless "friction drive" transmission. Some drivers disliked the unusual feature. As Gothberg's business interests continued to expand, he could easily see the advantages of greater mobility. At the end of June, he made his decision and struck a deal with Webel to buy his nearly new touring car.[29]

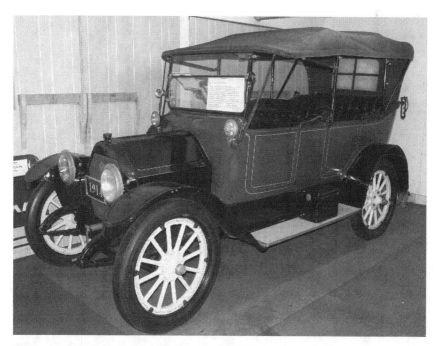

Martin J. Gothberg's first automobile was a 1914 Cartercar similar to the one shown here. Built in Wisconsin, this Model 7 Touring car sported a 195-cubic-inch side-valve engine and Carter's famous "friction drive" transmission. It appears that all Cartercars were equipped for right-hand drive. This wonderfully restored example belongs to the LeMay Collection at Marymount in Tacoma, Washington.
PHOTOGRAPH COURTESY OF THE LEMAY COLLECTION AT MARYMOUNT

In mid-July, Walt Blackmore's profits from properties contracted with the Hjorth Oil Company greatly improved when the company committed the sale of all of their oil on the Blackmore leases to the Midwest Oil Company's refinery in Casper. Midwest erected storage tanks at the Hjorth Well that they connected to their pipeline system for transport to the refinery.[30]

As the Ideal Apartments neared completion, the project was all the rage. Newspapers lauded over the facility at every opportunity. The *Casper Press* called it "a modern and commodious apartment house," then added, "When finished, this building will undoubtedly be the handsomest structure of its kind in the city." A year later, in retrospect, they concluded, "The $40,000 Ideal apartments, is a very handsome building of press brick. It is well furnished and centrally located. Heated by the city heating plant, it is modern in every respect."[31]

As Martin's apartment house came to fruition, the family brass works in New Jersey also flourished. In August, his brothers advertised for additional office help as well as for people in shipping and in the polishing

The Ideal Apartment building nearing completion in 1914.
COURTESY OF THE NATRONA COUNTY PIONEER ASSOCIATION COLLECTION, CASPER COLLEGE WESTERN HISTORY CENTER

shop. Besides the promising prospects of the apartment building, Martin Gothberg had a good year elsewhere in his business ventures. His lamb crop this year was outstanding and on August 29, Martin shipped seven of the twenty-seven railcar loads of sheep that left from Casper headed to the markets in Omaha. Four days later, he departed to Omaha himself to negotiate the sale of his flocks.[32]

In September, Mary Enid's mother and stepfather purchased a home on Center Street for two thousand dollars and moved from the rural community of Freeland, Wyoming, into Casper. Frank Sanders's health had seriously declined in recent years and they endeavored to live a less strenuous life in town. They also appreciated being closer to the Gothbergs. Mary Enid had been unable to visit their home in Freeland since her accident the previous year.[33]

Shortly after Martin's return from Omaha, Mary Enid's stepfather passed away in Idaho Falls, Idaho. After living in Casper only a few weeks, Frank and Dora Sanders had moved to Idaho Falls, presumably for medical treatment due to Frank's rapidly failing health. Dora had Frank buried at the soldiers' burial ground there and began closing out their affairs in the city. Dora planned to return to Casper as soon as was practical.[34]

At the end of the month, Martin's attorney, A. H. Cobb, and his wife leased their home in east Casper to P. N. Nunn, manager of the Wyoming Electric Company. They in turn rented an apartment at the Ideal Apartments, looking forward to a comfortable winter with efficient heating and close proximity to the courthouse and Mr. Cobb's law office during inclement weather. Two weeks later, Edwin Hall, president and general manager of the Hall Oil Company, rented a suite in the building. He then moved his wife and children from Lusk, Wyoming, to make their home in Casper. Martin and Walt's new venture was becoming a big hit with the middle- to upper-class residents of the city.[35]

In November, Martin Gothberg and Bill Clark received final patent on forty acres in Emigrant Gap that adjoined the 160 acres that Gothberg patented there in 1908. At the same time, Martin purchased another forty acres bordering the same property. This gave him 240 acres of deeded land surrounded by four sections of state and federal open rangelands, all in a prime area for winter grazing his flocks and only seven miles from the home ranch.[36]

—◆◆—

It was bitterly cold on the night of Tuesday, December 15, 1914. Tom Clayton rode his horse from his ranch the ten miles or so to Glenrock earlier that day. After having a drink for the road that became several drinks, Jerky Bill, bundled up for the weather, mounted his horse and headed home. It was nine o'clock. The next morning it was twenty degrees below zero when his son went to do his chores, and his father had not returned. Jerky Bill's wife, Annie, and their sons were not particularly worried, thinking that he had spent the night in town. It was not until they discovered his rider-less horse standing outside of the gate that they became alarmed. Backtracking the horse in the snow, they discovered Jerky Bill lying where he fell. He was unconscious and nearly frozen.[37]

Hitching a wagon, his family took him to Glenrock. His limbs nearly frozen solid, Dr. Williams thought it impossible that he could survive. On Friday, Jerky Bill rallied and presumably even regained consciousness, at least for a time. Up to this point, the story had been that he had either fallen or been thrown from his horse. Now a second version of events surfaced. At some point on his ride home, Jerky Bill dismounted to walk and try to get circulation in his cold feet. While walking he lost the reins from the grip of his numb fingers and his horse wandered off. He continued to walk through the night trying to keep warm through exercise. When the sun came up, he sat down to rest and fell asleep. There were no witnesses and it is difficult to ascertain the course of events.[38]

With new hope, Dr. Williams sent Tom to the hospital in Douglas on Friday. By Christmas Eve, nearly a week later, the doctors in Douglas reported his condition as good. Everyone involved presumed that amputations would be necessary to his survival. By December 27, Dr. Cantril determined that Jerky Bill had recovered sufficiently to survive the amputations necessary to save his life. On the morning of December 28, Dr.

Cantril amputated Jerky Bill's left foot above the ankle, and the front of his right foot, leaving the heel. "In the operation upon Mr. Clayton, the surgeon used the nerve blocking system, by which the patient was relieved of being given an anesthetic. He was conscious throughout the entire operation and seemingly suffered no ill effects. It is believed now he has chances for ultimate recovery."[39]

On the morning of December 30, Jerky Bill showed every sign of making a full recovery. Dr. Cantril removed the fingers of both hands as planned without complications. By that afternoon, Clayton's condition began to decline. In the evening, he lost consciousness for the last time. He gradually sank until the end came at an early hour the following morning.[40]

Thomas C. "Jerky Bill" Clayton was dead at fifty-nine years of age. It is ironic that the most famous horseman and bronc-rider that central Wyoming had seen to that day should die as a result of perhaps falling off his horse. There are many tales of his prowess. In the days before the use of a stopwatch, Clayton rode his broncs to a standstill. Many say that he could ride anything with hair on it and perform stunts from the back of a horse that were unsurpassed in skill and daring. He had ridden with the boys of the CY for several years before Martin Gothberg arrived in the area in 1883 and still performed at local events two decades later. Martin Gothberg knew him well and called him his friend. He ran a successful ranch on Boxelder Creek and left a loving wife and a half dozen adult children to carry on his legacy. Thomas Charles Clayton was laid to rest in the cemetery at Glenrock, Wyoming.

In August 1914, Germany declared war on both Russia and France. A half dozen western European countries declared neutrality. When Kaiser Wilhelm II invaded Luxembourg and Belgium preparing Germany's invasion of France, Great Britain protested that they were in violation of the Treaty of London. The German chancellor replied that the treaty was just a *chiffon de papier*, a scrap of paper. Great Britain declared war on Germany. Thus began what became World War I, the war to end all wars. The United States, though supportive of both Great Britain and France, declared neutrality.

CHAPTER 10

Wartime Boosts Patriotism
and the Economy

1915–1918

MANY YOUNG MEN OF HIGH SCHOOL AGE IN AMERICA BECAME INVOLVED in quasi-military organizations, preparing themselves to be ready to enter the war. Some of these groups later evolved into the Reserve Officers' Training Corps, or ROTC. Edwin Gothberg joined the Natrona County High School Cadet Corps in 1915. On March 17, the Cadet Corps elected officers for their company. They chose Bob Blackmore and Ed Gothberg, first and second sergeant, respectively. "The company is being rounded out into first class military style and the boys are taking great pride in their drills."[1]

The debutantes of the school strived to imitate their parents' social calendars. The evening of March 18, a day after the election, Edwin's younger sister Sis Gothberg attended a party at the home of Casper realtor William R. Woelfert and his wife, near the high school. Their daughter, Gladys Woelfert, hosted the party. Nine young ladies and an equal number of young gentlemen were present. Among the other young socialites was Patricia Sullivan, daughter of Senator Pat Sullivan, and Bob Blackmore. On her own social calendar, Mary Enid Gothberg hosted the ladies' aid meeting of the Methodist church at their home on April 16.[2]

Bill Noonan, who repaired anything from typewriters to tractors, entered into the automobile business as the motorized age progressed. He became the dealer in Casper for Chalmers Automobiles. Bill knew Edwin Gothberg and his fellow cadet, Orland Ormsby, since they were children. As adolescents, he helped them repair their bicycles and often sold parts to them. In May, he hired the two young men to ride the train to Denver on a Friday after school and take delivery on one of his brand-new Chalmers "Baby Six" automobiles. With cash in their pockets for expenses, they then had the weekend to drive the car back to Casper. Ed, the older of the two boys, was then nineteen, but imagine the thrill these young men experienced with the opportunity to drive a brand-new car some three hundred miles over a weekend. They probably would have made the trip without pay if Bill had asked them to.[3]

In June, Mr. and Mrs. A. H. Cobb returned from their winter at the Ideal Apartments to their home on East First Street. Walt and Minnie Blackmore moved their family to Hat-Six Ranch for the summer and Billie and Elmer Johnson became house sitters at the Blackmores' home in Casper.[4]

On Sunday, July 25, Walt and Minnie hosted the Cobbs and a dozen other guests to an outing at their ranch. The guests motored out in three automobiles that morning and shared a splendid day. An afternoon thunderstorm drove the visitors indoors where they enjoyed refreshments before their return to town on the muddied road that evening.[5]

The Casper Brewing Company incorporated in 1914 and elected Missou Hines among its directors in February. They asked farmers in Lander and Riverton, Wyoming, to begin growing the barley needed for their product. They already owned the land on West First Street, now Midwest Avenue, and expected to begin erecting the facility in March. Suffering continual setbacks, construction of the buildings finally began in August and managers announced completion of the first batch of beer by January. With much of their machinery already arriving in Casper, in September they moved up their forecast to November. No sooner had they publicized their plans than rumors surfaced of a state prohibition movement that halted construction for months.[6]

The company, initially capitalized with eighty thousand dollars, exceeded one hundred thousand dollars in expenditures before completing its buildings and locating all of the critical equipment needed to begin the process. Suppliers cancelled orders for delivery of several key components due to the ongoing war in Europe. On April 9, 1915, Missou Hines caught the train to Denver and then to Kansas City procuring the final key pieces. The company ultimately released their first batch of Wyoming Light Lager in a grand opening ceremony of the brewery on July 26, 1915. Missou Hines, who had sold everything from sheep dip to mine stocks, began selling beer. He advertised in the newspapers and called on potential clients. Traveling to Thermopolis and Basin, Wyoming, he took orders from numerous establishments then returned with their deliveries. Hines was a promoter and understood his customers. Of Wyoming Light Lager, he said it is "elevating and invigorating, but not intoxicating."[7]

In September, Martin Gothberg and his son Edwin journeyed to Jersey City, New Jersey, visiting their family there. Martin's father, Edwin Herman Gothberg, then living in nearby South Orange, New Jersey, was aging and his health declining. Herman had visited the family in Wyoming, but it was not likely that his health would permit a future excursion of that length. For lack of a better excuse, Martin and his son came for Grandfather's eighty-first birthday. This was Edwin's first chance to see the East. With the war in Europe in full swing, factories were turning out a multitude of arms and equipment for the Allied armies. New arms factories were under construction along every available railroad siding. Agents called on other plants to manufacture parts for shrapnel bombs.

The Gothberg Foundry had been making chandeliers for over forty years there, but solicitors regularly called on them to produce the special copper rings used to fit around the nickel-steel shrapnel shells. The demand was almost limitless. If they would refit to build these parts, and guarantee daily deliveries, contracts awaited to create millions of the item at a handsome profit. Virtually every type of manufacturing boomed in wartime. The volume and pace of business there was frantic and practically overwhelming to Edwin, who had never seen anything like it.[8]

After a month's absence, nineteen-year-old Edwin Gothberg was not disappointed to return home and go back to school. The excursion to

New Jersey had certainly been exciting, but the slower tempo of life in the West was worthy of its own praise. He now began to understand why his father had so desperately longed to resume his lifestyle in Wyoming after returning to the culture of his boyhood in 1892.[9]

—◦—

When Martin returned home, he received final proof on another forty acres at Emigrant Gap with Ben Thompson, George Houck, and Ira Lake. He then left for Riverton with architect A. M. Garbutt. Garbutt showed him numerous agricultural and industrial areas in the Wind River valley mostly owned by the Wind River Indian Reservation. The trip highlighted the new Riverton Irrigation Ditch No. 2, two alfalfa mills, a flourmill and a railroad tie–mill, treating plant, and landing owned by the Wyoming Tie and Timber Company. The *Riverton Chronical* named Gothberg a "Casper capitalist," who was favorably impressed with the community and the industries, sparking contemplation for future investments.[10]

Martin Gothberg purchased Fred L. Haughton's Sheep Creek Ranch in northwest Albany County, Wyoming, around 1916. The ranch was twenty miles southeast of Gothberg's operations on Stinking and Lone Tree Creeks. The livestock included 1,600 head of sheep and eighty head of cattle and the land made up the home base for Haughton's summer range. It appears to have been 320 deeded acres and several thousand acres of open range access. This seems to be about the same time that Samuel Frank Service and Verner D. Dewey merged with the Gothbergs in the Lone Tree Creek Sheep Company, which Martin and Mary Enid had established in 1902.[11]

While Martin maintained financial control of the company, Sam Service oversaw the daily business of the ranching operations for the corporation by January 1916. Sam Service had only two months earlier returned home to Wyoming after an extended trip to Missouri and Oklahoma. To everyone's surprise, he brought with him a new bride. While in Oklahoma, Sam had married Maud Mae Moore. All of Sam's friends were anxious to get to know his new wife. On January 11, Walt and Minnie Blackmore entertained a small gathering of friends with an informal party at their home in the newlyweds' honor. The Gothbergs, of course, were among the guests.[12]

⬤⸰⬤

Martin Gothberg was never one to boast or flaunt his wealth. He was not above boasting on his children, however. Edwin, his eldest son, was about to graduate from high school. Not only that, but he was valedictorian of his graduating class. Martin was overflowing with pride. Edwin had overcome a poor educational beginning and flourished. A few weeks before graduation, Martin paid Earl C. Boyle a visit at his Ford garage on North Center Street. There, he bought a shiny new Ford Runabout for Edwin's graduation. The cost was $345.00, plus $47.90 freight from Detroit.[13]

Martin's father, Edwin Herman Gothberg, passed away in New Jersey on May 10, 1916, at the age of eighty-one. He had long suffered from multiple ailments. In his lifework in brass and bronze manufacturing, he was exposed to smoke and most likely asbestos and a multitude of other materials known to be health hazards today. Martin probably attended the funeral, held on May 21 at his parents' home in South Orange, then rushed home for his son Edwin's high school graduation. Ed was the only male graduate in his class. He gave his valedictory address for the class exercises the evening of May 31, at the Natrona County High School auditorium. The following evening, June 1, 1916, he and his classmates received their diplomas in their graduation ceremony at the same venue.[14]

⬤⸰⬤

On July 11, 1916, Martin Gothberg and four other Casper businessmen filed articles of incorporation for the Wyoming Drilling Company. With an initial investment of thirty thousand dollars, the five men planned to purchase drilling equipment and contract with oil companies to drill wells on their properties. Their original plans were to restrict their operations to Natrona County.[15]

⬤⸰⬤

Though the United States remained neutral in the war in Europe, it was clear that the majority of Americans sided with the Allied forces. As

American factories continued to manufacture arms and ammunition for their support, they gained a growing scrutiny from the kaiser. On July 16, German agents sabotaged multiple New Jersey munitions factories resulting in an explosion on Black Tom Island. It is unknown if the H & E Gothberg Manufacturing Company was a target of the saboteurs.

━◦━

About the time of the explosion at Black Tom, Martin's sister Sophia and her husband, Edward C. Fuller, departed Casper with their nephews Ed and Walt Gothberg on an automobile expedition through Yellowstone National Park. The Fullers had relocated from Attleboro, Massachusetts, to Roseville Park, New Jersey, a few years earlier. Also sharing the adventure were Walt and Minnie Blackmore and their family. The entourage traveled in Walt Blackmore's Dodge, Ed Gothberg's Ford Roadster, and two other cars with camping gear and supplies for a month. They had a splendid trip, and all remarked that the scenery was unsurpassed. They exited the park at the south entrance and wishing to avoid the wiles of Hoback Canyon, chose the route over Togwotee Pass on their return. Arriving in Lander on August 12, the company anxiously partook in baths and lodging at the hotel.

While in Lander, Walt Blackmore reacquainted himself with local business associates and introduced the other gentlemen in the party to them. Their recent journey was the primary subject of conversation and road conditions in the area were a central topic. Blackmore highly emphasized how improvements in the roads to the southern entrance of the park would greatly improve the number of visitors passing through their town. Logistics would make Lander, Wyoming, a primary departure point from the railroad if automobiles were available and a passable road existed. Walt expressed that old-timers in that area told him that his Dodge was the first automobile to make it across Togwotee Pass under its own power, but he boasted with a smile that not everyone drove a Dodge.[16]

As soon as Walt Blackmore was back in Casper, he was back to work planning his next investments. In November, he joined Pat O'Connor, B. B. Brooks, and others in forming the Jupiter Oil Company, for which Blackmore served on the board of directors. A few weeks later, he was in Cheyenne filing papers to incorporate the Antigo Oil Company with another group of Casper businessmen, for which he was elected president. The founders of each company invested one million dollars in capital.[17]

—◆—

In December, Martin Gothberg again expanded his acreage when he purchased 280 acres from W. F. Witt. This parcel was the first of his acquisitions on Bear Creek in southern Natrona County. At the same time, he bought forty acres from Anna Hench on Iron Creek, fifteen miles west of the home ranch. This also was a new region of development for the Gothberg Ranch.[18]

—◆—

Martin Gothberg's Wyoming Drilling Company had two National No. 2 drilling rigs idle in their yards in Casper when Myron C. Dutton, manager of the drilling company, had the opportunity to acquire a lucrative lease on three sections of the Powder River Dome, ten miles west of Salt Creek. Charles Liebenstein, president of the Associated Oil and Land Company, specified the terms of the lease, including the condition that drilling commence by December 29, 1916. With a two-month window to work with, Myron was certain of their success. Just as Mr. Dutton prepared to begin moving equipment to the operation in the north, a contract with the Northwest Oil Company arose to drill two wells immediately in the Big Muddy Field of western Converse County. Martin Gothberg and the other directors of the Wyoming Drilling Company considered purchasing another drilling rig to comply with the requirement, but Mr. Dutton was certain the shallowness of the wells in the Big Muddy Field would still allow ample time to send one of the rigs to meet the obligation of the lease at Powder River Dome.

The Wyoming wind blew in constant waves of winter storms of a ferocity unsurpassed in recent years. As the deadline approached, the weather finally seemed to abate slightly, and Myron Dutton breathed a sigh of relief. No sooner had he regained a slight confidence in accomplishing the mission than a flurry of mechanical breakdowns besieged the rigs on both of the wells at Muddy. This now made certain that they would miss their deadline and default on the Associated Company lease. With hat in hand, Myron called on the president of Associated Oil and Land. Understanding the situation, Wyoming Drilling Company received a thirty-day reprieve on the cut-off date.

The Casper Daily Tribune wrote:

> *A race between capital, exemplified in almost superhuman efforts to comply with the terms of a lease on valuable oil properties in Powder River Dome...*
>
> *And in this struggle is again shown that capital, once satisfied with the merits of a property and possibilities of reward from the expenditure of goodly sums in development, knows not the word "Can't."*
>
> *The occasion of long strings of four and six-horse teams hauling out supplies and machinery is the absolute necessity of M. C. Dutton of the Wyoming Drilling Company, having a camp established, drilling outfit set up and in action...*[19]

This undated photograph pictures a string team preparing to cross the North Platte River Bridge at the Midwest Oil Company's refinery in Casper, Wyoming. The twenty-eight horses and mules are moving a twenty-one-thousand-pound steam-powered engine to the Salt Creek Oil Field, forty miles north of Casper. The photograph, attributed to Martin J. Gothberg, has a note stating, "Probably Coleman's string team."
COURTESY OF THE BLACKMORE COLLECTION, CASPER COLLEGE WESTERN HISTORY CENTER

Myron Dutton told the newspaper:

With properties so favorably reported on, so choicely located, and with such high-class neighbors, it isn't going to be a question of money, work or hours to hold that lease. Unforeseen conditions prevented our operations being under way at the first specified time, but Mr. Liebenstein has no doubt been up against just such things in his years of experience in the game, and is cooperating fully with me, and, unless the great unexpected happens, I am confident that the first deep well on the east arm of the Powder River anticline will be completed by the end of May with most favorable and gratifying results.[20]

Two weeks later the Northwestern Oil Company announced that the Wyoming Drilling Company drilled in Well No. 1 in the Big Muddy Field and Well No. 2 was not far behind.[21]

With the rapid success of the Wyoming Drilling Company, Martin Gothberg began preparing for his next investment. With Walt Blackmore, Harold Banner, Tom Majors, and C. L. Rhinemuth as directors, Gothberg incorporated the Casper Petroleum Company on February 1, 1917. They formed the corporation with capitalization of one million dollars in stock and direction by Martin Gothberg, president.[22]

The owners of the Casper Petroleum Company prided themselves in their credibility, and former newspaperman-turned-stockbroker Alfred J. Mokler advertised that "some of Casper's most conservative and responsible business men are backing this company, and it is strictly a Casper corporation." Mokler added P. C. Nicolaysen, C. H. Townsend, and H. G. Duhling to the list of prominent and reliable stockholders. He went on to say, "There are no salaried officers, no promotion stock, and not one cent will be expended except but for legitimate and actual development work.[23]

After completing Northwest Oil Company's Well No. 2 at Big Muddy, the Wyoming Drilling Company moved their second drilling rig to the Interstate Petroleum Company's Veitch Well. The Veitch Well was located on the north side of the North Platte River approximately seven miles east of Casper. In February, Interstate Petroleum temporarily abandoned work on the Veitch Well and Myron Dutton moved the drilling rig to the Powder River Dome to work in the same proximity as their other rig. Breakdowns, no matter how small, invariably haunt an oil well drilling operation. A few days after the second rig was on location, a breakdown beyond repair in the field prompted a rapid trip to Casper by driller Frank Kershaw. After a short respite, he returned to Powder River Dome with the restored tool in good working order.[24]

━ ⁓

Emulating their parents in social circles, a congenial gathering of high school friends took possession of the Jourgensen home at the invitation of Miss Charlotte Jourgensen. The guests had the best of times enjoying themselves in a thoroughly informal manner. They sang and listened to piano music, danced and talked, and there were refreshments provided for them. Among those present were Sis Gothherg, Norma Jourgensen, Helen Banner, Glen Littlefield, George Jourgensen, and Edwin Gothberg.[25]

On Valentine's Day, Mary Enid filed for final proof on 160 acres on the southern border of Natrona County. The parcel adjoined 120 acres that the Gothbergs acquired from John Harris in 1907 and forty cares patented with John Scott in 1904. The Gothbergs now held 320 deeded acres along Lone Tree Creek on which to center their summer grazing operations.[26]

At the end of February, Martin ventured to Thermopolis, Wyoming, for a ten-day sojourn. He took in the baths of the hot springs there for benefit of his health. In his absence, his daughter Sis and her classmate Adeline Moore hosted a large dance and party for over one hundred members of the junior and senior classes and a number of other invited guests. It was the largest and most important social event of the school year. Held at the high school gymnasium, both the girls' mothers and six members of the faculty chaperoned the affair. There was music and dancing throughout the evening and refreshments served by several young ladies of the freshman class. Among the many attendees were Charlotte and Norma Jourgensen, Marie Bishop, Alfa Mokler, Patricia and Kathleen Sullivan, Glen Littlefield, Roy Dinneen, Floyd Blackmore, and Walter Storrie.[27]

━ ⁓

Dr. C. C. Clark of Casper formed a new type of oil exploration company in 1917. The Two Hundred Oil Club was just that—a club—starting with fifty stockholders. Upon his return from Thermopolis, Martin Gothberg attended the first meeting of the stockholder/members of the club, held in Casper. At the meeting, the members confirmed Dr. Clark as president and elected Martin Gothberg as one of the five directors.[28]

Two weeks later, Martin was having mechanical problems with his Cartercar. He brought the car to Roy Dinneen's garage. Unfortunately, the automobile needed major repairs. Pleased with the sturdiness of the Ford Runabout he bought for Edwin the previous year, he paid a visit to Earl Boyle. Opting for the bonus of an enclosed vehicle over his present open touring car, Martin chose to purchase a new Ford Sedan from Mr. Boyle. The Ford was less luxurious than the Cartercar with its "gearless" transmission and larger engine, but the comfort of a weather-resistant passenger compartment had its advantages in Wyoming's unpredictable climate. Satisfied with the more popular Ford, Gothberg sold his Carter-car to Roy Dinneen.[29]

On March 2, Margaret Knittle and Myrtle Reavill rode the train from Douglas to Casper where they spent the weekend with Sis Gothberg. Sis and Norma Jourgensen spent the following weekend in Douglas with Margaret Knittle and her family. Both the Knittle and Reavill families lived on North Third Street in Douglas. On Saturday evening, Myrtle Reavill hosted dinner for the young ladies.[30]

On April 5, 1917, Martin Gothberg, Archibald D. MacFarlane, and Mary Enid Gothberg incorporated the Dobbin Sheep Company. Not to be confused with the Dobbin Springs Sheep Company formed in 1906 with Harry Parsons, the Dobbin Sheep Company utilized summer range that Archie MacFarlane established northeast of Arminto, Wyoming, in the Big Horn Mountains. This business incorporated with twenty-five thousand dollars in capital. Martin Gothberg served as president and Mary Enid Gothberg as secretary.[31]

President Woodrow Wilson did his best to keep the United States out of the war in Europe. Even after German U-boats sank the British liner

RMS *Lusitania* in 1915, in which 128 Americans died, he continued to preach against American involvement. Wilson narrowly won reelection in 1916 on the campaign slogan "He Kept Us Out of War." In January 1917, Germany resumed its submarine attacks on civilian ships in the Atlantic. Wilson held fast to his vow.

On January 19, 1917, German foreign minister Arthur Zimmermann sent a coded telegram to the German consulate in Mexico City. British intelligence intercepted the wire and decoded it. In the message, Zimmermann invited Mexico to join Germany as an ally against the United States. In return, Germany would finance Mexico's military in an offensive to recover the territories of Texas, New Mexico, and Arizona from the United States. The United Kingdom presented the communication to the United States and President Wilson released the message to the press. After German submarines sank seven United States merchant ships and the publication of the telegram to Mexico, Wilson called for a declaration of war on Germany. Four days later, on April 6, 1917, Congress obliged the president's request.[32]

With the declaration of war came a frenzy of activity in the already chaotic oil fields. Martin Gothberg's Casper Petroleum Company immediately boosted activity on their 3,200 acres in the promising Big Muddy Field. By the end of April, they had drilling rigs working on three wells there. The first well was already down 1,300 feet. From the property Casper Petroleum controlled, considered the best in the field, the owners expected to produce generous volumes of crude oil.[33]

Bernard and Herman Gothberg had more orders at the brass works in New Jersey than they could fill. In March, they already needed lathe operators, and when the United States entered the war, nearly all of their young and able-bodied employees left their positions to join the military. The shortage of workers necessitated the Gothbergs to advertise incessantly for help. They needed punch and drawing press operators, platers and polishers, spinners and machinists, tinsmiths, solderers and braziers, and clear down to shipping clerks and janitors. Initially they asked for boys over eighteen years of age, then over sixteen, then fourteen. They even resorted to advertising for elderly men able to work part-time. Initially they offered starting salaries at six to seven dollars per week, and by the end of the war they offered up to eighteen dollars per week, always advertising steady, reliable employment and the opportunity to learn a trade. The factory literally became a vocational school for anyone willing to work as the company struggled to fill wartime orders.[34]

Martin Gothberg's attorney and his wife, Mr. and Mrs. A. H. Cobb, again rented a suite at the Ideal Apartments as they had for the previous winter. In their absence, they rented their home to Edward F. Massam, an investor in multiple petroleum-related ventures. Mr. Massam's sister and daughter came to Casper to stay with him from Seattle, Washington, through the winter months. Mrs. Cobb spent several months in Lawrence, Kansas, visiting their son who had been studying law at the university there. He since enlisted in the Officers' Reserve Corps and in March was in training at Fort Riley, Kansas. Mrs. Cobb returned to Casper at that time but was happy to return to their East First Street home in May.[35]

One of Sis Gothberg's closest friends since childhood, Adeline Moore, married Carl M. Parcell at her parents' home on South Walnut Street in Casper on June 3, 1917, a few days before the two young women's high school graduation. Sis was a bridesmaid. Mary Enid, Ed, and Emma Gothberg were all in attendance, as well as Walter Storrie, who recently moved to Casper from Lusk, Wyoming.[36]

Two weeks earlier, Walt Blackmore retired to his ranch for a few days under the guise of looking after spring planting in the fields. In reality, he needed a break. He just completed filing the incorporation of the two-million-dollar Wyoming National Oil Company with six other Casper investors. Walt also was a primary member of the board of directors for that company. More importantly, he was in the midst of the largest oil business deal of his career to date.[37]

On May 21, 1917, Walt Blackmore and his board of directors closed a deal with the Ohio Oil Company in which the Ohio Company purchased a half interest in Blackmore Oil Company's holdings in the Salt Creek Oil Field. The consideration paid for their share of these assets is unknown. Part of the agreement included that the Ohio Company would immediately develop wells on all of the properties in the least possible time. It was noted that several productive wells were already established on these and adjacent locations. The two companies made arrangements the next day to locate the first of the new oil wells.[38]

The young and prosperous Blackmore Oil Company already planned to share with stockholders a return on their investments. On June 14, they announced they would pay a dividend of 20 percent cash and 100 percent stock to each stockholder of record as of July 4. The company scheduled the mailing of dividend checks and paperwork supporting the two-to-one stock split on July 14. They planned to allot a separate dividend with moneys coming from the Ohio Oil Company purchase. Not stopping there, they planned to distribute an additional 10 percent dividends in thirty and sixty days based on the new issuance of stock. Early investors like Martin Gothberg not only doubled their shares of stock, but also received several handsome checks over the next few months.[39]

Blackmore Oil Company did not hold a monopoly on good fortune in Wyoming. The oil business was booming. The Canary-Stilwell Oil Company asked the Wyoming Drilling Company for bids on drilling several oil wells in Fremont County. Mr. W. W. Rhea, general manager of that company's operations in the area, announced that his company expected to be active by mid-July. He added that Wyoming Drilling should have tools in the ground shortly.[40]

<hr />

When thirty-one-year-old Augustus J. "Gus" Hardendorf came to Casper, Wyoming, in 1917, he had already worked on and around oil well drilling equipment for a decade and a half. Born in Coffeyville, Kansas, in 1886, he followed his father's example after two years of high school in Chanute, Kansas, and began his career in the oil field. In 1910, Gus was a top paid drilling tool dresser in the bustling oil fields near Bakersfield, California. A year later while visiting his family in Kansas, a drilling company from Oklahoma recruited him into a job drilling oil wells in South

America, then in Colon, Panama, before returning to New Orleans on the steamship *Cartago* in 1912.[41]

Gus arrived in Basin, Wyoming, in April 1916, where he and his old friend W. H. "Cap" Baker opened the Oil Exchange, a pool hall and rooming house. Managed by Baker's wife, they catered to the hardworking men from nearby oil fields. In September Gus was working in Bridger, Montana, and a week later he and Baker sold their "gentleman's club." In February 1917, Gus passed through Basin on his way to Chanute, Kansas, to marry his longtime sweetheart, Miss Margaret Cox. He and his bride returned to Bridger, Montana, where he resumed his position as oil well driller for the Elk Basin Oil Company. In the fall of 1917, Mr. and Mrs. Hardendorf relocated to North Maple Street in Casper, Wyoming, where they purchased a home. By then, Gus had quite a reputation as an oil field prospector, also known as a scout or wildcatter. When he arrived, he held the position of "scout" for the Shiloh Oil Company, who was drilling for oil in the West Salt Creek field, forty miles north of Casper. It was not long before Gus Hardendorf and Martin Gothberg became acquainted. Neither man had any formal education in geology, but both had an instinct for the oil business. Most likely, Martin saw in Gus a younger version of himself and remembered the time twenty years ago when he, himself a wild, young cowboy, had chosen to marry Adolphena Spalding and settle down to raise a family.[42]

Martin Gothberg's old friend Missou Hines also prospered that year. Hines went to work as a representative of the E. T. Williams Oil Company from its onset. Early on, he purchased a substantial volume of stock in that company at sixty cents per share. Since their success in the Big Muddy Oil Field, that stock was selling for three dollars per share. The company held significant acreage in prime oil districts and speculators forecasted the value of their stock to continue climbing. With limited stock in that company available, investors reportedly offered Missou Hines ninety thousand dollars for his shares, but he refused the bid. Missou felt certain that it would be worth far more in the future.[43]

As if Martin Gothberg's life was not busy enough in 1917, his peers also urged him to run for a seat on the Casper City Council. Always a member of the Democratic Party, his friend Dr. John F. Leeper suggested running on the Casper nonpartisan ticket. When November rolled around, Dr. Leeper won the mayoral race for the party. With Martin's reputation and popularity, he easily won his position on the council, also.[44]

Gothberg and his associates' Wyoming Drilling Company continued to stay busy. When the Atlas Crude Oil Company was drilling a well west of Salt Creek, their drilling contractor shut down in October, unable to procure equipment to continue. In November, Mr. Eshelman, general manager of the Wyoming Drilling Company, contracted to complete the drilling job. With his crew and equipment on location, Mr. Eshelman calculated that by working both day and night, his company could reach oil in forty-five days with favorable weather conditions. Wyoming Drilling planned to continue the sixteen-inch hole that the previous contactor had started and to carry on at that dimension as far as possible. C. E. Littlefield's Bessemer Oil Company was also drilling a deep well nearby. The Wyoming Company would continue to monitor the progress of the Bessemer well and adjust their strategy as necessary.[45]

As the Casper Petroleum Company, Blackmore Oil Company, and the Wyoming Drilling Company continued to prosper, Martin Gothberg invested a portion of his profits into expanding his ranch. In November 1917, he purchased 2,720 acres in Natrona County from Carl G. Carlson. One thousand six hundred of these acres were near the 280 acres he purchased the previous year from W. F. Witt. This land is in southern Natrona County near Bear Creek. The other 1,120 acres were fifteen miles northwest of the home ranch.[46]

A week before Thanksgiving Day, Mary Enid Gothberg attended the wedding of her half-brother in Casper. Perry Sanders married Miss Helen Bestel on the evening of November 22. The ceremony was small, as they were married in Judge Tubbs's office at the Casper Hotel. The couple planned to make their home in Casper where both had resided for quite some time. A week later, Edwin G. Gothberg, while attending college at Boulder, Colorado, enlisted in the United States Army. Soon after, Edwin became a member of the 352nd Aviation Corps and began training at Kelly Fields, San Antonio, Texas.[47]

Amid all of the hustle and bustle, Martin spent a week in Kansas visiting various oil fields. The nature of his business there is unknown. He returned to Casper two weeks before Christmas to a continuing swarm of activity.[48]

It is unknown when Sis Gothberg became engaged to Walter Storrie. After Christmas, Walter traveled to Fort Logan, Colorado, where he took his examination for the Aviation Corps. Sis accompanied her fiancé and future mother-in-law on a several days' visit to Walter's aunt and uncle. Mr. and Mrs. Andrew Falconer ranched at Hat Creek, Wyoming. An old haunt of Martin Gothberg from his early days of riding the range and roundups, Hat Creek is about fifteen miles north of Lusk, Wyoming. Walter's parents, John and Mary L. Storrie, and the Falconers home-steaded there around 1890.[49]

Walter received a degree in engineering from the University of Wyoming and moved to Casper. When his father passed away, his mother moved to Lusk. In 1917, Walter Storrie came to work for Wheeler and Worthington Engineers in Casper. In June, he purchased the home of Mr. and Mrs. W. Fred Neuman there. His mother sold her house in Lusk and came to Casper to keep house for her son a short time later. Walter also operated the Hupmobile Sales Agency from the Townsend Building when he first arrived in Casper.[50]

In 1918, Ichabod Sargent Bartlett wrote volume III of his *History of Wyoming*. He had this to say about Martin Gothberg:

*Martin J. Gothberg is a capitalist residing at Casper. He is promi-
nently identified with the sheep industry in Natrona County and is
also closely connected with the oil interests of this section of the state, his
investments having been so judiciously made as to place him among
the most prosperous residents of his locality . . .*

*He is a very prominent business man and is numbered among
Casper's wealthiest residents, for at all times his investments have
been judiciously made and his interests carefully conducted. He has
ever been watchful of indications pointing to success, and with the
development of the oil fields he became an important factor in promoting the oil industry and is now president of the Casper Petroleum
Company, president of the Bantry Oil Company, a director of the
Blackmore Oil Company and a director in several other large business
interests. He is likewise half owner of the Ideal apartments, one of the
most modern, complete and attractive apartment buildings in Casper.
He likewise has many other real estate holdings in the city, having
made extensive and judicious investments in property, from which he
now derives a most gratifying annual income.*[51]

Bartlett added:

*At this writing, in 1918, his holdings comprise about twelve hun-
dred acres of patented land in Natrona county and about four hundred
acres in Carbon county.*[52]

As was typical for Martin Gothberg, while there was no hiding many
of his ventures and investments, he tried to downplay his wealth and prosperity. By 1918, his ranch in fact had grown to over five thousand acres
of deeded land in Natrona County and he leased over 1,400 additional
acres. In Carbon County he owned 1,200 acres, and over three hundred
in Albany County. It was quite an achievement considering the modest
160 acres and half dozen heifers he started with at Dobbin Springs three
decades earlier. Nevertheless, success was not a given condition. He and
Mary Enid had earned everything that revealed their success through
years of hard work and careful management.

In recent years, Martin Gothberg had lost his father, an older brother, and a younger sister. His widowed mother lived in New Jersey, as did his surviving siblings. Martin had lived in Wyoming over two-thirds of his life. He had lost a loving wife, but later remarried. Mary Enid was every bit as devoted and engaging as Adolphena had been. In addition to an effective partnership in their ranch, businesses, and home, they raised a wonderful family together. His careful scrutiny of business risks and prudent speculations continued to provide prosperity for the Gothberg family.

The Gothberg family. Standing (L–R): Emma, Sis, Edwin, and Walt; Seated: Martin John Gothberg and Mary Enid Gothberg
COURTESY OF GEORGE EVANS AND LORETTA BAYOUN, SUSAN LITTLE-FIELD HAINES COLLECTION

Near the end of January, Sam Service, partner and manager of Martin Gothberg's Lone Tree Creek Sheep Company, and his wife, Maud, hosted a dinner party at the Henning Hotel in Casper. The dinner was in honor of Sis who was leaving for Colorado to attend college, and for her fiancé, Walter Storrie, who was leaving for Berkley, California, for training in the US Army Aviation Corps. Mary Enid Gothberg and Mary L. Storrie were also guests. Before his departure, Walter Storrie received final proof on a forty-acre homestead with Henry Lightle. This property is forty miles west of Casper on Horse Creek north of Independence Rock.[53]

—◦—

Regardless of what their intentions were earlier, on February 4, 1918, Walter Storrie and Adolphena D. Gothberg purchased a marriage license in Denver, Colorado. Eight days later, twenty-six-year-old Walter married nineteen-year-old Adolphena in the apartment of a friend on Logan Street. Like the dinner party a short time ago, Mary Enid Gothberg and Mary L. Storrie both attended the ceremony. Sis chose not to return to college, and the following week, Lieutenant and Mrs. Walter Storrie left Denver for Casper en route to Berkley, California, where Lieutenant Storrie trained for the Army Aviation Corps.[54]

—◦—

Amid the flurry of events surrounding Sis and Walter Storrie's marriage, Walt Blackmore's son Bob traveled to Panama for the Sinclair-Panama Oil Company. This five-million-dollar company sent a team of geologists to the Atlantic side of that county exploring for oil. Bob Blackmore was among the Americans working there. Headquartered in Cristobal, in the Panama Canal Zone, the young Mr. Blackmore was in charge of a division of the company's work in opening up the new field.[55]

—◦—

Martin Gothberg and his one-time cow-boss at the CY Ranch, Missou Hines, were both in their mid-fifties. The two men were total opposite personalities. Martin was reserved and clinical in both personality and business undertakings. Missou was flamboyant and carefree in his. What they shared was their work ethic. Both men were hard workers at physical labors when necessary and neither shied away from putting in many long hours at the business table.

Missou retained his status as a self-proclaimed cowboy philosopher. He loved to entertain friends with jokes and yarns. He acquired his own wealth from knowledge and investments in mining and oil claims, and in 1918 the Wyoming Wool Growers Assocation elected Hines to an honorary lifetime membership in thanks for his many years of service to the organization. Missou was a colorful character; age and financial success did not strip him of his "pep and ginger." Not afraid to don a coat and tie, his bowed legs and Missouri vernacular revealed his sagebrush aristocracy.[56]

Jim Dahlman was a counterpart of Martin Gothberg and Missou Hines in their roundup days. Dahlman entered into politics in later years and held the office of mayor in Omaha, Nebraska, in 1918. When dining with Dahlman in Omaha, Hines entertained his old friend with tales of wildcatting in the Wyoming oil fields and they reminisced over the good old days of longhorn cattle on the open range of Nebraska and Wyoming. When asked of their reunion, Mayor Jim told the *Omaha Mediator*, "It made me jealous when he told me what he had struck. Hines is one of the finest fellows with whom I ever rode the range and he knows how to handle a gun and lariat, too."[57]

Mrs. Louise Foster came to Casper and purchased the Sprague Hotel in 1918. It was not long before she discovered an old acquaintance from her youth living in Casper. She had not seen the young man she called Billy Hines since he left their old stomping ground of Vernon County, Missouri, thirty-eight years earlier. Discovering her old chum was a divorcee and had recently developed a significant bank account may have also influenced her interest. Regardless, in April she held a dinner in Missou Hines's honor, complete with the Hawaiian Orchestra. Dinner was at eight o'clock followed by dancing and it appears that everyone had an enjoyable time.[58]

Walter Storrie distinguished himself in his service to his country. *The Denver Post* reported that Lieutenant Storrie stood out among his peers as a student in the aviation school at the University of California. Carrying on the family tradition inherited from his father of integrity and hard work, young Walt Gothberg also celebrated a banner year with his high school basketball team. During the state tournament in Laramie, Wyoming, they beat the tough University of Wyoming Prep School and Powell High School early on, but lost to Laramie High School in the semi-finals.[59]

Apart from his accomplishments in the petroleum industry, Martin Gothberg continued to expand his ranching operations. On April 29, he received his final proof on forty acres between Lone Tree Creek and the Bates Hole Stock Trail. This claim was in partnership with John W. Clark and again added to his holdings along the border between Natrona and Carbon Counties.[60]

A week later, Mary Storrie left Lusk to visit Walter and Sis in Berkley, California. Walter had nearly completed his training for the US Aviation Corps and expected to leave California soon. When he completed his training at the University of California, Lieutenant Storrie would be stationed in Egypt. His mother was anxious to see him before his departure.[61]

When Bob Blackmore returned from Panama, he enlisted in the US Army. After attending basic training in Fort Snelling, Minnesota, he was home on furlough in July. While on leave, he received his first decree with the Masonic lodge before leaving for Europe. He felt sure that he would be in France with his younger brother before the end of summer.[62]

While Bob was at home, Walt Blackmore, vice president, and associates from Casper and Denver incorporated the Wyoming National Oil Company capitalized for two million dollars. They immediately negotiated acquisition of the Toltec Oil & Gas Company with eight thousand to ten thousand acres of oil holdings in Albany and Carbon Counties. Toltec had a well drilled to 450 feet in Albany County when they shut down. Wyoming National placed a standard drilling rig and six thousand feet of casing at the site and planned to continue drilling the well without hesitation. Toltec, however, delayed finalizing the agreement and left Wyoming National hanging with the expense of moving the drilling rig into place.[63]

In June, Martin's sister-in-law Wilhelmina "Minnie" Gothberg passed away in Jersey City at the age of fifty-four. She had never fully recovered from the loss of her husband, Ernst, seven years earlier. They had no children, but they had had each other, and the recent years had been terribly lonely for her. Her sisters and brother posted a "card of thanks," in the *Jersey Journal* the day following the funeral, expressing gratitude for flowers and condolences offered by their beloved sister's many friends and relatives.[64]

On July 15, 1918, the E.T. Williams Oil Company, only one year old and based in Thermopolis, Wyoming, issued their first quarterly dividend. Now vice president of the company, Missou Hines proudly announced the 5 percent disbursement to the people of Casper. The following evening a group of his friends in Casper held a large banquet in honor of Missou's fifty-sixth birthday.[65]

On Saturday afternoon, July 27, Mary Enid Gothberg and a group of the prominent ladies of Casper met in the club room of the Natrona County Library. The Delphian Society was a national organization formed in 1910 to promote the education of women in the United States. At this first meeting in Casper, the field secretary from California and Mrs. Huntington of Texas explained that the purpose of the society was to help its members better understand the world's important events and the arts of civilization. Four dozen of the ladies in attendance joined the association and voted to charter the Natrona Delphian Chapter. They elected Clementina Nicolaysen as local president and Martha P. Littlefield as vice president.[66]

Walt and Minnie Blackmore got a letter in August from their son Floyd in France. He told them that his unit, the Second Anti-Aircraft Division, arrived there on June 30. Floyd told them that he was well and pleased with the training he received before leaving the States. He liked his work there and the equipment that they were using preformed splendidly in the field.[67]

On the evening of August 6, Mary Enid Gothberg, Maud Service, and Mrs. Elva Anderson hosted a banquet at the Midwest Hotel in

Casper on behalf of the Mothers' League. Twelve young men selected to enter military service were the honorees. Nine of the men departed that night and the other three left the next day. Governor B. B. Brooks spoke with power and enthusiasm to them. The Mothers' League presented each man with a Red Cross Comfort Kit made by members of the league.[68]

The following morning Mary Enid, Walt and Emma Gothberg, Maud Service and her daughter Hazel, and Mrs. F. E. Grippen and her three children all left Casper for a weeklong camping trip. Mrs. Grippen of Omaha was Mrs. Service's sister. Their destination was the head of Bates Creek, thirty miles directly south of Casper, but closer to fifty miles by their likely route. The area was an excellent place to evade the summer heat. Besides the increase of two thousand feet in elevation, proximity to the cool mountain stream made for a splendid campsite. Martin Gothberg and Sam Service may have been overseeing some of their flocks of sheep in the vicinity at the time, but there is no mention of it. It may have been a hen party, in which case if Walt was the only male in the group, he probably spent as much time fishing as possible. Regardless, camping was a popular respite for families at the time and the women were obviously up for it.[69]

Near the end of August, the Two Hundred Oil Club of Casper invested fifteen thousand dollars in stock of the Casper-Ranger Oil Company. Gothberg's Casper-Ranger company recently obtained several lucrative oil leases in the Ranger Oil Field in Texas. The company already had a drilling rig in the area and prepared to begin drilling when the directors of the Two Hundred Club elected to purchase the stock. Though Martin Gothberg obviously felt it a wise venture, he abstained from voting due to a conflict of interest.[70]

As Martin's business interests prospered, his sister Teresa Koezly continued to be less fortunate. Lack of sufficient income still forced her and her daughter to depend on her widowed mother for support. They resided in her parents' home on Walton Road in South Orange, New Jersey, when on August 26, her daughter, Helen Doretta Koezly, passed away. At twenty-four years old, Doretta was Teresa's only child.[71]

—◦—

In September, Minnie Blackmore's nephew Case J. Conlee was in Casper on military leave before deployment to Europe. Case was the son of Minnie's brother F. C. Conlee, who was foreman for the Blackmores' Hat-Six Ranch. Mr. and Mrs. Conlee made their home at the ranch and Case enjoyed the fall weather at the base of the mountain. For several weeks, he had been in training with the Machine Gun Battalion at Camp Sheridan, Alabama, where the heat and humidity were relentless for the young man from Wyoming.[72]

Mary Enid Gothberg actively supported the troops in Europe. September found her, Maud Service, Leone Blackmore, and dozens of other ladies working hard for the Red Cross in a mass linen drive. They needed everything imaginable from small to large to supply the hospitals in France with bandages, towels, and bedding. The American Red Cross asked Natrona County to supply 1,960 pieces of linen from handkerchiefs to bedsheets. The city was divided into sectors of several blocks and groups of two or three ladies went door to door requesting donations and bringing them to a collection point. Three weeks later, Mary Enid, Minnie Blackmore, and Maud Service were busy soliciting subscriptions for bonds to the Fourth Liberty Loan. The ladies were well on their way to meeting the quota with nearly 60 percent already subscribed for.[73]

—◦—

After twelve years in business, the owners of the Gothberg-Harris Sheep Company chose to dissolve the corporation. Attorney A. H. Cobb had acquired John Harris's interest in the company sometime earlier. Martin, Mary Enid, and Mr. Cobb paid all debts of the company and liquidated the assets. On October 10, 1918, the company closed its books.[74]

As November neared, Martin Gothberg assessed his position as city councilman in Casper. He strongly believed in the necessity of good government, but his place on the city council was quite demanding of both time and energy. Scheduling business trips, family matters, and overseeing the ranch around the agenda of the council was trying to say the least. He had nearly fulfilled his current one-year term of office and seriously considered opting out of the race for reelection. When discussing the matter with Walt Blackmore, he was overwhelmed with Walt's boyish enthusiasm and his speech on civic duty, and he signed the docket to run for a second term. Walt himself had entered the race for county commissioner.[75]

In the closest race of the year, Walt Blackmore narrowly lost his race for commissioner to his Republican opponent. With 49 percent of the vote, his defeat left him aggravated and disappointed. Martin, too, lost his bid for reelection, but the loss was practically a blessing. His devotion to his community aside, he would not miss his twelve dollar per month salary as a councilman nor the headaches that often came with the office. It was easy to console his friend Walt. Walt was resilient and enthusiastic, two characteristics that helped drive him though occasional pitfalls in financial ventures, which confronted his aggressive business style.[76]

To add to Walt and Minnie Blackmore's emotional havoc, their daughter Leone received an appointment from the US surgeon general as a reconstruction aide. She left Casper on Election Day to her position in the military recuperation hospital at Fort Bayard, New Mexico. There she taught occupational and industrial arts to the wounded soldiers who returned from the front. With Leone's appointment, all three of the Blackmores' children were serving their country in the war effort. Floyd Blackmore was somewhere in France with the Second Anti-Aircraft Division and Robert was with the medical department at Fort Snelling, Minnesota.[77]

A short time later, the *Fort Bayard News* reported that Miss Blackmore took up this new line of work, having received her training at Columbia University in New York. Her position at the fort involved instruction in metalwork, carving, art, design, and a variety of occupational therapy and vocational training based on her particular artistic background. While Leone settled in at Fort Bayard, Walter Storrie received his commission of second lieutenant in the US Army Aviation Corps. Almost simultaneously, the war ended in Europe and the kaiser fled Holland. Mary Enid Gothberg never slowed in her patriotic crusade as she began the groundwork for organizing a Casper chapter of the Society for Fatherless Children of France. By early December, the group received their charter. Mary Enid and Maud Service served on the original committee governing the assembly, which sponsored providing aid and protection for one hundred French children in 1919.[78]

While Eugene T. "Gene" Williams, president of the E. T. Williams Oil Company, was in Denver on business, the Nebraska Commercial Club of Omaha contacted the company requesting a "reliable report" on the stature of the oil fields in Wyoming. In his absence, vice president Missou Hines responded by telegram, "The E. T. Williams Oil Company will gladly furnish all information of an authentic nature to the Commercial Club of Nebraska or any other state. Our oil fields are delivering the goods, and in fact, the entire state of Wyoming is prepared to show and not tell you of its great oil, mineral, field, and stock-raising resources."

Gene Williams followed up Missou's message with a wire from his hotel in Denver, "It now seems that Nebraska people are looking forward to a great future in the production of Wyoming oil and the E. T. Williams Company has taken the initiative in showing the faith of local corporations in the merits of the productive state."[79]

Minnie Blackmore braced herself for the reality that all of her children were away from home for Christmas. She and Walt would share their empty nest for the first time since living in Bessemer. As she reminisced over holidays past, she busied herself to balance the loneliness by hosting a meeting of the Casper Women's Club. Attempting a better understanding of the Great War in Europe, the subject of discussion was the "stronghold of the Ottoman." The ladies debated on Turkish activities in the war and their effect on American soldiers there. They concluded their meeting with lunch, at which time they decided to sponsor a French orphan through Mary Enid Gothberg's Society for Fatherless Children.[80]

Captain John A. Sexon was commander of the hospital at Fort Bayard, New Mexico. In mid-December, he wrote to a former associate who lived in Casper. In speaking of Leone Blackmore's exemplary service, Captain Sexon said, "You can assure Casper people that she is making good here. It is a tribute to women like her who undergo the hardships of military service, run the risks of exposure, etc., and who do unselfish service in the military hospitals."[81]

The words of praise for their daughter were uplifting for Walt and Minnie to hear, but not nearly as exciting, however, as the telegram received on December 19 from their son Floyd. His ship had landed at Camp Merritt, New Jersey. It appears that the Blackmores were unaware that Floyd was even on his way home. He told them that he would be home as soon as he was mustered out of the Army, hopefully by Christmas. He added that he could use a "fifty," a request to which his father jumped to comply. He knew where he could pull a few strings. Walt contacted J. S. Mechling of the Oil Well Supply Company. Mr. Mechling arranged for Floyd to pick up the money at the company's New York office. When Mechling found out that Blackmore could not leave the post, he had his New York office deliver the funds directly to Private Floyd C. Blackmore at Camp Merritt, New Jersey. Walt and Minnie were thankful beyond apprehension for the safe return of their youngest child from the front line of the battlefields in France.[82]

Martin and Mary Enid Gothberg were also blessed for the holiday. Their son Sergeant Edwin Gothberg arrived home on Christmas Eve night on furlough. Edwin trained with the Aviation Corps in California and since then was stationed at Roosevelt Aviation Field, Long Island, New York, awaiting assignment in Europe. With a hold on deployment, Edwin was granted a short leave to visit his family for Christmas.[83]

With the fighting in Europe ended, most of the servicemen and women were being mustered out and on their way home. Though many missed Christmas dinner with their families, most were home within a few days after. It seems almost certain that the Blackmores and Gothbergs spent time together over the holidays. Perhaps almost miraculously, all of the members of both families escaped the gruesome conflict virtually unscathed. While praising the birth of the Christ child, they gave thanks for their salvation.

Martin Gothberg was experiencing great success in his Casper-Ranger Oil Company. At times, it almost seemed he had the Midas touch. Nearly every venture he invested in became prosperous. He, however, would have been modest in describing his good fortune. Though rightly deserved, his prosperity resulted from a lifetime of hard work and diligence. Every move he made was carefully planned and all possibilities weighed before making a decision. Thus, his speculations often came to a positive conclusion.

CHAPTER 11

Expanding the Empire

1919–1920

IN RECENT MONTHS, THE CASPER-RANGER OIL COMPANY GREW EXPO-
nentially. On January 7, 1919, they filed a change of capital stock with the
Wyoming secretary of state's office. The certificate signified an increase
from 250,000 shares of capital stock with a par value of one dollar to two
million shares at the same par value. The document effectively signified an
eight-to-one stock split. Not knowing exact daily values of shares on the
stock market, we can only suspect that the fifteen thousand dollar investment made by the Two Hundred Oil Club in the company had grown to
something near $120,000 in a very short time period.[1]

It appears that everyone was following Martin Gothberg's success in
the oil fields of Ranger, Texas, and many were anxious to get in on the
action. Missou Hines spent several weeks scouting the field for the E. T.
Williams Oil Company. When he returned to Casper in February, Hines
said that they had a wealth of oil there and that activity in the field beat
anything he had ever seen before. "Never saw so many operators, scouts,
promoters, near-promoters, grafters, and stock peddlers in my life," he
said, adding that the wells averaged over three thousand feet in depth.[2]

Gus Hardendorf accepted the position of field superintendent for the Producers and Refiners Corporation. In November 1918, they relocated him
and his family to Rawlins, Wyoming, and the Hardendorfs leased their
home in Casper to Mr. and Mrs. Charles Douds. In January, Margaret
and their infant daughter accompanied Gus to Medicine Bow, Wyoming,

and spent several days there visiting friends while Gus attended to business. On this trip, Gus contracted smallpox. Upon diagnosis, the family was quarantined in their home in Rawlins. They hired a specially trained nurse from Denver who stayed with them and cared for Gus who began to recover. Shortly thereafter, Margaret developed a rash, which initially was also thought to be smallpox, but turned out to be erysipelas. As Margaret's condition worsened, the rash became infected. Her circumstance grew dire and soon proved to be fatal. As Gus fully recovered from his illness, he arranged to take his deceased wife home to Chanute, Kansas, to be buried in her family's plot. Margaret's sister, Miss Gladys Cox, arrived in Rawlins from her home in Portland, Oregon. She took charge of the Hardendorfs' thirteen-month-old daughter and accompanied Mr. Hardendorf and her sister's remains to Kansas.[3]

In January, the Red Cross asked the people of Casper for two thousand dollars to feed the starving civilians in war-torn Armenia and Syria. Casper had met the goal for every campaign before and during American involvement in the war. However, on this drive they fell short by 30 percent. Many of the residents felt that since the war was over, they should not need to donate to the humanitarian efforts that resulted from the conflict. Mary Enid Gothberg, Maud Service, and two dozen other Casper ladies joined the campaign. They called on local businesses and residents until they raised the additional six hundred dollars.[4]

The young Floyd Blackmore both proudly and honorably served his country as a member of the crack Second Anti-Aircraft Battalion in France. The battalion selected Floyd for their team due to his understanding of motorized vehicles, a necessary credential when engaging the enemy with an extremely mobile battery of equipment. His unit earned repeated praise for record numbers of enemy aircraft hits and their skill in shooting by expending nearly 70 percent fewer rounds of ammunition per German plane brought down than their French counterparts. In appreciation for their exemplary performance in the field, he and his peers received rapid returns home and early discharges from their service.[5]

———

In February, Mary Enid Gothberg and Sis Storrie, encouraged by Emma Gothberg, were among the ladies who organized the Young People's Good Time Club in Casper. They elected Sis as secretary. Establishing the group provided young people an opportunity to congregate and socialize in a positive environment. The organization held its first event, a dance followed by refreshments, at the Masonic auditorium on February 6. The ladies even managed to recruit Martin to assist in managing the affair.[6]

Mary Enid seemed a never-ending center for organizing Casper's social groups. Following the end of combat for American forces in Europe, the Mothers' League refocused their objectives. Acquiring the Oil Exchange Building, the mothers established the Soldiers and Sailors Club for returning veterans. Always a successful fundraiser, they placed Mary Enid in charge of procuring furnishings. With her usual resolve, she scoured Casper for donations of comfortable furniture, books, magazines, and a host of other accoutrements necessary to outfit and operate the clubrooms. Inviting the public to attend, the ladies held their grand opening on the evening of February 26.[7]

A few days later Mrs. Mary L. Storrie arrived from her home in Lusk, staying with the Gothbergs for a visit in Casper. On the third, she hosted a small dinner party at the Henning Hotel. Her guests were Martin and Mary Enid Gothberg, Walter and Sis Storrie, Sam and Maud Service, and Mrs. Nell Davis of Harrison, Nebraska. Mrs. Storrie spent time with Walter and Sis as well as other friends in Casper before returning home two weeks later.[8]

While the Gothbergs hosted Mrs. Storrie at their home in Casper, Walt Blackmore was in Ranger, Texas representing the Two Hundred Oil Club. After Martin Gothberg's success with the Casper-Ranger Company, they too recently invested in the Ranger boom. On March 1, 1919, their first well in the field came in with a vengeance. It instantly vaulted the group to among the largest oil producers in the Ranger field. Two days later the well was still not under control and it "gushed over the top of the derrick several times." Conservative estimates for production were of five hundred barrels per day. On the strength of reports emanating from the field the unit shares in the club jumped to a five-hundred-dollar bid on the afternoon of March 2, but no one was selling. Every shareholder anxiously awaited definitive reports on production. Only then would anyone consider a sale of stock.[9]

When Walt returned from Texas, F. C. Conlee immediately summoned him to his Hat-Six Ranch. After a couple of days taking care of business there, he made good a stint in Casper to catch up on affairs there.[10]

With the popularity of the dances for the Young People's Good Time Club, Mary Enid and Maud Service decided to do something similar for adults. In April, they suggested the idea to the Mothers' League and it became unanimously approved. On April 11, they held their first dance at the Masonic Temple. They charged a nominal fee of those attending, the proceeds going to a building fund for a permanent home for the Soldiers and Sailors Club. The dance was widely enjoyed by those present. Martin Gothberg was not among them. M. J. left for Thermopolis to take in the baths for a few days, possibly in order to avoid the festivities, but more likely to relieve is aging body.[11]

Martin may not have been able to avoid too many of Mary Enid's future Friday night dances. The first event was so successful that Maud Service and Mary Enid expanded their event the following Friday to include music provided by the Iris Theater Orchestra. The opening night dance may have gotten a bit rowdy causing the ladies to announce, "Every effort will be made by the managers, Mrs. Sam Service, Mrs. C. T. Boone and Mrs. M. J. Gothberg to keep the crowd as select as possible."[12]

After hanging Walt Blackmore's Wyoming National Oil Company out to dry nearly a year earlier, the Toltec Oil & Gas Company held a stockholders meeting in Laramie in April. The purpose of the meeting was to discuss Wyoming National's offer further and other propositions received since. After spending many hours behind closed doors, the meeting adjourned without reaching any decisive agreement.[13]

It was not all bad news for Walt Blackmore, just days after the failed Toltec meeting; the New York Oil Company brought an offer to him and Martin Gothberg to lease their mineral claims on Spindle Top Dome.

Martin and Walt had been very successful in their oil ventures but did not have the capital to begin exploration at Spindle Top anytime soon; the New York Oil Company did. Martin and Walt held the mineral rights on two thousand acres at Spindle Top. New York Oil had the finances to drill it. They signed the lease and the New York Oil Company began moving in a drilling rig. They scheduled drilling to begin within ten days.[14]

On April 24, Walt and Minnie Blackmore received a telegram notifying them that their daughter Leone had a severe case of pneumonia and was hospitalized. She had been bedridden at Fort Bayard for a week. Minnie had her bag packed and boarded the train for New Mexico the same day. Walt followed a few days later. After another week, Leone's health improved significantly enough to allow her to sit up in bed for the first time since contracting the illness and Walt returned to Casper. As Leone's condition improved, Minnie made plans to bring their daughter home to recuperate. On May 22, Minnie and Leone arrived in Casper where Leone could convalesce while on a thirty-day medical leave from her position at the military hospital.[15]

On May 1, 1919, Martin J. Gothberg, Mary E. Gothberg, and Frank S. Service dissolved the corporations of both the Dobbin Springs Sheep Company and the Lone Tree Creek Sheep Company. It is unknown what Sam Service's position was resulting from these decisions. Martin Gothberg was clearly the president of both corporations and had the final say in all financial decisions. Mr. Service, however, had been the manager of daily affairs for all of Martin Gothberg's ranching operations for the past few years. It appears that he continued in the employment of the Gothbergs.[16]

In lieu of the new Friday Night Dance Club's regular popular weekly event, the ladies of the Mothers' League organized a full-blown Military Ball for the evening of May 9 at the Masonic Temple. With assistance from the Masons and members of the Soldiers and Sailors Club, Mary Enid Gothberg and Maud Service planned the gala. In addition to the regular fanfare, the military men decorated the hall with patriotic embellishments and the Masons provided the orchestra. Ladies from the Mothers' League furnished refreshments. The hosts requested all veterans meet in the Army and Navy clubrooms in uniform prior to the ball for a special novelty show.[17]

Lieutenant Walter Storrie was unable to attend the Military Ball. Subsequent to his discharge from military service, he accepted a position with the engineering department for the Midwest Refining Company. The Midwest Company located Walter in their facility at Elk Basin, twelve miles north of Powell, Wyoming. He recently had several days in Casper, which he spent with Sis, family, and friends. His work, however, necessitated embarking on his 250-mile return journey to the northern field prior to the grandiose celebration.[18]

In the early days of summer, Martin Gothberg and Walt Blackmore put together a very profitable real estate undertaking. The two men owned a sizeable piece of land in the foothills of Casper Mountain just west of Garden Creek Falls. The area had been a popular site for picnickers for some time. A mixture of pine-covered hills and grassy meadows mingle with mountain springs that feed small rivulets that trickle into the two forks of Garden Creek. Initially coveted for its quality spring and fall grazing, more recently it offered refuge to residents of the city to travel in their motorcars above the heat of the Platte River valley during the warmest days of summer.

With this development, the land became more valuable for recreation than pasture. With that in mind, and perhaps without fully understanding its impact, Martin and Walt created Casper's first subdivision. They named their mecca Gothmore Park and immediately laid out the park into sizeable lots, "many of which are located among the pines and rocks with cool mountain springs running through them." The county had already proposed an extension of the Garden Creek Road to the vicinity of the park, and Martin and Walt planned to construct a reservoir and stock it with fish as well as to erect playgrounds for children, horseshoe pits, and other places of amusement for summer residents of the colony.[19]

Gothberg and Blackmore contracted Ben L. Scherck and his See Ben Realty Company to market the lots. Ben set about spreading the word, boasting the many attributes of the recreational wonderland. He purposely withheld sales of any lots prior to a specified time on Sunday, July 13. That day he set up a table in the park and waited as motorists rushed to the location, anxious to secure one of the choicest sites to build their summer cabin. The company sold twenty lots in the first twenty-four hours, many to Casper's most prominent citizens. "One man who came to buy a lot brought his tent along and as soon as he had closed the deal, he set up his residence in the tent he had carried out to the addition."[20]

A few days later Charles C. McCandless, field manager for the Casper-Ranger Oil Company, announced that eight-inch casing had been set in the company's Evans No. 2 well in the Caddo Field in Stephens County, Texas. Scheduled for completion within the next two weeks, he expected substantial production based on that of the first well, which was already piling up significant earnings. Additionally, the company recently acquired fifteen acres amid a dozen other high production wells. With the derrick already erected, they expected to begin drilling there within a week. Present predictions anticipated a skyrocket in stock prices, "in true Texas style," almost immediately.[21]

In the meantime, the real estate market in Casper remained very active. Walt Blackmore sold two more lots in Gothmore Park to Ben Scherck and Cecil Bon. A week later Mary Enid's mother, Dora Sanders, purchased a lot and a half in the Butlers' west addition of Casper. Mrs. Sanders sold another lot in Casper to Oscar Mohr a short time later.[22]

At the end of August, Casper-Ranger Oil Company announced that the Evans Well No. 2 was producing six hundred barrels of oil per day. Equipment was in transit to their next well and this location sat among other wells producing from 1,500 to five thousand barrels per day. The company released one hundred thousand shares of treasury stock on the market at twenty-five cents per share. The purpose of the release was to raise capital for the development of their newly acquired properties.[23]

Martin Gothberg was very calculating in all avenues of business. On September 4, he was in Omaha with Alec Mills selling lambs. Most likely a result of Martin's careful analysis, it appears that they caught the peak market. Gothberg sold at $16.50 and Mills reported getting a good price also. Both the previous and following weeks' prices were in the twelve-dollar range.[24]

In October, Walt Blackmore was rushing the construction of his new apartment house on the corner of Delaware and Wolcott Streets. He and Gothberg's Ideal Apartments venture had proven very successful, prompting this latest investment. Demand for reasonably priced housing was at a premium in Casper and he hoped to have the new establishment ready for occupancy by Thanksgiving. He constructed the new facility along similar principals as the Ideal building and Blackmore expected the location to be as popular a residence as its predecessor had been.[25]

Martin and Mary Enid Gothberg along with their daughter Sis traveled to Colorado in mid-October. There, on Sunday October 12, Edwin George Gothberg married Margaret Martha Lewis in a spectacular ceremony at the bride's parents' home in Denver. A reception followed the ceremony with a five-course dinner attended by family members and a few intimate friends. The couple met three years earlier while attending the University of Colorado at Boulder. Walt Gothberg came home from the University of Wyoming to keep his younger sister, Emma, company while the rest of the family was gone for the weekend. Emma spent Sunday night with the Service family while Walt returned to Laramie to attend classes Monday morning. Following the ceremony Ed and Margaret came to Casper where they spent a few days at the Gothberg home on South Wolcott Street before visiting the Gothberg Ranch on an extended honeymoon.[26]

In October, Martin Gothberg posted a notice for a special meeting of stockholders of the Casper-Ranger Oil Company. Scheduled for November 1, the meeting was deferred to a later date, yet to be determined.[27]

—‿—

About the same time, the American Red Cross named Maud Service as the chairperson of their annual membership drive. They also appointed Mary Enid Gothberg and Mary N. Brooks, wife of former governor B. B. Brooks, as her assistants on the management committee. Since the culmination of the war in Europe, demands on the organization had drastically increased. Assistance to widows and orphans in countries torn by war required momentous support. A large corps of Red Cross nurses and student nurses worked in American hospitals with disabled veterans and others provided comfort and entertainment for these men.[28]

—‿—

After overcoming every conceivable obstacle, The New York Oil Company brought in the Spindle Top Well No. 1 on November 21, 1919. They made the strike rather unexpectedly at 2,300 feet. With the bit only one revolution into the sand, rock pressure filled seven hundred feet of casing with oil almost instantly. After the initial surge, oil filled the casing at one hundred feet per hour. The company estimated production at one hundred barrels per day. When the New York Oil Company began drilling in May, they encountered five water sands, which they cased off before reaching the oil. At the time of the discovery, the road to the area was nearly impassable, but the company already had a well-established camp at the site and planned to continue drilling the field as rapidly as weather permitted. Martin Gothberg and Walt Blackmore were majority owners of all the claims in the field, which consisted of over two thousand acres. The New York Oil Company leased the rights to drill the entire field.[29]

The oil strike made at Spindle Top was of particular interest to shareholders of the Poison Spider-Bolton Syndicate. The two geological structures share the same anticlinal axis, which extends on through the Carter Field with the Bolton structure midway between the others. The syndicate's first well was well underway and to date had not encountered any water at the levels, which caused so many problems for the Spindle Top well. From the reports coming from the New York well, the syndicate expected to reach the oil-bearing sands within a few days. Martin Gothberg and Walt Blackmore also held the rights to the entire Bolton structure that they had leased to the Poison Spider-Bolton Syndicate. Martin Gothberg owned the particular quarter section the syndicate was drilling on outright. This was a portion of the ranch Gothberg purchased from Pancake Charley Stevens in 1906.[30]

Throughout his lifetime, Martin Gothberg's ranch was never far from his thoughts. In 1919, he renewed the registration of the brand and earmarks for his livestock. Taking a break from the oil business in late November, he took seventeen head of cattle to auction at the Denver Stockyards. Prices faltered slightly due to the Thanksgiving holiday, but he still received respectable values from his sales. He sold one bull, two heifers, four calves, seven cows, and three steers for just under $750, equivalent to about eleven thousand dollars today.[31]

This excerpt from the 1919 brand book shows Martin Gothberg's "T-Flying E" brand and earmarks for his livestock.[32]

Two weeks later in Texas, a fire consumed the drilling rig owned by the Casper-Ranger Oil Company. Drilling was underway on the second well of the company, known as the McCleskey well, when they struck a large gas pocket. A spark from the rig ignited the gas. The resulting fire immediately engulfed the operation, burning the derrick to the ground and damaging the drilling equipment. Martin Gothberg left for Texas to evaluate the situation the same evening he received word of the fire. Upon assessment, Gothberg arranged to have the rig rebuilt and a new derrick constructed. The company intended the well in progress to extend deeper than their first well, which was currently producing oil quite successfully. A local facility quickly repaired their machinery and they planned to resume drilling as soon as the crew could erect a new derrick.[33]

On Martin's return to Casper, the Casper-Ranger Oil Company finally held their stockholders' meeting deferred nearly two months earlier. At the forefront of the agenda, the stockholders elected a new board of directors at the meeting. Martin J. Gothberg retained his position as president. R. L. Mitchell, Peter C. Nicolaysen, George F. Stilphen, and Harry Adams filled out the remainder of the board.[34]

❦

While Martin Gothberg was in Denver selling cattle, Gus Hardendorf was in Cheyenne incorporating a new oil company. Gus and four partners from Salt Lake City, Rawlins, and Rock River, Wyoming, established the San Juan Petroleum Company headquartered in Rawlins. They capitalized with $150,000 in stock. Two weeks later, Gus announced his resignation as field superintendent for the Producers & Refiners Corporation, stating that he had not completed plans for his future, but that he expected to continue residing in Rawlins. Newspapers speculated that he would contract with one of the many oil companies operating in central Wyoming in an executive position.[35]

While bitter cold weather and near blizzard conditions brought nearly every oil field in central Wyoming to a standstill, Gus Hardendorf announced his new position as secretary-treasurer and general manager of the new San Juan Petroleum Company. While field managers in Wyoming hoped that water supplies would not freeze solid before the snow subsided enough to resume drilling, Gus began assembling equipment to begin drilling on two thousand acres of oil leases belonging to the San

Juan in southern Utah. For Christmas, he boarded an eastbound train to spend the holidays with his daughter and family in southeastern Kansas.[36]

———

Earlier in the month, the Gothbergs had intended to spend Christmas as the onset of an extended visit to southern California. Mary Enid planned a vacation of sorts, soaking in the warm winter days there. Martin could not justify to himself relaxing for any extended period of time. He had their automobile shipped by train to Los Angeles enabling him to investigate oil exploration in the surrounding area. But the Casper-Ranger drilling rig caught fire in Texas causing Martin to modify his plan. Leaving for Ranger, Texas, he told Mary Enid to go ahead to California and he would catch up to her there. Understanding her husband's habit of getting heavily involved in his work and losing track of family plans in the process, Mary Enid postponed her departure while she awaited news of Martin's quick detour to Texas. As she had suspected, Martin's short stopover in Ranger turned into several days.

As Christmas drew near, she made her own change of plans for the family. Always the organizer, Mary Enid convinced Martin that returning to Casper would allow him to reschedule the stockholders' meeting. It also allowed her the opportunity to gather her chicks for the holiday. Walt Gothberg arrived in Casper from college at the University of Wyoming in Laramie about the same time that his father returned from Texas. Later in the week, Sis returned to her parents' home from Elk Basin. On Christmas Day, Ed and Margaret Gothberg drove in from the family ranch where they had made their home. With fourteen-year-old Emma still at home, all of Mary Enid's children had returned to the nest to celebrate the day together.[37]

On New Year's Day, Sam and Maud Service hosted a dinner in the Gothberg family's honor. The evening was a bon voyage of sorts for Martin and Mary Enid, who were departing on their postponed vacation to southern California. In attendance were Mary Enid Gothberg, Walter and Sis Storrie, Ed and Margaret Gothberg, Sam's mother, Mrs. Nancy Service of Jennings, Oklahoma, Mrs. Mary Storrie of Lusk, Emma and

Walter Gothberg, Helen Michie, and Mary Long. Martin Gothberg planned to attend, but was peculiarly absent for unknown reasons.[38]

Following the dinner, Mary Enid, Emma, and Margaret Gothberg all departed for Denver. The ladies spent a few days shopping there as guests of Margaret's parents. Emma particularly enjoyed the adventure, especially being treated as a young adult. The weather was unseasonably pleasant, and they all had a wonderful time. From there Mary Enid continued on her journey to Riverside, California. While Mary Enid traveled to California, Margaret accompanied Emma back to Casper where she stayed with the Service family and returned to school. Margaret then returned to Denver for another week before rejoining Ed in their home at Gothberg Ranch.[39]

While Mary Enid and Emma shopped in Denver, Martin Gothberg returned to Ranger, Texas, to oversee the resumption of drilling on the McCleskey well before joining his wife in California. The New York Oil Company had a steady stream of materials and supplies delivered to

The Gothbergs' "town" home as it appeared circa 1920
COURTESY OF MARTIN MOHR, IN THE DEBORA GLASS COLLECTION

Spindle Top as they prepared to drill their second well there. On January 10, 1920, the Casper-Ranger Oil Company announced that they had been back over the hole and drilling for ten days. Gas pressures increased daily on the well and field manager McCandless reported that as a result the well was nearly drilling itself. He added that "news of a big strike may be expected from the McCleskey well at almost any hour."[40]

On January 16, Casper-Ranger had a major gas strike on the McCleskey well. The next day, the Texas Oil Company offered to build a pipeline to the property and immediately purchase 100 percent of the gas produced. Charley McCandless prepared to have the gas headed off in order to continue drilling deeper for oil. With the new gas strike, the Casper-Ranger and the Two Hundred Club expected a joint income in excess of sixteen thousand dollars per month. The Evans well already earned the company over three thousand dollars per month. The strike instantly catapulted Casper-Ranger into the crowd of the largest producers in the region. This new increase also allowed the company to broaden their development campaign from operating capital without dipping into the treasury. Wyoming investors financed both organizations almost entirely. News of the big strike brought many cheers and toasts in Casper's saloons. Martin did not miss the celebration. He also received his share of congratulations from friends and acquaintances in Riverside.[41]

In February, Sam and Maud Service along with Sam's mother, Nancy Service, moved to the Service Ranch in Bates Hole. They leased their home on South David Street to former county treasurer M. C. Price and his wife. Their daughter, Hazel Service, moved into the Gothberg home on South Wolcott Street with her friend Emma until the end of the school year. Presumably, the young girls were being chaperoned while Martin and Mary Enid were in California, probably by Sis Storrie or perhaps Margaret Gothberg.[42]

In the meantime, the New York Oil Company was drilling on the Spindle Top Well No. 2. They were progressing at about 150 feet per day and by February 5 had reached a depth of 2,312 feet. Experiencing some gas pressure and nearing an oil sand, oil had already risen to fifty feet from the surface in the well. There they waited until marketing facilities were set in place before continuing.[43]

On February 24, Gus Hardendorf and Al Gokel of the San Juan Petroleum Company arrived in Casper along with representatives of the Keoughan-Hurst Drilling Company from Greybull, Wyoming. Gus had worked with Keoughan in Basin, Wyoming, and Bridger, Montana, and respected their opinions on oil exploration. By the end of their stay, San Juan had leased 480 acres in the Bolton Creek Field from Gothberg, Blackmore, and associates. When George W. Jarvis representing the Casper group announced the deal, he provided no details except that "the terms were very satisfactory to all concerned and that the development work would start at once." Indeed, this was true. Two days later crews of the San Juan began moving equipment and materials to the location. With increasing interests in the area, the San Juan Petroleum Company also began preparing to move their headquarters from Rawlins, Wyoming, to Casper.[44]

Martin Gothberg was an assiduous businessman. Considering the developments taking place within his various companies, he must have been excruciatingly anxious to return to the center of the action. In early March, he and Mary Enid left their temporary home in Riverside, California, heading for Wyoming. The overland journey today is lengthy; in 1920, it was a trek. Roads were muddied by rains in the lowlands and snow-covered in the mountains. A week into their travels, the *Casper Herald* reported, "Mr. and Mrs. Gothberg are motoring through in their car and expect to reach Casper early this month."[45]

As Martin and Mary Enid made their way to Casper, Walt Blackmore took the train to New Mexico. The specifics of the dealings are unknown. It is thought that he negotiated an important oil contract on the Bolton Creek properties that he and Martin owned.[46]

When Martin arrived back in Casper, Gus Hardendorf contracted another lease for his San Juan Company on a portion of the quarter section the Poison Spider-Bolton Syndicate were developing that Martin owned individually. Besides the Bolton Creek Field, the San Juan Petroleum Company then held leases on 2,500 acres in southern Utah and 320 acres in the Rock River Field northwest of Laramie, Wyoming.[47]

Not long after Martin and Mary Enid's return to Casper, their daughter-in-law Margaret came into town from the ranch and spent several days with the family. In April and May, Mary Enid's mother, Dora Sanders, had several real estate transactions in Casper. She exchanged multiple city lots with Mary Enid's brother, Arthur Brandt, and his wife, Ella, in the Butler and North Burlington Additions. A few weeks later, she purchased two lots on what then was West 28th Street in Nelson's Addition.[48]

With so many activities in the oil business centered in Casper, Gus Hardendorf moved back into his home on North Maple Street. The Poison Spider-Bolton Oil Syndicate was heavily invested in exploration of the Bolton Creek Field in May 1920. Gus, Al Gokel, and R. O. Meents, all shareholders in the syndicate, guided a tour of inspection of operations in the field for three of the organization's top investors. They left Casper for Bolton Creek on the morning of the twentieth and returned very pleased with the progress they observed there.[49]

A month later, doctors admitted Gus Hardendorf to a hospital in Denver, Colorado. He had suddenly become blind in his right eye and doctors feared he would lose sight in his left eye also. Both the cause and the treatment eluded chroniclers of the time, but within a few weeks he seemed to have recovered.[50]

Walt Blackmore's brother Bill was killed in an automobile accident in early June near his home in Pomona, California. Walt immediately checked train schedules allowing his arrival there in time for the funeral. His earliest possible departure from Casper would result in missing the burial by nearly a day. If he could make it to Rawlins, Wyoming, in time, however, he could catch a westbound Union Pacific Pullman that would allow connections to southern California in time. With his son behind the wheel of Walt's high-powered Dodge, he threw a valise in the rear seat and the two sped off in a cloud of dust. They missed their connection in Rawlins but raced on westward. Overtaking the train while crossing the Red Desert, Walt secured his ticket in Rock Springs, Wyoming, in time to await the locomotive's arrival moments later. Like Walt, Bill Blackmore began his career in Nebraska in pharmaceuticals. Bill visited Walt and Minnie in Casper on several occasions and was well liked by the locals. Eventually he moved his family to Pomona and ran a very large and successful drug store there. He later invested in a prosperous orange grove. His hospitality was unsurpassed when the Gothbergs and other Casper residents visited his home there over recent years.[51]

While Walt Blackmore was in Pomona, officers and stockholders of the Poison Spider-Bolton Oil Syndicate held a two-day meeting in Casper. In the end, the syndicate became the Iowa-Wyoming Oil Company. Martin Gothberg as well as George Jarvis and Mark Weber, partners with Martin and Walt in the Bolton Creek Oil Field, all became members of the board of directors in the new company. With the No. 1 well in the Bolton Field pumping four hundred barrels of crude oil per day, the syndicate expanded its operation, putting three additional drilling rigs to work in the vicinity. The syndicate, already a five- million-dollar operation, added an additional two million dollars in stock on the market with the forming of the new company.

The Bolton Creek Oil Field camps were nearly becoming a town. In addition to the Iowa-Wyoming and the San Juan operations, the Chappell-Victor Oil Company, Casper-Bolton Creek Syndicate, and two other companies were moving into nearby locations. Not counting barns, garages, and blacksmith shops, there were a dozen buildings in the field and the new company arranged to take panoramic photographs of the camps. Gothberg, Blackmore, and their associates' income continued to grow from both mineral royalties and investments in oil exploration and production companies. On July 2, Gothberg, Blackmore, and Weber escorted two executives from the Iowa-Wyoming Oil Company to the Bolton Field to observe the explorations in progress there.[52]

The arrival of extremely hot weather in late July drove many Casper residents to Casper Mountain in pursuit of cooler temperatures. Several of those who purchased property in Gothmore Park the previous year took advantage of their private resorts among the pines. Ben Scherck, the realtor Gothberg and Blackmore contracted to sell the lots in their development, was among the first to move his family into the cabin he erected there the previous year. Dr. Keith leased the cabin belonging to E. J. Sayles for the summer and moved his family there, and Bill Kocher made improvements on his rustic cabin to better accommodate his family for an extended stay. Seeing the success of Gothberg and Blackmore's vision, Ben Scherck and his partner Cecil Bon acquired a tract adjacent to Gothmore Park and immediately began selling lots in this new addition.[53]

When the secretary-treasurer of the San Juan Petroleum Company was a business visitor in his recent hometown of Rawlins the last week of July, recovered from his loss of eyesight, Gus reported that they had a rig in the Bolton Creek Field and expected to begin drilling any day. On Tuesday of that week, the Iowa-Wyoming Oil Company reportedly brought in its well No. 2, only about one thousand feet from the San Juan well. The company, however, opted to drill deeper and cased the well past the depth of their first showing of oil. On the evening of August 4, Gus left for Kentucky, where the San Juan considered acquisition of considerable new acreage.[54]

In mid-August, Mary Enid and Emma Gothberg, Sis Storrie, Ed and Margaret Gothberg, and guests from the East embarked on a trip to Yellowstone National Park. The party loaded themselves, camping gear, and provisions into two motorcars and planned for an extended vacation there.[55]

While his family enjoyed the scenery and adventure of the Yellowstone country, Martin Gothberg expanded his oil interests. As they relished the recent success of the Iowa-Wyoming No. 3 well, on August 24, 1920, Gothberg, Blackmore, Jarvis, and Weber filed four oil and gas claims on an additional 1,800 acres in the proximity of the Bolton Creek Oil Field. At the same time, Martin and Walt Blackmore, joined by Bill Evans and a dozen other area ranchers and businessmen, filed another oil and gas claim on over 2,500 acres in eastern Natrona County north of the Platte River and in the vicinity of Evans's sheep range. Gothberg and Blackmore also took notice with smiling approval when their sons entered into petroleum speculating by filing a claim on 320 acres five miles north of the Bolton Field.[56]

In the meantime, the New York Oil Company continued to have setbacks on their Spindle Top No. 2 well. They were, however, making progress. In July, they were at the nine-hundred-foot level and three weeks later, they reached one thousand feet. Although the Spindle Top Field had not yet become the massive producer they hoped for, other areas of the county, showed splendid results and profits mirrored that success. In September, they published a report in *Wyoming Oil World* stating that in the past five years, stock in the company had showed gains in value from divisions and dividends of over 5,000 percent. They presently held ten thousand acres under oil and gas contracts with seventy-six producing oil wells and fourteen producing gas wells in operation. They recently received a franchise to provide natural gas for the city of Casper and were currently installing a fifty-mile pipeline and distribution system to meet that demand. It is unknown how much money Martin Gothberg invested in the company from the onset, but whatever the amount, it continued to multiply.[57]

When Gus Hardendorf made his next visit to Rawlins to look after business matters of the San Juan Petroleum Company, he told reporters that he had been spending the past few weeks at Casper and in the Bolton Creek Field, where his company was now putting down their first well. He reported that their well was down about four hundred feet and progressing very favorably.[58]

Only days later, on September 2, the Iowa-Wyoming Oil Company well No. 2 in the Bolton Oil Field came gushing in at a conservatively estimated 1,500 barrels of oil per day with nine hundred pounds of pressure blasting it to the surface. Engineers were not prepared to find such gas pressure when they struck the Embar sand at the depth of 2,050 feet and the well suddenly became a producer. Crews scrambled to build earthen dams to contain the oil spewing from the well. It was the largest producing well in the area to date. Martin Gothberg and his partners were gaining wealth by the minute and the *Casper Herald* reported it this way:

> *Vision and foresight, stirred by confidence in the ultimate development as a great oil producing state climaxed Thursday morning for M. J. Gothberg when he visited the Bolton field, a structure that was located years ago thru his efforts, and saw liquid gold, in gusher proportions, streaming from reservoirs far beneath the earth.*
>
> *A story of confidence repaid, summarizes Mr. Gothberg's interest to the Bolton field. Now he has potential wealth added to his many successful enterprises as a result of the strike for in the wide area of the Bolton field there is little land, which he and associates had not located.*
>
> *The hurried preparations which were necessitated to conserve the oil overflow following the bringing in of the Iowa-Wyoming Oil company well No. 2 in the Bolton field by throwing up temporary earth dikes, proved of no avail yesterday when the rudely constructed dam broke and the vast quantity of oil found its way to the river, representing a loss of thousands of dollars.*
>
> *Rapidity with which the oil traveled was evidenced by an oily coat which the Platte river carried thru Casper yesterday. This oil had come from the new well of the Bolton field, over 30 miles distant, by the river course.*
>
> *Additional precautions to conserve the oil were made at the field yesterday and huge pumps are now being installed to take the oil from the earth reservoir to permanent storage tanks.*[59]

The article erupts with praise for Gothberg's foresight in recognizing the potential strength of the oil formations in the vicinity, yet there are no evident concerns with thousands of barrels of oil escaping into the North Platte River beyond the financial loss to the investors. The strike was the most sensational in the vicinity to date. The Midwest Refining Company immediately contracted to construct a pipeline to the field that fall and sent pumps to transfer the oil from the makeshift reservoirs to nearby storage tanks owned by the company. The tankage, however, was not adequate to hold more than an eighteen-hour run from the spewing well. The situation was further complicated in that this was the first well in the field that had developed any considerable gas pressure. The heavy gas showing with the oil was significant enough to warrant cordoning off an area around the well to keep out sightseers and avoid the danger of a fire. In spite of the drama created by the discovery and thirty miles of extremely rough road to access the site, it was not long before crews installed a wellhead and controlled the flow.

—

Not as enthusiastic as his brother Ernst had been but an automobile enthusiast nonetheless, Martin Gothberg joined over three hundred other members of the Casper Auto Club in promoting the regional enjoyment of motorized vehicles. The membership roster comprised those of all ages and lifestyles from prominent ranchers and businessmen to newsboys. While Martin attended a meeting of the club, a much more relaxed atmosphere than his usual business affairs, his son Walt prepared to return to the University of Wyoming for fall classes. Walt checked in for the night of September 20 at the Connor Hotel pending arrangements for more permanent lodging for the school year.[60]

—

That fall Ed and Margaret Gothberg traveled throughout much of the East while seeing the sites of several major cities. After visiting our nation's capital, their tour moved on to New York City. While there, they ventured across the river to New Jersey to see Ed's Grandmother Sophie, Aunt Minnie and Uncle Willis Lund, and other members of his father's family. From there they journeyed on to Massachusetts, where they saw the Old North Church and other historic sites in Boston and stopped over in Attleboro to see Ed's Aunt Sophia and Uncle Clint Fuller before returning home to Wyoming.[61]

—

On November 11, Gus Hardendorf published a notice to stockholders of the San Juan Petroleum Company. One month later, on December 11,

1921, the company scheduled its first annual meeting of stockholders at the company's headquarters in Rawlins, Wyoming. They proposed to elect officers, discuss operations, and vote on necessary transactions pertaining to the conducting of business for the coming year.[62]

Walt and Minnie Blackmore planned to spend the winter in warmer environs than Wyoming as they investigated the purchase of a vacation cottage in Hollywood, California. At the same time, the Blackmores prepared for the wedding of their daughter. On the morning of October 12, Marion Leone Blackmore married Walter Ronald MacGregor in an elaborate ceremony at St. Mark's Episcopal Church. Walt and Minnie hosted a striking breakfast at their home for the wedding party following the rite. The new Mr. and Mrs. MacGregor prepared to reside in their new home on South Wolcott Street and planned for a honeymoon trip later in the fall.[63]

By the fall of 1920, Walt Blackmore had long since traded off his Dodge for a Franklin touring car. Walt was a fervent motorist, perhaps as passionate as Martin Gothberg's brother Ernst had been. On November 13, he departed Casper in the Franklin destined for southern California. Minnie was less keen on the adventure and chose to stay home until Walt arrived at his destination. She preferred to travel comfortably by train later. Walt, however, was enthusiastic enough for both of them. He chose a southern route. Leaving Casper, he drove through Denver to Trinidad, Colorado, and on south to New Mexico. From there, he ventured west across Arizona through Flagstaff, then Needles, California, arriving in Pomona nine days later. Walt reported that though the roads were often rough, he encountered no rain or muddy conditions throughout his route, and he had no car trouble at all. Minnie Blackmore expected to leave Casper as soon as Walt secured a home for them. Prospects for housing were slim, especially in Los Angeles. Even apartments were scarce. While Walt scoured the area in search of a home to purchase or rent, she supposed it might be two or three weeks before her departure.[64]

Martin and Mary Enid Gothberg hosted a turkey dinner in a belated Thanksgiving Day celebration on Friday, November 26. Sarah Cheney and her daughter Ruth, ranch neighbors from Freeland, were among the guests, as well as Mrs. A. L. Ford who motored in from Salt Creek. Also present were Maud Service, Ed and Margaret Gothberg, Emma Gothberg, and Sis Storrie.[65]

The following Monday, Martin Gothberg received notice that he had been awarded a prospecting permit on 1,060 acres in southern Utah. The area of his permit was in central Garfield County along the Circle Cliffs anticline, part of the present-day Glen Canyon National Recreation Area.[66]

Martin, Mary Enid, and their daughter Emma left Casper for Denver, Colorado, on December 10, 1920. They spent several days there visiting friends and the ladies took the opportunity to shop at a variety of merchants. From there the ladies went on to California for a month's vacation. Martin stopped over for a week in Salt Lake City handling business affairs in conjunction with his newly acquired prospecting permit. When the family reunited in California, they enjoyed the warm climate and relaxed in the pleasant atmosphere. They may have shared lodging with the Blackmores during the stay. Martin and Walt undoubtedly met during the time, as these two addicted workaholics could not have abstained from discussing business dealings for an entire month.[67]

If Walt and Martin lacked in subject matter for productive conversation, on December 15, Gus Hardendorf returned to Casper from an extended scouting trip to the Mid-Continent Oil Fields in Kansas. There, Gus kept multiple geologists busy looking over tracts of interest to the San Juan Petroleum Company and the Chappell Oil Company. Gus held stock in both companies and they both held leases in the Bolton Creek Oil Field. Drilling of the San Juan's well at Bolton Creek progressed nicely and they were confident that it would become a producer.[68]

It is obvious that both the Gothberg and Blackmore families were flourishing. Without flaunting their wealth, they both took advantage of somewhat frequent and often prolonged vacations. They owned rather large, yet not extravagant homes, and it appears that both Martin and Walt enjoyed motoring about in reasonably new automobiles. Life was good for them and it seems that both couples enjoyed each other's company. While Emma may have missed having a white Christmas in Wyoming, it made for a pleasant holiday for all as they relaxed in the mild climate of southern California.

The pause in California was short-lived. Developments in Utah were about to explode into a spectacle of men and machines moving into the area. Not unlike the gold rush in California of 1849, stories of fortunes being made flooded newspapers across the nation. Once again, Martin Gothberg and several of his associates were right in the midst of the flurry of the activity.

CHAPTER 12

The Oil Business Booms in Utah

1921

As the New Year dawned, Martin Gothberg's warm winter vacation may have seemed long ago. In a matter of weeks, his expanding investments found him spending much more time traveling out of state to negotiate and oversee a multitude of business ventures. As had been his history, he did not throw money at every scheme that was presented to him. He did, however, invest wisely in a variety of businesses while maintaining his primary focus on oil and ranching.

Details are unknown, but new developments reported from the Iowa-Wyoming Oil Company at Bolton Creek on the morning of January 11 caused quite a stir, and Gus Hardendorf left immediately for the field to investigate the situation. After scrutinizing operations at the San Juan Petroleum Company well, Gus returned to Casper.[1]

Missou Hines, nearing sixty, married Mrs. Mary D. Jackson of Lander, Wyoming, on January 18, 1921. Mrs. Jackson was the daughter of Lander, Wyoming pioneer P. P. Dixon. It had been some time since Missou Hines and Martin Gothberg had been very close and the couple's history has escaped chroniclers, but Missou had been a frequent visitor to Lander for many years. The couple married in Denver, Colorado, and Missou, now a wealthy man, did not hesitate to share his fortune with his new bride.

Following the wedding, Mr. and Mrs. Hines embarked on an extended honeymoon trip to Honolulu.[2]

—〰—

Maud Service seemed to have loved hosting a party. She took advantage of many opportunities to do so. On January 21, Maud sponsored an engagement party for Miss Evelyn Lowe, a friend of her daughter Hazel and Emma Gothberg. Miss Lowe and her family were recent arrivals to Wyoming. Immigrants to America from England ten years earlier, The Lowes had been in Casper only a year or so. Roy Beaver, the young foreman of the Bates Creek division of the Two Bar Ranch, had met Evelyn shortly after her arrival and they were soon courting. The announcement of their engagement at the party gave the guests plenty of time to congratulate them before the wedding date in June. Mary Enid Gothberg surprised everyone there with her late arrival accompanied by several more friends of the young couple. The celebration went on through the evening and the hostess served refreshments at midnight. Perhaps the biggest surprise of all was Mary Enid's attendance. She had suffered a serious fall since her return from California and had not been about.[3]

—〰—

In mid-February, Emma Gothberg took the train to Denver for a week-long vacation and shopping trip. Perhaps a special gift for her father's upcoming fifty-seventh birthday was on her shopping list. Details of her excursion are unknown, but at age fifteen it is likely she spent her time in Denver with her sister-in-law's family, the Lewises.[4]

—〰—

February 26 found Gus Hardendorf at the Connor Hotel in Laramie. While there, he oversaw matters with one of the San Juan's properties in the Rock River Field. He then proceeded west to look in on other assets. After a tour of several days, Gus returned to Casper on March 3. The nature of his business is unknown, but prompted several days of consultation with the San Juan's attorney in Rawlins a short time later. Following his trip to Rawlins, Gus met up with Martin Gothberg and they traveled together on business to Salt Lake City, Utah.[5]

In their absence, the *Casper Daily Tribune* published an article announcing that several Casper interests would dominate the development of the petroleum industry in the oil fields of Utah. The newspaper claimed that news was finally sifting "through the secrecy that is maintained in the district." Foremost of this secret intelligence was that Green River, Utah, would become a rallying ground and the supply hub for the exploration of numerous fields in the region. The *Tribune* added that this small hamlet was bursting at the seams with an oil boom that surpassed any recently seen in Wyoming. The first major development in the town was the new sixty-room Midland Hotel. Among the honored guests to attend the grand opening were Martin Gothberg, Walt Blackmore, Gus Hardendorf, and George Jarvis. The *Tribune* failed to deny the implication that these four men mentioned may have financed the Midland Investment Company that erected the structure.[6]

After their extended business trip, Martin Gothberg and Gus Hardendorf returned to Casper on March 28, 1921. The *Casper Daily Tribune* reported that members of the Circle Cliffs Oil Company and Midland Investment Company also were returning to Casper that day. They failed, however, to mention who those men were. Two days later the *Salt Lake Mining Review* reported that the Gothberg Syndicate of Salt Lake City shipped an eighty-four-foot Standard drilling rig into southern Utah. The unit was en route to Martin's oil lease in the Circle Cliffs district. Gus Hardendorf's former employer, the Elk Basin Oil Company, also shipped two National No. 2 drilling rigs into Utah, one to Circle Cliffs and one to the San Rafael Swell.[7]

Within days of Gus and Martin's return from Utah, Ed Meents of the Iowa-Wyoming Oil Company and Carl McCutcheon of the Victor-Wyoming Oil Company arrived in Casper. During their visit, the men looked in on their operations in the Bolton Creek Oil Field, but primarily met with Gothberg and Hardendorf, who were major stockholders in both companies, to discuss developments in Utah.[8]

Several of Casper's wealthiest oilmen were heavily involved in the development of oil fields in Utah. The Mountain States Petroleum

Company, Midland Petroleum Company, Utah Consolidated Royalties Company, and Midland Investment Company were all new Utah corporations backed almost entirely by Casper investors. The men behind these companies were Martin Gothberg, Walt Blackmore, Gus Hardendorf, Mark Weber, and George Jarvis. The officers of the Iowa-Wyoming Oil Company, San Juan Petroleum Company, Chappell Oil Company, and the Victor-Wyoming Oil Company bolstered these men.[9]

On April 3, 1921, the *Salt Lake Tribune* announced that at least fifteen drilling rigs were at work in Utah. The Circle Cliffs Oil Company was bringing the second Standard drilling rig into the Circle Cliffs Oil Field within a matter of weeks. By this time, it was known that Martin Gothberg was a primary stockholder in the company. In addition to Gothberg, several investors from Utah, Wyoming, and Iowa made up the Circle Cliffs Company. They were locating the rig on Martin Gothberg's permit area, near the Ohio Oil Company's well. The Ohio's drilling rig had reached a depth of 750 feet and already encountered both oil and gas pockets as they continued drilling to deeper levels.[10]

A few days later, F. F. Hintze, a geologist for Gus Hardendorf's former employer, the Producers and Refiners Company of Denver, and F. W. Weeks, geologist for United States Smelting, Refining, and Mining Company both were in Green River, Utah. Walter Storrie, representing his father-in-law Martin Gothberg, was also there. As the geologists made plans to tour the Circle Cliffs area, Walter arranged to join them, hence creating an opportunity to learn how the two scientists rated the region. The management of the Midland Hotel was not disappointed in losing their clients, as another two dozen guests anxiously awaited any vacancy. Business was so brisk for the inn, they purchased two railcar loads of tents and set them up adjacent to the hotel to aid in handling the overflow. The establishment had not had an overnight vacancy since they opened.

Roads to the Utah oil fields were a shambles. As crews unloaded the first drilling rig assigned to the new San Rafael Oil Field to come through Green River, J. L. Humble contemplated his route. He elected to move the 24 Star drilling rig through Black Dragon Canyon, west of Green River. The road within the canyon was barely passable. Even today, the route is not recommended for anything less than four-wheel-drive vehicles. An arduous task lay ahead, to say the least. The drilling rigs for Gothberg's Circle Cliffs Oil Company and the Elk Basin Oil Company had yet to arrive in Green River.

The Ohio Oil Company was building a new road into the Circle Cliffs with the assistance of local communities. A new route to the Black Dragon Canyon was also under construction. Crews promised to furnish a road without sand sufficient to allow an automobile to cover the distance from town to the mouth of the canyon in forty-five minutes. Plans were in the works to extend the new road through the San Rafael Swell so that it would become the main highway to most of the San Rafael region, Caineville, and Circle Cliffs.[11]

While all was swarming in Utah, in Wyoming the Midwest Refining Company absorbed the Greybull Refining Company. Agents for the Midwest offered holders of Greybull stock of one thousand dollars per unit. Most shareholders considered the proposal generous and they sold their units. Mr. E. E. Lonabaugh declined the offer. When talking to fellow shareholder John Arnott, Arnott told Lonabaugh that he thought one thousand dollars was a fair price. At that, Lonabaugh offered the same to Arnott, who sold his unit to him. Mr. Lonabaugh ended up with two units of stock, which turned out to be of much greater value than the Midwest Company suggested. The only other outstanding shares belonged to Missou Hines, who had not yet returned from his honeymoon, and W. C. Irvin, each holding one unit. All three men savored their good fortune.[12]

On return from the Hawaiian Islands, Missou and Mary Hines continued their honeymoon in southern California. While there, they visited the lots of the fledgling motion picture industry. Missou's gregarious personality and natural inclinations to entertain those around him sparked the interest of movie producers there. In his colloquial jargon, he amused the entourage with colorful tales of the West. Most certainly, he would not have missed the opportunity to exploit the accepted claim that he and a cohort were Owen Wister's inspiration for the legend of the baby exchange revealed in *The Virginian*. Thus armed, the legend grew to the point that he, Missou, was in fact the Virginian. As a result, a large production company reportedly made Missou "a good offer" to play himself in a movie rendition of the novel.[13]

In mid-April, the Standard oil drilling rig of the Circle Cliffs Company finally arrived by train in Green River, Utah. As crews prepared to transport the equipment overland to Martin Gothberg's prospecting claim in southern Utah, Martin and his family entertained his older sister in Casper. For unknown reasons, the Gothbergs had temporarily vacated their home on South Wolcott Street at the time and taken up residence in Walt Blackmore's nearby new apartment building. Teresa Koezly had never been to Wyoming prior to 1921. Her life had been tumultuous. The loss of her husband in 1890 had been an extreme blow emotionally and she suffered from financial difficulties compounded by his early demise. She and her daughter resided with her aged parents when her father passed away in 1916, followed by the loss of her only child just two years later. The respite at her brother's home in Wyoming was overdue and long needed. While she visited, she enjoyed a ride with Martin when they motored to Bates Hole where he showed her his ranching operation, and she got her first view of an oil well drilling rig working on his property on Bolton Creek. In town, Mary Enid and Maud Service hosted a number of social events in her honor. After taking pleasure in a very relaxing vacation, Teresa departed for her home in New Jersey on April 18.[14]

In early May, Gus Hardendorf and Mark Weber were in Oklahoma negotiating an oil contract. The following week Gus was in Texas attending to business dealings of his San Juan Petroleum Company before returning to Denver to meet with financial interests of the company. Concluding his affairs, he returned to Casper on May 11. In the meantime, crews were hard at work moving their Standard drilling rig from Green River, Utah, to Martin Gothberg's prospecting claim in the Circle Cliffs of southern

Utah. At the same time, the Ohio Oil Company was working near the Gothberg claim. Their crew had lost a piece of drilling equipment down-hole and was busy with fishing tools trying to extract it. Meanwhile, several other companies with claims in the vicinity anxiously awaited results from the Ohio and Circle Cliffs Companies before beginning operations of their own in the area.[15]

As temperatures warmed along the Platte River in the valley around Casper, investors in Walt and Martin's Gothmore Park in the foothills of Casper Mountain were hard at work constructing summer cottages on their properties. Ben Scherck finished his log cabin and Cecil Bon had nearly completed his. A small fire in the massive fireplace of Polly Lloyd's shingled bungalow quickly erased the morning chill in the mountain retreat as G. R. Hagens dug the foundations of his prospective summer domicile nearby. Dr. and Mrs. Frost hosted a golf picnic on their property for four couples who motored out for the fun. With all of the activity in the new summer colony, plans were made for road improvements that would allow a timelier commute to the city for seasonal residents in the neighborhood.[16]

Walter Storrie arrived in Casper in mid-July to visit family and confer with his father-in-law on oil prospects in Utah. A few days later Walt Blackmore received an oil-prospecting permit in Utah. On August 3, Gus Hardendorf's San Juan Petroleum Company struck oil in the Bolton Creek Field. At 2,032 feet in the Embar sand, they estimated the well to produce four hundred barrels of oil per day. The strike was great news for shareholders in the San Juan Company was well as for Martin Gothberg, who owned the land and mineral rights. The San Juan Company was also drilling a well in Logan County, Kansas, on land that Gus had recently secured. All was not good news, however, and two days later, the New York Oil Company abandoned the well they were drilling in the Spindle Top Field at 1,260 feet and skidded their drilling rig to a new location.[17]

The New York Oil Company hired Charles Gokel to direct the drilling of their test well on the Spindle Top Dome. With marginal success in the field, the company sought someone with greater experience in the area and Gokel had significant results while overseeing the drilling of several wells in the Bolton Creek Field, part of the same geological structure. On August 27, the parties met in Casper to negotiate the terms of the contract.[18]

———

Martin's sister Sophia Fuller arrived in Casper from Attleboro, Massachusetts, early in June. After hearing of her sister Teresa's visit, she and her twenty-two-year-old son, Clint, decided it was time for them to return to Wyoming also. Nineteen-year-old nephew Willis Lund Jr. also accompanied the Fullers to Wyoming from his home in Long Branch, New Jersey. They planned an extended visit with Martin's family while taking in the sights and culture the state had to offer. Sis Storrie also arrived from her home in Salt Lake City to join in the affairs with her parents.[19]

On July 2, 1921, Margaret Gothberg gave birth to a son, Edwin K. Gothberg. Edwin was the first grandchild born to Martin and Mary Enid. With much pride, Martin quite likely envisioned his grandson as the future patriarch of the Gothberg family.[20]

At the end of July, Mary Enid Gothberg, both of her daughters, Sophia and Clint Fuller, and Will Lund embarked on a two-week excursion through Yellowstone National Park. The entourage returned to Casper on August 16, and all reported having a delightful adventure. In the interim, Walt Gothberg, who spent that summer in Rawlins, paid Cheyenne a visit on the tenth. Two days later, his father arrived in Rawlins where he spent a few days on business matters before traveling on to California to oversee his investments there. Among this somewhat mysterious chain of events, Walt Gothberg married Dorothy S. Stitt in Casper on August 14, 1921. The two were both twenty years old. Peculiarly, the proceeding appeared to have missed mention in local newspapers and all of Walt's family was out of town at the time, other than Ed and Margaret residing at the ranch. The marriage may have been kept secret. On August 25, Dorothy attended a social event at the home of Mrs. Glen Littlefield. She appeared on the guest list under the name of Stitt, not Gothberg.[21]

Around 1920, Martin erected a stone and concrete fence around the house at the ranch. He reportedly commented with pride that there was finally a sturdy fence, sufficient to keep the livestock out of the yard. On a stone gatepost carved in granite is a pictorial history of Martin J. Gothberg's time in the West. With only a beginning date of 1880, it is suspected that he intended to continue recording his saga in stone.
COURTESY OF SUSAN LITTLEFIELD HAINES

The same day, representatives of United Artists arrived in Casper scouting shooting locations for their upcoming motion picture, *The Virginian*, based on Owen Wister's novel. The famous movie couple of Douglas Fairbanks and Mary Pickford would star in the movie and Missou Hines play the part of Lin McLean in the baby exchange scene. Crews planned to film the scene in the very room that the original exchange allegedly took place at the old stone house headquarters of the Goose Egg Ranch. The studio planned to resurrect much of the ghost town of Atlantic City, Wyoming, for the movie, and chose several other sites around Wyoming for shooting. Doug and Mary would stay in Casper while filming.[22]

Margaret Gothberg's mother, Frances Lewis, was visiting her daughter and son-in-law at the Gothberg Ranch when her daughter Ethel Lewis arrived in Casper. It seems likely that Mrs. Lewis had arrived in Casper shortly after the birth of her grandson and stayed to assist the new mother with housekeeping and caring for the baby. In late August, Ethel was concluding an extensive trip in which she toured much of the East Coast before returning to her home in Denver. After visiting New York City, Washington, DC, and walking the boardwalk of Atlantic City, New Jersey, she welcomed the quiet interval spending time with her mother, sister, brother-in-law, and new nephew at the peaceful Gothberg Ranch at the foot of Casper Mountain.[23]

Martin Gothberg returned to Casper following his lengthy trip to California on oil business. Upon his arrival, the family moved from the Blackmore apartment back into their spacious home on South Wolcott Street. After Martin and Walt Blackmore spent several days looking after business affairs, Blackmore left on a business trip expected to consume several weeks. Martin and Mary Enid then left on an overland journey to Detroit, Michigan. Walt Blackmore's daughter Leone and her husband, Walt MacGregor, accompanied them. In Detroit, Martin Gothberg and

Walt MacGregor endeavored to obtain a contract for an automobile deal-ership in Casper. Negotiations with automakers were evidently unsuc-cessful and the two men returned home empty-handed.[24]

Two weeks later, Walter Storrie arrived in Casper from Salt Lake City, where he spent a week with his wife, Sis, at her parents' home. From there he continued on to Kansas and Texas on oil business before return-ing to Utah.[25]

- ~ -

To the pleasure of the owners of the New York Oil Company, Charles Gokel had reached the depth of eight hundred feet with 12½-inch cas-ing on their latest well at Spindle Top when Walt Blackmore's son Rob-ert received an oil lease on 640 acres from the state eleven miles north of Natrona, Wyoming, on September 24. Having returned from Detroit, Martin Gothberg and Gus Hardendorf left on an overland journey to the Circle Cliffs region in southern Utah. They continued on to southern California where Martin planned to oversee his extensive interests in the operations of the Iowa-Wyoming and the Victor-Wyoming Oil Com-panies there. In their absence, federal oil examiner Roy Thomas from the US Land Office in Washington, DC, arrived in Casper. Mr. Thomas investigated several oil claims in central Wyoming including Martin Gothberg's claims on Bolton Creek. Nothing appeared out of order on Gothberg's properties.[26]

- ~ -

Mary Enid Gothberg became ill during their trip to Detroit, Michigan. Upon returning to Casper, she took a break at Thermopolis, Wyoming, where she rested and recuperated, soaking in the hot springs while Mar-tin traveled again to the West Coast.[27]

In mid-October, Ed and Margaret Gothberg hosted a Sunday gath-ering at the ranch in honor of Sis Storrie. The occasion prompting the celebration is unknown, but several guests enjoyed the luxury of a splen-did waffle breakfast to begin the day. On his return from California, Mar-tin had gathered up Sis's husband, Walter, in Salt Lake City and brought him to Casper in time for the affair. Among the attendees were Frances

Lewis, who was still a visitor of the ranch at the time, and Sis's longtime friend from Douglas, Wyoming, Margaret Knittle. Sis's mother-in-law was staying with Martin and Mary Enid in Casper later that week and had most likely been at the party. After spending the day relishing each other's company and their pleasant surroundings, the guests enjoyed a fabulous chicken dinner before departing.[28]

Walt Blackmore was always a proactive person. When the Warren Construction Company paved the street in front of his home, they only laid down half the depth of base below the asphalt specified in the contract. Blackmore complained to the city council. The city still paid for the work sending Walt into a fury and causing him to suspect corruption within the city government. Armed with threats of legal action, he compelled the construction company to tear out their faulty work and repave the street. A short time later, he chose to reenter politics and joined in a three-way race for mayor. In an open letter to the people of Casper, Martin Gothberg pledged his support.

> *To the people of Casper:—I favor W. A. Blackmore for mayor of Casper for the following reasons. I have known him for over thirty years and during that time have had many business dealings with him and know him to be strictly reliable and honest in every way. He is also progressive as to the welfare of Casper. I think he has built more up-to-date buildings in Casper than any other individual and if elected mayor of Casper he can be depended upon to look after the interests of all Casper citizens and see that the taxpayers get full value for their taxes on all contracts that are let, the same that he demanded from the paving contractors on the street at his residence which he made them tear out and rebuild. I also know the other men on the ticket and I recommend their support.*
>
> *M. J. GOTHBERG*[29]

Walt Blackmore's run for mayor was an aggressive crusade. Regional newspapers published several lengthy articles in his backing. Always progressive, he was devoted to Casper's growth and improvement. Being a staunch Democrat like Gothberg, he ran on the ticket of the Casper Party and unlike greedier businessmen, Blackmore had a reputation of strongly supporting union labor when contracting the building of his many business structures. His business experience, honesty, and integrity always held the forefront of his campaign and Walt refused to enter into a slugfest of mudslinging. His party summed him up, concluding in an advertisement in the *Casper Daily Tribune*, "He is just a plain American gentleman of splendid business equipment, sound judgement, with a high sense of honor and is not afraid to maintain it under any and all circumstances."[30]

The three candidates in the race each carried the vote of at least one of Casper's precincts. On November 8, 1921, Walt Blackmore won the election by only sixty-three votes, the narrowest margin on record to date.[31]

Amid the bluster of Walt's mayoral campaign, Martin and Mary Enid Gothberg, Walt and Minnie Blackmore, Marvin and Lona Bishop, and Bill and Wealthy Evans were among the guests of Pete and Clementina Nicolaysen when they celebrated their thirtieth wedding anniversary in Casper. All of the men as well as Minnie Blackmore and Lona Bishop had attended the wedding ceremony thirty years earlier. Martin Gothberg and Bill Evans, both widowed, had since remarried. The festivity was an opulent affair including music and a sumptuous dinner held at the Henning Hotel. Former governor B. B. Brooks read congratulations from Missou Hines and many other of the Nicolaysens' longtime friends who were unable to attend.[32]

In the final tumultuous days leading up to the election, the Natrona County Stock Growers Association held their annual convention in Casper. Several important topics were on the agenda. Like Gothberg, most of the stockmen had begun their ranches on a 160-acre desert homestead claim in the previous century. With the vast open ranges available of that era significantly diminished, however, many foresaw the extinction of public grazing. They argued that future homestead expansion into the rangeland jeopardized their livelihood and the industry as a whole. In an effort to thwart further encroachment of new homesteading settlers, the members drafted a resolution to Congress to introduce a bill authorizing the sale of unoccupied federal land within the state of Wyoming to cattle and sheep ranchers. They proposed to pay either collectively or individually $1.25 per acre for all of the millions of acres of vacant federal land in Wyoming. For many ranchers like Martin Gothberg who were becoming quite wealthy in the petroleum industry, this would enable them to increase their ranch holdings by thousands of acres almost instantly. Legislators from more densely populated states, however, could not favorably grasp the concept.[33]

Another resolution adopted by the association requested from Congress an increase in appropriations for the control of predators. Members estimated depredations had cost them over fifty thousand dollars that year even though the six government trappers assigned to the county had caught or shot over two thousand coyotes and poisoned another 1,200 already that year. In addition, they had exterminated nearly five hundred other predators including wolves, bobcats, and mountain lions. By this time, Martin Gothberg had considerably expanded his ranching operation into Converse County, reporting to the members a loss of one thousand head of sheep near Glenrock to coyotes and wolves that year.[34]

Before closing the convention, stockmen endorsed a standard wage scale for ranch workers at forty-five dollars per month including room and board with an additional five dollars per month for rangers. They also agreed to sponsor the annual meeting of the Wyoming Wool Growers the following January. They appointed Martin Gothberg and Ben Scherck to the hosting committee. Mary Enid Gothberg, Maud Service, and Clementina Nicolaysen made up the ladies' committee for hosting the wool growers.[35]

A day after the election, over seventy of Wyoming's independent oil producers met in the banquet room of the Henning Hotel in Casper and formed the Wyoming Independent Oil Association. Among the founders were Martin Gothberg, Walt Blackmore, Gus Hardendorf, B. B. Brooks, Clarence Littlefield, Pat Sullivan, Missou Hines, Pete Nicolaysen, and George Jarvis. One of the key topics of concern among the oilmen was the inequities in price given for Wyoming crude oil. The Wyoming producers often received 60 percent less per barrel for a higher grade of crude oil than those in other markets. All the while, Wyoming's refineries manufactured 12 percent of the total gasoline consumed in America. The Wyoming oilmen hoped to affiliate themselves with the Mid-Continent Oil Association and invite more competition among pipeline companies and encourage construction of more refineries to improve their margins of profit.[36]

As if mayor-elect Walt Blackmore was not busy enough at the time, he and former superintendent of the Midwest Refinery in Casper, W. H. Leavitt, helped organize the Wyoming Refining Company. The purpose of the company was to construct a refinery in the Casper vicinity. The proposed twenty thousand barrel per day refinery planned an eight-inch pipeline from the Salt Creek Oil Field and filed articles of incorporation in Denver with an authorized capital stock of ten million dollars. The Harry O. Ryan Company directed the proposed financial underwriting of the business establishing headquarters in Casper with connections to investment houses in Chicago, Cleveland, Boston, and New York City. With the exception of three eastern investors, the directorate was composed of prominent Wyoming executives.[37]

On November 29, Walt Blackmore concluded a deal for the Wyoming Refining Company to purchase 320 acres of land three miles east of Casper between the Burlington Railroad right-of-way and the North Platte River from B. B. Brooks. The site for the new refinery lay west of the property recently purchased by the Producers and Refiners Corporation for its planned refinery and immediately east of Bill Evans's sheep ranch. Neither party disclosed the terms of the sale, but the *Casper Daily Tribune* reported "it was a cash deal, the land selling at a new high figure for unimproved property in this vicinity." They went on to say that there was "no possibility of a town being built between the proposed refinery and the city of Casper and the construction of the plant should be beneficial in extending Casper along the eastern border."[38]

Walt Gothberg filed a homestead on 640 acres adjoining the land his father bought in 1916 from Anna Hench on Iron Creek west of Casper. It may have been his intention to branch out on his own or to contribute to the expansion of the Gothberg family's ranching operation. He came into Casper for the week of Thanksgiving from his ranch there. On Monday evening, Martin and Mary Enid hosted a dinner party in Walt's honor inviting family friends as well as many of Walt's friends. There also was no mention of Walt's wife, Dorothy, further suggesting that the marriage had been made in secret and had yet to be revealed at that time.[39]

The following week, Martin Gothberg was in Thermopolis, Wyoming, attending to oil business in the vicinity. When he returned, Gothberg, Blackmore, and the Casper Rotary Club made a formal dedication and presentation of "Camp Rotary" to the Casper Boy Scout Council. When establishing Gothmore Park, Martin and Walt donated five acres at the northeast corner of the park to the local area council of the Boy Scouts of America. With the help of the Casper Rotary Club, the scouts erected a twenty-four-by-thirty-six-foot cabin on the site. As the cabin neared completion, executives of the Scout Council and the Rotary Club visited the project. On November 22, the men noted that the floor was finished, all four walls erected, and the porch around two sides of the building were completed. They planned six triple-bunk cots in furnishing the cabin, allowing eighteen boys to enjoy the facility for weekends or extended outings. Workers expected to finalize construction before winter except for the stone fireplace that Troop 2 planned to build the following summer. When completed the next month, volunteers installed mattresses on the bunks, a cook stove and utensils in the kitchen, and curtains and other furnishing adorned the cabin. An elaborate ceremony held on Sunday, December 11, inaugurated the facility. Dozens of scouts, their families, Rotarians, and dignitaries made the trip to the foothills to attend the affair. Of course, Martin Gothberg and Walt Blackmore were among the honored guests.[40]

The next day, Casper dentist Dr. William Kocher advised residents with cabins in Gothmore Park to keep a closer eye on their properties there. He, however, did not issue the warning due to the increasing activity of the Boy Scouts in the area. After Sunday's ceremony at the Scout Cabin, Dr. Kocher stopped in to check on his own nearby cabin. To his surprise, he discovered ninety-five gallons of moonshine stored in his abode. Vacant for the season, it appeared to bootleggers that they had discovered a perfect warehouse for their merchandise. Its close proximity to the city made it an ideal candidate for the purpose, which prior to Dr. Kocher's discovery and notification of the authorities had probably been quite convenient.[41]

The next morning, Mark Weber, Gus Hardendorf, and two others traveled together by automobile to Salt Creek to look after their oil interests there. Soon after, the weather turned bitterly cold with temperatures plunging to twenty degrees below zero for several days. It was not long before water supplies were frozen solid and drilling operations in the entire district ground to a halt. Hardendorf told reporters that the Mosher Syndicate was the only well that managed to keep drilling through the frigid cold. In the meantime, the New York Oil Company's latest test well at Spindle Top southwest of Casper extended to the depth of 2,400 feet and the company expected to reach oil any day.[42]

The cold snap not only hampered progress in drilling for the oil companies, but also posed a physical danger to their employees. Charles Gokel, field manager for the San Juan Petroleum Company, had a heavy oil tool fall on his foot in the Bolton Creek Field. Poor circulation in the swollen member resulted in a brutal case of frostbite during the extremely cold weather. The complication to the injury landed Gokel in the hospital in Casper and threatened possible amputation. When released, he returned to work, but still returned to Casper for periodic treatments over the next several months.[43]

Martin Gothberg's nephews Willis Lund and Clint Fuller had remained guests with the Gothberg family since the previous summer. Shortly before Christmas, Willis returned to his home in New Jersey to spend the holidays with his family. His cousin Clint, however, remained at the home of Ed and Margaret Gothberg at the Gothberg Ranch. Margaret's mother, Frances Lewis, was also a guest at the ranch. It is not known if Mrs. Lewis had returned to visit her daughters and grandson or had remained at the ranch for several weeks. The day after Christmas, Ed and Margaret hosted a party at the ranch in honor of Margaret's younger sister Rachel Lewis who had been teaching school at Bridgeport, Nebraska, and was visiting for the holidays. Two dozen guests packed the house for the evening. Martin and Mary Enid with daughter Emma, Walter and Sis Storrie, Sam and Maud Service, and Marvin Bishop were among those who spent a festive evening dining and dancing.[44]

CHAPTER 13

Becoming a Legacy

1922–1947

THE CITY OF CASPER AND THE NATRONA COUNTY STOCK GROWERS Association hosted the annual meeting of the Wyoming Wool Growers Association. Mary Enid Gothberg, Maud Service, and Lona Bishop headed the wives of local ranchmen in greeting the women of Wyoming attending the convention with their husbands. They asked other local wives to join them in welcoming the ladies from around the state upon their arrival with a reception held at the Henning Hotel banquet room on the evening of January 6, 1922. Following the greeting with hors d'oeuvres and punch, the hostesses presented a special bill of vaudeville at the Iris Theater for the entertainment of those in attendance. Later, a dinner served back at the Henning Hotel in the visitors' honor capped the pleasant evening.[1]

A week later, in a letter from the National Association of Rotary Clubs in America, Martin Gothberg and Walt Blackmore received kudos for their generosity in donating the site for the Boy Scout Camp. In the letter to local chapter officials, Howard R. Hancox congratulated the club in their success of promoting harmonious life and education in the young men of the area. He continued, adding, "Casper is certainly fortunate in having such public spirited men as Messrs. Blackmore and Gothberg, for a camp is one of the most necessary things to the development of an all-round character for the boys."[2]

While Martin Gothberg prospered in the West, his family's business in New Jersey suffered. Following the passing of Martin's father, the company fell into financial trouble. By the end of January, the H & E Gothberg Manufacturing Company had collapsed into receivership and attorneys posted a legal notice for creditors to file on debts owed by the company. In mid-February, they announced the sale of the company. The auction included all real estate together with the factory, machinery and equipment, inventory, patents and inventions, and all other property "together with the business and good will of said corporation as a 'going concern.'"[3]

When the day of the auction arrived, the Chancery Court accepted a bid of $8,625 for the entire assets, which carried an estimated value of between thirty and forty thousand dollars. Elmer W. Demarest, attorney for the family, was outraged and immediately filed a complaint that the whole deal had been a "frame-up." Upon review, Vice-Chancellor Griffin revoked the transaction and advised Mr. Demarest to instruct his client to return the deposits and advertise a new sale.[4]

When the property returned to the auction block on March 10, Vice-Chancellor Griffin found himself amid a heated controversy between the bidders. When the bidding reached a little over ten thousand dollars, Lee Cohen of New York thought that he had won the sale. After a short lull, however, another flurry of bidding ensued, and DeWitt Ryder appeared to have taken the bid at twelve thousand dollars. When the competitors appeared before the vice-chancellor, Cohen, who had arrived late for the proceeding, accompanied by his attorney, Emanuel Weitz, requested a delay in order to inspect the property and probably increase his bid over Ryder's. An animated discussion followed. Mark Sullivan, Ryder's counsel, insisted they finalize the sale and confirm Ryder the winner. Weitz, in turn, insisted that his client was not through bidding. At that point, Griffin suggested the contestants adjourn to a private room and settle the issue. The bidding was sharp and lively. In conclusion, Cohen received the property for $14,100.[5]

For reasons unknown, this sale could not be finalized either and the property again went on the auction block on March 30. This time neighboring manufacturer James Dart purchased the real estate for $7,700 and the Woodcraft Machinery Company won the bid for inventory and equipment at $3,100. If the poor price received for their company was not disappointing enough, the same day the family received notification of $874.50 in overdue property taxes. It is unknown if they were held liable for the debt. As if there was no end to the frustration, three days later the Woodcraft Company sold the inventory and a portion of the machinery at a handsome profit.[6]

While Martin's siblings waded through the financial woes of liquidating the family business, affairs were much less dismal in Wyoming. Martin's nephew Clint Fuller went to work with Mary Enid's brother, Arthur Brandt, at the water department for the city of Casper, and fifteen-year-old Emma Gothberg, youngest of the Gothberg children, hosted a Valentine's Day party a few days before the holiday. A longtime student of social entertainment, she had well learned the lessons of hospitality from her mother and family friend Maud Service, distributing formal invitations to twenty-four of her dearest friends. The throng of adolescents enjoyed an evening of games and refreshments, invading the family home on South Wolcott Street.[7]

The previous day, Walt Blackmore left for New York City to attend a series of meetings and conferences with executives of the Wyoming Refining Company. Important decisions pertaining to future policies and the development of the company dominated the agenda. Reporters were disappointed upon his return ten days later when he refused to comment on the results of the meetings. Blackmore deferred any announcements prior to conferring with local investors in the company.[8]

In February, Martin Gothberg received a rebate on a portion of his property taxes for ranchlands in Albany County. It appears that there was an error in calculating the amount owed. Two weeks later, he, J. P.

Christensen, and George Jarvis were in Sioux City, Iowa, on business of the Iowa-Wyoming Oil Company. Upon his return, Martin and Mary Enid hosted a surprise birthday party for their son Walt. Walt continued to reside at his homestead on Iron Creek west of Casper. At the time, he had come to town for supplies and a weekend sojourn. Mary Enid invited two dozen friends who enjoyed dancing, playing cards, and socializing before feasting on a splendid meal.[9]

In April, the Casper Chamber of Commerce brought a petition before the city council calling for additional streetlights at several points in the city. Walt Blackmore campaigned on reining in unnecessary expenditures by the governing body. The request prompted a response from Mayor Blackmore that the city paid fifteen thousand dollars annually for municipal lighting, a figure that he considered more than sufficient for a city of twelve thousand people.[10]

Casper Mayor Walter Albert Blackmore
(1922–1923)
COURTESY OF CITY OF CASPER COLLEC-
TION, CASPER COLLEGE WESTERN HISTORY
CENTER

A week later, while Ed and Margaret Gothberg hosted a visit from Mrs. Gladys Morris of Denver and her son Kenneth, Ben Scherck advertised his cabin in Gothmore Park for sale at a "very reasonable" price. For reasons not mentioned, he claimed that he had been unable to use the retreat for over two years and would entertain cash offers. It seemed at first that perhaps he found its location less convenient to the city than he had previously stated when promoting the sale of lots in the development. Contrary to his advertisement though, both he and his partner Cecil Bon had just completed their respective cabins the previous May. Perhaps there were other reasons to separate his investments from Gothberg and Blackmore.[11]

Since 1865, various methods of fracturing underground geological formations to increase production in oil wells have been in use. Some techniques were as simple, and dangerous, as dropping a canister filled with nitroglycerin down the casing of a well. With luck, the collision at the bottom of the hole would be sufficient to cause the explosive to detonate on impact and thus fracture the rock at the bottom. The risk in the process was that the canister might strike a joint in the casing near the surface and explode prematurely, before "the shooter" had the opportunity to escape the vicinity. Many devices and procedures were patented over the decades following to increase reliability and safety.

On the perhaps ominous day of May 13, 1922, Gus Hardendorf, Mark Weber, and J. T. Wilson incorporated the Mid-Western Torpedo Company with one hundred thousand dollars in capital and headquartered in Casper, Wyoming. It is unknown what patents or methods these experienced oilmen may have brought to the fracturing business. In their articles of incorporation, they stated the "purposes of the corporation are to conduct the business of manufacturing, buying, selling, and dealing in nitroglycerin and other explosives, and the blasting and shooting of oil wells and mines."[12]

On June 5, Gus Hardendorf's San Juan Petroleum Company brought in a 1,400 barrel per day gusher in the Bolton Creek Oil Field. The land was leased from Martin Gothberg's Iowa-Wyoming Company. The strike was reported at 2,043 feet in depth. A year previous, the well was at a depth of 2,026 feet and producing three hundred barrels per day. The production of the well was now expected to level off at around 1,300 barrels per day after the initial strike subsided. It can only be suspected that products or services of the Mid-Western Torpedo Company may have been introduced and contributed to the vast increase in production of the well after increasing the depth a mere seventeen feet.[13]

⁓

In June, the Natrona County Wool Growers pooled nearly half a million pounds of wool and offered it up for auction at the second and largest sale of the season on June 15. Reports varied that the wool amassed for the pool totaled between four hundred and five hundred thousand pounds, but most agreed on a sum near 470,000 pounds. The flock-masters elected Martin Gothberg, Tom Cooper, and P. C. Nicolaysen to a committee to oversee the sale and look after the growers' interests. Prior to the sale, Professor J. A. Hill, a wool expert from the University of Wyoming, accompanied G. M. Penley, county agriculture agent and secretary of the Natrona County Wool Growers, in examining the fleeces accumulated by the membership. Professor Hill visited the various shearing pens throughout the county and demonstrated methods of grading and determining shrinkage of the fleeces, consequently validating the need for a vigilant culling and selection process.[14]

On the morning of the fifteenth, buyers representing nine large purchasers were busy examining the clips gathered at the Bishop, Burlington, and Northwestern warehouses. Due to the high demand in the industry, particularly in the manufacture of clothing, members of the pool were encouraged by experts' predictions of record high prices ranging from forty to forty-five cents per pound for their clips. The warehouses bustled with growers, buyers, financiers, and onlookers. The pool arranged the sale on a sealed-bid basis. Organizers received the bids at a special car near the Northwestern Depot and all waited anxiously for the opening of the envelopes that afternoon at a meeting of the growers and buyers.[15]

With anticipation of the best wool prices ever, the sale resulted in what most considered a complete failure. It was obvious that the buyers conspired to drive the prices down, so much so that the majority of growers rejected their bids completely. In each circumstance, there was one high bid accompanied by several drastically lower bids, the bidders taking turns as to which would be the high bidder on any particular clip. The highest price paid, thirty-seven cents a pound for the fifty-two-thousand-pound clip of Josendahl, Parsons, and Klockseim, was by the Jeremiah Williams Company of Boston, Massachusetts. The lowest price accepted was thirty-three cents per pound by Albert Majors from the same buyer. Only Jeremiah Williams and the Chicago Wool Company made successful purchases. All three committee members along with Marvin Bishop and a half dozen other growers refused to accept the bids offered by the buyers. In complete frustration, Tom Cooper confronted the buyers: "We gathered here under the impression that we were dealing with a number of real wool buyers. Your manner of bidding makes us believe that you are here to take up the time of the growers, and I for one am willing to call the sale a failure and put up no more clips."[16]

In the end, several of the growers persuaded Tom Cooper not to stop the sale, but transactions on more than half of the wool on hand were not completed. Four of the growers received no bids at all on their clips and every grower involved in the entire pool was disgusted by the deceit exhibited among the buyers.[17]

On June 14, the *Casper Daily Tribune* announced Martin Gothberg's acquisition of the Buick dealership in Casper. In partnership with his son-in-law Walter Storrie and mechanic/machinist L. D. Branson, they formed the L. D. Branson Auto Company. Initially the agency operated from the L. D. Branson Garage repair shop on South David Street, but immediately began construction of a new facility at First and Wolcott Streets. The trio hired Ben Lummis, longtime employee of the former Buick dealership, as sales manager. It seems likely that Gothberg was the financier of the company and Branson, well known regionally as an automotive expert, was the perfect figurehead for the company. Walter Storrie also brought his experience from the earlier operation of his short-lived Hupmobile Sales Agency in Casper. The Branson Company incorporated on June 13, 1922, with fifty thousand dollars in capital stock. They named

Walter Storrie as secretary of the corporation with offices in the Consolidated Royalty Building in Casper.[18]

One might think that representing his fellow wool growers during the
wool sale and purchasing an automobile dealership were enough to keep
the energetic Martin Gothberg busy for the month, but amid his other
responsibilities was an important meeting of the stockholders of the Iowa-
Wyoming Oil Company. They dealt with several key issues involving the
Bolton Creek Oil Field during the meeting. Since the San Juan Petroleum Company's recent increase in production, the need for an efficient
pipeline system became more necessary. With five other wells working
the same formation the San Juan well had been in earlier, most assuredly
the owners of those wells would endeavor to tap the third oil sand that
the San Juan Company had. The Iowa-Wyoming Company had already
installed a massive pumping system to handle the increased production,
and several major interests were anxious to build a new pipeline directly
to the markets in Casper.

The directors appointed a committee with the authority to finalize
negotiations with one of the several companies vying for the contract.
They also entertained the possibility of building their own pipeline to
Kansas City, Omaha, or Chicago where there was more demand for their
grade of crude oil. The company ensured that whatever the outcome, it
would be advantageous to themselves and the city of Casper.

They reported that since Carl Newman, former manager of operations in the Mid-Continent Field, had taken over production for the
Iowa-Wyoming Oil Company, results had been flattering. Based on the
accessing of the third sand, they expected production of existing wells
to increase by up to three times if deepened. Drilling companies might
complete these procedures in as little as ninety days if initialized. Mr.
Newman also had improved conditions in pollution of nearby streams
and stockmen's water supplies.

Concluding the meeting, they held elections of officers and directors.
Martin Gothberg was reelected to the board of directors and his friend
Mark Weber elected as vice president of the company.[19]

On June 30, the New York Oil Company was at a depth of five thousand feet on their latest well in the Spindle Top Field. With the positive results showing recently in nearby Bolton Creek Field, they were anxious to see the results on this latest test well. On July 11, the drillers struck oil at 1,035 feet in the Sundance Formation. Not quite a gusher, the oil rose to within five hundred feet of the surface. It was the company's intention to drill a deep test well and thus they made the decision to drill past that oil sand and case off the well past the formation, which they expected to be between 160 and 178 feet in thickness. They continued to bore the 12½-inch hole. At a later date, they planned to return and sink another test well into the Sundance sand. As his potential royalties began to mount in the Bolton Creek Field, Martin Gothberg kept a careful eye on operations at Spindle Top, where he also had a stake. At 1,310 feet, they exited the formation and the New York Company cased the well to that depth. On July 15, they continued drilling with a ten-inch bit and on August 24, they were at 2,465 feet and still making headway.[20]

On July 8 and 9, Mary Enid Gothberg, daughter Sis Storrie, and Mary Storrie spent the weekend as guests of Mrs. Olive Clelland and Susie Love Hames in Douglas, Wyoming. Mrs. Clelland's husband, L. W., had recently passed away, but the nature of their stay was not recorded. Perhaps the visit was concerning affairs coming up at the Wyoming Wool Growers Convention in Sheridan, Wyoming. Mary Enid attended the convention a few weeks later, apparently without Martin. L. W. Clelland was a long-time sheep rancher in the Fort Fetterman area and had served in various capacities in county and state governments for some thirty years.[21]

A week later, Walt Blackmore officially announced the dissolution of the Wyoming Refining Company and a calling in of the stock. Unable to secure adequate contracts for sufficient amounts of crude oil to operate their proposed refinery, the directors opted to liquidate the company's assets and dissolve the corporation. They sold the land they had acquired east of Casper to the Civic Land Company, who in turn sold it to the

Texas Oil Company, later known as Texaco. They sold the property for an ample amount to refund 100 percent of the original purchase price for the stock to their stockholders.[22]

It is interesting to note that the contingency of the original purchase not to establish a town near the new refinery was evidently negated in the later transfers of ownership. Bill Evans, friend and former business associate of Martin Gothberg, had homesteaded the area some twenty years earlier and established a sheep ranch there. Even before Blackmore left for New York to meet with investors in the company in March, Evans and the Guaranteed Investment Company platted 120 lots on Evans's ranch adjacent to the proposed refinery and founded the town of Evansville, Wyoming. The Texas Company had originally planned a refinery near Glenrock, Wyoming, but when the Wyoming Refining land became available, they reconsidered. They required a larger parcel of land for their proposed operation than Blackmore's company had procured. With Bill Evans already planning to establish a new town there, the oil company quickly negotiated the purchase of an appropriate portion of his ranch that when added to the Wyoming Refining property would fit their needs.

By the second week of August, all of the lots in Evansville were sold and an additional 137 lots platted. By fall, those lots were also sold and a second addition of eighty-two lots was platted. In September, founders incorporated the water company to supply the needs of the town and refinery with their primary source being Elkhorn Spring at the foot of Casper Mountain. When the refinery went into operation, they also provided natural gas utilities to the public. The original streets of Evansville were Evans, Leavitt, Williams, King, and Texas, running north and south. The Yellowstone Highway and First through Fifth Streets ran east and west. Evans Street was the main street and boasted a dozen businesses occupying both sides of the street. Several other businesses thrived along the Yellowstone Highway serving both residents and passersby. The Burlington Railroad constructed a siding to serve the new refinery and the Northwestern passed at the southern outskirt of the town. The little town boomed with the bustle of construction and refinery workers.[23]

Martin and Mary Enid Gothberg, Walt and Minnie Blackmore, and George Jarvis and Mark Weber along with their wives joined in speculating on prospective oil properties and applied for several land patents. In September, they received mineral and placer patents on 480 acres of land near the Spindle Top and Bolton Creek Oil Fields. They were awarded an additional mineral and placer patent on an adjoining 160 acres in December.[24]

In September, Walt and Minnie Blackmore, sons Robert and Floyd Blackmore, and son-in-law Walter MacGregor incorporated the Blackmore Company. They founded the new company with two hundred thousand dollars in capital and designed it to consolidate an array of real estate investments owned and managed by the family. Walt Blackmore held the position of president and Robert that of secretary of the company.[25]

In October, Martin Gothberg and P. C. Nicolaysen were beckoned to serve on the grand jury in the federal court in Cheyenne along with two other Casper jurors. In their absence, Edwin Gothberg filed intention for final proof on six hundred acres adjoining the home ranch. In his petition, he named his cousin Clint Fuller among the witnesses to his claim.[26]

From October 23 through the twenty-sixth, Casper automobile enthusiasts held the first annual Casper Auto Show at the Arkeon Building on North Center Street. The Buicks shown by the L. D. Branson Auto Company were a big hit. The boys showed one or two Buicks every night of the event, changing them out every day. Unable to keep ahead of the demand for new vehicles, the directors of the company showed cars recently purchased by their proud customers. Sales manager Ben Lummis showed his own Model 55 five-passenger sport car along with N. A. Tyler's Model 48 four-passenger coupe. Next, Lummis pulled his auto and showed Gus Hardendorf's Model 45 five-passenger touring car with Tyler's coupe.

Mr. Tyler's coupe was then replaced with Jeff Crawford's Model 54 three-passenger sport roadster to finish out the show.[27]

—◦—

Shortly after Martin Gothberg returned from jury duty in Cheyenne, house burglars struck his home on South Wolcott Street. In the early morning hours of Saturday, November 11, the family was absent from the home when the robbers entered. It seems they may have expected to find a fair amount of cash receipts from the Buick dealership kept over the weekend. Those moneys, however, were securely stowed in the safe at the garage downtown. The thieves did manage to make off with an adding machine from Martin's home office and an old "six-shooter" he kept in his desk. There were two other robberies in Casper earlier in the week. The authorities thought the suspects to be members of the same group that burglarized six homes in Wheatland the previous week. Casper police arrested one suspect Saturday afternoon and one of the victims identified him. Police Captain William Clayton turned him over to the sheriff's office pending the placement of formal charges against him.[28]

—◦—

A few days later, the L. D. Branson Auto Company opened the doors of their new facility at the corner of First and Wolcott Streets. The new building offered a showroom large enough to display a variety of new Buicks, if they could ever manage to keep ahead of the supply of available automobiles long enough to display any of them. They also had a state-of-the-art garage where authorized Buick mechanics could service the motorcars supported with a brand-new parts department with a sophisti-cated inventory management system, the first of its kind in central Wyo-ming. The concrete and steel structure was heated by steam and claimed to be completely fireproof. They also offered a complete gasoline filling station with air and water available free to the public. Walter Storrie, Ben Lummis, and L. D. Branson occupied the light and airy new business and sales offices located on either side of the Wolcott Street entrance, boast-ing large French-style windows. The new L. D. Branson Auto Company building was complete and modern in every conceivable way for its time.[29]

⊷

While the Gothberg family delighted in the success of the Buick dealership, celebrations were interrupted with tragedy. On November 19, 1922, Mary Enid Gothberg's sister-in-law died from complications of appendicitis. Ella Brandt, the wife of Mary Enid's brother, Arthur, had been ill for several days and had grown progressively worse when her doctor performed an operation to remove her appendix at their home on South Walnut Street. The exact cause of death is unknown, but the twenty-eight-year-old did not survive the surgery.[30]

⊷

Martin's siblings in New Jersey continued to struggle with the bankruptcy of the family's foundry. His brother Herman petitioned the court for previous salaries he claimed were due to him of $1,400. Vice-Chancellor Griffin refused to grant the claim. Griffin pointed out that Herman had owed the company eight hundred dollars at the time of its closure. Herman admitted to the debt and the court held that lacking sufficient evidence otherwise, the amounts cancelled each other out and dismissed the claim.[31]

⊷

On April 20, 1923, Walt Blackmore and his son Bob drove to the communities of Bucknum and Cadoma northwest of Casper. It was Friday. The tour presumably involved business, perhaps checking on oil developments or real estate investments for the Blackmore Company. They may have been inspecting the intended route for the new railroad planned to serve the Salt Creek Oil Field. On their return, their automobile apparently stalled while crossing the tracks of the Northwestern Railroad near Illco Station, a rail siding fifteen miles northwest of Casper between Cadoma and Bucknum. The malady occurred precisely as the Northwestern Railroad's daily westbound passenger train approached. For unknown reasons, the Blackmores failed to abandon their vehicle in time to escape the arriving locomotive. The collision was horrendous. Walt and Bob were both gravely injured. Employees of the Illinois Pipeline Company, who were working nearby, brought the two men to the Illco Station and administered what aid they were able until medical help arrived.[32]

Dr. H. R. Lathrop sped to the scene in a motor ambulance, followed soon after by Casper Police Chief Alexander Nisbet and other city officials in a high-powered automobile. The Northwestern dispatched a local train to Illco on which they transported the mayor and his son to Casper. Walt Blackmore failed to regain consciousness following the accident and died about 5:30 p.m. while en route to the city. Ironically, the end to Walt's life was not dissimilar to that of his brother Bill Blackmore less than three years earlier. Walt's son Bob was badly injured in the accident, but eventually recovered.[33]

Walt Blackmore had been a good friend to Martin Gothberg for over thirty years. Walt's flamboyant personality and voracious flair for business led him and Martin into many business ventures that both men benefitted from over their years of working together. Walt had tended to prod Martin into ventures that were slightly more volatile than Martin felt comfortable with. On the other hand, Martin had injected caution into Walt's schemes and pointed out details that he tended to overlook when the idea for a new enterprise entered his thinking. Their mindsets complemented each other in both their investments and their friendship. Both Martin Gothberg and the community would greatly miss Walt Blackmore's presence.

—◦—

The Gothberg Ranch continued to grow. A week later Ed Gothberg received patent on the 602 acres adjoining the home ranch that he had filed for final proof on the previous year. While mourning the loss of his friend, Martin began looking back toward his ranching roots. He perhaps took solace in the solitude of that lifestyle and re-evaluated the possibility of directing more of his investments to that end.[34]

As L. D. Branson advertised a string of used automobiles for sale to oil workers in the Salt Creek Oil Field, the bankruptcy of the H & E Gothberg Manufacturing Company in New Jersey ended. The assets of the company sold for a total of approximately fourteen thousand dollars and an additional $2,700 in receipts was collected. Taxes and court costs deducted from that totaled $8,600. The attorneys for the company received two thousand dollars and stockholders $2,600. The balance, approximately $3,500, was dispersed among the creditors. It was the end of July 1923. The long process was over. The company that Martin's father had started some sixty years earlier was gone. Built from the decades of hard work performed by Martin, his brothers, and father, it was all gone. Whether the failure of the company resulted from mismanagement, greed, or any of a multitude of possible difficulties is unknown. Martin Gothberg did not intend the outcome of his lifetime of toils to meet a similar defeat.[35]

Over the next few years, Martin did not significantly change his investment philosophies. In May 1925, Sam Service, Martin's former partner and friend, died from tick fever. Sources believed he had contracted the disease from ticks on the rabbits he had shot to eat. Sam was sixty. That same year, with the encouragement of his aviator son Ed and son-in-law Walter Storrie, Martin studied the possibility of purchasing an airplane. Growing up in the mechanized world of the brass manufacturing industry, Martin and his brothers all shared a keen interest in mechanical wonders. The prospects of owning an aircraft were intriguing to him to say the least. In his meticulous method of studying other ventures, Martin investigated a multitude of viable candidates. After careful consideration, his interest focused on the Alexander Eaglerock Bi-Plane. The Alexander Company was located in Colorado Springs, Colorado. He and Ed took the train there to study the machines firsthand. After the two admired the quality of the aircraft at their facility, Ed flew one of the planes around the area and was significantly impressed. Following a brief barter, a price was agreed upon, and the Gothbergs flew home, following the railroad lines to Casper.[36]

By 1926, L. D. Branson had left the Buick dealership and returned to operating his former repair shop on South David Street. Martin continued to control the Buick garage. Walter Storrie presumably remained as manager of the business.[37]

Martin continued to expand his ranching operation. In 1927, the Gothbergs acquired an additional 477 acres adjoining their other property in Gothberg Draw. Walter Storrie received the final patent on this livestock homestead in January 1927. Martin's nephew Clint Fuller also received final patent for 640 acres with a coal and mineral claim on Casper Mountain in March that adjoined two and a half sections of Gothberg land southeast of the home ranch. With this procurement, those lands now connected to the home ranch through two sections of land that the ranch leased from the State of Wyoming. In January 1928, Walt Gothberg received a stock raising homestead patent on his 640 acres on Iron Creek. It appears that this good winter rangeland, eleven miles west of the home ranch, was also destined to become part of the Gothberg family's ranching operation.[38]

In July 1928, Martin Gothberg again confronted officials regarding highway access across his ranch. In 1912, Natrona County built a new road across two sections of his ranch and assessed the loss of property at $175. Gothberg claimed a loss of one thousand dollars. After a two-year battle, the court dismissed the case and for an undisclosed amount, Gothberg deeded to the county that portion of land required for their road right-of-way. Now the state of Wyoming was building a new highway across his ranch consuming a considerable increase in width to the previously agreed right-of-way. The ownership of the roadway belonging to the county had been transferred to the state. When Martin challenged state officials, they claimed legal ownership granted to them from the county. Gothberg confronted the county, claiming they had transferred ownership of land that did not belong to them. With that, the land in question was condemned and an expanded right-of-way established. The board of county commissioners appraised Martin's condemned property at four hundred dollars. The quiet man did not remain quiet at this, and Gothberg filed suit against both the state and the county asking for damages of $15,710 for the acreage lost in the process and requested a restraining order against the highway commission and their crews pending settlement of the case. The result of the procedure is unknown, but the case was of high enough profile to make mention in the *Denver Post*.[39]

There is no question that the Wall Street Crash of 1929 effected in some way every person in America. In Martin Gothberg's case, the impact on his financial condition was far less severe than many other American

Walt Gothberg and his son, Martin John Gothberg II, at the Gothberg Ranch sheep camp
on Sheep Creek in 1929

COURTESY OF MICHAEL C. STITT, SUSAN LITTLEFIELD
HAINES COLLECTION

businessmen. He had not invested in the stock market based on unfounded rumors. His investments were in tangible assets and companies that he knew well, most of which he had a strong voice in the management. Consequently, his hardships were from the backlash of the devastation. The public no longer had money to spend on many commodities that his income was drawn from: oil, beef and lamb, wool, and automobiles.

By 1930, Sis Storrie was living with her parents in Casper and her husband, Walter Storrie, lived in Denver. Rumors flourish to this day of the rift between the couple. The key gossip suggested to have caused the breakup was an alleged love affair between Walter Storrie and another man's wife. Regardless of the circumstances, a bitter divorce battle ensued that dragged on for several months. During the course of the divorce, Sis received a desert homestead patent on 160 acres in Gothberg Draw that adjoined already well-established grazing land owned by the family.[40]

Sis's divorce became final in April 1931. Youngest daughter Emma added to the acreage of Gothberg Ranch that year when she received patent on an additional 160 acres adjoining the home ranch in October. Coincidently, the twenty-six-year-old maiden married George Dewey

Evans in the quaint Northeastern Utah town of Randolph on the same day the homestead patent was finalized.[41]

As the Great Depression continued, no one could foresee that it was still years from an end. As the economy slumped there was sufficiently less demand for fuel, and Gothberg withdrew from oil exploration and somewhat from the petroleum industry in general. He was nearing seventy years old and found the hectic and stressful life of the oil business less appealing than he had when he was younger, though he still owned a fair amount of oil producing property.

It was about this time that Martin acquired approximately fifteen thousand acres of land located between the property he owned on Iron Creek and the home ranch. Details of the purchase are sketchy. Since the New York Oil Company owned or leased a large percentage of the land in that area, the acquisition may have in some way been connected with them.

Two Gothberg grandchildren play at the sundial in the yard at the home ranch. Engraved in the face is the inscription, "My face marks the sunny hours. What can you say of yours?"
COURTESY OF GEORGE EVANS AND LORETTA BAYOUN, SUSAN LITTLEFIELD HAINES COLLECTION

Oil royalties paid by the New York Company on the Spindle Top and other wells to Martin Gothberg had long been a significant annual income.[42]

In January 1932, Martin received a stock raising patent on 474 acres of land adjoining his other property on Casper Mountain. The following month, he received a desert patent through a cash sale on another 160 acres in the same area. Later that year he sold his interest in the Buick dealership. Although he had occasionally coaxed his son Ed or son-in-law Walter Storrie to fly him to Denver to pick up a new car and drive it back to Casper, a jaunt that he considered a joy ride, he had rarely taken an active interest in the day-to-day operation of the business. Since Walter left the company pending his and Sis's divorce, Martin took little pleasure in activities at the shop.[43]

When Martin's older sister Teresa Koezly passed away in 1934 while visiting the Gothberg home on South Wolcott Street, the realization of

Wyoming Pioneers' annual party, 1934, at Gothberg Ranch. Martin Gothberg was a founding member of the organization and over the years hosted several annual parties at his ranch.
COURTESY OF GEORGE EVANS AND LORETTA BAYOUN, SUSAN LITTLEFIELD HAINES COLLECTION

his own age and mortality struck bitterly close to home. He was seventy. His sons took care of most of the operation of the ranch, but Martin felt his age. The years spent on horseback on the open range and the decades of hard physical labor it took to build the ranch took their toll. Aches from old injuries were more prominent as each year passed and the length of his and Mary Enid's winter vacations in southern California grew longer in recent seasons.[44]

Ed and Walt Gothberg had run the family ranch together for several years, but by the early 1930s, Ed Gothberg had lost interest in ranching and moved to California. Before leaving Wyoming, he filed on a stock raising homestead on another forty-acre parcel of land adjoining the Gothberg Ranch on Casper Mountain.[45]

Wyoming is usually not included in discussions on the era that became known as the Dust Bowl. When the second wave of drought and dust storms struck the central plains in 1936, Wyoming, too, suffered the severe drought. A reporter from the International News Service visited Wyoming that summer and interviewed Walt Gothberg among the ranchers he visited. Walt had observed that the normally lush summer pastures were baked for eleven consecutive weeks under an unrelenting sun with temperatures often over the century mark and reaching 110 degrees on at least one occasion. There was practically no water left anywhere. Thirsty cattle bawled for water day and night.

On August 4 the reporter described, "Gothberg, himself burned to a leather crisp, said such scorching weather had been virtually unbroken since June 1." The Gothberg Ranch had shipped thousands of cattle and sheep to very weak markets in a desperate attempt to preserve what little grass remained on the ranges. In addition to the severe conditions suffered in the drought of 1934, an infestation of grasshoppers in 1936 had devoured most of the grass that survived the lack of water. Desperate for rain, Gothberg Ranch trucked water up to fifty miles to much of their thirsty livestock. Officials declared that twenty-four thousand square miles of Wyoming were suffering from extreme drought conditions. The circumstance was so intense that it made headlines in southern California.[46]

The Gothberg Ranch survived the droughts of the Dust Bowl era, but not without consequences. The family sold off a large percentage of their livestock during that time. It not being economically feasible to purchase vast numbers of sheep and cattle, they opted to replenish their herds naturally by relying on breeding, a lengthy process. In the meantime, Walt converted a portion of the unused livestock barns into a mink farm with moderate success. In 1938, Sis married Harold C. Campbell in Billings, Montana. A Casper native, Harold had been foreman of the Gothberg Ranch previously and the couple had known each other for a long time. For a while, they lived and worked in Montana, but eventually moved to Casper and returned to work the family ranch with Walt.[47]

By 1940, Martin and Mary Enid were living about half of the year in Long Beach, California, but still considered Wyoming home. In January

Martin J. and Mary Enid Gothberg in California
COURTESY OF THE FRANCES SEELY WEBB COLLECTION,
CASPER COLLEGE WESTERN HISTORY CENTER

1940, Sis received patent on a stock raising homestead of 618 acres. The homestead included tracts on Casper Mountain, Iron Creek, and at the home ranch, all adjoining lands already owned by the Gothberg Ranch.[48]

Ben Scherck and his See Ben Realty Company sued Martin Gothberg over a property line between Gothmore Park and the tract Scherck's company had developed adjacent to the park in 1920. The properties in question were originally homesteaded by Jane McNelly and Charley Hawks and patented in 1904 and 1912, respectively. They may have changed hands prior to Gothberg and Scherck purchasing them. The boundary between these homesteads was based on the original government survey from 1883. It seems that the original surveyor, Mr. Owens, strayed a little over two hundred feet from the eighth parallel when marking a section corner, effecting the two properties. When a new government survey was performed in 1922 to correct errors from Owens's survey, Scherck discovered that the corrected section line between the parcels then included just under thirteen acres of land within Gothmore Park. Scherck felt that this land belonged to him. Disregarding commissions paid to him by Gothberg and Blackmore for the marketing of Gothmore Park, and profits from his own real estate development that resulted from the establishment of the park, Scherck took possession of the parcel in question. It is unknown when this conflict actually began, but this may explain Scherck's sudden sale of his cabin in Gothmore Park in 1922.[49]

After a lengthy and consequently expensive court battle, the case came before the Wyoming Supreme Court in January 1941. Justice Blume determined that the boundaries had been established and cleared title to the lands issued to Mr. Hawks and Ms. McNelly prior to the survey of 1922. Those titles were issued, and corners established prior to the patenting of the claims based on the 1883 survey. Thus, even though that survey was in error, a line on a piece of paper did not supersede the actual boundary. He also concluded that a government survey that corrected such errors did not affect public lands that had previously passed into private ownership.

Counsel for the plaintiff then argued that the plaintive had possession of the disputed property and that this was *prima facie* evidence of title. This the judge rejected based on evidence that Gothberg had proof of ownership preceding Scherck's possession of the plot, thus proving better title. After both sides produced a string of surveyors and witnesses, Justice Blume found insufficient evidence to overturn the decisions of lower courts. At seventy-six, Martin Gothberg may not have been as spry as in earlier years, but even after days in the courtroom and numerous trips to the witness stand, it was clear he had lost none of his mental faculties. Justice Blume of the Wyoming Supreme Court ruled in favor of the defendant on January 21, 1941.[50]

As the war in Europe escalated, Martin's twenty-year-old grandson Edwin K. Gothberg traveled from his home in San Francisco to Casper. Ed was probably planning to spend his summer vacation from art school at his boyhood home, Gothberg Ranch. Martin perhaps reminisced with his grandson of his own youth and his days in the saddle on the open range. Whatever the circumstances, young Ed developed a plan and began preparing to ride horseback from Casper back to his home in San Francisco. He selected a ranch-bred horse he called Trigger to make the trip and apparently packed light enough for his horse to carry both him and his gear. He mounted up and pointed Trigger's nose west along the old Oregon Trail on July 15, 1941. Making a flamboyant image wearing buckskin clothing, one might think the entire journey a publicity stunt; there is no record, however, of any such arrangement. When asked why he took on the challenge, he responded, "to find out what the old timers went through."[51]

Ed followed the Oregon Trail into Idaho, and then took the California Cut-Off across Nevada. Making twenty-five miles per day most of the time, they made the 1,300-mile trek in seventy-five days. Ed tried to avoid the highways when possible, claiming that tourists took up too much of his time with silly questions. He occasionally helped host ranchers along the way to pay for his horse's feed and spent most nights in a bedroll under the open skies. In the process, Trigger wore out three sets of horseshoes, and though the weather was pleasant for the most part, other than an occasional rain shower, they did however encounter an early snowstorm when crossing the infamous Donner Pass. The duo arrived at the foot of Oakland Bay Bridge on October 5, where they unavoidably boarded a pickup truck and horse trailer for the first time in the trip to cross the bay.[52]

As Christmas approached in 1942, Walt Gothberg's wife, Dorothy, supplied the boys in the motor pool at the Army Air Base at Casper with lights and ornaments to decorate their Christmas trees and wreaths. Some

The Gothberg family; Standing (L–R): Ed and Walt Gothberg; Seated (L–R): Emma (Gothberg) Evans, Martin J. Gothberg, Mary Enid (Brandt) Gothberg, and Sis (Gothberg) Campbell
COURTESY OF GEORGE EVANS AND LORETTA BAYOUN, SUSAN LITTLEFIELD HAINES COLLECTION

of the soldiers stationed there had taken a truck up Casper Mountain, cut down trees to embellish several of the buildings, and made wreaths from evergreen branches also taken from the mountain. Sometime afterward, Walt abandoned his mink farm and moved his family to California where he went to work in the defense industry. Sis and Harold Campbell took over sole operation of the ranch.[53]

During World War II, the Army Air Base bustled with continual waves of young aviators honing their skills behind the sticks of a variety of military aircraft, receiving their final training before shipping out to join in the battle. Most of the young flyers who trained in Casper ended up in Europe battling the able pilots of the Luftwaffe. While the men at the Casper airfield enjoyed Dorothy Gothberg's Christmas ornaments, a young aircraft mechanic, Private Charles Yeager, was beginning pilot training in a new program of the US Army Air Force dubbed the "Flying Sergeants." Within a few months, Yeager received his wings, a promotion to non-commissioned officer (a warrant officer in today's classifications), and a transfer to the Air Base at Casper for his final six months of fighter pilot training. When Chuck and his squadron shipped out to join the war in Europe in November 1943, he stowed away five hundred pounds of Christmas candy hidden in military washing machines to share with the British children. Not unlike Martin Gothberg's venture west sixty years earlier, after high school Yeager joined the Army Air Corps seeking adventure. What began as a two-year hitch prior to the bombing of Pearl Harbor became a career of over thirty years for Yeager. At his retirement in 1975, Brigadier General Charles E. "Chuck" Yeager was one of the most celebrated fighter and test pilots in aviation history.[54]

On October 14, 1947, twenty-four-year-old test pilot Chuck Yeager set a new world speed record when he broke the sound barrier for the very first time in history. His speed was Mach 1.07, just short of eight hundred miles per hour. It was Yeager's ninth powered flight in Bell's rocket driven X-1 experimental aircraft. Eight days later, Martin John Gothberg passed away at his home on South Wolcott Street in Casper. Much had happened in America since Martin Gothberg had rode the plains on half-wild mustangs chasing herds of cattle numbering in the tens of thousands on the wide-open range of Wyoming. Then, steam locomotives were the fastest machines created, yet it still took several days to ride the rails from coast to coast. Now a man could theoretically travel the same distance in a matter of a few hours if the aircraft could carry enough fuel.[55]

Chuck Yeager's achievements were probably not terribly surprising to the aged Martin Gothberg. He did not object to evolvement. In fact, he had been a rather progressive man throughout his life. He welcomed advances in transportation with the coming of the automobile and then the airplane. As long-distance communication grew beyond newspapers, mail, and telegraph services, Gothberg Ranch was one of the first in the region to acquire a telephone. A farsighted man, Martin may have remarked that the accomplishment of Yeager's historic feat was only a matter of time.

Mary Enid, his wife of over fifty years, was by Martin's side at his death, as well as his daughter Sis and son Walt. Walt had relocated his family to Casper after the war. Martin had suffered from a heart condition for quite some time and had not been well for most of the previous year. He and Mary Enid had spent winters in California and summers in Casper for a number of years and probably planned again to venture to that climate as soon as his condition improved. Over more than six decades of ranching and business investments, Martin Gothberg amassed a ranch of over thirty thousand deeded acres spread over four Wyoming counties, no small accomplishment considering his modest beginning.[56]

Primarily a sheep rancher, Gothberg, however, never forgot his roots in the West. His days as a range rider for the big cattle outfits of the previous century engrained in him a respect for the ranchers, the riders, and the bovine they grazed on the wild and open rangelands of Wyoming. No matter how large his flocks of sheep grew, Martin always maintained a few hundred head of beef on the ranch, perhaps only as a reminder of his humble beginnings.[57]

Martin Gothberg spent a lifetime building a sizeable ranch by the standards of the mid-twentieth century, something beyond that by today's measures. His children planned to continue that legacy. Through times of both pitfalls and fortune, they held it together for another decade and a half. As they aged, it became more difficult for them to operate. Eventually after several conversations among the Gothberg siblings, they opted to sell the ranch to a man who planned to carry on their father's legacy.

CHAPTER 14

The Legacy Continues

1948–2019

A YEAR AFTER HER FATHER'S DEATH, SIS CAMPBELL AND HER HUSBAND, Harold, faced the most brutal winter in operating the ranch since 1887, remembered only by the oldest of the region's residents at the time. Sis was reminded of stories as a child of that deadly winter told by her father as she and Harold braced themselves for the worst. Later dubbed "the Blizzard of 1949," the storm began on January 2 of that year. By January 7, the first two deaths resulting from the storm were reported in Wyoming. No one had any idea that the storm was destined to continue for eight more weeks. "Forecasts in advance of the storm had not given the warning of a storm of this magnitude. In the following weeks, relentless snow, brutal winds and dangerously frigid temperatures cost the lives of cattle and people across the plains."[1]

On January 14, the second wave of the storm hit and Peggy Ann DesEnfants of Goshen County, Wyoming, recorded in her diary feelings that many Wyoming ranch families like hers and the Gothbergs shared: "Everyone is wondering will there be any cattle left in the morning because it is another 'northwester.'"[2]

Ralph Barton, the Natrona County emergency chairman, knew that they could not wait for the storm to subside. Something had to be done now. On January 27, he announced that three hundred tons of hay was being flown in from Fort Riley, Kansas, to the Air Base at Casper to help feed stranded sheep and cattle. He recruited every available aircraft in the area to assist in airdropping feed to the starving livestock. No doubt,

Martin would have pressed Ed and the Eaglerock into service had the disaster occurred a couple of decades earlier.[3]

It was not enough to save the Gothbergs' livestock. Frozen sheep carcasses were piled like cordwood in the ravines and draws where they had sought refuge from the bitter winds. It became a trap for many who were buried in the rapidly drifting snow that they could not escape. Whether they suffocated from being buried, inhaling the fine crystalized snow, or died from exhaustion trying to escape the pit nature created for them made little difference. "That year killed off so many of the Gothberg sheep that it was a matter of completely re-stocking [the ranch] or selling off the land." The family chose the second option, selling perhaps half of their land in order to raise enough capital to restock the remainder of the ranch. Fifteen thousand acres of land west of the home ranch became part of the Diamond Ring Ranch and Mills Livestock Company. All of the land homesteaded and purchased on Iron Creek and more was gone.[4]

Two years later, Mary Enid died in Long Beach, California, while visiting her daughter Emma Evans for the winter. Following their mother's death, the children incorporated the ranch, each owning an equal share. Sis and Harold Campbell continued to run the ranch, only consulting with the Gothberg siblings concerning major financial issues. Sis was a strong willed and independent woman. She had been single for a number of years when she and Harold married. Harold and Sis were both experienced ranchers and perhaps overly set in their own ways of doing things. Both were totally dedicated to the success of the Gothberg Ranch and family tales speak of many clashes of opinion between them. "It is rumored that Harold slept many a night out in the spring house." Their temperaments did not shrink the prosperity of the ranch however and "the pair kept the ranch running quite successfully for many years."[5]

As the Gothberg children grew older, the ranch became less profitable and more work than the aging Campbells were able to maintain. Ed and Emma had now been gone from Casper for more than half their lives. Emma lived in California and Edwin, upon retiring from the Pacific Gas and Electric Company, purchased a small ranch near Baker, Oregon, to live out his days. In 1961, the siblings agreed that it was time to liquidate the ranch that their father founded nearly eighty years earlier. Martin and Mary Enid had built the ranch literally from the ground up. Through blood, sweat, and tears they thrived and bore four children there who all grew to be prosperous, educated adults worthy of the Gothberg name, their family's legacy.[6]

— ⁓ —

In December 1961, retired newspaperman Earl P. Hanway purchased the remaining thirteen thousand acres of the Gothberg Ranch. His acquisition included Martin Gothberg's original homestead claim at Dobbin Springs and all that had consisted of the home ranch for many years. The parties did not disclose the purchase price. Three hundred fifty head of cattle and Martin Gothberg's beloved "T flying E" brand were included with the purchase. Martin had designed his brand as a variation on the old Searight brothers' "Lazy flying E" brand, which they sold with the last of their herds to the Carey brothers in 1886. Hanway planned to continue raising cattle on the ranch and to add his hobby of breeding Quarter horses to the operation.[7]

As often happens, things did not work out as Mr. Hanway so optimistically envisioned. Within a few years, Hanway's marriage ended, along with his interest in the ranch. He had sold his shares in the newspaper earlier and following his divorce, he sold off the ranch in smaller parcels, subdividing much of the property adjoining the original home ranch into small "ranchettes" of just a few acres. For some reason, this rural residential subdivision was named Indian Springs and references to Dobbin Springs have all but disappeared.

— ⁓ —

Over the next three decades, the old Gothberg home ranch changed hands several times and continued to shrink in size. In 1999, Susan Littlefield Haines purchased the last of the Gothberg Ranch. Her acquisition consisted of the surviving ranch structures in various stages of disrepair, the spring and eighty-six acres, about half of Martin Gothberg's original 1885 desert-homestead claim. Mrs. Haines's family has their own history in the vicinity. Her great-grandfather, Clarence Littlefield, was an early Casper newspaperman and oilman. Consequently, he was also a contemporary of Martin J. Gothberg.

First on the checklist was to evaluate the condition of each structure on the ranch. As Susan and her husband, Roy, began assessing the condition of the many buildings they had attained, they began devising a plan to save them. Several log structures literally sat on the dirt and were slowly rotting away from the ground up. Some required more urgent care than others did. A first necessity was to replace the roofs on nearly every building on the property. Once everything was somewhat weatherproof, the rest of the process could begin. The first two contractors they called recommended demolishing most of the structures. She and Roy were not willing to accept their recommendation. While living temporarily in a mobile home set up nearby, Susan and Roy along with two hired carpenters began the process themselves. First, they needed a place to work. They refurbished the large calving barn and converted it into a garage and machine shop.

The most urgent need was to resurrect the residence, but before tackling the log main house, they opted to "practice" on a smaller building. They chose the bunkhouse that Martin Gothberg had constructed by adding Lou Spalding's original ten-by-ten homestead cabin to his own creating a single building a century earlier. The structure had no foundation; the bottom logs were literally sitting in the dirt. With jacks and timbers, they raised the building and poured a concrete foundation. After sliding the bunkhouse over its new base, they completely refurbished it into a guesthouse.

The next order of business was the main house. The procedure was not a speedy one, but a strong desire to save the heritage of the ranch kept them moving forward. Eventually they succeeded in salvaging the original log house that Martin Gothberg built for his wife, Adolphena, in 1889. In order to accommodate their family, the Haineses also constructed a matching 1,600-square-foot log addition to the original house.

As soon as they had a permanent home to live in, they set the carriage house on a stable foundation and refurbished it. They also updated the stone springhouse that was built in 1905.

The bunkhouse, 2017
COURTESY OF SUSAN LITTLEFIELD HAINES

The main house at Gothberg Ranch. The portion to the left is the original 1889 house built by Martin Gothberg; to the right is the addition built by Susan and Roy Haines. Notice the original chimneys visible through the trees on the left.
PHOTOGRAPH BY DEBORA GLASS, 2016

The carriage house restored and repurposed into a residence. A history of Gothberg brands burned into the logs over the years and iron rings imbedded in the walls remain from the days of hitching horses, 2017.
COURTESY OF SUSAN LITTLEFIELD HAINES

Springhouse, 2016
PHOTOGRAPH BY DEBORA GLASS

They stabilized Martin Gothberg's large sheep barn that was converted to a horse barn in later years, probably during Mr. Hanway's days of ownership. With the danger of losing that structure minimized, the Haineses reconstructed a number of corrals on the east of the property to accommodate a small cow-calf operation.

Susan Littlefield Haines is an avid genealogist. Infatuated with family histories, she began researching the Martin John Gothberg family genealogy. Through local sources and snippets of information about the family, it was not long before she discovered that her new home had once been the headquarters of what today would be considered a quite large ranch. She was able to contact some of the Gothberg descendants and began piecing together the family history.

Since their original purchase, the Haineses have been able to acquire additional remnants of the old Gothberg home ranch, totaling about 660 acres. They also lease 330 acres from the State of Wyoming, part of the same school section that Martin Gothberg leased over a century ago. Plans for the future include a major renovation of the aforementioned building. In the meantime, as Susan says, "The place is small for Wyoming standards but plenty big to keep us always busy."[8]

The Gothberg Ranch, 2013
COURTESY OF SUSAN LITTLEFIELD HAINES

Appendix A

The Kenneth McRae Murder Trial, 1897

On June 7, 1897, the coroner held an inquest in the case of Kenneth McRae and the death of Robert Gordon. The following key witnesses testified to the coroner's jury.

Duncan McLain's Testimony:

> *Duncan McLain testified that he had known Robert Gordon since childhood in Scotland and that Gordon had been in the country since the previous spring. He positively identified the body as that of Robert Gordon.*

Peter Keith's Testimony:

> *Peter Keith testified that Kenneth McRae had cursed Robert Gordon when he came in for breakfast on the morning of May 29 for being late the night before. He supposed that Gordon had gone to look for sheep that he was tending. Keith had gone to bed about eight o'clock that morning. When he arose about 11 a.m., Gordon was not in camp. Keith asked McRae if Gordon had eaten his dinner before he went out since Keith was the cook that day. McRae replied that he had sent him down to Souter's sheep camp. When Keith asked again if Gordon ate before he left, McRae answered, "That ___ ___ ___ will come in when he gets hungry!"*
>
> *Keith ate his dinner and left to look after McRae's sheep, as McRae was sick in bed. At four o'clock, Keith returned to camp and noticed that Gordon still had not eaten his dinner. When he asked*

McRae where Gordon was, he retorted, "That __ __ __ has not been home yet!"

Keith said, "Surely you have been saying too much to him, if he is afraid to come here for his meals." McRae did not answer.

As Keith cooked supper, Gordon came up past the camp wagon. After Gordon came in to eat his supper, McRae told him to go to Souter's sheep camp and get him some whiskey. McRae told Gordon to wait there until he could get it, and bring it home, then go after his sheep. Gordon left the camp and Keith did likewise a short time later to watch the sheep awaiting Gordon's return. Keith returned to camp about five o'clock on the morning of the trouble. When he asked where Gordon was, McRae reacted, "That __ __ __ has not brought me my whiskey!" He said, "I will never be satisfied until I have that __ __ __ heart's blood!"

Later Keith brought McRae his breakfast. McRae stopped him on his way out and told Keith to bring him the coffee pot. When Keith returned with the pot, he also brought Gordon's breakfast, left it on the stove in the camp wagon and said, "This is Gordon's breakfast."

"That __ __ __ will never eat breakfast here again!" he said. Keith stayed in the warm wagon while he ate his own breakfast and McRae did not utter another word. When Keith left, he climbed under the supply wagon and curled up in his bedroll.

A short time later he heard a commotion in the camp wagon and heard McRae, "You __ __ __ why did you not bring my whiskey from Souter's camp?"

Gordon replied, "I waited at the camp until the sheep had strayed away, and then came away, as I did not want to lose them."

"You __ __ __, what is it to you where the sheep went to?" McRae asked.

"I will go for it now, then," Gordon said.

McRae made a response that Keith could not understand then and as the camp quieted he went to sleep.

Sometime later, there was a loud noise then he heard a man scream, "Peter! Peter! I am shot! I am shot!"

As Keith startled awake, he saw Gordon facing him about half-way between the camp wagon and the supply wagon. As he scrambled from his bed, Gordon fell to his knees. "He did not seem to come down easy, nor very hard," Peter Keith remembered in his testimony. Then he fell headlong right over Keith. "When I turned him over and looked in his face, I saw that he was hurt. I called to McRae that Gordon was hurt. He came out in about a half-minute or so. He stood about six feet away from the supply wagon where Gordon was lying at the time. I said to him, 'Surely to God, you haven't shot the boy, have you?' He was carrying the rifle at the time, holding it in his two hands."

In his testimony, Peter Keith reported, "I was trying to push him out of the wagon with the rifle, and the gun went off and shot him," said McRae. "I told him to go and fetch some water, and when he came back with the water, he carried the water in one hand, and the rifle in the other. He stood about six feet away from the body."

Keith said, "He is dead."

"What shall we do with him?" he asked.

"He is dead and we can't do anything with him."

As Keith retrieved his shoes from beneath the supply wagon, McRae said, "Go for John Landon." Keith told him that he did not know where Landon was, but that he knew where Souter's camp was and he would go and get him. As he left, McRae called him to come back. Keith stopped and told him there was no use in coming back, that Gordon was dead and they needed to report it to somebody. He continued walking not knowing whether to expect a bullet coming from his direction. After a short distance, he turned and looked back, just in time to see McRae climbing back into his camp wagon.

They then asked Keith a few minor questions and told him to share any other information that he thought might be of importance to the jury. Keith told them that about a week prior to the incident, McRae had told him that he would beat Gordon to death with a club. Keith had later shared this information with Gordon and told him to watch his back.

William Clark's Testimony:

William Clark, also an employee of Kenneth McRae and father of McRae's fiancé, testified that on the evening of May 29, he came into camp for supper about eight o'clock. McRae had asked him if he had seen Robert Gordon. Clark told McRae that indeed, he had seen Robert Gordon that evening and Gordon had told him that Mr. Souter was not at home. Clark said that hearing this, McRae used violent language. McRae said, "That ___ ___ ___, that ___ ___ ___! I will kill that ___ ___ ___! I will never be satisfied until I do kill him! I long to kill that ___ ___ ___!" Clark left the camp wagon at that point and went back to look after the band of ewes that he was tending. He came back later and McRae had quieted down. Clark then had his supper and went to bed. At about 3:30 a.m. Clark arose and returned to his band of ewes that were lambing. About seven o'clock, Peter Keith, being extremely excited, came down to where Clark had his band of sheep and told him that McRae had shot and killed Robert Gordon. Keith had said that he thought it was an accident, that McRae had been pushing Gordon with the rifle when it went off and killed Gordon. Keith told Clark that he was going down to Souter's camp and Clark told him to hurry, run if he needed to.

Clark stated that shortly thereafter, McRae showed up. Clark testified, "I said, 'My God Mac, what have you done?'

"He says, 'Ain't in fearful, ain't in fearful,' three times. He says, 'It will cause me lots of trouble, but I've got a clear conscience.'"

McRae then told Clark that the gun was lying on the bed and that he threw it on the bed roughly, and the gun had gone off. The shotgun was lying beside it. When asked, Clark identified the .45-70 Winchester that the court had in evidence as the gun belonging to Kenneth McRae, that McRae told him killed Robert Gordon.

They asked Clark if he had fired the gun that morning. He told them that he had fired two shots from the gun that morning. When he finished using it, he had placed it on the bed with the muzzle pointing toward the back of the wagon. After a few questions, it was determined that the supply wagon and camp wagon were situated at the time about sixteen feet apart, facing north and south, and that Peter Keith's bed was under the supply wagon.

Pat Fagan's Testimony:

Pat Fagan testified that when he arrived at the camp Gordon's body was lying beneath the supply wagon with his feet extending out near the rear wheel. He did not know if that was where the body had fallen. He continued that when McRae first spoke to him he said, "It is a sad accident," and Fagan had agreed. When examining the condition of the body, Fagan realized that flies were already despoiling the wounds so he, Sam Haynes, Charley Souter, and perhaps another man moved the body from under the wagon, cleaned the wounds and wrapped the body in a tarpaulin, then placed the body back under the wagon. During the process, Fagan had noticed what looked like powder burns around the entry wound.

When done, Fagan asked McRae how the accident happened. McRae led him into the camp wagon where the rifle and a shotgun lay at the foot of the bed, to the right as they entered. McRae picked up the rifle, swung it around, and pitched it back on the bed. "That is the way it happened," McRae said, "when he pitched the gun on the bed, it went off." McRae then told Fagan that he was considering putting the body in a wagon and taking it to Casper and asked what Fagan thought. Fagan told him that under the circumstances, McRae should request a coroner's investigation.

Later, Fagan saw Peter Keith and asked him if he was going back to McRae's camp. Keith told him that he was afraid to return and was going to Casper. Fagan offered him a job and Keith stayed at Fagan's camp until Sheriff Patton called on Keith to testify.

John F. Landon's Testimony:

When John Landon rode into Kenneth McRae's sheep camp around 11:30 on the morning of May 31, 1897, he was unaware that anything out of the ordinary had occurred. Standing in the door of the camp wagon was a young herder named Burns who worked for Charley Souter. Before Landon had dismounted his horse, McRae hollered from the wagon for Landon to come in. As Landon entered the wagon, McRae, seated on the bed, said, "I suppose you have heard of the accident?"

Landon asked, "No, what was it?"

"We have a dead man here," McRae said.

"What was the matter?" Landon asked.

"He got shot," McRae answered.

Landon asked, "Who?"

"Bob," McRae said.

When asked how it happened, "accidently," was the reply.

McRae went on to explain that Gordon and he had spoken only a few minutes earlier and McRae had rolled over and gone back to sleep. Gordon was the last to eat breakfast and as was his habit, he must have been cleaning and straightening things up afterward. Evidently, the rifle was in his way and as he moved it, the gun discharged. McRae felt the jolt of the gun by his feet, but the noise seemed more like that of a cap gun. Then Gordon hollered, "I am shot! I am shot!" and jumped clear out of the wagon and fell on his face. Then McRae went out and turned him over. Even Peter did not hear the shot, McRae told Landon, and he was asleep under the supply wagon.

Landon told McRae that it was incredibly careless for someone such as McRae, who had spent many years camping, to leave a loaded rifle lying about. McRae explained that they fired the rifle last thing every night when they went to bed and first thing every morning when they got up. McRae went on to say he had just fired the gun twice to turn a band of sheep that were going away.

Landon testified that McRae said nothing more after that.

Sam Haynes's Testimony:

McRae said the boy came into the camp wagon with the gun in his hand. He tossed the rifle on the bed causing it to discharge, hitting him in the body. When asked by the jury, Haynes clarified that McRae had told him, Fagan, and Souter what had happened.

Charles Souter's Testimony:

"He told me that the fellow that is dead came in and throwing his gun on the bed, and it accidently went off and shot him."

Testimony of Drs. Leeper, Garner, and Dean:

The bullet first struck the right arm midway between the elbow and the wrist. Passing through the arm it entered the right side of the chest and passed through the lower order of the right lung. It then passed through the heart splitting it in two at the middle and passed through the lower order of the left lung breaking the sixth rib on the left side. The bullet then passed through the fleshy part of the left arm midway between the shoulder and the elbow.

The victim could not have survived more than thirty seconds, even in the most perfect circumstances.

This concludes the testimony heard by the coroner's jury resulting in Kenneth McRae being charged for the murder of Robert Gordon.

Appendix B

The Jailbreak, 1905

AFTER EVADING CAPTURE AT BIG MUDDY, LEE CLUBB DISAPPEARED. Two days later on May 18, he stole a saddled horse belonging to the VR Ranch. There were eight horses at the hitching rail in front of a saloon in Glenrock, Wyoming, at eleven o'clock that night. Clubb mounted the best of the bunch and trotted into the darkness. The next morning, he took some food and provisions from a cabin on the headwaters of Little Deer Creek and rode away. That was the last track Sheriff Webb saw from him. He continued to scour the country for several days, but to no avail. Webb believed that Marty Trout made his way to the Union Pacific Railroad and left the country. A sheepherder near Lone Tree Creek was the last to see Trout a day or two after Bill Wardlaw's capture.

Lee Clubb spent three years in prison for cattle rustling in Colorado. Released around 1900, he came to Wyoming where he took up the name of Ed Lee. He worked as a cowboy for the CY Ranch for about a year before becoming a deputy sheriff where for a time his service was exemplary. In 1903, he was instrumental in the capture of outlaw Tom O'Day. Over the next couple of years, he organized a ring of horse thieves. Between January and May 1905, they stole seven railcar loads of horses, then shipped and sold them outside of Wyoming. Deputy Sheriff Ed Lee signed all of the paperwork for brand inspections on the horses at the railroad station, but never turned the copies in at the county clerk's office. At his preliminary hearing the day before his escape, Judge Tubbs held his case over for trial in district court and set bond at six thousand dollars.

Bill Misters's stolen horse was standing without saddle or bridle by his gate one morning a few days after it disappeared and before the end of May, as rumors circulated of rewards for the capture of Trout and Clubb.

Sheriff Webb rode out again before the rumors were substantiated. He returned from the northwest on June 4. Everyone suspected he had been on the trail of the escaped men, but Webb was too sullen to be confronted with questions.

On June 13, Guy Burson found the saddle stolen from Bill Misters at the same time as the horse. Concealed in some brush east of the cemetery in Casper, the blanket and bridle were not there with it. A few days later, a young boy found the blanket while playing not far from where Burson had found the saddle. The boy said that there was a long letter with the saddle blanket, but he lost it before he made it back to town.

On June 22, 1912, Sheriff Frank Webb ended the rumors about a reward for Lee Clubb when he posted in the *Natrona County Tribune:*

$250 Reward

Will be paid for information that will lead to the capture of Lee Clubb
(alias Ed Lee), who escaped from the Natrona County, Wyoming, jail
on May 12, 1905. Address all information to
F. K. Webb, Sheriff.
Casper, Natrona County, Wyo.

A short time later, several ranchers, victims of Clubb's gang, together upped the ante. They added one thousand dollars to the reward making the total of $1,250, about thirty-six thousand dollars in today's money. The county also added a reward of fifty dollars for the capture of Martin Trout. Some newspapers added "dead or alive" to their reports, but this option was never legally extended except in extreme cases for murderers.

Shortly before Christmas, the sheriff of San Bernardino, California, picked up Martin Trout on an unknown charge. He soon learned that Trout was a wanted man in Wyoming for horse and cattle rustling, and a reward offered. The California sheriff notified Sheriff Webb in Casper that he had Trout in custody. When Frank Webb petitioned the county commissioners for funds to bring Marty Trout back to Casper to face justice, the commissioners balked. When questioned about the affair, the sheriff told the *Wyoming Derrick* that he was ready to go after Trout whenever the county commissioners would guarantee the necessary expenses. The county never appropriated the money and it appears that Martin Trout never paid the consequences for his crimes in Wyoming.

In late January 1906, Sheriff Webb received a tip that Lee Clubb was in southern New Mexico. From there Webb tracked him to Texas, then Mexico. Deputy United States Marshal Joe Lafors from Cheyenne assisted in the pursuit. When located south of Juarez, Mexico, they applied in Chihuahua for authority to arrest Clubb in that country. Lafors returned to Cheyenne while Frank Webb awaited the Mexicans' approval. Lee Clubb heard of his detection by the Wyoming officers and left the area four days before Webb received his sanction from the Mexican authorities. On Sheriff Webb's return, an official at the border recognized Clubb from a photograph. The agent told Webb that Clubb had crossed into the United States a few days earlier. Again, Frank Webb had lost his trail.

In September, Sheriff Webb received word that the sheriff in Garden City, Kansas, had Abe Macklay, alias Dan Meckley, alias J. E. Clark, in custody. Macklay was an accomplice of Lee Clubb in the horse thieving operation. On September 25, 1906, Sheriff Webb left Casper with three prisoners en route to the Wyoming State Penitentiary in Rawlins. From there he took the train to Cheyenne, where Governor Bryant B. Brooks handed him the extradition papers for Abe Macklay. Webb was elated. He was nearly certain that Macklay would turn the state's evidence against Lee Clubb, particularly his whereabouts, in trade for leniency. Anticipating trouble, Frank Webb tried keeping Macklay's location secret until he had him in his own custody, but that effort failed. Possibly, as a result, Abe Mackay escaped from the Kansas jail, just hours before Webb's arrival.

Sometime after his sojourn in Mexico, Lee Clubb returned to Wyoming. Using his given name, Clubb located in Carbon County. There he herded sheep for nearly two years. Afterward he moved to Wamsutter, Wyoming, where he operated a saloon for about another year. During this time, he often visited Rawlins where he saw a number of people that he had known from Casper, but he did not speak to them and remained unrecognized. From there, Clubb moved to Rock Springs, Wyoming, where he ran another saloon. While in Rock Springs, he married a woman from Colorado. After a year there, Lee Clubb operated a saloon in Great Falls, Montana. The proprietor of the saloon he ran in Rock Springs later requested his return to that position, which he accepted. Then former sheriff Frank K. Webb received information of Clubb's expected arrival in Rock Springs. Webb procured a bench warrant from District Court Judge Charles E. Carpenter for the arrest of Lee Clubb.

On Wednesday, February 2, 1910, former sheriff Frank K. Webb served the warrant to Lee Clubb when he arrived in Rock Springs without incident. From there the two men traveled by train to Casper where a large crowd met them. Upon their arrival, they walked to a nearby restaurant where they had dinner. Before they had finished eating, Sheriff J. A. Sheffner sat down with them. He told them both that he had no grounds on which to hold Clubb. Since Webb's departure to arrest him, Sheffner had tried to collect enough evidence to charge Clubb, but had not succeeded. The district court case had dropped from the docket some time ago. When Sheffner approached several of the victims of the thefts, none wished to press charges.

The outlaws had marketed the animals across the country. Five years earlier, Sheriff Webb accumulated evidence from several recipients of the stock in Pocahontas, Iowa; East St. Louis, Illinois; St. Joseph, Missouri; and Omaha, Nebraska. He recovered dozens of the horses and shipped them back to their rightful owners. The ranchers had long since withdrawn the subscriptions that made up their one-thousand-dollar reward, and the county commissioners rescinded the $250 offered by their predecessors.

Sheriff Sheffner could not even hold Clubb for escaping jail since there were no statutes for that offense on the books at the time. Mrs. Clubb arrived in Casper on Sunday, February 6, and the two remained for a few days, giving the county every opportunity to review their options.

Rumors ran rampant around Casper that Sheriff Webb had been a party to the whole operation and even the jailbreak was a ruse. Some even suggested that Webb's many trips around the country in pursuit of Lee Clubb were actually planned opportunities for the two men to meet and spend their ill-gotten gains undetected. Both men proclaimed their innocence and Lee Clubb suggested that his alleged co-conspirators, George Jones and Abe Macklay, had succeeded in framing both he and Webb for crimes neither committed.

Prosecuting Attorney John B. Barnes stated that without a complaint filed by the victims he would not reinstate the case against Clubb unless authorities produced competent witnesses to testify against him. The board of county commissioners remained unwilling to relinquish funds to pursue the case further. It appears that nothing ever became of the case and Frank Webb wasted several years of his career in pursuit of a man that was never prosecuted.

In 1911, Frank K. Webb sued Natrona County for $83.30, expenses due to him for the capture of Ed Lee Clubb. It is unknown if he ever received compensation.

Appendix C

The Salt Creek Oil Field War, 1910

MISSOU HINES MAY HAVE FOUND HIMSELF MORE DEEPLY INVOLVED IN the oil business than he had bargained for. The Franco-Wyoming Oil Company acquired most of the assets of the Belgo-American Company about the same time that the California Oil Syndicate began drilling for oil, early in 1910. Franco-Wyoming, a subsidiary of the Petroleum Maatschappij Salt Creek Company, or Dutch Company as it was called, and the California Oil Syndicate along with others all laid claim to a prime piece of real estate in the Salt Creek Oil Field. The California oilmen contested earlier claims to the land and filed their own claims when they began drilling there. Armed horsemen employed by the California group prevented others from entering the area, claiming they were trespassing. This prompted a lawsuit filed by Franco-Wyoming on May 14, 1910, against the others in district court.

On May 29, Mr. Coenraad Kerbert of the Franco-Wyoming, with S. A. Lane and two others, drove to their operations at the Salt Creek field. At their request, Sheriff J. A. Sheffner accompanied them to ensure their safety. Upon their arrival, William Fitzhugh of the California Company, backed by his entourage of well-armed and mounted men of which Missou Hines almost certainly was a party, ordered the men of the Franco-Wyoming off the property. After considerable argument, they agreed to allow Kerbert's group to occupy half of the house, which Mr. Lane actually owned, while those of the California Company occupied the other half. As evening approached, Mr. Fitzhugh returned to Casper and immediately filed charges of trespassing against Kerbert and his men, including Sheriff Sheffner.

On Tuesday, Mr. Fitzhugh accompanied Casper Marshal William Jones back to Mr. Lane's house near Salt Creek, where Marshal Jones served warrants to the four men of the Franco-Wyoming Company and Sheriff Sheffner, arresting them all for trespassing. Back in Casper on Thursday, the men appeared before Justice Warren E. Tubbs. There were many unanswered questions regarding Marshal Jones's authority outside of Casper and especially presiding over Sheriff Sheffner. The men each posted five hundred dollars bond and Justice Tubbs bound the case over to district court. Upon his release, Con Kerbert left immediately for Cheyenne on the next available train "on business."

A week later, the district court granted an injunction against Mr. William Fitzhugh, his partner Mr. Henshaw, and their California Oil Syndicate, forbidding them from denying access by the Franco-Wyoming Company to lands in the Salt Creek Oil Field claimed by both firms. Missou Hines then traveled to Lincoln, Nebraska, on other company business. By mid-June, the Franco-Wyoming Company began hauling new machinery to the location from the railyard in Casper, planning to continue development of the property. Messrs. Kerbert and Vander-Gracht of the Dutch Company and Mr. Otis, New York attorney for the company, returned to Casper from visiting the field a week later reporting that all was quiet at the wells.

While awaiting a hearing, the court appointed Frank Wood, vice president of Stockman's National Bank in Casper, as receiver for the Franco-Wyoming Company. On July 20, Mr. Wood accompanied Messrs. Young and Wallace of Franco-Wyoming delivering supplies to the disputed territory. B. A. Elias drove the three men from Casper in his automobile. When approaching the site, the car was stopped by armed horsemen representing the California people. They left their conveyance at the Dutch Company camp and Wood, Young, and Wallace continued toward their destination on a four-horse supply wagon. Missou Hines, John A. Jones, and J. F. Harris again stopped the men and told the party that they could not proceed. Frank Wood climbed down from the wagon attempting to convince the trio that as court-appointed receiver for the company, he could continue ahead and had every legal right to be on the land in question. Wood and Jones's conversation then began to deteriorate prompting Jones to pick Wood up and carry him back from the disputed property where he put Wood down and sat on him. When this was going on, Young and Wallace tried to proceed with the wagon, but Hines and Harris again stopped them. There was no violence nor threats made. The Franco-Wyoming men withdrew and returned to Casper. Frank Wood caught the train to Cheyenne the next morning planning to put the case before the United States Circuit Court.

On Friday, July 22, Deputy United States Marshal Les Snow from Cheyenne arrived in Casper. He went to Salt Creek and summoned Missou Hines, John A. Jones, and J. F. Harris to appear before Judge Riner in the United States Circuit Court in Cheyenne on July 28 to show cause why they should not be held in contempt of court. On Saturday, Marshall Snow summoned Judge E. Nusbaumer, attorney for the California Oil Syndicate, to appear in Cheyenne before Judge Riner on the same date and upon the same charge.

After hearing arguments, Judge Riner felt that the men charged were not guilty of contempt and dismissed them. It appears that by this time, the trespassing charges against Sheriff Sheffner, Messrs. Kerbert and Lane, and the other men had also been dropped. Judge Riner then issued a stop work order on the disputed quarter section to both companies. The grounds for the California Oil Company's contest of the Franco-Wyoming Oil Company's claim to the property were that the latter had never developed a producing oil well on the property. He then gave Franco-Wyoming forty days to submit affidavits to the court that they or their predecessor, the Belgo-American Oil Company, had in fact made valid discoveries of oil on the quarter section in question before the old company filed on those locations. Judge Riner then gave the California Oil Company twenty days in which to file counter affidavits.

As representatives of the California Company in the courtroom smiled ear to ear with an apparent victory, Judge Riner continued. He reprimanded the men of the California Company, stating that their use of force in the field was deplorable and it was the purpose of the court to protect the public. The courts were open to both parties and were the proper place to settle such differences. Assault was not an option and if it were used again in the future, appropriate charges would be filed against those responsible, and they would be prosecuted with due process in a court of law and suffer the prescribed sentence.

On October 10–11, Judge Riner heard the case of the controversy between the Franco-Wyoming Oil Company and the California Oil Company in the United States Circuit Court at Cheyenne. The court determined that there was strong proof of oil springs and seepages on the land, together with sandstone cuttings on adjoining lands. While the geological character of this land and surrounding country had evidence to strongly indicate that it was oil-bearing land, all did not constitute a discovery so far as the Franco-Wyoming Company was concerned. Therefore, the Franco-Wyoming Company never acquired any title to the land and the California Company was granted release to resume drilling on the disputed property without interference from the Franco-Wyoming Company.

Franco-Wyoming apparently took the loss in stride. A week later the *Casper Press* reported, "The Dutch company report another good well, in which the oil pressure is so strong it is impossible to cap the casing for a long continued time. Each day looks better for the field and all the camps are getting ready for a strenuous winter's work. The Dutch company is putting up some substantial buildings, making their camp more comfortable."

Judge Carpenter in Casper heard the suit filed in district court by the Franco-Wyoming Oil Company against the California Oil Company on October 31, 1910. That afternoon he suspended litigation when both parties agreed that the two companies could probably reach a compromise. The *Natrona County Tribune* announced, "If they get together it will advance the development of the Salt Creek oil lands a number of years and no doubt will result beneficially to both companies."

Thus, the story ends. Beyond a few bruised feelings and a couple of bloodied reputations, there were no fatalities and no one received serious injury.

Notes

Chapter 1

1. Martin John Gothberg was the fourth child of Edwin Herman and Sophia (Kretch-mer) Gothberg. His elder siblings were Ernst or Ernest, born in 1857; Teresa, born in 1859; and Bernard, born about 1860. Younger sisters and brother were Lillian, born in 1867; Sophia, born in 1870; Minnie, born in 1873; and Herman Edward, born in 1876. The older children were all born in Germany, and the younger in New York or New Jersey. Susan Littlefield Haines, *Gothberg Family Genealogy* – Primary Reference – FGR-1; Rex G. Lewis, *M. J. Gothberg, Pioneer Range Rider and Rancher*, (WPA Subject #755), 1; Martin Gothberg's father, known as Herman, was an artisan from Sweden who had migrated to Germany, where he met and married Sophia. In Germany, Herman studied art and entered into the brass trade. The circumstances regarding the young family's decision to come to America are unknown, but Herman came to New York in advance of Sophia and the children. Upon arriving in New York City, Herman opened his own small brass foundry where he began producing chandeliers. A short time later, Sophia, Ernst, Teresa, Bernard, and Martin boarded the *Barussia* in Hamburg and sailed in the steerage compartment to America. Crossing the Atlantic Ocean, the Gothbergs arrived in New York harbor on September 22, 1866. Within a few months, Herman's business was sufficient to require additional help. He contacted his close friend and former co-worker Louis Kuhne in Germany, who soon became Herman's first employee. In 1870, with his family growing by two new daughters since their arrival in America, he relocated his family across the river to Bartholdi Avenue in the Greenville district of Jersey City, New Jersey. Ichabod Sargent Bartlett, *History of Wyoming* (Chicago: S. J. Clarke Publishing Company, 1918), v. III, 259–260; "Gothberg, Long Resident Here, Taken by Death—Pioneer Rancher and Businessman Came Here Five Years Before Casper Founded," *Casper Tribune-Herald*, (October 22, 1947), 1; "New York Passenger Lists, 1820–1891," *FamilySearch*. "Whirled to Death," *Jersey City News*, (June 13, 1894), 2; The Gothberg Foundry continued to prosper and grow. In addition to chandeliers, they cast "gladiators which popularly stood on each side of a fireplace mantle, or statuettes of graceful ladies holding a lamp to stand on a newel post to light the stairway." It has been reported that the foundry cast the famous lions that guard the entrance to the New York Public Library. This is in error; the lions mentioned are sculpted from marble. Jo Mohr, editor, "Starting at Dobbin Springs: The Gothbergs, pioneering, ranching, and art." *Casper Magazine*, (Dec.–Jan. 1983, Vol. 5 No. 6), 3; As the business grew, they expanded

into brass sheet work and began manufacturing bedsteads, as well as stamping and punching a multitude of brass ornaments and decorations. They began spinning vases and fixtures, which led to turning heavier brass objects on lathes. All of Herman's sons worked in the factory as they grew up, learning not only the craft of a variety of manufacturing techniques, but the artistry behind the complex designs of their merchandise. As the young men gained in age and experience, Herman moved the factory to Cator Avenue in Jersey City and renamed the business H. E. Gothberg and Sons Manufacturing Company. In 1880, Herman and his sons Ernst, Bernard, and Martin all were listed on the New Jersey census as "mould makers," as the enumerator spelled the occupation in that era. Four-year-old Herman Jr. was the only male member not working at the family brass works. Being a mold maker in their area of proficiency not only required a great deal of skill, but also required a gifted artistic touch and knowledge of metallurgy. Census of Jersey City, Hudson County, New Jersey, 1880.

2. Bartlett, 260; Lewis, 1; "bull cook": a handyman in a camp (as of loggers); *especially*: one who does caretaking chores and acts as cook's helper. *Merriam-Webster.com.* Merriam-Webster, n.d. Web. 19 Feb. 2017.

3. Lewis, 1; US Census, 1880; Ernest Staples Osgood, *The Day of the Cattleman*, (Chicago and London: University of Chicago Press, 1929), 42; John K. Rollinson, *Wyoming Cattle Trails* (Caldwell: Caxton Printers, 1948), 61, 248–251, 256; "The 'Club' Cup," *Cheyenne Daily Sun*, (September 6, 1887), 6; Adolphena Gothberg Campbell, *Martin J. Gothberg—Notes*, unpublished manuscript, (Casper: circa 1947), 2; While Martin knocked around Cheyenne, his older sister Teresa married Theodore Frederick Koezly. The wedding took place at the Gothberg family home on January 26, 1881. Theo was a mechanical engineer with a keen interest in electricity. In 1876 at age twenty, he already had a reputation for his expertise on the subject. "A fine paper has been translated by Theo. F. Koezly, M. E. entitled, *On the Use of the Gamma Magneto Electric Machines for Lighting Railroad Depots*. All of these articles are ably written and carry with them high scientific worth." *New Jersey Marriages, 1670–1980*; "Van Nostrand's Eclectic Engineering Magazine," *Boston Traveler* (June 28, 1876), 4.

4. Campbell, 2; "Gothberg . . ." *Casper Tribune-Herald*, (October 22, 1947), 1; Bartlett, 260.

5. Lewis, 1.

6. Other terms like *buckaroo* (originally derived from the Spanish word *vaquero*) and *waddy* are usually more regional titles tagged to those men of the same vocation from the Southwest or working in the basin country of northern Nevada and California, eastern Oregon, and western Idaho. These men often use slightly different techniques, equipment, and clothing than others of their trade. Winfred Blevins, *Dictionary of the American West* (New York: Facts on File, 1993), 45–46, 93–96; Bruce Grant, *The Cowboy Encyclopedia*, (Chicago: Rand McNally & Co., 1951), 32, 53, 155–156; Lewis, 1.

7. Lewis, 1; Campbell, 2; Jefferson Glass, *Reshaw: The Life and Times of John Baptiste Richard* (Glendo: High Plains Press, 2014), 249–50; While Martin kicked around in Wyoming, his elder siblings began settling into family life in New Jersey. The marriage of their sister Teresa early the previous year set Martin's eldest brother Ernst Gothberg to contemplate settling down and rearing a family of his own. On September 4, 1882,

Ernst married Wilhelmina "Minnie" Lauer at St. Paul's Catholic Church in Jersey City. *New Jersey Marriages, 1678–1985*.

8. Lewis, 1; Land Patent, Alexander H. Swan: #WYWYAA 007553, October 1, 1878; "_____," *Cheyenne Weekly Leader*, (July 27, 1882), 10; "Gothberg ..." *Casper Tribune-Herald*, (October 22, 1947), 1; *Wyoming Platte County Heritage* (Wheatland: Platte County Extension Homemakers Council, 1981), 161; John Baptiste Richard, a trader of French descent, established a horse and cattle ranch on Richard Creek in 1863. The tributary to Chugwater Creek is five miles northwest of present day Chugwater, Wyoming. Richard Creek and the surrounding hills were renamed Richeau in later years due to a misunderstanding of the French pronunciation of "Richard." Glass, *Reshaw*, 150–151, 157–158; Campbell, 2.

9. Tom Lindmier, *Drybone: A History of Fort Fetterman, Wyoming*, (Glendo: High Plains Press, 2002), 145–146, 159–161; Larry K. Brown, *The Hog Ranches of Wyoming: Liquor, Lust, and Lies Under Sagebrush Skies*, (Glendo: High Plains Press, 1995), 85–91.

10. The Searight brothers established the Goose Egg Ranch on the North Platte River at the mouth of Poison Spider Creek, or Poison Creek as it was sometimes called. The ranch acquired its name when a group of cowboys found a nest of wild goose eggs along the river and took them to the cook. The oval Goose Egg brand that was registered was primarily used on horses while the Searight brothers continued to use their well-known "Lazy flying E" brand on cattle. Mae Urbanek, *Wyoming Place Names* (Boulder: Johnson Publishing, 1967), 88; Lindmier, 148; Brown, 91–92; "A Brutal Murder," *Cheyenne Weekly Leader*, (October 19, 1882), 7; "The Fetterman Tragedy," *Cheyenne Daily Leader*, (October 20, 1882), 2.

11. Lindmier, 148–149; Brown, 92–93; "A Brutal Murder," *Cheyenne Weekly Leader*, (October 19, 1882), 7.

12. Lindmier, 148–149; Brown, 92–93; "A Visitor at Fetterman," *Cheyenne Weekly Leader*, (June 21, 1883), 5.

13. "Arrivals at the Inter Ocean Hotel," *Cheyenne Daily Sun* (March 3, 1882), 4; Lindmier, 148–149.

14. "More About Capp," *Cheyenne Weekly Leader*, (October 19, 1882), 5; "A Brutal Murder," *Cheyenne Weekly Leader*, (October 19, 1882), 7; "The Fetterman Tragedy," *Cheyenne Daily Leader*, (October 20, 1882), 2.

15. Campbell, 2; Lewis, 1; "Glenrock Items," *Natrona County Tribune*, (Casper: October 7, 1897), 4; Mollie Wolf worked as a cowpuncher throughout central Wyoming for several years. He established a sheep and horse ranch near the mouth of the Sweetwater River in the 1890s. Mollie was one of the best sheepshearers in the state. He consistently sheared over one hundred sheep per day. When Pathfinder Reservoir submerged his ranch on the Sweetwater, he purchased another on Bates Creek. In later years, he worked at times as a stock detective and part-time deputy sheriff. In 1891, the *Newcastle Journal* reprinted a column from the *Casper Derrick* explaining the evolution of Mollie Wolf's nickname: "'Mollie' Wolf, who is now working for the YU outfit came down from the Big Horn last week, and spent several days in town. In 'Mollie,' we find a most expressive illustration of the evolution of a name as it passes through the cowboy vocabulary. His proper name is Myrian Wolf, but when he arrived in Wyoming and went to punching

cows, Myrian was too aesthetic for a calf rustler and broncho buster so the boys changed it to Mary Ann, which in time was abbreviated to Mary and as they became more familiar it finally resolved itself down to 'Mollie,' by which name he is now known all over central Wyoming." "Casper Derrick," *Newcastle Journal,* (August 21, 1891) 1; Known by all as "Jerky Bill," Thomas Charles Clayton was also sometimes called William Clayton. He arrived with his brother on the North Platte in 1871. Clayton acquired his perhaps somewhat cruel nickname due to continuous involuntary spasms suffered most of his life caused by chorea, a condition more commonly known as St. Vitus's dance. In addition to his riding feats, he owned and operated a successful cattle and horse ranch on Boxelder Creek southeast of Glenrock, Wyoming, for many years. "William Clayton," *Bill Barlow's Budget,* (Douglas: August 09, 1905), 4; William P. Hines grew up in Missouri and came west as a cowpuncher around 1880. He had a cowboy sense of humor and once commented that in the early years, "he moved his home every day ... all he had to do was throw a bucket of water on it [his campfire] and move on." Hines was also quite renowned for his prowess with a lariat and a six-shooter. His tenure with Judge Carey and the CY continued for several years. "'Missou' Hines Now a Benedict," *Douglas Budget* (January 20, 1921), 1; James H. Bury passed by the old Fort Casper in the early 1870s and later recalled, "there was nothing there but the charred remains of the old adobe trading post." Glass, *Reshaw,* 255.

16. Lewis, 1; "Mr. R. Davis Carey," *Cheyenne Daily Sun,* (July 24, 1877), 4; "Tusler Bros. Shipped 27 Cars," *Cheyenne Daily Leader,* (September 15, 1877), 4; "Cattle Notes," *Cheyenne Daily Leader,* (September 15, 1877), 4; "Stock Notes," *Cheyenne Daily Leader,* (November 29, 1878), 4; http://www.wyomingtalesandtrails.com/nplatte3.html.

17. Bessemer Bend took its name from the town of Bessemer, Wyoming (1888–1892). Urbanek, 21; Alfred James Mokler, *History of Natrona County Wyoming 1888–1922,* (Chicago: Lakeside Press, 1923), 221–225; John Baptiste Richard established a trading post and road-ranch along the Overland Trail at the crossing of Rock Creek west of present day Laramie, Wyoming, in 1865. When the Union Pacific Railroad was constructed, they built a railway station there. Glass, *Reshaw,* 176; Rock Creek was the southern terminus of the Fort Fetterman Road. About forty miles from Laramie, Rock Creek was the major supply hub of central Wyoming for forty years. In the early days, passengers could board a stagecoach there and travel all the way to Miles City, Montana. When the Union Pacific changed its route in 1901, the community of Rock Creek was abandoned and the new town of Rock River was founded a few miles south of the original site. Urbanek, 176; Lewis, 2; http://www.wyomingtalesandtrails.com/bessemer.html.

18. Lewis, 2; Maud Kerns Garton, "Word Picture of Old Goose Egg Ranch," *Casper Chronicle*s, (Casper: Casper Zonta Club, 1964), 27; Mrs. Renfro's son was probably the man known as "Ogallala" Renfro and later as "Dad" Renfro. Known to have ridden the range in central Wyoming as early as 1880, he competed in a Sheridan, Wyoming, rodeo in 1897. "Casper Cowboys," *Sheridan Post,* (June 17, 1897), 4; Charles Lajeunesse, also known as Cemineau, was a mountain man and trader working for the American Fur Company at Fort John in the 1840s. By 1852, he and his partners had established a trading post, Fort Seminoe (an Americanized spelling of his nickname) at Devil's Gate west of Independence Rock along the Oregon Trail in what later became Wyoming. The

nearby Seminoe Mountains and Seminoe Reservoir also carry his name. Glass, *Reshaw*, 29, 78; "Our nearest neighbors were a family of Indians. That is, the woman was a Shoshone Indian, who had two sons and a daughter, Bouquet, who looked white and was a pretty girl. The two boys were expert horsemen." Bryant Butler Brooks, *Memoirs of Bryant B. Brooks: Cowboy, Trapper, Lumberman, Stockman, Oilman, Banker and Governor of Wyoming*, (Glendale: Arthur H. Clark Company, 1939), 158.

19. "G. A. Searight," *Cheyenne Weekly Leader*, (January 16, 1879), 8; Rollinson, 233, 314, 319–322.

20. "Round Up Racket," *Cheyenne Weekly Leader*, (June 12, 1879), 8; "Cattle Notes," *Cheyenne Daily Sun*, (August 3, 1879), 4; "Personal Points," *Cheyenne Daily Leader*, (August 5, 1879); 4.

21. Lewis, 2.

22. Lewis, 2–3; "Round Ups, Wyoming Stock Growers Association, 1883," *Cheyenne Weekly Leader*, (April 19, 1883), 5; A remuda (ruh-MOO-duh) is a herd of saddle horses. Large-scale cattle ranches had dozens, if not hundreds of saddle horses (usually geldings) used by the cowboys to complete their daily tasks. Each cowboy would have his own *string* of six or more horses assigned to him for his daily use. During the roundup their *string* would need to increase in numbers to compensate for the extreme exertion the animals endured. When not being ridden the remuda was herded by a wrangler or kept in a corral. Blevins, 284; Grant, 118.

23. Lewis, 2–3.

24. Ibid.

25. Ibid; "Gothberg . . ." *Casper Tribune-Herald*, (October 22, 1947), 1; In 1883, the railroad shipped up to one hundred cars of cattle daily from the stockyards at Rock Creek, while ranchers held their herds on the plains waiting their turn. Urbanek, 176; On June 13, 1883, the Searight brothers filed articles of incorporation for the Searight Cattle Company with Secretary Morgan of the Wyoming Territory. "The amount of capital stock is $1,500,000, or 3,000 shares at $500 each. The trustees of this corporation are: Gilbert A. Searight, of Cheyenne; Francis W. Searight and George P. Searight, of Carlisle, Pennsylvania; Robert M. Searight and W. W. Corlett, of Cheyenne." *Weekly Boomerang*, (Laramie: June 14, 1883), 8.

26. Campbell, 3–5.

27. Gothberg is credited with inventing a type of horse-hobble that worked like a Chinese puzzle in order to keep Indians from stealing the ranch's horses. Mohr, 3.

28. Campbell, 5.

29. Lewis, 4; Campbell, 5–6.

30. Lewis, 4–5; Campbell, 6; "Gothberg . . ." *Casper Tribune-Herald*, (October 22, 1947), 1–2.

31. Campbell, 6.

32. "A Devoted Daughter," *Democratic Leader*, (Cheyenne: March 13, 1884), 10.

33. "Personals," *Northwestern Live Stock Journal*, (Cheyenne: June 27, 1884), 3; "Stock Cars Ordered," *Daily Boomerang*, (Laramie: August 11, 1884), 4; "Stock Shipments—Within 20,000 Head of Last Year—Thursday's Sales & Yesterday's Orders," *Cheyenne*

Daily Sun, (September 27, 1884), 3; "Stock Cars Ordered," *Daily Boomerang*, (Laramie: October 14, 1884), 4.

34. "Minor Mention," *Weekly Boomerang*, (Laramie: July 12, 1883), 8.

35. In the far away world of New Jersey, Martin's sister Teresa Koezly gave birth to a daughter, Doretta Helen, in July 1884. Within a few days, her husband Theo purchased a home for his growing family on Claremont Avenue in Jersey City from George Tompkins for the unusual sum of $1,406. *New Jersey State Census, 1905*, database, *FamilySearch*; "Real Estate Transfers—Jersey City," *Jersey Journal*, (Jersey City: July 25, 1884), 3.

Chapter 2

1. Campbell, 6–7; Declaration of Intention, Laramie County District Court (April 4, 1885: volume A, page 107) Laramie County, Wyoming; Land Patent, Martin J. Gothberg: #WYWYAA 012142, April 29, 1893.

2. "The Fattening Herds," *Cheyenne Daily Sun*, (May 21, 1885), 3; "Cattle Notes," *Daily Boomerang*, (July, 16, 1885: Laramie), 3.

3. "Local Lines," *Sundance Gazette*, (August 8, 1885), 8; "_____," *Sundance Gazette*, (September 5, 1885), 5.

4. "_____," *Sundance Gazette*, (September 19, 1885), 4; "October Oddities," *Cheyenne Daily Sun*, (October 23, 1885), 3; http://www.in2013dollars.com/1885-dollars-in-2017?amount=1000000; "Cattle Notes," *Democratic Leader*, (Cheyenne: November 20, 1885), 3.

5. Lewis, 4; Campbell, 6–7; A corduroy road was built by laying slabs of logs across soft surfaces to keep heavy wagons from sinking and bogging down. The name was derived from its appearance, similar to the wales in corduroy fabric. Crossing a corduroy road with a steel-tired wagon and no form of suspension undoubtedly was a very bumpy ride.

6. Mohr, 3; Jefferson Glass and Susan Littlefield Haines, *Letter to the Wyoming State Historic Preservation Office*, February 6, 2017, 2; Lewis, 5–6.

7. *Boston Daily Advertiser*, July 28, 1885. Cited in William E. Deahl, "Buffalo Bill's Wild West Show, 1885," *Annals of Wyoming*, Vol. 47, No. 2, Fall 1975, 145; Karen Roles, *Letter to Jefferson Glass, July 6, 2018*, (Cody: Buffalo Bill Center of the West).

8. Thirty-two-year-old Thomas C. Clayton married twenty-two-year-old Alice B. Young on November 24, 1886, in Madison, Illinois. "Illinois, County Marriages, 1810–1940," database, *FamilySearch* (https://familysearch.org/ark:/); Land Patent, Thomas C. Clayton: #WYWYAA 009844, October 6, 1894.

9. Lewis, 4; Campbell, 7.

10. "Gothberg . . ." *Casper Tribune-Herald* (October 22, 1947), 2; John R. Pexton, "Douglas," *Pages From Converse County's Past*, (Douglas: Wyoming Pioneer Association, 1986), 683–686; "Personal Intelligence," *Bill Barlow's Budget*, (December 1, 1886: Douglas), 5.

11. "Gothberg . . ." *Casper Tribune-Herald*, (October 22, 1947), 2; "Fetterman Notes," *Northwestern Live Stock Journal*, (Cheyenne: December 24, 1886), 5.

12. "It Was Only the Watchman," *Jersey Journal*, (Jersey City: April 6, 1887), 4.

13. Campbell, 7; Mokler, 221.

14. "Roundup Racket," *Bill Barlow's Budget*, (Douglas: June 15, 1887), 5; "Stray Horse Column," *Northwestern Live Stock Journal*, (Cheyenne: June 10, 1887), 11; "Douglas Items," *Northwestern Live Stock Journal*, (Cheyenne: July 22, 1887), 5.

15. "Glenrock appeared on legal documents on December 7, 1887 for the first time as one word instead of two." Pexton, "Douglas," 690.

16. Haines, FGR-1; "Home Happenings," *Carbon County Journal*, (Rawlins: October 22, 1887), 3; Lewis, 4; "Nicknames Labeled Rough and Tough Rugged Men of '86: Early Days of Cowpunching are Told by 'Molly' Wolfe," *Douglas Enterprise*, (June 23, 1936), 1.

17. _____, *Mrs. Blackmore Looks Back*, unpublished manuscript, (Wyoming Pioneer Memorial Museum: circa 1951); Cora M. Beach, *Women of Wyoming, Vol. 1*, (Casper: S. E. Boyer, 1927), 333–334; "Vote for Decency and Municipal Economy," *Casper Daily Tribune* (November 7, 1921), 7; "_____," *Bessemer Journal*, (August 1, 1889), 4.

18. Mokler, 115, 202; While newcomers hustled to found the new town of Casper, back in New Jersey Martin's older brother Bernard married Ellen Corcoran, known by friends as Nellie. Haines, FGR-5.

19. Bartlett, 260.

20. _____, *Mrs. Blackmore Looks Back*; "Local Notes," *Casper Weekly Mail*, (February 1, 1889), 6.

21. Robert Bruce Blackmore, *Letter to Wyoming Pioneer Association Museum*, September 16, 1966, Wyoming Pioneer Memorial Museum, Douglas, Wyoming; Minnie Blackmore's "Full Square Grand" piano made by McCammon Co., Albany, New York is on display in the lower level of the Wyoming Pioneer Memorial Museum in Douglas, Wyoming. It is still in good condition and said to have a soft mellow tone.

22. Mokler, 264–272.

23. Lewis, 5.

24. Natrona County Clerk Abstract Book #1 R77-82 1890–1905, 210; Campbell, 7.

25. Lewis, 2; Campbell, 3; Mokler, 410–414.

26. Mokler Historical Collection, Casper College Western History Center.

27. Theodore Koezly was a scientist and engineer of considerable knowledge. He was particularly interested in properties of electricity. "Mortuary Notice," *New York Herald*, (June 1, 1890), 1.

28. "Society Notes," *Jersey Journal*, (Jersey City: May 1, 1891), 3.

29. "Arrested at Glenrock," *The Graphic*," (Douglas: August 1, 1891), 1.

30. Martin J. Gothberg, *Letter to Edward T. David, July 2, 1891*, David Collection, Casper College Western History Center.

31. "This Week Twenty Years Ago," *Natrona County Tribune*, (Casper: July 12, 1911), 4; "Local Notes," *Natrona Tribune*, (Casper: August 5, 1891), 4.

32. "Notice for Publication," *Natrona Tribune*, (Casper; July 22, 1891), 4; In his testimony, Martin stated that his house was fifteen feet by thirty-two feet with a twenty-by-twenty addition. He also claimed that he had built a barn and that both buildings were made of logs with shingle rooves. He estimated their value well in excess of four hundred dollars. Martin J. Gothberg, *Homestead Proof—Testimony of Claimant*, (US Land Office, Douglas: September 4, 1891); Land Patent, William P. Hines: #WYWYAA 011416, June 10, 1891.

33. "Local Notes," *Natrona Tribune*, (Casper: September 16, 1891), 4.
34. Casper's first church, the historic building was moved in later years to the Natrona County Fairgrounds and is often rented for special occasions. Jefferson Glass, "Founder of Evansville: Casper Builder W. T. Evans," *Annals of Wyoming: The Wyoming History Journal*, Autumn 1998, Vol. 70, No. 4, 20–22; "Nicolaysens Celebrate Wedding Anniversary," *Casper Daily Tribune*, (October 29, 1921), 3.
35. "Wedding Bells," *Wyoming Derrick*, (Casper: November 19, 1891), 1; Campbell, 8.
36. "County Notes," *Saratoga Sun*, (December 3, 1891), 3; "Local Notes," *Natrona Tribune*, Casper: December 9, 1891), 4; "Derrick Darts," *Wyoming Derrick*, (Casper: December 10, 1891), 8.
37. 1893 City Directory for Jersey City, New Jersey; Haines, FGR-1; "Local Notes," *Natrona Tribune*, (Casper: February 17, 1892), 4.
38. Death Certificate of Adolphena Gothberg, Haines, FGR-1.
39. "State Topics," *Bill Barlow's Budget* (March 16, 1892: Douglas), 5.
40. Local Notes," *Natrona Tribune*, (Casper: May 25, 1892), 4.

Chapter 3

1. Eugene Potter, "Wolcott, Frank and Adelaide," *Pages From Converse County's Past*, (Douglas: Wyoming Pioneer Association Converse County, 1986), 648–650; It is difficult to ascertain which Mr. Wister suffered more from: his incessant (likely migraine) headaches or the nightmares and hallucinations he experienced when taking the narcotics prescribed by his family physician to ease his pain. Regardless, the clean air and relaxed lifestyle of the American West became his cure, not only from the headaches but also from a probable addiction to the narcotics. He so loved his extended stay that he made numerous subsequent visits to various locations throughout Wyoming and the western United States over the subsequent several years. Ben Merchant Vorpahl, *My Dear Wister: The Frederic Remington-Owen Wister Letters*, (Palo Alto: American West Publishing, 1972), 17–20.
2. A few weeks before the invasion, Frank Canton deeded over the property he owned in Buffalo, Wyoming, to his sister for the consideration of one dollar. Potter, 648–650; Mokler, 344–362.
3. In an interview several years later, Gothberg remembered both men, though in his recollection he called Nate Ray, Harve Rae. Lewis, 5.
4. "Derrick Darts," *Wyoming Derrick*, (Casper: January 28, 1892), 8; "Personal," *Cheyenne Daily Sun*, (March 12, 1892), 3; "Quarter of a Century Ago," *Douglas Budget*, (April 5, 1917), 4; "Short Stops," *Bill Barlow's Budget*, (Douglas: November 23, 1892); "Personal and Local News," *Lusk Herald*, (November 24, 1892), 5; "Short Stories," *Cheyenne Daily Sun*, (October 8, 1892), 3.
5. "Local News," *Graphic*, (Douglas: July 11, 1891), 8; "Short Stops," *Bill Barlow's Budget*, (Douglas: February 24, 1892); "_____," *Bill Barlow's Budget*, (Douglas: July 6, 1892).
6. "Wild West Shows," *Boomerang*, (Laramie: August 25, 1892), 11.
7. "Historical Decennial Census Population for Wyoming Counties, Cities, and Towns," http://eadiv.state.wy.us/pop/citypop.htm; Glass, "Founder of Evansville," 21.
8. Glass, "Founder of Evansville," 20, 22–26; Lewis, 1.

9. Harold Hutton, *Doc Middleton: Life and Legends of the Notorious Plains Outlaw*, (Chicago: Swallow Press, 1974), 175–191.

10. "A Central Wyoming Celebrity," *Bill Barlow's Budget* (Douglas: April 5, 1893), 5; "Quarter of a Century Ago," *Douglas Budget*, (May 30, 1918), 4; To substantiate that Jerky Bill possibly performed in Chicago, it may have been there that he met Doc Middleton following the Chadron to Chicago race. "Black Hills Items," *Sundance Gazette*, (December 1, 1893), 3.

11. Beach, 334.

12. "A Journal 'Fake' Nailed," *Jersey City News*, (August 5, 1893), 3.

13. "City News Notes," *Jersey City News*, (August 9, 1893), 5; "E. Gothberg's Employees' Dance," *Jersey City News*, (August 21, 1893), 4; In a review of popular picnic sites in Jersey City, "On the slope of McAdoo Avenue, Greenville . . . is J. Gantner's Passaic Garden. The place is completely shaded by a grove of horse-chestnut trees. Its other attraction is a dancing platform." "Local Picnic Grounds," *Jersey City News*, (May 17, 1889), 2.

14. Land Patent, Louis A. Spalding: #WYWYAA 012143, August 14, 1893; Lewis, 4; "Town Topics," *Natrona Tribune*, (Casper: May 10, 1894), 3.

15. Mary Helen Hendry, *Tales of old Lost Cabin and Parts Thereabout*, (Lysite: privately printed, 1989), 10–13.

16. Brooks, 197–198; Edward Norris Wentworth, *America's Sheep Trails*, (Ames: Iowa State College Press, 1948), 321, 451–452.

17. Jefferson Glass, "Marvin Lord Bishop, Sr., Pioneer Sheep Rancher (1861–1939)," *Annals of Wyoming*, autumn 2000, Vol. 72, No. 4, 29.

18. "Hudson County Orphans' Court," *Jersey City News*, (December 1, 1893), 4; "Administratix Sale of Real Estate," *Jersey City News*, (July 14, 1894), 5.

19. "Greenville Gossip," *Jersey City News*, (January 2, 1894), 3; There is little known of Ariel Martin Childs. His father died before he was ten years old and he was twenty-three at the time of his marriage to Lillie. According to census records, his older brother Albert was a press-hand in a brass works. Ariel presumably fit comfortably into the Gothbergs' social circles. "Greenville Gossip," *Jersey City News*, (February 21, 1894), 3.

20. "Town Topics," *Natrona Tribune*, (Casper: May 10, 1894), 3.

21. "_____," *Natrona County Tribune*, (Casper: June 3, 1908), 6; "Town Topics," *Natrona Tribune*, (Casper: June 7, 1894), 3; "Town Topics," *Natrona Tribune*, (Casper: June 28, 1894), 3; "Town Topics," *Natrona Tribune*, (Casper: July 5, 1894), 3; "Town Topics," *Natrona Tribune*, (Casper: July 19, 1894), 3.

22. "Whirled to Death," *Jersey City News*, (June 13, 1894), 2; "In Greenville," *Jersey Journal*, (Jersey City: August 16, 1894), 7.

23. "Wyoming Wisps," *Salt Lake Tribune*, (Salt Lake City: May 6, 1895), 7; "Our Eastern Neighbors," *Salt Lake Herald-Republican*, (Salt Lake City: April, 22, 1895), 7.

24. "Sanders-Brandt," *Laramie Weekly Boomerang*, (January 7, 1886), 3; "Letter List," *Casper Weekly Mail*, (February 8, 1889), 6; "Local Notes," *Natrona Tribune*, (November 11, 1891: Casper), 2.

25. Haines, FGR-2; Edward L. McGraugh was the Natrona County Assessor in 1890–1894 and 1911–1914. He was a county commissioner for a time in the interim. Mokler, 10–11, 16, 292; The McGraugh ranch on Big Red Creek was one mile west

of the Sanders homestead on Pitchpine Creek. Land Patent, Edward L. McGraugh: #WYO180.077, December 27, 1895; Land Patent, Frank A. Sanders: #WYO270.445, December 17, 1903; "Martin Luther Brandt, a famous frontier lawyer written about in Bill Nye's book (in 1891) where Mr. Nye called him an 'eccentric jurist.'" Mohr, 3–4.

26. "Greenville Gossip," *Jersey City News*, (April 23, 1895), 4; "Wedding Bells," *Jersey Journal*, (Jersey City: May 2, 1895), 3.

27. "An Old Trick—How Gothberg Lost His Big Diamond Stud," *Jersey Journal*, (Jersey City: June 3, 1895), 1.

28. "Society Notes," *Jersey Journal*, (Jersey City: July 8, 1895), 5.

29. Glass and Haines, *Letter*, 2017, 2.

30. Mohr, 3–4.

31. There is no known record of Tom Horn being in Wyoming prior to 1892. He could not have visited the Gothbergs in 1885 when Martin built his first cabin nor in 1889 when he built the second. Chip Carlson, *Tom Horn: Blood on the Moon: Dark History of the Murderous Cattle Detective*, (Glendo: High Plains Press, 2001), 71–72; "Local Happenings," *Natrona Tribune*, (Casper: February 28, 1895), 5.

32. "Local Happenings," *Natrona Tribune*, (Casper: October 4, 1894), 5; "Unofficial Vote of Natrona Co," *Natrona Tribune*, (Casper: November 8, 1894), 1; "Cattle Cars Ordered," *Democratic Leader*, (Cheyenne: September 1, 1885), 3; "Stock Cars Ordered," *Democratic Leader*, (Cheyenne: October 9, 1885), 3; C. Kutac, "The Carlisle Cattle Company," http://www.elbowcreek.com/html/the_carlisle_cattle_company__c.html; Tales abound of a ring of cattle rustlers employed as respectable riders for the Hat-Six Ranch. The gang, who allegedly operated from the picturesque headquarters for several years undiscovered by their employers, may have contributed to the demise of the Carlisle brothers' success.

33. "Short Stops," *Natrona Tribune*, (Casper: July 11, 1895), 5; "Quarter of a Century Ago," *Douglas Budget*, (July 29, 1920), 6.

34. Meteorologist, *University of Wyoming, Agricultural College Department, Wyoming Experiment Station, Laramie, Wyoming, Meteorology For 1895, and Notes on Climate From 1891–1896*, Bulletin No. 27, (Laramie: 1896), 15–16.

35. "Lost in a Snowstorm," *Semi-Weekly Boomerang*, (Laramie: December 16, 1895), 8.

36. "Wedding Bells," *Jersey Journal*, (Jersey City: February 8, 1896), 8.

37. "Jersey City Mortgages," *Jersey Journal*, (Jersey City: July 14, 1896), 5; "Real Estate Works," *Jersey Journal*, (Jersey City: July 14, 1896), 5; "F. J. Koezley's Will," *New York Tribune*, (October 6, 1896), 7; *United States Census, 1900*.

38. Letter, Bob Devine to Hugh Patton, March 29, 1896. Cited in, Margaret Brock Hansen, Powder River Country (Kaycee: Margaret Brock Hansen, 1981), 430.

Chapter 4
1. "Throughout Wyoming," *Daily Boomerang*, (Laramie: February 25, 1897), 2.
2. "Memorial Day—Casper People Observe it for the First Time," *Natrona County Tribune*, (Casper: June 3, 1897), 1.

3. "City and County News," *Natrona County Tribune*, (Casper: July 1, 1897), 5; "_____," *Wyoming Derrick*, (Casper: July 22, 1897), 8; "Stock Movements," *Wyoming Derrick*, (Casper: September 16, 1897), 4.

4. "Land Lease Hearing," *Wyoming Derrick*, (Casper: August 5, 1897), 1 & 4; "City and County News," *Natrona County Tribune*, (Casper: August 26, 1897), 5; "City and County News," *Natrona County Tribune*, (Casper: September 9, 1897), 8; "_____," *Wyoming Derrick*, (Casper: November 11, 1897), 8; "Died," *Jersey Journal*, (Jersey City: August 31, 1897), 1; The fate of Lillian's widowed husband Ariel is sketchy. They apparently had no children together. Many years later, he was a real estate agent and remarried in Illinois. At the time, he again was widowed and like his mother before him, raising five children from his second marriage alone. He died in Decatur, Illinois, in 1940. *United States Census, 1920; United States Census, 1930; Illinois Deaths and Stillbirths, 1916–1947.*

5. "Glenrock Items," *Natrona County Tribune*, (Casper: October 7, 1897), 4.

6. "Large Sheep Shipments," *Wyoming Derrick*, (Casper: December 2, 1897), 1.

7. Mokler, 283–284; "Shot to Death," *Natrona County Tribune*, (Casper: June 3, 1897), 1.

8. "Shot to Death," 1. "Accused of Murder," *Cheyenne Daily Sun-Leader*, (June 7, 1897), 1.

9. "McRae Held for Murder," *Natrona County Tribune*, (Casper: June 10, 1897), 1; "Kenneth McRae's Trial," *Natrona County Tribune*, (Casper: November 18, 1897), 1.

10. Mokler, 284.

11. "_____," *Wyoming Derrick*, (Casper: March 3, 1898), 4; Haines, FGR-2.

12. "News of the West—Wyoming," *Salt Lake Herald-Republican*, (Salt Lake City: March, 24, 1898), 6; "Wyoming," *Salt Lake Herald-Republican*, (Salt Lake City: April 19, 1898), 5.

13. "Weekly Roundup," *Cheyenne Daily Sun-Leader*, (April 16, 1898), 4.

14. "_____," *Natrona County Tribune*, (Casper: May 12, 1898), 5; "_____," *Natrona County Tribune*, (Casper: May 26, 1898), 5.

15. The Gothberg family attended the Methodist Episcopal Church in Casper with the family of pioneer sheep rancher Marvin L. Bishop. Bishop often shared with Gothberg the potential advantages of raising sheep on his ranch over that of cattle. As beef prices continued to falter, Bishop further urged him to make the transition. With Bishop's influence along with the success of several other peers, Martin made his decision. Glass, "Marvin Lord Bishop . . ." 28–31; "Personal Mention," *Daily Boomerang*, (Laramie: June 06, 1898), 2; Campbell, 8; Lewis, 4; Bartlett, 260.

16. "Little Locals," *Natrona County Tribune*, (Casper: June 16, 1898), 8; Natrona County Clerk Abstract Book #1 R77–82 1890–1905; Glass and Haines, *Letter.*

17. "Little Locals," *Natrona County Tribune*, (Casper: June 23, 1898), 5; "_____," *Wyoming Derrick*, (Casper: August 18, 1898), 1, 5.

18. "The Democratic County Convention," *Natrona County Tribune*, (Casper: September 22, 1898), 1; "Democratic Convention," *Wyoming Derrick*, (Casper: September 22, 1898), 4; "_____," *Wyoming Derrick*, (Casper: June 30, 1898), 5; "Little Locals," *Natrona County Tribune*, (Casper: July 7, 1898), 5.

19. "Official Returns," *Natrona County Tribune*, (Casper: November 17, 1898), 1.

20. "_____," *Wyoming Derrick*, (Casper: September 29, 1898), 8; "_____," *Wyoming Derrick*, (Casper: July 27, 1899), 5.

21. "Personal and Local News," *Converse County Herald*, (Lusk: October 27, 1898), 5.

22. Land Patent, Martin J. Gothberg: #TC 0432-051 January 14, 1899.

23. "The Bittner Theater Company," *Wyoming Derrick*, (Casper: February 2, 1899), 5; "_____," *Wyoming Derrick*, (Casper: February 9, 1899), 5.

24. "_____," *Natrona County Tribune*, (Casper: December 29, 1898), 5.

25. "School 20 in Flames," *Jersey Journal*, (Jersey City: February 13, 1899), 1.

26. "Greenville Snowed In," *Jersey Journal*, (Jersey City: February 13, 1899), 1.

27. Glass, "Marvin Lord Bishop ..." 31.

28. John Brandt does not appear to be a sibling of Mary Enid (Brandt) Gothberg, but he did seem to reside near her family on Bates Creek. "_____," *Natrona County Tribune*, (Casper: April 6, 1899), 1; "Sheep Losses," *Wyoming Derrick*, (Casper: May 25, 1899), 1, 5.

29. "Sheep Losses," *Wyoming Derrick*, (Casper: May 25, 1899), 1.

30. Campbell, 8. "_____," *Wyoming Derrick*, (Casper: July 6, 1899), 4; "_____," *Wyoming Derrick*, (Casper: July 27, 1899), 5.

31. Charles Kelly, *The Outlaw Trail: A History of Butch Cassidy & His Wild Bunch*, (Lincoln: University of Nebraska Press, 1996), 239–248; Mokler, 318–323; "Robbery and Murder! Bold Bandits Flag and Rob the Union Pacific Flyer," *Bill Barlow's Budget*, (Douglas: June 7, 1899), 5; "Fight With Train Robbers—Robbers Still at Large in Powder River—Passed Through Casper Sunday Morning," *Natrona County Tribune*, (Casper: June 8, 1899), 1, 8.

32. "Robbery and Murder! Bold Bandits Flag and Rob the Union Pacific Flyer," *Bill Barlow's Budget*, (Douglas: June 7, 1899), 5; "Fight With Train Robbers—Robbers Still at Large in Powder River—Passed Through Casper Sunday Morning," *Natrona County Tribune*, (Casper: June 8, 1899), 1, 8.

33. "E. T. Payton's Story," *Cheyenne Daily Sun-Leader*, (June 7, 1899), 4; "Fight With Train Robbers ..." *Natrona County Tribune*, (Casper: June 8, 1899), 1, 8.

34. "E. T. Payton's Story," and "Sheriff Hazen," *Cheyenne Daily Sun-Leader*, (June 7, 1899), 4.

35. "Fight With Train Robbers ..." *Natrona County Tribune*, (Casper: June 8, 1899), 1, 8.

36. Mokler, 319–320; "Fight With Train Robbers ..." *Natrona County Tribune*, (Casper: June 8, 1899), 1, 8.

37. "Fight With Train Robbers ..." *Natrona County Tribune*, (Casper: June 8, 1899), 1, 8.

38. Mokler, 320.

39. Jefferson Glass, "The Sunny Sheriff—Joe Hazen left a deep hole in the heart of Wyoming after the Wild Bunch shot him down," *True West Magazine*, September 2017, Vol. 64, No. 9, 52–53; Bartlett, 260.

Chapter 5

1. "_____," *Wyoming Derrick*, (Casper: July 13, 1899), 5.

2. "_____," *Wyoming Derrick*, (Casper: July 27, 1899), 5.

3. Jean Lassila, editor, "Life in Natrona County, 1899–1900. Recollections of Myrtle Chalfant Gregg," *Annals of Wyoming*, Spring 1974, Vol. 46, No. 1, 117; "Little Locals," *Natrona County Tribune*, (Casper: October 5, 1899), 8; "_____," *Natrona County Tribune*, (Casper: October 5, 1899), 4.

4. "Wedding Bells," *Jersey Journal*, (Jersey City: February 24, 1900), 10.

5. "Local News," *Natrona County Tribune*, (Casper: March 22, 1900), 8; The *Wyoming Derrick* reported that Herman had married since leaving Wyoming the previous July. "_____," *Wyoming Derrick*, (Casper: March 22, 1900), 4; "_____," *Wyoming Derrick*, (Casper: September 6, 1900), 4.

6. "Little Locals," *Natrona County Tribune*, (Casper: January 25, 1900), 5; "_____," *Bill Barlow's Budget*, (Douglas: April 4, 1900), 5; "Mineral Land Contest," *Wyoming Derrick*, (Casper: April 5, 1900), 4; "Little Locals," *Natrona County Tribune*, (Casper: June 7, 1900), 5.

7. "Sheep and Sheep Men," *Bill Barlow's Budget*, (Douglas: May 2, 1900), 5; "Local News," *Natrona County Tribune*, (Casper: July 5, 1900), 8.

8. "Local News," *Natrona County Tribune*, (Casper: August 23, 1900), 8.

9. "_____," *Wyoming Derrick*, (Casper: August 16, 1900), 5; "_____," *Bill Barlow's Budget*, (Douglas: September 19, 1900), 7.

10. "_____," *Wyoming Derrick*, (Casper: September 20, 1900), 1; "Local News," *Natrona County Tribune*, (Casper: October 18, 1900), 12.

11. "Hotel Arrivals," *Salt Lake Herald-Republican*, (Salt Lake City: January 17, 1901), 6; "La Grippe," *Natrona County Tribune*, (Casper: January 31, 1901), 5.

12. "Local News," *Natrona County Tribune*, (Casper: January 31, 1901), 5

13. "Freeland Notes," *Natrona County Tribune*, (Casper: February 21, 1901), 8.

14. Haines, FGR-2; "Society Notes," *Jersey Journal*, (Jersey City: July 15, 1901), 7; "_____," *Natrona County Tribune*, (Casper: September 12, 1901), 1.

15. "Glenrock News," *Bill Barlow's Budget*, (Douglas: November 20, 1901), 4; "_____," *Natrona County Tribune*, (Casper: December 5, 1901), 8.

16. "Woolgrowers Meet," *Natrona County Tribune*, (Casper: December 5, 1901), 1.

17. "Woolgrowers Meet," *Natrona County Tribune*, (Casper: February 27, 1902), 5.

18. "This 'Detective' Came to Grief," *Jersey Journal*, (Jersey City: April 21, 1902), 12.

19. Vorpahl, 303–308; "'Virginian' Characters Get a Write-up From the Eastern Newspaper Correspondents," *Lander Eagle*, (October 20, 1911), 1.

20. "Was Writing Fiction and not Geography," *Wyoming Oil World*, (Casper: May 14, 1921), 3.

21. "Bates Park Telephone," *Natrona County Tribune*, (Casper: May 29, 1902), 1.

22. "Local Telephone Lines," *Wyoming Derrick*, (Casper: August 7, 1902), 1.

23. "_____," *Wyoming Derrick*, (Casper: July 31, 1902), 5.

24. "_____," *Natrona County Tribune*, (Casper: August 28, 1902), 5.

25. "_____," *Wyoming Derrick*, (Casper: July 17, 1902), 5. "_____," *Wyoming Derrick*, (Casper: September 18, 1902), 5; "Vote for Decency . . . ," *Casper Daily Tribune*, (November 07, 1921), 7.

26. "Court in Session," *Wyoming Derrick*, (Casper: December 4, 1902), 1; "Murphy's Trial," *Wyoming Derrick*, (Casper: July 30, 1903), 1; "Murphy Murder Trial," *Natrona County Tribune*, (Casper: July 30, 1903), 1; Mokler, 291–292.

27. *Sixth Biennial Report of the State Engineer to the Governor of Wyoming for the Years 1901 and 1902*, (Laramie: 1902), 120, 130.

28. "Stock Shipments," *Natrona County Tribune*, (Casper: October 2, 1902), 1; "_____,"
Natrona County Tribune, (Casper: November 13, 1902), 5; "Gothberg . . . ," *Casper
Tribune-Herald*, October 22, 1947, 2; Campbell, 8;

29. "Operation on Mr. Gothberg," *Jersey City News*, (October 23, 1902), 4.

30. "Freeland Telephone Line Completed," *Natrona County Tribune*, (Casper: December
25, 1902), 1.

31. "_____," *Natrona County Tribune*, (Casper: November 13, 1902), 8; "In Realms of
Society," *Natrona County Tribune*, (Casper: December 11, 1902), 4; "Society," *Wyoming
Derrick*, (Casper: January 8, 1903), 8.

32. "_____," *Wyoming Derrick*, (Casper: January 15, 1903), 8; "Vote for Decency . . . ,"
Casper Daily Tribune, (November 7, 1921), 7; "_____," *Natrona County Tribune*,
(Casper: January 15, 1903), 4.

33. "His Automobile Went on Rampage," *Jersey Journal*, (Jersey City: March 20, 1903), 6.

34. "_____," *Natrona County Tribune*, (Casper: April 9, 1903), 5; "_____," *Natrona
County Tribune*, (Casper: April 16, 1903), 9; "Vote for Decency . . . ," *Casper Daily Tri-
bune*, (November 7, 1921), 7; "_____," *Wyoming Derrick*, (Casper: May 7, 1903), 5;
"_____," *Natrona County Tribune*, (Casper: May 14, 1903), 8.

35. "Selling Oil Lands," *Rawlins Republican*, (October 22, 1902), 1; "Oil Men Meet,"
Wyoming Derrick, (Casper: January 8, 1903), 1; "Will Drill Oil Wells at Alcova," *Natrona
County Tribune*, (Casper: April 16, 1903), 8.

36. "Murphy Trial," *Wyoming Derrick*, (Casper: July 30, 1903), 1; "Hung Jury," *Wyoming
Tribune*, (Cheyenne, August 4, 1903), 4; "The Evidence," *Wyoming Derrick*, (Casper:
August 6, 1903), 1, 8; Mokler, 291–293.

37. "New Corporations," *Wyoming Tribune*, (Cheyenne: July 31, 1903), 5.

38. "Greenville Motorists' Trip," *Jersey Journal*, (Jersey City: July 7, 1903), 3.

39. "Mining Notes," *Rawlins Semi-Weekly Republican*, (September 20, 1899), 2; "John
Landon Dead," *Wyoming Tribune*, (Cheyenne: August 21, 1903), 4.

40. "_____," *Natrona County Tribune*, (Casper: August 13, 1903), 5; "Death of John
Landon," *Wyoming Derrick*, (Casper: August 20, 1903), 1.

41. "Dam at AlcovaGovernment Reservoir Will Probably be Built at Grand Canyon-
Sheep to be Dipped," *Wyoming Derrick*, (Casper: August 20, 1903), 1.

42. "Alcova Hot Springs Of Central Wyoming," *Wyoming Commonwealth*, (Cheyenne:
May 10, 1891), 1; Urbanek, 8.

43. "A Health Resort," *Wyoming Derrick*, (Casper: September 3, 1903), 1; Land Patent,
Marion Wolf: #WYWYAA 014500, October 1, 1903; "_____," *Bill Barlow's Budget*,
(Douglas: November 11, 1903), 6.

44. Around 1893, the F, E & M. V. Railway discontinued regularly scheduled passenger
trains between these points due to lack of sufficient business. Passengers rode in appropriate cars coupled with freight cars for about ten years. Mokler. 47; "Stock Shipments,"
Natrona County Tribune, (Casper: September 24, 1903), 1; "Children Must Stay Away
from Stock Yards," *Natrona County Tribune*, (Casper: September 24, 1903), 1.

45. "Society Notes—Greenville," *Jersey Journal*, (Jersey City: October 17, 1903), 10.

46. "Improvements at Alcova," *Wyoming Derrick*, (Casper: November 19, 1903), 1.

47. Land Patent, Frank A. Sanders: #WYWYAA 012062, December 17, 1903; "United States Land Office," *Natrona County Tribune*, (Casper: February 4, 1904), 4; Land Patent, Martin J. Gothberg: #WYWYAA 012082, April 13, 1908.

Chapter 6
1. "Prospects Good," *Wyoming Tribune*, (Cheyenne: January 25, 1904), 2.
2. "_____," *Natrona County Tribune*, (Casper: January 28, 1904), 5; "Society," *Natrona County Tribune*, (Casper: February 4, 1904), 8.
3. Mokler, 327–328.
4. "O'Day's Third Trial," *Natrona County Tribune*, (Casper: February 25, 1904), 1; Mokler, 328; "O'Day Gets Six Years," *Natrona County Tribune*, (Casper: March 3, 1904), 1.
5. "_____," *Wyoming Derrick*, (Casper: February 25, 1904), 5; "_____," *Natrona County Tribune*, (Casper: March 3, 1904), 5; "Lander for Casper," *Wyoming Derrick*, (Casper: March 10, 1904), 1; "_____," *Natrona County Tribune*, (Casper: March 31, 1904), 5; "Vote for Decency and Municipal Economy," *Casper Daily Tribune*, (November 07, 1921), 7; "_____," *Wyoming Derrick*, (Casper: March 17, 1904), 5.
6. "_____," *Natrona County Tribune*, (Casper: April 7, 1904), 5.
7. Ibid., 5; "Stock & Range," *Wyoming Derrick*, (Casper: May 5, 1904), 1; "Personal Paragraphs," *Laramie Republican*, (May 17, 1904), 4; "Local Brevities," *Laramie Boomerang*, (May 18, 1904), 4.
8. "_____," *Natrona County Tribune*, (Casper: May 26, 1904), 5; "_____," *Wyoming Derrick*, (Casper: June 2, 1904), 5.
9. "_____," *Wyoming Derrick*, (Casper: June 9, 1904), 5.
10. Mokler, 75; "The Railroad is Getting Interested," *Natrona County Tribune*, (Casper: June 16, 1904), 1.
11. "Society Notes—Lower Jersey City," *Jersey Journal*, (Jersey City: June 27, 1904), 10; Clinton Gothberg Fuller was born November 25, 1898 in Attleboro. *Massachusetts Births, 1841–1915*, database with images, *FamilySearch*.
12. "'Molly' Wolf Married," *Natrona County Tribune*, (Casper: July 14, 1904), 4; *United States Census, 1900*, database with images, *FamilySearch*.
13. "Brooks: His Life and His Labors," *Natrona County Tribune*, (Casper: August 25, 1904), 6.
14. "Casper Man Will go to Penitentiary," *Cheyenne Daily Leader* (July 30, 1904), 6; "_____," *Wyoming Derrick*, (Casper: September 24, 1903), 5.
15. "Children Not Wanted at the Stock Yards," *Natrona County Tribune*, (Casper: September 1, 1904), 1.
16. "The Big Industrial Convention is Now On," *Natrona County Tribune*, (Casper: September 22, 1904), 1; "Ranchmen Will Exhibition," *Wyoming Derrick*, (Casper: September 8, 1904), 8; "Wyoming State Fair," *Bill Barlow's Budget*, (Douglas: July 9, 1902), 6; "_____," *Grand Encampment Herald*, (October 7, 1904), 2.
17. "_____," *Natrona County Tribune*, (Casper: June 9, 1904), 5; "_____," *Natrona County Tribune*, (Casper: October 27, 1904), 5; "_____," *Natrona County Tribune*, (Casper: January 29, 1908), 5.

18. "Mr. and Mrs. Willis E. Lund of Pearsall Avenue had as their guests Sunday, City Treasurer and Mrs. Louis McCloud of East Orange and Mrs. J. Van Note of Point Pleasant, N. J." "Society Notes—Greenville," *Jersey Journal*, (Jersey City: January 13, 1905), 12; "Arrested for Perjury," *Natrona County Tribune*, (Casper: January 19, 1905), 1.

19. "Case Against Gothberg Dismissed," *Natrona County Tribune*, (Casper: February 2, 1905), 5.

20. "Gothberg Dismissed on Perjury Charge," *Cheyenne Daily Leader*, (February 4, 1905), 1.

21. Mokler, 75–76; Urbanek, 72, 89.

22. Mokler, 248–249.

23. "An Old Landmark Removed," *Natrona County Tribune*, (Casper: March 2, 1905), 1; Charles C. P. Webel was the same Webel who co-owned the Altman & Webel's Saloon at Fort Fetterman when Martin Gothberg and Lou Spalding first ventured up the Platte River twenty years earlier. Lindmier, 147–148, 182; Con Trumbull and Kem Nicolaysen, *Images of America—Casper*, (Charleston, SC: Arcadia Publishing, 2013), 45; Blackmore's Market on Second Street was later known as the Blue Front Market. "Vote for Decency . . ." 7.

24. "Vote for Decency . . ." 7; "_____," *Wyoming Derrick*, (Casper: March 2, 1905), 5; "Wholesale House," *Wyoming Derrick*, (Casper: April 13, 1905), 1; "Commissioner's Proceedings," *Wyoming Derrick*, (Casper: April 13, 1905), 8; "Wholesale House," *Wyoming Derrick*, (Casper: April 20, 1905), 8.

25. "Survey Bought," *Wyoming Derrick*, (Casper: March 23, 1905), 1; "_____," *Natrona County Tribune*, (Casper: April 13, 1905), 5.

26. Mokler, 49; Glass, "Marvin Lord Bishop, Sr., . . .," 32.

27. "Bates Hole and Alcova," *Wyoming Semi-Weekly Tribune*, (Cheyenne: June 9, 1905), 2.

28. In fact, Martin Trout and William Wardlaw remained together off and on until Wardlaw's capture.

29. "Headed For Hole-In-Wall," *Cheyenne Daily Leader*, (May 16, 1905), 8; "Prisoners Escape," *Wyoming Derrick*, (Casper: May 18, 1905), 1 & 8; "Wardlaw's Story," *Wyoming Derrick*, (Casper: May 18, 1905), 8; Prisoners Break Jail," *Natrona County Tribune*, (Casper: May 18, 1905), 1 & 4; "Offered a Reward," *Wyoming Tribune*, (Cheyenne: February 11, 1910), 2.

30. Glass and Haines, *Letter*; *Wyoming State Business Directory, 1910–1911*, 159 Cited in, Glass, "The Founder of Evansville . . ." 26.

31. Haines, FGR-2; Land Patent, Martin J. Gothberg, and John Billingsly: #WYWYAA 012079, May 23, 1905; "_____," *Natrona County Tribune*, (Casper: June 1, 1905), 1.

32. "The Trail at Portland Will be the Best Ever," *Wyoming Tribune*, (Cheyenne: May 16, 1905), 1.

33. "Bates Hole and Alcova," 2.

34. "Stock Shipments," *Natrona County Tribune*, (Casper: October 19, 1905), 1.

35. "_____," *Natrona County Tribune*, (Casper: June 22, 1905), 5.

36. "The Big Parade," *Natrona County Tribune*, (Casper: June 22, 1905), 1; "Will Be Well Treated," *Wyoming Tribune*, (Casper: June 27, 1905), 8; "Society Notes—Bergen," *Jersey Journal*, (Jersey City: July 3, 1905), 8.

37. "Alcova," *Wyoming Derrick*, (Casper: July 13, 1905), 1; "_____," *Wyoming Derrick*, (Casper: July 13, 1905), 5.

38. "District Court News," *Natrona County Tribune*, (Casper: July 21, 1905), 1; "_____," *Natrona County Tribune*, (Casper: July 21, 1905), 5; "'Jerky Bill' is Promoting," *Wyoming Tribune*, (Cheyenne: July 25, 1905), 8.

39. Mokler, 49; Glass, "Marvin Lord Bishop . . . ," 32–33, 35.

40. "_____," *Natrona County Tribune*, (Casper: August 24, 1905), 5; "Miller Wakes Up," *Wyoming Tribune*, (Cheyenne: August 21, 1905), 1; "Guy Holt the High Man," *Wyoming Tribune*, (Cheyenne: September 5, 1905), 1.

41. "Load of Logs Rolled Over Him," *Natrona County Tribune*, (Casper: August 31, 1905), 1.

42. "_____," *Natrona County Tribune*, (Casper: September 28, 1905), 5.

43. "Stock Shipments This Week," *Natrona County Tribune*, (Casper: September 14, 1905), 1.

44. "Proposals for Bids," *Natrona County Tribune*, (Casper: October 5, 1905), 3.

45. "Stock Shipments," *Natrona County Tribune*, (Casper: October 19, 1905), 1; "Bates' Park Items," *Natrona County Tribune*, (Casper: November 9, 1905), 1.

46. "Bates' Park Items," *Natrona County Tribune*, (Casper: November 9, 1905), 1; "Bates' Park," *Natrona County Tribune*, (Casper: December 7, 1905), 1.

47. "District Court," *Natrona County Tribune*, (Casper: January 18,1906), 1.

48. In 1905, the New Jersey State Census listed Willis E. Lund's occupation as "Jobber in Brass." *New Jersey State Census, 1905*, database with images, *FamilySearch*. "Society—Greenville," *Jersey Journal*, (Jersey City: March 3, 1906), 14.

49. This property being in her daughter's name may indicate the result of Martin's sister Teresa Koezly's effort to keep from losing it in bankruptcy; "Conveyances—Jersey City," *Jersey Journal*, (Jersey City: April 4, 1906), 13; "Conveyances," *Jersey Journal*, (Jersey City: April 23, 1906), 15; "Conveyances—Jersey City," *Jersey Journal*, (Jersey City: May 8, 1906), 13; "Building Contracts, Jersey City," *Jersey Journal*, (Jersey City: May 11, 1906), 15.

50. "Shriners Were Much Delighted," *Riverside Daily Press*, (May 9, 1906), 4.

51. "_____," *Natrona County Tribune*, (Casper: May 10, 1906), 5. "Railroad News Notes," *Natrona County Tribune*, (Casper: May 10, 1906), 5. "_____," *Natrona County Tribune*, (Casper: May 31, 1906), 8.

52. "Stocks and Bonds," *Jersey Journal*, (Jersey City: June 16, 1906), 6.

53. "Big Wool Sales," *Wyoming Tribune*, (Cheyenne: July 6, 1906), 7; Lewis, 4; Campbell, 8; Land Patent, Charles Stevens: #WYWYAA012015, April 14, 1906; Land Patent, Charles O. Stevens: #WYWYAA 015829, July 3, 1902; Land Patent, Charles O. Stevens: #WYWYAA 015830, December 1, 1905; Mohr, 3–4.

54. "Two Deaths at Pathfinder," *Natrona County Tribune*, (Casper: August 2, 1906), 1.

55. "_____," *Natrona County Tribune*, (Casper: August 2, 1906), 5.

56. "_____," *Natrona County Tribune*, (Casper: September 6, 1906), 5.

57. Campbell, 8; "Notice of Incorporation," *Natrona County Tribune*, (Casper: October 31, 1906), 4; Land Patent, Harry E. Parsons: #WYD 0001971, June 26, 1918; Land Patent, Noah Lindsey: #WYWYAA 012866, February 27, 1908.
58. "Commissioner's Proceedings," *Natrona County Tribune*, (Casper: December 19, 1906), 4; "Blackmore's Market," *Natrona County Tribune*, (Casper: December 19, 1906), 1.

Chapter 7
1. "District Court," *Natrona County Tribune*, (Casper: February 27, 1907), 1.
2. "_____," *Natrona County Tribune*, (Casper: January 30, 1907), 5; "Millinery and Dressmaking," *Natrona County Tribune*, (Casper: March 20, 1907), 5.
3. "Notice," *Natrona County Tribune*, (Casper: April 3, 1907), 5; "Want Water Rights," *Wyoming Tribune*, (Casper: May 7, 1907), 7.
4. "Caught in the Snow Storm," *Natrona County Tribune*, (Casper: May 15, 1907), 1.
5. Land Patent, Martin J. Gothberg and Franklin J. Deuel: #WYWYAA 012081, May 25, 1907; Land Patent, Martin J. Gothberg and James M. Silver: #WYWYAA 011715, May 25, 1907.
6. "_____," *Natrona County Tribune*, (Casper: June 12, 1907), 5.
7. "Northwestern Officials," *Wind River Mountaineer*, (Lander: June 14, 1907), 3; "Henderson Oil Wells," *Laramie Republican*, (August 13, 1907), 2.
8. "Northwestern Surveyors Working Towards Pinedale From Lander," *Pinedale Roundup*, (September 18, 1907), 1.
9. "Found Dead in Bed," *Natrona County Tribune*, (Casper: September 25, 1907), 1.
10. "Notice of Incorporation," *Natrona County Tribune*, (Casper: November 6, 1907), 8; Land Patent, John Harris: #WYWYAA 011702, October 22, 1908.
11. "Northwestern Lays Off Two Good Men," *Wyoming State Journal & Lander Clipper*, (November 22, 1907), 1.
12. "Missou's New Position," *Riverton Republican*, (December 14, 1907), 1; "Personal and Local News," *Lusk Herald*, (December 26, 1907), 5.
13. Westerners in Chicago," *Salt Lake Tribune*, (Salt Lake City: December 18, 1907), 9; http://www.encyclopedia.chicagohistory.org/pages/11591.html. In 1866, the entire building was raised four feet, two inches to accommodate a change in the grade of Chicago's streets. https://chicagology.com/prefire/chicagoillustrated/1866jul02/. Built in 1854 by William Briggs, Esq., the Briggs House burned to the ground in the Chicago fire of 1871. Reconstructed in 1873, owners utilized the same architect, John M. Van Osdel, who designed the original structure. https://www.greatchicagofire.org/landmarks/briggs-house/.
14. Land Patent, Mary E. Gothberg: #MV-0718-153, January 27, 1908; Land Patent, Mary E. Gothberg and Charles Stevens: #WYWYAA 012017, January 27, 1908; "Notice of Lands to be Leased," *Saratoga Sun*, (March 12, 1908), 3; "Legal Notice," *Natrona County Tribune*, (Casper: March 11, 1908), 8.
15. "Local Mention," *News Journal*, (Newcastle: February 7, 1908), 5; "Notice of Incorporation," *Natrona County Tribune*, (Casper: February 19, 1908), 4.
16. "_____," *Natrona County Tribune*, (Casper: February 5, 1908), 5; "Notice of Quarantine," *Natrona County Tribune*, (Casper: February 12, 1908), 4.

17. "_____," *Natrona County Tribune*, (Casper: April 15, 1908), 5. "Proclaims Quarantine," *Semi-Weekly Enterprise*, (Sheridan: April 3, 1908), 6.
18. "Killed Diseased Sheep, State Veterinarian Slaughters Bunch of Sheep With Incurable Disease," *Natrona County Tribune*, (Casper: May 13, 1908), 1.
19. "Democrats Nominate a Winning Ticket," *Cheyenne Daily Leader*, (May 14, 1908), 1; "_____," *Natrona County Tribune*, (Casper: June 3, 1908), 6.
20. "Wedding at Freeland," *Casper Press*, (July 3, 1908), 5.
21. "Charged with Stealing Sheep at Casper," *Laramie Republican*, (July 3, 1908), 3; "Lost on Prairie," *Wyoming Tribune*, (Cheyenne: March 14, 1906), 4.
22. "_____," *Natrona County Tribune*, (Casper: July 15, 1908), 7.
23. "Three Alleged Crooks Caught," *Cheyenne Daily Leader*, (January 28, 1909), 2; "District Court News," *Natrona County Tribune*, (Casper: January 20, 1909), 1; "Local and Personal," *Casper Press*, (June 25, 1909), 5.
24. "Resolution," *Natrona County Tribune*, (Casper: July 15, 1908), 5; "Young Fish from the Laramie Hatchery," *Laramie Republican*, (July 24, 1908), 3.
25. "The Western Inn," *Natrona County Tribune*, (Casper: July 22, 1908), 4.
26. "Notice," *Natrona County Tribune*, (Casper: July 22, 1908), 6.
27. "_____," *Natrona County Tribune*, (Casper: August 5, 1908), 6.
28. "Department of the Interior," *Natrona County Tribune*, (Casper: August 5, 1908), 4; Bartlett, 260; "Local News," *Natrona County Tribune*, (Casper: August 19, 1908), 1; "Town Council Proceedings," *Natrona County Tribune*, (Casper: September 16, 1908), 5.
29. Land Patent, Martin J. Gothberg and Grandeson Dorsey: #WYWYAA 012084, October 22, 1908; Land Patent, Martin J. Gothberg and William Shelton: #WYWYAA 012083, September 3, 1908; Natrona County Clerk Abstract Book #2 R77-82 1906–1917, 186; "Stock Shipments," *Natrona County Tribune*, (Casper: September 23, 1908), 1.
30. "Notice to Appropriators of Water," *Natrona County Tribune*, (Casper: November 4, 1908), 8.
31. "_____," *Casper Press*, (October 9, 1908), 8.
32. "Park Addition has Many New Homes," *Casper Press*, (December 11, 1908), 1.
33. Natrona County Clerk Abstract Book #2 R77-82 1906–1917, 186, 188.
34. "Quarantine Notice," *Natrona County Tribune*, (Casper: January 20, 1909), 4; https://parasitipedia.net/index.php?option=com_content&view=article&id=2541&Itemid=2817.
35. "Sheepmen's Meeting," *Natrona County Tribune*, (Casper: February 17, 1909), 1.
36. "At the Hotels," *Los Angeles Daily Herald*, (February 25, 1909), 13; *United States Census, 1910*, database with images, *FamilySearch*.
37. "Elizabeth Robinson Convicted," *Natrona County Tribune*, (Casper: February 10, 1909), 1.
38. "New Law is a Freak," *Natrona County Tribune*, (Casper: March 17, 1909), 1.
39. "Short Court Session," *Casper Press*, (July 16, 1909), 1; "Bond Forfeiture Set Aside," *Natrona County Tribune*, (Casper: August 11, 1909), 1.
40. "Lady Defendant," *Wyoming Tribune*, (Cheyenne: November 17, 1909), 2; "Elizabeth Robinson Case Reversed," *Natrona County Tribune*, (Casper: January 12, 1910), 4; "Court is in Recess," *Natrona County Tribune*, (Casper: August 3, 1910), 1.

41. "_____," *Natrona County Tribune*, (Casper: May 12, 1909), 5; "Blackmore & Gue Co. Sold," *Natrona County Tribune*, (Casper: May 19, 1909), 1; "Local and Personal," *Casper Press*, (May 21, 1909), 5.

42. "Please Settle Your Accounts," *Natrona County Tribune*, (Casper: May 19, 1909), 5.

43. "Win Their Point," *Casper Press*, (May 21, 1909), 1.

44. "Sheepmen Attention," *Natrona County Tribune*, (Casper: May 26, 1909), 5; "Sheepmen Attention," *Natrona County Tribune*, (Casper: August 18, 1909), 5.

45. "Sheepmen Attention," *Natrona County Tribune*, (Casper: July 7, 1909), 5; "Sheepmen Attention," *Natrona County Tribune*, (Casper: July 28, 1909), 5.

46. "Local and Personal," *Casper Press*, (June 18, 1909), 5.

47. "No Isle of Pines for Them," *Casper Press*, (July 9, 1909), 1.

48. "Missou Hines Selling Stock for a Casper Asbestos Mine," *Casper Press*, (June 25, 1909), 1.

49. "Additional Local News," *Casper Press*, (July 23, 1909), 4.

50. "Additional Local News," *Casper Press*, (July 23, 1909), 8.

51. "_____," *Natrona County Tribune*, (Casper: July 14, 1909), 5.

52. "_____," *Wyoming Derrick*, (Casper: July 9, 1903), 5; "District Court in Session," *Wyoming Derrick*, (Casper: July 16, 1903), 1; "_____," *Natrona County Tribune*, (Casper: August 4, 1909), 5.

53. "Local and Personal," *Casper Press*, (August 20, 1909), 5; "Local Mention," *News-Journal*, (Newcastle: September 17, 1909), 5; "Newcastle," *Sheridan Post*, (September 17, 1909), 8.

54. "Contest Notice," *Natrona County Tribune*, (Casper: August 25, 1909), 4.

55. "Local and Personal," *Casper Press*, (September 3, 1909), 5; "Lander's Leading Local Items of Interest to All," *Wyoming State Journal*, (Lander: September 10, 1909), 1.

56. "Bucks For Sale," *Natrona County Tribune*, (Casper: September 15, 1909), 5; "_____," *Natrona County Tribune*, (Casper: September 8, 1909), 5; "Notice of Appropriations of Water," *Natrona County Tribune*, (Casper: October 20, 1909), 5.

57. "_____," *Natrona County Tribune*, (Casper: October 27, 1909), 5; "Local and Personal," *Casper Press*, (November 12, 1909), 9.

58. "The Burlington Machine Shops," *Natrona County Tribune*, (Casper: December 8, 1909), 1; Alfred J. Mokler cited that all of the parties insisted on $150 per acre. The railroad then held the town at ransom threatening to build their facility a mile east of town. He made it sound as if when hearing this, the people of Casper raised by donation seemingly several thousands of dollars in subscriptions to appease the wealthy land barons with their greedy profits. In his rendition, you can almost visualize small children emptying their piggy banks into a barrel of cash in front of the courthouse, with tearstained cheeks, saving their town and families. Mokler, 53–54.

59. "Bought a Bates Hole Ranch," *Natrona County Tribune*, (Casper: December 8, 1909), 1.

60. Land Patent, George Madison: #WYWYAA 012085, May 17, 1909; Natrona County Clerk Abstract Book #2 R77-82 1906–1917, 186.

61. "More Local," *Casper Press*, (December 17, 1909), 4.

Chapter 8

1. "Local and Personal," *Casper Press*, (January 14, 1910), 5; "Wholesale House," *Wyoming Derrick*, (Casper: April 13, 1905), 1; "Blackmore is Back," *Casper Press*, (April 1, 1910), 8.

2. "District Court," *Natrona County Tribune*, (Casper: January 26, 1910), 1; Land Patent, Robert S. Weston: #WYWYAA 012158, June 9, 1910.

3. "Local and Personal," *Casper Press*, (January 14, 1910), 5; "Missou is Selling Asbestos," *Wyoming Semi-Weekly Tribune*, (Cheyenne: January 28, 1910), 3; "Oil Machinery Arrives," *Casper Press*, (February 18, 1910), 1.

4. "Local Events," *Natrona County Tribune*, (Casper: April 13, 1910), 1.

5. Though his position was that of a security manager, many considered him an "Enforcer" of William Fitzhugh and William Henshaw's will and their tyrannical rule of the California Oil Company's empire. Trumbull and Nicolaysen, 14.

6. "Will Enforce Hide Inspection Law," *Natrona County Tribune*, (Casper: July 20, 1910), 1. "_____," *Natrona County Tribune*, (Casper: July 27, 1910), 5. "Commissioner's Proceedings," *Wyoming State Journal*, (Lander: September 23, 1910), 4. "Commissioner's Proceedings," *Buffalo Bulletin*, (October 13, 1910), 1. "Commissioner's Proceedings," *Wyoming State Journal*, (Lander: October 14, 1910), 6. "Commissioner's Proceedings," *Buffalo Voice*, (October 14, 1910), 4. "Commissioner's Proceedings," *Wyoming State Journal*, (Lander: December 16, 1910), 6.

7. "Lightning Shocks Many People," *Natrona County Tribune*, (Casper: June 15, 1910), 1; "Narrow Escape from Lightning," *Casper Press*, (June 17, 1910), 1.

8. William Kittredge, *Owning it All*, (St. Paul: Greywolf Press, 1987), 26.

9. "_____," *Natrona County Tribune*, (Casper: August 17, 1910), 5.

10. "Stock Shipments," *Natrona County Tribune*, (Casper: September 7, 1910), 4.

11. Land Patent, Gothberg, Martin J. and Scott, Benjamin F and Scott, John D.: #WYD0000945, November 8, 1909; "Notice of Publication," *Natrona County Tribune*, (Casper: September 14, 1910), 4; Robert P. Fuller, Commissioner of Public Lands, *Appendix to Third Annual Report of Robert P. Fuller*, (Cheyenne: 1910), 47, 161, 163–164.

12. "Bucks For Sale," *Natrona County Tribune*, (Casper: November 16, 1910), 5; "Local Happenings," *Casper Press*, (December 16, 1910), 5.

13. "Commissioner's Proceedings," *Buffalo Bulletin*, (January 5, 1911), 4; "Commissioner's Proceedings," *Wyoming State Journal*, (Lander: January 6, 1911), 4; "Commissioner's Proceedings," *Buffalo Bulletin*, (February 16, 1911), 1.

14. "_____," *Natrona County Tribune*, (Casper: November 2, 1910), 5; "_____," *Natrona County Tribune*, (Casper: March 15, 1911), 5; "Local Happenings," *Casper Press*, (March 17, 1911), 5.

15. "_____," *Natrona County Tribune*, (Casper: May 3, 1911), 5; "Order," *Natrona County Tribune*, (Casper: June 21, 1911), 6.

16. "_____," *Natrona County Tribune*, (Casper: June 21, 1911), 7; "Flockmaster's Wife Injured," *Cheyenne State Leader*, (June 22, 1911), 2; "Local Happenings," *Casper Press*, (June 23, 1911), 5.

17. "Cashed Forged Check," *Natrona County Tribune*, (Casper: August 16, 1911), 1; "Forger Escapes," *Cheyenne State Leader*, (August 19, 1911), 2.

18. "All Over Wyoming," *Basin Republican*, (August 25, 1911), 5; "What's Doing Over the State," *Thermopolis Record*, (August 31, 1911), 3; "The Court is Working Fast," *Bill Barlow's Budget*, (Douglas: September 13, 1911), 1.
19. "Lightning Kills Herder," *Bill Barlow's Budget*, (Douglas: August 23, 1911), 7; "Herder Killed by Stroke of Lightning," *Laramie Republican*, (August 25, 1911), 3.
20. "Mortgages–Bayonne," *Jersey Journal*, (Jersey City: June 27, 1910), 13.
21. "Dr. Finn and E. Gothberg Better To-Day," *Jersey Journal*, (Jersey City: August 22, 1911), 1.
22. "E. Gothberg, Hurt in Auto Crash, Dead," *Jersey Journal*, (Jersey City: September 12, 1911), 1; "Funeral of Ernest Gothberg," *Jersey Journal*, (Jersey City: September 15, 1911), 8.
23. Land Patent, William I. Ogburn, WYWYAA #012150, May 12, 1903; Natrona County Clerk Abstract Book #2 R77-82 1906–1917, 190.
24. Mokler, 54, 253–254; "District Court Doings," *Natrona County Tribune*, (Casper: July 19, 1911), 1; "Dain not Guilty: Verdict Formed in Short Order," *Wyoming Tribune*, (Cheyenne: July 21, 1911), 7; "Local News," *Casper Record*, (November 14, 1911), 7.
25. "_____," *Natrona County Tribune*, (Casper: December 27, 1911), 5; "Personal Paragraphs," *Casper Record*, (January 2, 1912), 8.
26. "In Society's Realm," *Natrona County Tribune*, (Casper: December 13, 1911), 5; "In Society's Realm," *Natrona County Tribune*, (Casper: December 27, 1911), 1.

Chapter 9
1. "Casper Ten Years Ago," *Casper Herald*, (March 5, 1922), 4.
2. "Graduation Exercises," *Casper Press*, (May 10, 1912), 1.
3. "Local News," *Natrona County Tribune*, (Casper: May 15, 1912), 1; "Hotel Arrivals," *Cheyenne State Leader*, (May 15, 1912), 2.
4. "Commissioner's Proceedings," *Natrona County Tribune*, (Casper: July 10, 1912), 5; "Commissioner's Proceedings," *Casper Press*, (July 12, 1912), 1; "District Court Convenes Today," *Natrona County Tribune*, (Casper: January 16, 1913), 1; "Doings of the District Court Today," *Casper Daily Press*, (October 7, 1914), 1; About this time, Mollie Wolf received his first appointment as Bailiff for the District Court in Natrona County. He held other positions between court sessions, but continued to hold this office for over a decade. "First Cases Set for Trail by Court Today," *Casper Daily Tribune*, (March 1, 1921), 8.
5. "In Chancery of New Jersey," *Jersey Journal*, (Jersey City: June 25, 1912), 10.
6. "Mortgages–Jersey City," *Jersey Journal*, (Jersey City: February 1, 1913), 15.
7. "Apartments to let—continued," *San Francisco Chronicle*, (November 24, 1912), 29.
8. "_____," *Natrona County Tribune*, (Casper: September 11, 1912), 5; Ben H. Pelton, "Midwest Oil Company," *Annals of Wyoming*, Vol. 22, No. 1, January 1950, 91.
9. "Struck a Gusher," *Natrona County Tribune*, (Casper: October 9, 1912), 1.
10. "Natrona's Legislative Candidates," *Natrona County Tribune*, (Casper: July 24, 1912), 1; "1st Primary Election," *Casper Press*, (August 23, 1912), 1; "Campaign Expenses," *Natrona County Tribune*, (Casper: September 25, 1912), 1; "Unofficial Returns," *Natrona County Tribune*, (Casper: November 06, 1912), 1.

11. "_____," *Natrona County Tribune*, (Casper: November 6, 1912), 5.

12. "Notice of Incorporation," *Casper Press*, (December 13, 1912), 8.

13. Natrona County Clerk Abstract Book #2 R77-82 1906–1917, 191.

14. "Ade Irwin in Trouble Again," *Natrona County Tribune*, (Casper: September 11, 1912), 1.

15. "Arrest is Sensational," *Cheyenne Daily Leader*, (May 24, 1908), 1.

16. "Local and Personal," *Casper Press*, (August 07, 1908), 5; "Fugitives Returning," *Natrona County Tribune*, (Casper: September 30, 1908), 1.

17. "Ade Irwin in Trouble Again," 1.

18. "Judge Carpenter Dies," *Casper Record*, (December 31, 1912), 1. "District Court Convenes Today," *Natrona County Tribune*, (Casper: January 16, 1913), 1. "One Man Convicted, Another Acquitted," *Natrona County Tribune*, (Casper: February 06, 1913), 4.

19. "Captured Two Safe Blowers," *Natrona County Tribune*, Casper: March 20, 1913), 1.

20. Campbell, 9.

21. "Blackmore Oil Company Strikes Big Gusher," *Casper Record* (March 18, 1913), 1.

22. "Blackmore Company Gets Gusher," *Natrona County Tribune*, (Casper: March 20, 1913), 1.

23. "Blackmore Rig at Well No. 2 Burned Down," *Natrona County Tribune*, (Casper: June 5, 1913), 1.

24. "Hotel Arrivals," *Cheyenne State Leader*, (June 21, 1913), 5; "Hotel Arrivals," *Cheyenne State Leader*, (June 27, 1913), 5; "Notice of Foreclosure of Chattel Mortgage," *Natrona County Tribune*, (Casper: July 3, 1913), 8.

25. "Notice of Incorporation," *Natrona County Tribune*, (Casper: December 18, 1913), 5.

26. "Apartment House Next," *Casper Press*, (February 6, 1914), 1; "_____," *Casper Press*, (February 6, 1914), 5; "Vote for Decency . . . ," *Casper Daily Tribune*, (November 7, 1921), 7; Campbell, 8.

27. As they grew, the county moved the courthouse to its current location and the city changed the name of Fourth Avenue to "A" Street. Thus, the Ideal Apartments were located nearly across the street from the current courthouse and immediately north of the current Townsend Justice Center building. "Local News Notes," *Natrona County Tribune*, (Casper: March 12, 1914), 6.

28. "Apartment Contract Let," *Casper Press*, (May 8, 1914), 1.

29. "With the Motorists," *Natrona County Tribune*, (Casper: July 2, 1914), 6.

30. "Midwest Will Buy Hjorth Oil Company's Product," *Casper Daily Press*, (July 17, 1914), 1.

31. "Apartment House Next," *Casper Press*, (February 6, 1914), 1; "Apartment Contract Let," *Casper Press*, (May 8, 1914), 1; "Notable Improvements Show Growth of City," *Casper Daily Press*, (October 9, 1915), 25.

32. "Help Wanted—Male," *Jersey Journal*, (Jersey City: August 12, 1914), 11, 13; "Local and Personal," *Casper Daily Press*, (September 2, 1914), 4; "27 Cars of Sheep to Omaha," *Casper Weekly Press*, (September 4, 1914), 6.

33. "_____," *Natrona County Tribune*, (Casper: September 4, 1912), 5; "The Week's Doings," *Casper Record*, (September 10, 1912), 5.

34. "Local News and Personal Items," *Natrona County Tribune*, (Casper: October 1, 1914), 8.

35. Ibid. "Spray of the Oil Area," *Casper Record*, (October 13, 1914), 5.

36. Land Patent, Gothberg, Martin J. and Clarke, William: #WYD 0000337, November 27, 1914; Natrona County Clerk Abstract Book #2 R77-82 1906–1917, 271.

37. "William Clayton Frozen," *Douglas Budget*, (December 17, 1914), 1.

38. "Broncho Buster Badly Frozen," *Casper Daily Press*, (December 17, 1914), 1; "Nearly Freezes to Death," *Douglas Enterprise*, (December 22, 1914), 1.

39. "William Clayton Will Recover," *Douglas Budget*, (December 24, 1914), 3; "Performed Two Delicate Surgeries," Douglas *Enterprise*, (December 29, 1914), 1.

40. "William Clayton is Dead," *Douglas Budget*, (December 31, 1914), 1.

Chapter 10

1. "High School Notes," *Casper Record*, (March 23, 1915), 5.

2. "Spray of the Oil Area," *Casper Record*, (March 23, 1915), 5; "Local and Personal," *Casper Daily Press*, (April 15, 1915), 4.

3. "High School Notes," *Casper Record*, (May 18, 1915), 1; Chalmers automobiles were developed by Hugh Chalmers, former owner of the National Cash Register Company. The company later merged with the Maxwell Motor Company which eventually was absorbed by the Chrysler Corporation.

4. "Spray of the Oil Area," *Casper Record*, (June 08, 1915), 5; "Local and Personal," *Casper Weekly Press*, (June 25, 1915), 8.

5. "_____," *Casper Record*, (July 27, 1915), 5.

6. "Casper Brewing Co. Formally Organized," *Casper Press*, (February 27, 1914), 1. "Local News and Personal Items," *Natrona County Tribune*, (Casper: September 24, 1914), 4.

7. "Spray of the Oil Area," *Casper Record*, (April 27, 1915), 5; "Casper Brewery Opens Monday," *Casper Daily Press*, (July 24, 1915), 1; "Local and Personal," *Casper Daily Press*, (August 13, 1915), 4; "Local Happenings," *Thermopolis Independent*, (September 3, 1915), 12; "Local Happenings," *Thermopolis Independent*, (September 24, 1915), 8; "Local News," *Basin Republican*, (October 29, 1915), 2.

8. "Says East is Busy With War Orders," *Casper Record*, (November 9, 1915), 1.

9. "High School Notes," *Casper Daily Press*, (November 10, 1915), 2.

10. Land Patent, Martin J. Gothberg, Benjamin F. Thompson, George C. Houck, and Ira S. Lake: #WYD 0007686, November 19, 1915; This is the first known reference to Martin Gothberg that journalists identified him by the term *capitalist*. *Riverton Chronicle* cited in "Local and Personal," *Casper Daily Press*, (November 20, 1915), 4.

11. Lewis, 4; Campbell, 8; Mohr, 4; Fred Haughton's Sheep Creek Ranch seems to be that which was originally homesteaded by Novia Beaver in S. 23 & 24, T26N, R76W; Land Patent, Novia S. Beaver: #WYWYAA 010644, December 16, 1907.

12. "Personals," *Casper Daily Press*, (January 25, 1916), 4; "Personals," *Casper Daily Press*, (January 12, 1916), 4.

13. "Spray of the Oil Area," *Casper Record*, (April 18, 1916), 5.

14. "Obituary, Edwin H. Gothberg," *Jersey Journal*, (Jersey City: May 19, 1916), 9; "Twelve in 1916 Graduating Class," *Casper Record*, (May 23, 1916), 1.

15. "Drilling Company Files its Papers," *Laramie Republican*, (July 13, 1916), 3; "Notice of Incorporation," *Casper Weekly Press*, (August 4, 1916), 8.

16. "Automobiles—Motorists You Know," *Wind River Mountaineer*, (Lander: August 18, 1916), 4.

17. "Notice of Incorporation," *Casper Record*, (November 14, 1916), 5; "Notice of Incorporation," *Casper Record*, (December 19, 1916), 4.

18. Natrona County Clerk Abstract Book #2 R77-82 1906–1917, 250 & 305; Land Patent, John M. Hench: #WYWYAA 012966, May 1, 1906.

19. The Powder River Dome is also known as the Tisdale Dome. Carroll H. Wegemann, The Salt Creek Oil Field, Wyoming—Bulletin 670, (Washington: US Government Printing Office, 1918), 6; "Expense Is Without Limitations When Capitalists Seek Choice Holdings In Powder River Field," *Casper Daily Tribune*, (January 5, 1917), 1.

20. "Expense Is Without Limitations . . ." *Casper Daily Tribune*, (January 5, 1917), 1.

21. "Northwest Oil Co. Brings in its First Well in Big Muddy," *Casper Daily Tribune*, (January 20, 1917), 1.

22. "3 Corporations Filed Yesterday," *Cheyenne State Leader*, (February 3, 1917), 8; "Notice of Incorporation," *Casper Record*, (March 6, 1917), 6.

23. "Casper Petroleum Co.," *Wyoming Tribune*, (Cheyenne: April 25, 1917), 6.

24. "Dutton Moving Rig," *Natrona County Tribune*, (Casper: February 8, 1917), 8.

25. "Merry Party Friday at Jourgensen Home," *Casper Daily Tribune*, (January 8, 1917), 8.

26. Land Patent, Mary E. Gothberg: #WYD 0008465, March 10, 1922.

27. "City News," *Natrona County Tribune*, (Casper: March 1, 1917), 4; "Happy Party at High School," *Natrona County Tribune*, (Casper: March 1, 1917), 2.

28. "Wyoming State News," *Guernsey Gazette*, (March 2, 1917), 2; "Directors Elected for Two Hundred," *Natrona County Tribune*, (Casper: March 1, 1917), 8.

29. "Fords in Big Demand," *Casper Record*, (March 13, 1917), 3; "Used Car Clearance," *Casper Daily Tribune*, (June 16, 1917), 5.

30. Frank Severn Knittle was a surveyor and owned a lumber and hardware business in Douglas. Ed A. Reavill was a building contractor there. Ed Reavill constructed the LaBonte Hotel and many other structures in Douglas. Myrtle Reavill married Harry Stevick shortly after World War I. Robert A. Knittle, "Knittle, Frank Severn and Mary," *Pages From Converse County's Past*, (Douglas: Wyoming Pioneer Association Converse County, 1986), 333–334; John R. Pexton, "David, Edward and Mary," *Pages From Converse County's Past*, (Douglas: Wyoming Pioneer Association Converse County, 1986), 143; Richard VanDine, "VanDine, William and Pearl Family," *Pages From Converse County's Past*, (Douglas: Wyoming Pioneer Association Converse County, 1986), 608; Vera Saul Trumper, "Saul, Henry and Willard Families," *Pages From Converse County's Past*, (Douglas: Wyoming Pioneer Association Converse County, 1986), 521; Honey Stevick DeFord, "Stevick, Harry and Agnes," *Pages From Converse County's Past*, (Douglas: Wyoming Pioneer Association Converse County, 1986), 579; "Local and Personal," *Douglas Budget*, (March 8, 1917), 5; "Spray of the Oil Area," *Casper Record*, (March 13, 1917), 5; "Local and Personal," *Douglas Budget*, (March 15, 1917), 5.

31. "Incorporated Yesterday," *Cheyenne State Leader*, (April 6, 1917), 5.

32. https://en.wikipedia.org/wiki/World_War_I.

33. "Casper Petroleum Co.," *Wyoming Tribune*, (Cheyenne: April 25, 1917), 6.

34. The H & E Gothberg Manufacturing Company placed dozens of classified ads for help throughout the war, far too many to cite individually here. "Help Wanted—Males," *Jersey Journal*, (Jersey City: April 20, 1917 to September 19, 1918).

35. "Society," *Casper Daily Tribune*, (May 4, 1917), 8.

36. "Society," *Casper Daily Tribune*, (June 8, 1917), 3.

37. "City News," *Casper Daily Tribune*, (May 15, 1917), 5; "Notice of Incorporation," *Casper Record*, (May 15, 1917), 8.

38. "Blackmore Oil Co. Makes Big Deal," *Casper Record*, (May 22, 1917), 7.

39. "Blackmore Oil Slices Melon," *Cheyenne State Leader*, (June 15, 1917), 2.

40. "Preparing for Operations," *Natrona County Tribune*, (Casper: June 18, 1917), 6.

41. *United States Census, 1910*, database with images, *FamilySearch*; "Prairie Queen," *Chanute Times*, (June 16, 1911), 9; "Prairie Queen," *Chanute Times*, (July 7, 1911), 9; *Louisiana, New Orleans Passenger Lists, 1820–1945*, database with images, *FamilySearch*.

42. "New Pool Hall," *Basin Republican*, (April 21, 1916), 1; "Weeks Oil News," *Basin Republican*, (September 8, 1916), 1; "Bought Pool Hall," *Basin Republican*, (September 15, 1916), 4; "Oil News of the Week," *Basin Republican*, (February 23, 1917), 1; "Hardendorf—Cox," *Big Horn County Rustler*, (Basin: March 9, 1917), 4; *United States World War I Draft Registration Cards, 1917–1918*, database with images, *FamilySearch*; "Local News," *Big Horn County Rustler*, (Basin: April 19, 1918), 9; "Scouts Perfect Organization," *Natrona County Tribune*, (Casper: April 4, 1918), 3.

43. "Oil Notes," *Buffalo Bulletin*, (August 30, 1917), 1.

44. "Non-Partisan Ticket Named at Casper," *Laramie Republican*, (October 30, 1917), 7; "Dr. Leeper is Casper Mayor," *Wyoming Tribune*, (Cheyenne: November 7, 1917), 1.

45. "Atlas Resuming Drilling," *Wyoming Tribune*, (Cheyenne: November 19, 1917), 6; "Drilling is Resumed on Atlas Well in West Salt Creek," *Casper Record*, (November 20, 1917), 6.

46. Natrona County Clerk Abstract Book #2 R77-82 1906–1917, 250, 297, 331.

47. "_____," *Casper Record*, (November 27, 1917), 7. Bartlett, 260–261.

48. "_____," *Casper Record*, (December 11, 1917), 5.

49. "City Briefs and Personals," *Casper Record*, (January 1, 1918), 6; "Lusk Local News," *Lusk Herald*, (January 10, 1918), 1.

50. "Lusk Local News," *Lusk Herald*, (May 10, 1917), 1; "_____," *Casper Daily Tribune*, (June 28, 1917), 5; "_____," *Casper Record*, (August 28, 1917), 10.

51. Bartlett, 259–260.

52. Bartlett, 260.

53. "Dinner Party Given at Henning Hotel," *Casper Record*, (January 29, 1918), 3; Land Patent, Walter Storrie and Henry Lightle: #WYD 0010437, February 1, 1918.

54. It is unknown if Martin Gothberg approved of the marriage of his daughter and Walter Storrie. He attended neither the dinner party in their honor nor the sudden wedding. "Wyoming Men Given Denver Licenses," *Laramie Republican*, (February 5, 1918), 6; "Storrie-Gothberg," *Lusk Herald*, (February 21, 1918), 1.

55. "Sinclair Panama Oil Attracting Attention," *Casper Record*, (February 12, 1918), 7.

56. "Convention Closed Last Friday afternoon," *Douglas Enterprise*, (January 15, 1918), 1; "Omaha Paper Writes Up Hon. Missou Hines," *Thermopolis Independent*, (March 8, 1918), 6.

57. Jim Dahlman was among the riders listed to ride in the Chadron to Chicago Cowboy Horse Race in 1893. The reason for his absence from the final roster is unknown. "Omaha Paper Writes Up Hon. Missou Hines," *Thermopolis Independent*, (March 8, 1918), 6.

58. "Mrs. Louise Foster Entertains at Dinner," *Natrona County Tribune*, (Casper: April 11, 1918), 3.

59. "Casper Young Man Distinguishing Himself," *Laramie Republican*, (March 18, 1918), 7; "Is Going Just Fine," *Laramie Republican*, (March 22, 1918), 4; "The Game For L. H. S.," *Laramie Republican*, (March 23, 1918), 1.

60. Land Patent, Martin J. Gothberg and John W. Clark: #WYD 0008488, April 29, 1918.

61. "Lusk Local News," *Lusk Herald*, (June 6, 1918), 1.

62. "_____," *Casper Daily Tribune*, (July 11, 1918), 6.

63. "Toltec Dome to be Proven," *Wyoming Oil World*, (Casper: July 13, 1918), 1.

64. "Died," *Jersey Journal*, (Jersey City: June 3, 1918), 11. "Card of Thanks," *Jersey Journal*, (Jersey City: June 6, 1918), 11.

65. "Missou Hines Passes Fifty-Sixth Stepping Stone and Celebrates," *Casper Record*, (July 17, 1918), 1.

66. "Natrona Delphian Chapter Organized," *Casper Daily Tribune*, (July 29, 1918), 3.

67. Floyd C. Blackmore was only seventeen years old when he enlisted in the Army the youngest of all the men to join from Natrona County at the time. "Society," *Casper Daily Tribune*, (August 6, 1918), 6.

68. The term *Selectives* was commonly used for draftees into the Selective Service system in that era. "Mothers' League Gives Dinner at Midwest to Selectives," *Casper Daily Tribune*, (August 7, 1918), 4.

69. "City News," *Casper Daily Tribune*, (August 7, 1918), 4; "City News," *Casper Daily Tribune*, (August 16, 1918), 3.

70. "Oil News," *Laramie Boomerang*, (August 24, 1918), 6.

71. Teresa's daughter most often went by "Doretta." Some sources list her name as Doretta H. Koezly and others as Helen D. Koezly. Her obituary, cited here, used Helen Doretta Koezly. "Deaths," *New York Daily Tribune*, (August 28, 1918), 11.

72. "City News," *Casper Daily Tribune*, (September 3, 1918), 8; "City Briefs," *Casper Daily Press*, (September 4, 1918), 4.

73. "Natrona County Must Furnish Red Cross with 1,960 Pieces of Linen for Hospital Supply," *Casper Daily Tribune*, (September 28, 1918), 8; "County Completes Half of Quota," *Casper Daily Press*, (October 8, 1918), 1.

74. "Notice of Dissolution," *Casper Daily Tribune*, (November 6, 1918), 7.

75. "Nine Candidates Representing Four Political Parties take the Field for Municipal Election," *Casper Daily Tribune*, (October 12, 1918), 1; "Chief Wolf Be Major Issue in

Fall Municipal Election," *Casper Daily Press*, (October 13, 1918), 1. "Democratic Commissioners," *Casper Daily Press*, (November 3, 1918), 12.

76. "Tribune Overlooks City Attorney Who Received Greatest Vote at Recent Election, Taken as Slight," *Casper Daily Press*, (November 21, 1918), 1; "District No. 4 of Casper Gives McGraugh Majority . . .," *Casper Daily Tribune*, (November 7, 1918), 4; "Council Proceedings," *Casper Daily Press*, (October 12, 1918), 7.

77. "Last of Blackmore Family Leaves for Duty with Nation," *Casper Daily Press*, (October 27, 1918), 6; "Leone Blackmore off for Hospital Activity," *Casper Daily Press*, (November 9, 1918), 4.

78. "Miss Blackmore Enter Upon Duties in School of Vocational Training," *Casper Daily Tribune*, (November 29, 1918), 8; "Lusk Local News," *Lusk Herald*, (November 14, 1918), 1; "War Ended at 6 Today," *Wyoming State Tribune*, Second Extra, (Cheyenne: November 11, 1918), 1; "Society Organized Here for Protection and Help Little French Children . . .," *Casper Daily Press*, (December 1, 1918), 8.

79. "E. T. Williams Company Designates Itself as Publicity Agent for State," *Casper Daily Press*, (December 7, 1918), 2.

80. "Meeting of Women's Club," *Casper Daily Press*, (December 7, 1918), 8.

81. "Leone Blackmore Makes Good in Sanitary Corps," *Casper Daily Tribune*, (December 11, 1918), 5.

82. "Floyd Blackmore on Transport Arriving at Jersey Yesterday," *Casper Daily Tribune*, (December 19, 1918), 3.

83. "Society Events," *Casper Daily Tribune*, (December 24, 1918), 3.

Chapter 11

1. "Notice of Change of Capital Stock," *Casper Daily Tribune*, (February 28, 1919), 3.

2. "Missou Hines Returns From Ranger Field," *Casper Daily Tribune*, (February 22, 1919), 5.

3. "City News," *Casper Daily Tribune*, (November 18, 1918), 3; "Local Notes," Rawlins Republican, (January 23, 1919), 12; "Rawlins Paper Gives Details of Late Death," *Casper Daily Tribune*, (February 26, 1919), 2; "Takes Body to Kansas," *Rawlins Republican*, (February 27, 1919), 1.

4. "Natrona Short $600 in Drive for Near East," *Casper Daily Tribune*, (January 20, 1919), 8.

5. "Blackmore Wins Early Return as Member of Crack Company in the Anti-Aircraft Service," *Casper Daily Tribune*, (January 30, 1919), 6.

6. "Society," *Casper Daily Tribune*, (February 3, 1919), 3.

7. "Soldiers and Sailors Club Ready to Open," *Casper Daily Tribune*, (February 25, 1919), 3.

8. "City News," *Casper Daily Tribune*, (March 3, 1919), 6. "Mrs. Story Entertains at Informal Dinner," *Casper Daily Tribune*, (March 4, 1919), 4. "City News," *Casper Daily Tribune*, (March 15, 1919), 2.

9. "200 Club Gets Big Producer," *Casper Daily Tribune*, (March 3, 1919), 4.

10. "City News," *Casper Daily Tribune*, (March 27, 1919), 2.

11. "New Dancing Club Makes Debut Friday," *Casper Daily Tribune*, (April 8, 1919), 3; "City News," *Casper Daily Tribune*, (April 8, 1919), 3.

12. "Friday Night Dancing Club to Start Dance Series," *Casper Daily Tribune*, (April 11, 1919), 6.

13. "Big Carbon County Deal is Pending," *Rawlins Republican*, (April 24, 1919), 6.

14. "Bates Hole Spindle Top Dome Leased For Test," *Laramie Daily Boomerang*, (April 26, 1919), 6.

15. "Leone Blackmore Ill at N. M. Army Hospital," *Casper Daily Tribune*, (April 25, 1919), 8; "Miss Blackmore Improving," *Casper Daily Tribune*, (May 3, 1919), 6; "Society Events," *Casper Daily Tribune*, (May 22, 1919), 3; "Miss Blackmore, Reconstruction Aide, to Recuperate Here," *Casper Daily Tribune*, (May 23, 1919), 3.

16. "Notice of Dissolution," *Casper Daily Tribune*, (May 19, 1919), 7; "Notice of Dissolution," *Casper Daily Tribune*, (June 16, 1919), 2.

17. "Elaborate Arrangements for Military Ball Friday," *Casper Daily Tribune*, (May 6, 1919), 3; "Military Ball Tomorrow Night," *Casper Daily Tribune*, (May 8, 1919), 3.

18. "Society Events," *Casper Daily Tribune*, (May 6, 1919), 3.

19. "Gothmore Park is Resort for Casper People," *Casper Daily Tribune*, (July 11, 1919), 3.

20. "Gothmore Lots Sell Like Bargain Offer," *Casper Daily Tribune*, (July 14, 1919), 8.

21. "Casper Ranger Will Finish Well in July," *Laramie Daily Boomerang*, (July 18, 1919), 6.

22. "Transfers are Filed at Rapid Rate in County," *Casper Daily Tribune*, (July 31, 1919), 8; "Real Estate Transfers Still Lively," *Casper Daily Tribune*, (August 4, 1919), 4; "Real Estate Transfers," *Casper Daily Tribune*, (September 16, 1919), 8.

23. "Casper Ranger Has Good Well," *Wyoming Oil World*, (Casper: August 30, 1919), 1.

24. "City News," *Casper Daily Tribune*, (September 4, 1919), 3; "City News," *Casper Daily Tribune*, (September 5, 1919), 3.

25. "New Blackmore Apartment Ready by Thanksgiving," *Casper Herald*, (October 5, 1919), 10.

26. "Gothberg-Lewis," *Casper Herald*, (October 22, 1919), 5; "Gothberg-Lewis Marriage," *Casper Daily Tribune*, (October 22, 1919), 3; Haines, Gothberg, FGR-2; "Around the Town," *Casper Daily Tribune*, (October 13, 1919), 2.

27. "Notice of Special Meeting of the Stockholders of the Casper Ranger Oil Company," *Casper Daily Tribune*, (October 22, 1919), 3.

28. "Mrs. Sam Service to Head Red Cross Drive Starting Sunday," *Casper Daily Tribune*, (November 1, 1919, 4.

29. "Spindle Top Field Added Proven Class by New York Oil Company," *Casper Herald*, (November 22, 1919), 8.

30. "Poison Spider-Bolton Syndicate Benefited by New York Oil Strike," *Casper Herald*, (November 23, 1919), 1.

31. "Denver Livestock," *Denver Rocky Mountain News*, (November 29, 1919), 12; "Friday, Nov. 28," *Rocky Mountain News*, (Denver: December 4, 1919), 5.

32. _____, *Official Brand Book of the State of Wyoming*, (State Board of Livestock Commissioners, Cheyenne: July 1, 1919), 101.

33. "Personals," Casper Daily Tribune, (Decemebr 12, 1919), 3; "Will Enjoy Southern California During the Winter," *Casper Herald*, (December 13, 1919), 5; "Casper Ranger Rig to be Rebuilt Soon Texas," *Casper Herald*, (December 18, 1919), 3.

34. "Elect Directors," Wyoming State Tribune, (Cheyenne: December 22, 1919), 8.

35. "New Oil Company Formed to Drill Carbon County," *Casper Daily Tribune*, (November 28, 1919), 4; "Field Supt. Resigns," *Rawlins Republican*, (December 11, 1919), 1.

36. "Notes From the Osage Field," *Wyoming Oil World*, (December 20, 1919), 4; "Utah Test Projected," *Casper Daily Tribune*, (December 27, 1919), 4; "Notes From the Southern Fields," *Wyoming Oil World*, (Casper: December 27, 1919), 2.

37. "Will Enjoy Southern California During Winter," *Casper Herald*, (December 13, 1919), 5; "Students Returning From School," *Casper Herald*, (December 13, 1919), 5; "Gothberg Reunion," *Casper Herald*, (December 25, 1919), 7.

38. "Mr. and Mrs. Sam Service Will Entertain," *Casper Herald*, (January 1, 1920), 5; "Dinner in Honor of Mrs. M. J. Gothberg," *Casper Daily Tribune*, (January 2, 1920), 3.

39. "Casper Locals," *Casper Herald*, (January 1, 1920), 5; "Return From Delightful Shopping Trip," *Casper Herald*, (January 6, 1920), 5; "Return from Delightful Trip," *Casper Herald*, (January 14, 1920), 5.

40. "Report of New York Oil Operations," *Wyoming Oil World*, (Casper: January 3, 1920), 1; "New York Oil to Pipe Gas," *Wyoming Oil World*, (Casper: January 10, 1920), 1; "Encouraging News From Ranger Field," *Wyoming Oil World*, (Casper: January 10, 1920), 1.

41. The Texas Oil Company later became more widely known as Texaco. "Casper Ranger in List Big Earning Concerns," *Casper Herald*, (January 18, 1920), 3.

42. "Society Events," *Casper Daily Tribune*, (February 2, 1920), 3.

43. "Wyoming State News," *Manville News*, (February 5, 1920), 7; "Drilling Goes Slowly," *Wyoming State Tribune*, (Cheyenne: February 11, 1920), 9.

44. "Personals," *Casper Daily Tribune*, (February 24, 1920), 3; The 480 acres leased from Gothberg, Blackmore, Jarvis, and Weber by San Juan comprised three quarters of section 4, township 29 N., range 81 W. Martin Gothberg owned the other quarter of that section outright, purchased in 1906 from Pancake Charley Stevens. Portions of that section were presently leased to the Poison Spider-Bolton Syndicate. "Bolton Field Scene of New Lease Deals," *Casper Herald*, (February 26, 1920), 3; "Bolton Creek Land Leased," *Casper Daily Tribune*, (February 27, 1920), 4.

45. "Returning From Western Coast," *Casper Herald*, (March 9, 1920), 5.

46. "Personals," *Casper Daily Tribune*, (March 13, 1920), 3.

47. "Secure Leases in Bates Hole," *Rock River Review*, (March 5, 1920), 9; "New Field Manager," *Wyoming State Tribune*, (Cheyenne: March 10, 1920), 7.

48. "Personals," *Casper Daily Tribune*, (May 17, 1920), 3; "Warranty Deeds," *Casper Herald*, (April 14, 1920), 6; "Realty Transfers," *Casper Daily Tribune*, (April 17, 1920), 10; "Warranty Deeds Recorded," *Casper Herald*, (May 29, 1920), 6.

49. "Personals," *Casper Daily Tribune*, (May 20, 1920), 3.

50. Hardendorf was perhaps suffering from alkali poisoning such as Missou Hines had contracted in 1892 or a similar malady. "Personals," *Casper Daily Tribune*, (June 24, 1920), 3.
51. With his sudden death, William C. Blackmore left behind his wife and two adult children. He and Walt also had a half-brother who lived in Detroit, Michigan. It is unknown which of Walt's two sons piloted the Dodge to Rock Springs, but younger brother Floyd's expertise with machinery hints toward his candidacy. "Blackmore in Race With Time to Attend Brother's Burial in Cal.," *Casper Herald*, (June 8, 1920), 1.
52. "Iowa-Wyoming Oil Company to Take Over Syndicates," *Casper Herald*, (June 12, 1920), 4; "_____," *Casper Daily Tribune*, (July 3, 1920), 7.
53. "Gothmore Park Popular With Casper People," *Casper Daily Tribune*, (July 22, 1920), 1; "Lots in Addition to Gothmore Park Selling," *Casper Daily Tribune*, (July 22, 1920), 1.
54. "San Juan Petroleum Co.," *Casper Herald*, (August 5, 1920), 6.
55. The "guests from the east" were presumably members of Martin's family but remain unnamed. "Party Leave for Yellowstone," *Casper Daily Tribune*, (August 10, 1920), 3.
56. "Department of Interior," *Casper Herald*, (August. 28, 1920), 6. "Department of the Interior," *Wyoming Oil World*, (Casper: August 28, 1920), 2. "Department of Interior," *Casper Herald*, (September 1, 1920), 3 & 9. "Department of Interior," *Casper Herald*, (September 2, 1920), 3. "Department of the Interior," *Casper Herald*, (September 4, 1920), 4.
57. "Oil Notes," *Laramie Daily Boomerang*, (July 23, 1920), 3. "Field Work," *Cheyenne State Leader*, (August 12, 1920), 6. "New York Oil Company," *Wyoming Oil World*, (Casper: September 4, 1920), 2.
58. "Drilling Progressing Nicely," *Rawlins Republican*, (August 26, 1920), 1.
59. "Confidence Repaid When Oil Gushes Forth Liquid Wealth 'Grease' Breaks Bolton Dyke," *Casper Herald*, (September 4, 1920), 12.
60. "Recent Wells Are Close to Mike Henry," *Douglas Enterprise*, (September 7, 1920), 4.
61. "Auto Club Shows Membership Over 300 in Statement," *Casper Herald*, (September 11, 1920), 6; "Guests at the Connor Hotel," Laramie Republican, (September 21, 1920), 5.
62. "Return From Delightful Visit in the East," *Casper Herald*, (October 23, 1920), 5; By 1920, Martin Gothberg's mother resided with his sister Minnie Lund and her family in Monmouth, New Jersey. Clint and Sophia Fuller had also returned to live in Attleboro, Massachusetts, where Clint resumed his trade as a gold plater of jewelry. *United States Census, 1920*, database with images, *GenealogyBank*.
63. "Notice of Annual Stock Holders' Meeting," *Rawlins Republican*, (November 25, 1920), 8.
64. "Society," *Casper Herald*, (October 1, 1920), 5; "St. Mark's Scene of Impressive Wedding," *Casper Herald*, (October 13, 1920), 5.
65. "W. A. Blackmore 9 Days Overland Casper to Coast," *Casper Herald*, (November 25, 1920), 3.
66. "Turkey Dinner at Gothberg Home," *Casper Herald*, (November 27, 1920), 5.
67. "Oil Prospecting in Southern Utah," *Salt Lake Telegram*, (Salt Lake City: November 29, 1920), 10.

68. "Society," *Casper Herald*, (December 11, 1920), 5.

69. "Hardendorf Back from South," *Casper Daily Tribune*, (December 15, 1920), 4.

Chapter 12

1. "Hardendorf Goes Into Field on Inspections," *Casper Herald*, (January 12, 1921), 1.

2. "Missou Hines Now a Benedict," *Douglas Budget*, (January 20, 1921), 1; "Hines—Jackson," *Wind River Mountaineer*, (Lander: January 21, 1921), 1.

3. "Complimenting Bride-Elect," *Casper Herald*, (January 23, 1921), 7, "Announcement of Engagement is Made at Dinner Party," *Casper Daily Tribune*, (January 24, 1921), 3; "Personals," *Casper Daily Tribune*, (January 28, 1921), 3.

4. "Society," *Casper Herald*, (February 19, 1921), 5.

5. "At the Hotels," *Laramie Republican*, (Semi-Weekly ed.), (February 26, 1921), 7; "Personals," *Casper Daily Tribune*, (March 3, 1921), 3; "_____," *Rawlins Republican*, (March 17, 1921), 12; "_____," *Casper Daily Tribune*, (March 18, 1921), 9.

6. "Market Gossip and Field News—Casper is interested in Utah," *Casper Daily Tribune*, (March 15, 1921), 7.

7. "Personals," *Casper Daily Tribune*, (March 28, 1921), 3; "Petroleum Notes," *Salt Lake Mining Review*, (Salt Lake City: March 30, 1921), 31.

8. "Personals," *Casper Daily Tribune*, (March 28, 1921), 3.

9. "Many Companies in Field," *Casper Daily Tribune*, (April 2, 1921), 9.

10. "At Least Fifteen Rigs at Work in Utah," *Salt Lake Tribune*, (Salt Lake City: April 3, 1921), 27.

11. "Activity Grows in Utah Fields," *Casper Daily Tribune*, (April 8, 1921), 9; The Black Dragon Canyon of Utah, known for its spectacular pictographs and petroglyphs, earned its name from the giant image of a black dragon on one of its canyon walls.

12. "Lonabaugh a Lucky Cuss," *Big Horn County Rustler*, (Basin: April 8, 1921), 2.

13. "Missou Hines May Enter Movies," *Casper Daily Tribune*, (April 25, 1921), 8.

14. "Petroleum Notes," *Salt Lake Mining Review*, (Salt Lake City: April 15, 1921), 31; "Prominent New York Matron Visits Relatives," *Casper Herald*, (April 15, 1921), 7.

15. "Field Notes," *Wyoming Oil World*, (Casper: May 7, 1921), 3; "Personals," *Casper Daily Tribune*, (May 10, 1921), 3; "Progress in Oil Development is Rapid," *Salt Lake Telegram*, (Salt Lake City: May 15, 1921), 26.

16. "Summer Homes Being Built at Gothmore Park," *Casper Daily Tribune*, (June 8, 1921), 8; "Golf Picnic at Gothberg Park," *Casper Herald*, (July 19, 1921), 5.

17. "Personals," *Casper Daily Tribune*, (July 14, 1921), 3; "Oil and Gas Permits," *Douglas Enterprise*, (July 26, 1921), 9; "San Juan Petroleum Company Strikes Oil," *Rawlins Republican*, (August 4, 1921), 1; "Field Report of New York Oil Company," *Wyoming Oil World*, (Casper: August 6, 1921), 1.

18. "Personals," *Casper Daily Tribune*, (August 27, 1921), 3; "Spindle Top Test Contracted," *Casper Daily Tribune*, (September 3, 1921), 9.

19. "Society," *Casper Daily Tribune*, (June 8, 1921), 3; "Gothberg Party Return Home," *Casper Herald*, (August 16, 1921), 5; "Personals," *Casper Daily Tribune*, (July 14, 1921), 3.

20. Haines, FGR-6.

21. "Gothberg Party Return Home," *Casper Herald*, (August 16, 1921), 5; "Society," *Casper Daily Tribune*, (August 16, 1921), 3; "News in Brief," *Wyoming State Tribune*, (Cheyenne: August 10, 1921), 6; "Local Notes," *Rawlins Republican*, (August 11, 1921), 12; Dorothy Stitt was the daughter of Albert and Belle (Hamilton) Stitt. Haines, Gothberg, FGR-10; "Home Guest is Honoree," *Casper Daily Tribune*, (August 25, 1921), 3.
22. "Doug and Mary to be Acting in Wyoming Scenes Soon," *Wyoming State Tribune*, (Casper: August 25, 1921), 5.
23. "Society," *Casper Daily Tribune*, (August 30, 1921), 3.
24. "Personals," *Casper Daily Tribune*, (September 2, 1921), 3; "Gothberg . . . ," *Casper Tribune-Herald*, October 22, 1947, 2.
25. "Personals," *Casper Daily Tribune*, (September 22, 1921), 3.
26. "New York Oil," *Wyoming Oil World*, (Casper: September 24, 1921), 3; "Market Gossip and Field News," *Casper Daily Tribune*, (September 28, 1921), 6; "Personals," *Casper Daily Tribune*, (September 29, 1921), 3; "Examiner Looking Over Claims," *Wyoming Oil World*, (Casper: October 1, 1921), 1.
27. "Society," *Casper Herald*, (October 2, 1921), 5; "Personals," *Casper Daily Tribune*, (October 4, 1921), 3.
28. "Entertained at Gothberg Ranch," *Casper Daily Tribune*, (October 18, 1921), 3; "Personals," *Casper Daily Tribune*, (October 21, 1921), 3.
29. "What Mr. Gothberg Thinks," *Casper Daily Tribune*, (October 27, 1921), 2.
30. "Why we are for Blackmore," *Casper Daily Tribune*, (November 1, 1921), 2; "An Ancient Canard," *Casper Daily Tribune*, (November 1, 1921), 2; "Blackmore and Details," *Casper Daily Tribune*, (November 4, 1921), 6; "Vote for Decency and Municipal Economy," *Casper Daily Tribune*, (November 7, 1921), 7.
31. "Blackmore Elected Mayor," *Casper Daily Tribune*, (November 9, 1921), 1.
32. "Nicolaysens Celebrate Wedding Anniversary," *Casper Daily Tribune*, (October 29, 1921), 3; William T. Evans's first wife, Elizabeth C. Evans, died in Casper from blood poisoning August 21, 1894. Bill Evans married Wealthy Stanley in November 1900. Glass, "Founder of Evansville . . . ," 21, 23, 26.
33. "Stockmen Petition US to Sell Them All Wyoming Lands," *Wyoming State Tribune*, (Cheyenne: November 8, 1921), 3; "Stockmen ask to Buy Lands," *Casper Daily Tribune*, (November 8, 1921), 2; The concept of ranchers purchasing vast amounts of public land that they were using as open range was not new. In 1883, Charles Goodnight and fellow ranchers of the Texas Panhandle proposed a similar agreement with the State of Texas. In their circumstance, Texas owned the majority of public land, a carryover from annexation of the Lone Star Republic into the United States. The Texas Legislature passed the Land Board Act of 1883 allowing the sale of up to seven sections of land per individual. It also allowed for leasing of these rangelands, the lease rate specified at four cents per acre annually. When ranchers jumped at the opportunity, the state doubled the rate to eight cents per acre. A political nightmare ensued prompting Goodnight at one point to deliver his annual payment to the Land Board office with a wheelbarrow load of cash.
J. Evetts Haley, *Charles Goodnight: Cowman and Plainsman*, (Norman: University of Oklahoma Press, 1949), 381–401.

34. Populations of predators naturally regulate themselves dependent on the supply of food. Prior to the introduction of domestic livestock into Wyoming, predators relied on wildlife for food. Slow moving cattle and especially sheep were virtually defenseless and made easy prey compared to fleet antelope, deer, and elk, thus predator populations increased exponentially in the late nineteenth century and continued to grow. By the 1920s, depredations on domestic livestock were out of control. The number of predators eliminated by the trappers during the first three quarters of the year seems phenomenal. In actuality, it was a small percentage of the perceptible population. Duncan Paul Grant, "Memoirs 1881–1975," Wheatland, Wyoming, 6; The fact that Gothberg lost one thousand head of sheep near Glenrock that year indicates that his ranch had grown much more in Converse County than other sources suggested. "Stockmen ask to Buy Lands," *Casper Daily Tribune*, (November 8, 1921), 2.
35. "Stockmen Petition US to Sell Them All Wyoming Lands," *Wyoming State Tribune*, (Cheyenne: November 8, 1921), 3.
36. "Independent Oil Operators Discuss Wyoming Situation," *Casper Herald*, (November 10, 1921), 1–2.
37. "New Refinery With 20,000 bbls. Crude Capacity for Casper," *Wyoming Oil World*, (Casper: November 12, 1921), 1.
38. "New Refinery Site Purchased, Location East of City, Report," *Casper Daily Tribune*, (November 29, 1921), 1.
39. "Party at Gothberg Home," *Casper Herald*, (November 22, 1921), 5.
40. "_____," *Casper Herald*, (December 1, 1921), 2; "Work on Scout Cabin Making Fine Progress," *Casper Daily Tribune*, (November 22, 1921), 12; "Dedication of Camp Rotary is Scheduled for Coming Sunday," *Casper Daily Tribune*, (December 7, 1921), 1.
41. "Mountain Cabin Proves Cache for 95 Gallons Hootch," *Wyoming State Tribune*, (Cheyenne: December 12, 1921), 1.
42. "Personals," *Casper Daily Tribune*, (December 13, 1921), 3; "Boone Dome Drilling to be Resumed," *Casper Daily Tribune*, (December 22, 1921), 10; "Market Gossip and Field News—Storm Slows up Well Drilling," *Casper Daily Tribune*, (December 22, 1921), 10.
43. "Injured Foot of Oil Man Frosted," *Wyoming State Tribune*, (Cheyenne: January 15, 1922), 12; "Personals," *Casper Daily Tribune*, (March 30, 1922), 3.
44. "City Briefs," *Casper Daily Tribune*, (December 22, 1921), 3; "Dance Enjoyed at Ranch Home," *Casper Daily Tribune*, (December 27, 1921), 3; "Dinner Served at Gothberg Ranch," *Casper Daily Tribune*, (December 29, 1921), 3.

Chapter 13
1. "Reception to Be Followed by Novel Entertainment," *Casper Daily Tribune*, (January 5, 1922), 3.
2. "Rotary Club Receives Congratulations on 'Back to School' Aid," *Casper Daily Tribune*, (January 17, 1922), 4.
3. "To the Creditors of H. & E. Gothberg Manufacturing co., Inc.," *Jersey Journal*, (Jersey City: January 30, 1922), 12; "Receiver Sale," *Jersey Journal*, (Jersey City: February 15, 1922), 6.
4. "Says Sale Was Frame-Up," *Jersey Journal*, (Jersey City: February 21, 1922), 1.

5. "Almost Make Court Auctioneer," *Jersey Journal*, (Jersey City: March 21, 1922), 4.

6. "Gothberg Plant Sold Second Time," *Jersey Journal*, (Jersey City: March 30, 1922), 17; "Personal Taxrears, 1921," *Jersey Journal*, (Jersey City: March 30, 1922), 17; "Auction Sales," *Jersey Journal*, (Jersey City: March 31, 1922), 21.

7. "Council Proceedings," *Casper Daily Tribune*, (April 25, 1922), 4; "Valentine Party for Tonight," *Casper Daily Tribune*, (February 11, 1922), 3.

8. "_____," *Casper Daily Tribune*, (February 11, 1922), 4; "Mayor Returns," *Casper Daily Tribune*, (February 20, 1922), 4.

9. "Commissioners' Proceedings," *Laramie Republican*, (February 22, 1922), 5; "City Briefs," *Casper Daily Tribune*, (March 18, 1922), 3; With still no mention of Walter's marriage to Dorothy Stitt, it is presumed that the union remained unannounced. "Party Recognizes Birth Anniversary," *Casper Daily Tribune*, (March 21, 1922), 3.

10. "Casper Has Spent Limit for Lighting," *Daily Boomerang*, (Laramie: April 20, 1922), 6.

11. "Personals," *Casper Daily Tribune*, (April 29, 1922), 3; "My Mountain Cabin," *Casper Daily Tribune*, (April 28, 1922), 11.

12. "Notice of Incorporation," *Casper Daily Tribune*, (May 16, 1922), 7.

13. "San Juan Company Strikes Big Gusher in Bolton Creek Field," *Casper Herald*, (June 06, 1922), 3.

14. "Casper Wool Pool to Sell Wool at Auction with an Expert Present," *Laramie Republican*, (June 10, 1922), 8.

15. "Many Bidders in Casper for Big Wool Sale," *Casper Daily Tribune*, (June 15, 1922), 1.

16. "Wool Sale is Failure Here," *Casper Daily Tribune*, (June 16, 1922), 1, 10.

17. Ibid. 1, 10.

18. Gothberg's daughter Sis reported several years later that her father, Walt Blackmore, and a third party established the Buick dealership in Casper together. Early research suggested that Blackmore's son-in-law Walt MacGregor might have been the third man involved in the company. Later research indicated that Sis's ex-husband Walter Storrie and L. D. Branson collaborated with Gothberg in the business, suggesting that Walt Blackmore might not have been involved at all. Campbell, 8; "Buick Agency Changes Hands, New Home Here," *Casper Daily Tribune*, (June 14, 1922), 2; "Notice of Incorporation," *Casper Herald*, (June 27, 1922), 5.

19. "Pipeline From Bolton Field Held Assured," *Casper Daily Tribune*, (June 20, 1922), 1, 8; "Iowa-Wyoming Elects New Officers Here," *Casper Daily Tribune*, (June 29, 1922), 8.

20. "New York Oil Operations," *Casper Daily Tribune*, (June 30, 1922), 10; "New York Strikes Oil in Test Well in Spindle Top District," *Casper Daily Tribune*, (July 11, 1922), 8; "Spindle Top Oil Well Holds Good Promise," *Casper Daily Tribune*, (July 12, 1922), 10; "Wyoming Oil News," *Wyoming State Tribune*, (Cheyenne: July 31, 1922), 2; "New York Oil Operations," *Casper Daily Tribune*, (August 24, 1922), 6.

21. "Local and Personal," *Douglas Budget*, (July 13, 1922), 5; "Wool Men in Large Meeting," *Sheridan Post*, (August 3, 1922), 4; John R. Pexton, "Clelland, L. W. and Olive," *Pages From Converse County's Past*, (Douglas: Wyoming Pioneer Association Converse County, 1986), 114.

22. "Wyoming Refining Co. Calls in Stock, Will Liquidate all Claims," *Casper Daily Tribune*, (July 15, 1922), 10.

23. Glass, "Founder of Evansville . . ." 27.

24. Land Patent, Martin J. Gothberg, Mary E. Gothberg, Walter A. Blackmore, Minnie A. Blackmore, George W. Jarvis, O. D. Jarvis, Mark U. Weber and V. S. Weber: #WYD 0029388, September 20, 1922; #WYD 0029389, September 20, 1922; #WYD 0029390, September 20, 1922 and #WYD 0029391, December 13, 1922.

25. "Notice of Incorporation," *Casper Daily Tribune*, (November 23, 1922), 11.

26. "Nine Casper Men Will Do Jury Service," *Casper Herald*, (October 19, 1922), 1; "Notice for Publication," *Casper Daily Tribune*, (October 23, 1922), 8.

27. "Automobile News," *Casper Herald*, (October 15, 1922), 2; "New Exhibits at Arkeon to Charm Second Nighters," *Casper Herald*, (October 25, 1922), 6; "Tonight," *Casper Daily Tribune*, (October 26, 1922), 8.

28. "House Bandits Made Hauls in Two Cities," *Casper Herald*, (November 14, 1922), 1.

29. "Buick Into New Branson Edifice," *Casper Herald*, (November 19, 1922), 1.

30. Arthur Eugene Brandt married Ella sometime before 1918. Ella had a brother, Charley Stewart. It was also reported that her mother was living in Glenrock, Wyoming, at the time of her death. A two-year-old daughter, Mary, also survived her. "Operation Fatal To Mrs. Brandt," *Casper Herald*, (November 20, 1922), 1.

31. "Denied $1,400 Salary Claim," *Jersey Journal*, (Jersey City: December 19, 1922), 10.

32. At the time, engineers for the Wyoming North and South Railroad were making their final assessments of their course from Illco Station northwest of Casper to the Salt Creek Oil Field and beyond. Construction of the line from Miles City, Montana, south had already begun and a substantial group of wealthy investors envisioned soon connecting Casper, Wyoming, to the Montana cattle town by rail via Buffalo, Wyoming. That fall, they completed the first leg of the southern end of the line from Illco Station, between the communities of Cadoma and Bucknum, to the Salt Creek Oil Field. The towns of Edgerton, Midwest, and Salt Creek, Wyoming, as well as the communities of Lavoye, Snyder, and Teapot, Wyoming, all received service from the new railroad. The Illco Station presumably earned its name as a conjunction of sorts of the "Illinois Pipeline Company." Jim Brown, "The Wyoming North and South Railroad, 1923–1935." WyoHistory.org, 2016, accessed May 24, 2019 at https://www.wyohistory.org/encyclopedia/wyoming-north-and-south-railroad-1923-1935; "Casper Mayor Killed; Train Strikes Auto," *Buffalo Bulletin*, (April 26, 1923), 1.

33. "Casper Mayor Killed; Train Strikes Auto," *Buffalo Bulletin*, (April 26, 1923), 1; Beach, 334.

34. Land Patent, Edwin G. Gothberg: #WYD 0014103, April 30, 1923.

35. "Buick," *Salt Creek Journal*, (May 10, 1923), 8; "Settle Affairs of Gothberg Co.," *Jersey Journal*, (Jersey City: July 24, 1923), 16.

36. Mohr, 6.

37. "_____," *Casper Tribune-Herald*, (January 31, 1926), 16.

38. Land Patent, Walter Storrie: #WYC 0036847, January 31, 1927; Land Patent, Clinton G. Fuller: #WYC 0037974, March 9, 1927; It should be noted that Walt did not receive mineral rights with this land patent. Land Patent, Walter A. Gothberg: #WYC 0038879, January 30, 1928.

39. "Wyoming Highway Commission Sued," *Denver Post*, (July 15, 1928), 12.
40. Haines, *Gothberg*, FGR-8; *United States Census, 1930*, database with images, *Family-Search*; Land Patent, Adolphena Storrie: #WYC 0051644, October 29, 1930; Hilery Walker, *A History of The Gothberg Ranch*, (unpublished manuscript, Casper: 2003), 20.
41. Haines, FGR-2, FGR-8; Land Patent, Emma L. Gothberg: #WYC 0051627, October 12, 1931.
42. Mohr, 3–4.
43. Land Patent, Martin J. Gothberg: #WYC 0040643, January 4, 1932; Land Patent, Martin J. Gothberg: #WYC 0051628, February 9, 1932; Campbell, 9; Mohr, 4.
44. "Died," *Jersey Journal*, (Jersey City: June 25, 1934) 12; Mohr, 4.
45. Edwin studied at the University of California at Berkley where he earned a degree in engineering. From there he went to work for the Standard Oil Company, and then the Pacific Gas and Electric Company. Mohr, 4; Land Patent, Edwin G. Gothberg: #WYC 0053210, July 20, 1937.
46. "Drought Effect Worse in Wyoming Than '34," *Riverside Daily Press*, (August 4, 1936), 2.
47. Mohr, 4; Haines, FGR-2, FGR-8; Walker, 20–21.
48. United States Census, 1940, database with images, GenealogyBank; Land Patent, Adolphena D. Storrie: #WYC 0055034, January 31, 1940.
49. Land Patent, Jane B. McNelly: #WYWYAA 011712, December 20, 1904; Land Patent, Charles M. Hawks: #WYD 0004742, July 11, 1912; "See Ben Realty Co. v. Gothberg, 109 P.2d 455 (Wyo.1941), Wyoming Supreme Court," https://www.case mine.com/judgement/us/5914cbd4add7b049348057da.
50. "See Ben Realty Co. v. Gothberg, 109 P.2d 455 (Wyo. 1941), Wyoming Supreme Court, https://www.casemine.com/judgement/us/5914cbd4add7b049348057da.
51. Some sources cite the horse's name as Trigger II. It could be supposed that the young Gothberg chose the name "Trigger" to emulate the horse that rising matinee idol Roy Rogers rode in his B-movies. It seems, however, that Rogers's horse Trigger was then known as Golden Cloud and though ridden in several of Rogers's earliest movies, was not renamed Trigger until Rogers purchased the horse himself from the studio in 1943. Walker, 23; "Trigger (horse)," *Wikipedia, the Free Encyclopedia*, accessed May 28, 2019, https://en.wikipedia.org/wiki/Trigger_(horse). _____," *San Francisco Chronicle*, (October 6, 1941), 11.
52. Ibid., 11.
53. "Motor Pool Highlites," *The Slip Stream*, (Casper: December 23, 1942), 3. Mohr, 4.
54. General Chuck Yeager and Leo Janos, *Yeager: An Autobiography*, (New York: Bantam Books, 1985), 12–14, 20–24.
55. Yeager and Janos, 129–135; "Gothberg . . ." *Casper Tribune-Herald*, (October 22, 1947), 1.
56. "Gothberg . . ." *Casper Tribune-Herald*, (October 22, 1947), 1–2; Martin's grandson Edwin K. Gothberg claimed the ranch consisted of double that amount of land, plus an additional 30,000 acres, "out west." Those figures are not substantiated. Mohr, 4.
57. Mohr, 4.

Chapter 14

1. James C. Fuller, *The Wyoming Blizzard of 1949: Surviving the Storm*, (History Press: Charleston, SC, 2018), 11–13.

2. Fuller, 109, 113.

3. Fuller, 113–114.

4. Mohr, 4.

5. Walker, 20–21.

6. On October 19, 1965, Adolphena D. (Gothberg) Campbell died in Hemet, California. Haines, FGR-2; On October 27, 1975, Walter A. Gothberg died in Casper, Wyoming. Haines, FGR-10; On January 11, 1993, Edwin G. Gothberg died in Baker, Oregon, and on August 2, 1993, Emma L. (Gothberg) Evans died in Riverside, California. Haines, FGR-2.

7. "Gothberg Ranch Is Sold To Former Newspaperman," *Casper Tribune-Herald & Star*, (December 31, 1961), 4.

8. Conversation with the author, July 18, 2019.

Bibliography

BOOKS:

Bartlett, Ichabod Sargent, *History of Wyoming, vol. III,* (Chicago: S. J. Clarke Publishing Company, 1918).

Beach, Cora M., *Women of Wyoming, Vol. 1,* (Casper: S. E. Boyer, 1927).

Blevins, Winfred, *Dictionary of the American West,* (New York: Facts on File, 1993).

Brooks, Bryant Butler, *Memoirs of Bryant B. Brooks—Cowboy, Trapper, Lumberman, Stockman, Oilman, Banker and Governor of Wyoming,* (Glendale: Arthur H. Clark Company, 1939).

Brown, Larry K., *The Hog Ranches of Wyoming: Liquor, Lust and Lies Under Sagebrush Skies,* (Glendo: High Plains Press, 1995).

Carlson, Chip, *Tom Horn: Blood on the Moon: Dark History of the Murderous Cattle Detective,* (Glendo: High Plains Press, 2001).

Fuller, James C., *The Wyoming Blizzard of 1949: Surviving the Storm,* (Charleston: History Press, 2018).

Garton, Maud Kerns, "Word Picture of Old Goose Egg Ranch," *Casper Chronicles,* (Casper: Casper Zonta Club, 1964).

Glass, Jefferson, *Reshaw: The Life and Times of John Baptiste Richard,* (Glendo: High Plains Press, 2014).

Grant, Bruce, *The Cowboy Encyclopedia,* (Chicago: Rand McNally & Co., 1951).

Haley, J. Evetts, *Charles Goodnight: Cowman and Plainsman,* (Norman: University of Oklahoma Press, 1949).

Hansen, Margaret Brock, *Powder River Country: The Papers of J. Elmer Brock,* (Kaycee: Margaret Brock Hanson, 1981).

Hendry, Mary Helen, *Tales of Old Lost Cabin and Parts Thereabout,* (Lysite: privately printed, 1989).

Hutton, Harold, *Doc Middleton: Life and Legends of the Notorious Plains Outlaw,* (Chicago: Swallow Press, 1974).

Kelly, Charles, *The Outlaw Trail: A History of Butch Cassidy & His Wild Bunch,* (Lincoln: University of Nebraska Press, 1996).

Kittredge, William, *Owning it All,* (St. Paul: Greywolf Press, 1987).

Lindmier, Tom, *Drybone: A History of Fort Fetterman, Wyoming,* (Glendo: High Plains Press, 2002).

Mokler, Alfred James, *History of Natrona County Wyoming 1888–1922,* (Chicago: Lakeside Press, 1923).

Osgood, Ernest Staples, *The Day of the Cattleman*, (Chicago and London: University of Chicago Press, 1929).
Pages From Converse County's Past, (Douglas: Wyoming Pioneer Association Converse County, 1986).
  DeFord, Honey Stevick, "Stevick, Harry and Agnes."
  Knittle, Robert A., "Knittle, Frank Severn and Mary."
  Pexton, John R., "Clelland, L. W. and Olive."
  Pexton, John R., "David, Edward and Mary."
  Pexton, John R., "Douglas."
  Potter, Eugene, "Wolcott, Frank and Adelaide."
  Trumper, Vera Saul, "Saul, Henry and Willard Families."
  VanDine, Richard, "VanDine, William and Pearl Family."
Rollinson, John K., *Wyoming Cattle Trails*, (Caldwell: Caxton Printers, 1948).
Trumbull, Con and Nicolaysen, Kem, *Images of America–Casper*, (Charleston: Arcadia Publishing, 2013).
Urbanek, Mae, *Wyoming Place Names*, (Boulder: Johnson Publishing, 1967).
Vorpahl, Ben Merchant, *My Dear Wister: The Frederic Remington-Owen Wister Letters*, (Palo Alto: American West Publishing, 1972).
Wentworth, Edward Norris, *America's Sheep Trails*, (Ames: Iowa State College Press, 1948).
Wyoming Platte County Heritage, (Wheatland: Platte County Extension Homemakers Council, 1981).
Yeager, Gen. Chuck and Janos, Leo, *Yeager: An Autobiography*, (New York: Bantam Books, 1985).

Periodicals:
Deahl, William E., "Buffalo Bill's Wild West Show, 1885," *Annals of Wyoming*, fall 1975, Vol. 47, No. 2.
Glass, Jefferson, "Founder of Evansville: Casper Builder W. T. Evans," *Annals of Wyoming*, autumn 1998, Vol. 70, No. 4.
Glass, Jefferson, "Marvin Lord Bishop, Sr., Pioneer Sheep Rancher (1861–1939)," *Annals of Wyoming*, autumn 2000, Vol. 72, No. 4.
Glass, Jefferson, "The Sunny Sheriff–Joe Hazen left a deep hole in the heart of Wyoming after the Wild Bunch shot him down," *True West Magazine*, September 2017, Vol. 64, No. 9.
Lassila, Jean, editor, "Life in Natrona County, 1899–1900. Recollections of Myrtle Chalfant Gregg," *Annals of Wyoming*, spring 1974, Vol. 46, No. 1.
Mohr, Jo, editor, "Starting at Dobbin Springs: The Gothbergs, Pioneering, Ranching, and Art," *Casper Magazine*, Dec.–Jan. 1983, Vol. 5 No. 6.
Pelton, Ben H., "Midwest Oil Company," *Annals of Wyoming*, January 1950, Vol. 22, No. 1.

Newspapers:
"_____," *Bessemer Journal*, (August 1, 1889), Courtesy of Wyoming Newspapers, Wyoming State Library, http://newspapers.wyo.gov.
"_____," *Bill Barlow's Budget*, (Douglas: July 6, 1892), Courtesy of Wyoming Newspapers, Wyoming State Library, http://newspapers.wyo.gov.

"_____," *Bill Barlow's Budget*, (Douglas: April 4, 1900), Courtesy of Wyoming Newspapers, Wyoming State Library, http://newspapers.wyo.gov.

"_____," *Bill Barlow's Budget*, (Douglas: September 19, 1900), Courtesy of Wyoming Newspapers, Wyoming State Library, http://newspapers.wyo.gov.

"_____," *Casper Daily Tribune*, (June 28, 1917), Courtesy of Wyoming Newspapers, Wyoming State Library, http://newspapers.wyo.gov.

"_____," *Casper Daily Tribune*, (July 11, 1918), Courtesy of Wyoming Newspapers, Wyoming State Library. http://newspapers.wyo.gov.

"_____," *Casper Daily Tribune*, (July 3, 1920), Courtesy of Wyoming Newspapers, Wyoming State Library.http://newspapers.wyo.gov.

"_____," *Casper Daily Tribune*, (March 18, 1921), Courtesy of Wyoming Newspapers, Wyoming State Library. http://newspapers.wyo.gov.

"_____," *Casper Daily Tribune*, (February 11, 1922), Courtesy of Wyoming Newspapers, Wyoming State Library. http://newspapers.wyo.gov.

"_____," *Casper Herald*, (December 1, 1921), Courtesy of Wyoming Newspapers, Wyoming State Library, http://newspapers.wyo.gov.

"_____," *Casper Press*, (October 9, 1908), Courtesy of Wyoming Newspapers, Wyoming State Library, http://newspapers.wyo.gov.

"_____," *Casper Press*, (February 6, 1914), Courtesy of Wyoming Newspapers, Wyoming State Library, http://newspapers.wyo.gov.

"_____," *Casper Record*, (July 27, 1915), Courtesy of Wyoming Newspapers, Wyoming State Library, http://newspapers.wyo.gov.

"_____," *Casper Record*, (August 28, 1917), Courtesy of Wyoming Newspapers, Wyoming State Library, http://newspapers.wyo.gov.

"_____," *Casper Record*, (November 27, 1917), Courtesy of Wyoming Newspapers, Wyoming State Library, http://newspapers.wyo.gov.

"_____," *Casper Record*, (December 11, 1917), Courtesy of Wyoming Newspapers, Wyoming State Library. http://newspapers.wyo.gov.

"_____," *Casper Tribune-Herald*. (January 31, 1926), Courtesy of Wyoming Newspapers, Wyoming State Library, http://newspapers.wyo.gov.

"_____," *Cheyenne Weekly Leader*, (July 27, 1882), Courtesy of Wyoming Newspapers, Wyoming State Library, http://newspapers.wyo.gov.

"_____," *Grand Encampment Herald*, (October 7, 1904), Courtesy of Wyoming Newspapers, Wyoming State Library, http://newspapers.wyo.gov.

"_____," *Natrona County Tribune*, (Casper: December 29, 1898), Courtesy of Wyoming Newspapers, Wyoming State Library, http://newspapers.wyo.gov.

"_____," *Natrona County Tribune*, (Casper: October 5, 1899), Courtesy of Wyoming Newspapers, Wyoming State Library, http://newspapers.wyo.gov.

"_____," *Natrona County Tribune*, (Casper: September 12, 1901), Courtesy of Wyoming Newspapers, Wyoming State Library, http://newspapers.wyo.gov.

"_____," *Natrona County Tribune*, (Casper: December 5, 1901), Courtesy of Wyoming Newspapers, Wyoming State Library, http://newspapers.wyo.gov.

"_____," *Natrona County Tribune*, (Casper: August 28, 1902), Courtesy of Wyoming Newspapers, Wyoming State Library, http://newspapers.wyo.gov.

"_____," *Natrona County Tribune*, (Casper: November 13, 1902), Courtesy of Wyoming Newspapers, Wyoming State Library, http://newspapers.wyo.gov.

"_____," *Natrona County Tribune*, (Casper: January 15, 1903), Courtesy of Wyoming Newspapers, Wyoming State Library, http://newspapers.wyo.gov.

"_____," *Natrona County Tribune*, (Casper: May 14, 1903), Courtesy of Wyoming Newspapers, Wyoming State Library, http://newspapers.wyo.gov.

"_____," *Natrona County Tribune*, (Casper: August 13, 1903), Courtesy of Wyoming Newspapers, Wyoming State Library, http://newspapers.wyo.gov.

"_____," *Natrona County Tribune*, (Casper: January 28, 1904), Courtesy of Wyoming Newspapers, Wyoming State Library, http://newspapers.wyo.gov.

"_____," *Natrona County Tribune*, (Casper: March 3, 1904), Courtesy of Wyoming Newspapers, Wyoming State Library, http://newspapers.wyo.gov.

"_____," *Natrona County Tribune*, (Casper: March 31, 1904), Courtesy of Wyoming Newspapers, Wyoming State Library, http://newspapers.wyo.gov.

"_____," *Natrona County Tribune*, (Casper: April 7, 1904), Courtesy of Wyoming Newspapers, Wyoming State Library, http://newspapers.wyo.gov.

"_____," *Natrona County Tribune*, (Casper: May 26, 1904), Courtesy of Wyoming Newspapers, Wyoming State Library, http://newspapers.wyo.gov.

"_____," *Natrona County Tribune*, (Casper: June 9, 1904), Courtesy of Wyoming Newspapers, Wyoming State Library, http://newspapers.wyo.gov.

"_____," *Natrona County Tribune*, (Casper: October 27, 1904), Courtesy of Wyoming Newspapers, Wyoming State Library, http://newspapers.wyo.gov.

"_____," *Natrona County Tribune*, (Casper: April 13, 1905), Courtesy of Wyoming Newspapers, Wyoming State Library, http://newspapers.wyo.gov.

"_____," *Natrona County Tribune*, (Casper: June 1, 1905), Courtesy of Wyoming Newspapers, Wyoming State Library, http://newspapers.wyo.gov.

"_____," *Natrona County Tribune*, (Casper: June 22, 1905), Courtesy of Wyoming Newspapers, Wyoming State Library, http://newspapers.wyo.gov.

"_____," *Natrona County Tribune*, (Casper: July 21, 1905), Courtesy of Wyoming Newspapers, Wyoming State Library, http://newspapers.wyo.gov.

"_____," *Natrona County Tribune*, (Casper: August 24, 1905), Courtesy of Wyoming Newspapers, Wyoming State Library, http://newspapers.wyo.gov.

"_____," *Natrona County Tribune*, (Casper: September 28, 1905), Courtesy of Wyoming Newspapers, Wyoming State Library, http://newspapers.wyo.gov.

"_____," *Natrona County Tribune*, (Casper: May 10, 1906), Courtesy of Wyoming Newspapers, Wyoming State Library, http://newspapers.wyo.gov.

"_____," *Natrona County Tribune*, (Casper: May 31, 1906), Courtesy of Wyoming Newspapers, Wyoming State Library, http://newspapers.wyo.gov.

"_____," *Natrona County Tribune*, (Casper: August 2, 1906), Courtesy of Wyoming Newspapers, Wyoming State Library, http://newspapers.wyo.gov.

"_____," *Natrona County Tribune*, (Casper: September 6, 1906), Courtesy of Wyoming Newspapers, Wyoming State Library, http://newspapers.wyo.gov.

"_____," *Natrona County Tribune*, (Casper: June 12, 1907), Courtesy of Wyoming Newspapers, Wyoming State Library, http://newspapers.wyo.gov.

"_____," *Natrona County Tribune*, (Casper: January 29, 1908), Courtesy of Wyoming Newspapers, Wyoming State Library, http://newspapers.wyo.gov.

"_____," *Natrona County Tribune*, (Casper: February 5, 1908), Courtesy of Wyoming Newspapers, Wyoming State Library, http://newspapers.wyo.gov.

"_____," *Natrona County Tribune*, (Casper: April 15, 1908), Courtesy of Wyoming Newspapers, Wyoming State Library, http://newspapers.wyo.gov.

"_____," *Natrona County Tribune*, (Casper: June 3, 1908), Courtesy of Wyoming Newspapers, Wyoming State Library, http://newspapers.wyo.gov.

"_____," *Natrona County Tribune*, (Casper: July 15, 1908), Courtesy of Wyoming Newspapers, Wyoming State Library, http://newspapers.wyo.gov.

"_____," *Natrona County Tribune*, (Casper: August 5, 1908), Courtesy of Wyoming Newspapers, Wyoming State Library, http://newspapers.wyo.gov.

"_____," *Natrona County Tribune*, (Casper: May 12, 1909), Courtesy of Wyoming Newspapers, Wyoming State Library, http://newspapers.wyo.gov.

"_____," *Natrona County Tribune*, (Casper: August 4, 1909), Courtesy of Wyoming Newspapers, Wyoming State Library, http://newspapers.wyo.gov.

"_____," *Natrona County Tribune*, (Casper: September 8, 1909), Courtesy of Wyoming Newspapers, Wyoming State Library, http://newspapers.wyo.gov.

"_____," *Natrona County Tribune*, (Casper: July 27, 1910), Courtesy of Wyoming Newspapers, Wyoming State Library, http://newspapers.wyo.gov.

"_____," *Natrona County Tribune*, (Casper: August 17, 1910), Courtesy of Wyoming Newspapers, Wyoming State Library, http://newspapers.wyo.gov.

"_____," *Natrona County Tribune*, (Casper: November 2, 1910), Courtesy of Wyoming Newspapers, Wyoming State Library, http://newspapers.wyo.gov.

"_____," *Natrona County Tribune*, (Casper: March 15, 1911), Courtesy of Wyoming Newspapers, Wyoming State Library, http://newspapers.wyo.gov.

"_____," *Natrona County Tribune*, (Casper: May 3, 1911), Courtesy of Wyoming Newspapers, Wyoming State Library, http://newspapers.wyo.gov.

"_____," *Natrona County Tribune*, (Casper: December 27, 1911), Courtesy of Wyoming Newspapers, Wyoming State Library, http://newspapers.wyo.gov.

"_____," *Natrona County Tribune*, (Casper: September 4, 1912), Courtesy of Wyoming Newspapers, Wyoming State Library, http://newspapers.wyo.gov.

"_____," *Natrona County Tribune*, (Casper: September 11, 1912), Courtesy of Wyoming Newspapers, Wyoming State Library, http://newspapers.wyo.gov.

"_____," *Natrona County Tribune*, (Casper: November 6, 1912), Courtesy of Wyoming Newspapers, Wyoming State Library, http://newspapers.wyo.gov.

"_____," *Rawlins Republican*, (March 17, 1921), Courtesy of Wyoming Newspapers, Wyoming State Library, http://newspapers.wyo.gov.

"_____," *San Francisco Chronicle*, (October 6, 1941), Courtesy of Genealogy Bank, https://www.genealogybank.com/doc/newspapers.

"_____," *Sundance Gazette*, (September 5, 1885), Courtesy of Wyoming Newspapers, Wyoming State Library, http://newspapers.wyo.gov.

"_____," *Sundance Gazette*, (September 19, 1885), Courtesy of Wyoming Newspapers, Wyoming State Library, http://newspapers.wyo.gov.

"_____," *Wyoming Derrick*, (Casper: July 22, 1897), Courtesy of Wyoming Newspapers, Wyoming State Library, http://newspapers.wyo.gov.

"_____," *Wyoming Derrick*, (Casper: November 11, 1897), Courtesy of Wyoming Newspapers, Wyoming State Library, http://newspapers.wyo.gov.

"_____," *Wyoming Derrick*, (Casper: March 3, 1898), Courtesy of Wyoming Newspapers, Wyoming State Library, http://newspapers.wyo.gov.

"_____," *Wyoming Derrick*, (Casper: June 30, 1898), Courtesy of Wyoming Newspapers, Wyoming State Library, http://newspapers.wyo.gov.

"_____," *Wyoming Derrick*, (Casper: August 18, 1898), Courtesy of Wyoming Newspapers, Wyoming State Library, http://newspapers.wyo.gov.

"_____," *Wyoming Derrick*, (Casper: February 9, 1899), Courtesy of Wyoming Newspapers, Wyoming State Library, http://newspapers.wyo.gov.

"_____," *Wyoming Derrick*, (Casper: July 6, 1899), Courtesy of Wyoming Newspapers, Wyoming State Library, http://newspapers.wyo.gov.

"_____," *Wyoming Derrick*, (Casper: July 13, 1899), Courtesy of Wyoming Newspapers, Wyoming State Library, http://newspapers.wyo.gov.

"_____," *Wyoming Derrick*, (Casper: July 27, 1899), Courtesy of Wyoming Newspapers, Wyoming State Library, http://newspapers.wyo.gov.

"_____," *Wyoming Derrick*, (Casper: March 22, 1900), Courtesy of Wyoming Newspapers, Wyoming State Library, http://newspapers.wyo.gov.

"_____," *Wyoming Derrick*, (Casper: August 16, 1900), Courtesy of Wyoming Newspapers, Wyoming State Library, http://newspapers.wyo.gov.

"_____," *Wyoming Derrick*, (Casper: September 6, 1900), Courtesy of Wyoming Newspapers, Wyoming State Library, http://newspapers.wyo.gov.

"_____," *Wyoming Derrick*, (Casper: September 20, 1900), Courtesy of Wyoming Newspapers, Wyoming State Library, http://newspapers.wyo.gov.

"_____," *Wyoming Derrick*, (Casper: July 17, 1902), Courtesy of Wyoming Newspapers, Wyoming State Library, http://newspapers.wyo.gov.

"_____," *Wyoming Derrick*, (Casper: September 18, 1902), Courtesy of Wyoming Newspapers, Wyoming State Library, http://newspapers.wyo.gov.

"_____," *Wyoming Derrick*, (Casper: July 31, 1902), Courtesy of Wyoming Newspapers, Wyoming State Library, http://newspapers.wyo.gov.

"_____," *Wyoming Derrick*, (Casper: January 15, 1903), Courtesy of Wyoming Newspapers, Wyoming State Library, http://newspapers.wyo.gov.

"_____," *Wyoming Derrick*, (Casper: May 7, 1903), Courtesy of Wyoming Newspapers, Wyoming State Library, http://newspapers.wyo.gov.

"_____," *Wyoming Derrick*, (Casper: July 9, 1903), Courtesy of Wyoming Newspapers, Wyoming State Library, http://newspapers.wyo.gov.

"_____," *Wyoming Derrick*, (Casper: September 24, 1903), Courtesy of Wyoming Newspapers, Wyoming State Library, http://newspapers.wyo.gov.

"_____," *Wyoming Derrick*, (Casper: February 25, 1904), Courtesy of Wyoming Newspapers, Wyoming State Library, http://newspapers.wyo.gov.

"_____," *Wyoming Derrick*, (Casper: March 17, 1904), Courtesy of Wyoming Newspapers, Wyoming State Library, http://newspapers.wyo.gov.

"_____," *Wyoming Derrick*, (Casper: June 2, 1904), Courtesy of Wyoming Newspapers, Wyoming State Library, http://newspapers.wyo.gov.

"_____,"*Wyoming Derrick*, (Casper: June 9, 1904), Courtesy of Wyoming Newspapers, Wyoming State Library, http://newspapers.wyo.gov.

"_____," *Wyoming Derrick*, (Casper: March 2, 1905), Courtesy of Wyoming Newspapers, Wyoming State Library, http://newspapers.wyo.gov.

"_____," *Wyoming Derrick*, (Casper: May 25, 1905), Courtesy of Wyoming Newspapers, Wyoming State Library, http://newspapers.wyo.gov.

"_____," *Wyoming Derrick*, (Casper: June 8, 1905), Courtesy of Wyoming Newspapers, Wyoming State Library, http://newspapers.wyo.gov.

"_____," *Wyoming Derrick*, (Casper: July 13, 1905), Courtesy of Wyoming Newspapers, Wyoming State Library, http://newspapers.wyo.gov.

"Accused of Murder," *Cheyenne Daily Sun-Leader*, (June 7, 1897), Courtesy of Wyoming Newspapers, Wyoming State Library, http://newspapers.wyo.gov.

"Activity Grows in Utah Fields," *Casper Daily Tribune*, (April 8, 1921), Courtesy of Wyoming Newspapers, Wyoming State Library, http://newspapers.wyo.gov.

"Additional Local News," *Casper Press*, (July 23, 1909), Courtesy of Wyoming Newspapers, Wyoming State Library, http://newspapers.wyo.gov.

"Ade Irwin in Trouble Again," *Natrona County Tribune*, (Casper: September 11, 1912), Courtesy of Wyoming Newspapers, Wyoming State Library, http://newspapers.wyo.gov.

"Administratix Sale of Real Estate," *Jersey City News*, (July 14, 1894), Courtesy of Genealogy Bank, https://www.genealogybank.com/doc/newspapers.

"Alcova," *Wyoming Derrick*, (Casper: July 13, 1905), Courtesy of Wyoming Newspapers, Wyoming State Library, http://newspapers.wyo.gov.

"Alcova Hot Springs of Central Wyoming," *Wyoming Commonwealth*, (Cheyenne: May 10, 1891), Courtesy of Wyoming Newspapers, Wyoming State Library, http://newspapers.wyo.gov.

"All Over Wyoming," *Basin Republican*, (August 25, 1911), Courtesy of Wyoming Newspapers, Wyoming State Library, http://newspapers.wyo.gov.

"Almost Make Court Auctioneer," *Jersey Journal*, (Jersey City: March 21, 1922), Courtesy of Genealogy Bank, https://www.genealogybank.com/doc/newspapers.

"An Ancient Canard," *Casper Daily Tribune*, (November 1, 1921), Courtesy of Wyoming Newspapers, Wyoming State Library, http://newspapers.wyo.gov.

"An Old Trick–How Gothberg Lost His Big Diamond Stud," *Jersey Journal*, (Jersey City: June 3, 1895), Courtesy of Genealogy Bank, https://www.genealogybank.com/doc/newspapers.

"Announcement of Engagement is Made at Dinner Party," *Casper Daily Tribune*, (January 24, 1921), Courtesy of Wyoming Newspapers, Wyoming State Library, http://newspapers.wyo.gov.

"Another Company Enters Oil Field," *Casper Press*, (October 21, 1910), Courtesy of Wyoming Newspapers, Wyoming State Library, http://newspapers.wyo.gov.

"Apartment Contract Let," *Casper Press*, (May 8, 1914), Courtesy of Wyoming Newspapers, Wyoming State Library, http://newspapers.wyo.gov.

"Apartment House Next," *Casper Press*, (February 6, 1914), Courtesy of Wyoming Newspapers, Wyoming State Library, http://newspapers.wyo.gov.

"Apartments to let—continued," *San Francisco Chronicle*, (November 24, 1912), Courtesy of Genealogy Bank, https://www.genealogybank.com/doc/newspapers.

"Around the Town," *Casper Daily Tribune*, (October 13, 1919), Courtesy of Wyoming Newspapers, Wyoming State Library, http://newspapers.wyo.gov.

"Arrest is Sensational," *Cheyenne Daily Leader*, (May 24, 1908), Courtesy of Wyoming Newspapers, Wyoming State Library, http://newspapers.wyo.gov.

"Arrested at Glenrock," *The Graphic*, (Douglas: August 1, 1891), Courtesy of Wyoming Newspapers, Wyoming State Library, http://newspapers.wyo.gov.

"Arrested for Perjury," *Natrona County Tribune*, (Casper: January 19, 1905), Courtesy of Wyoming Newspapers, Wyoming State Library, http://newspapers.wyo.gov.

"Arrivals at the Inter Ocean Hotel," *Cheyenne Daily Sun*, (March 3, 1882), Courtesy of Wyoming Newspapers, Wyoming State Library, http://newspapers.wyo.gov.

"At Home," *Gillette News*, (August 18, 1905), Courtesy of Wyoming Newspapers, Wyoming State Library, http://newspapers.wyo.gov.

"At Least Fifteen Rigs at Work in Utah," *Salt Lake Tribune*, (Salt Lake City: April 3, 1921), Courtesy of Utah Digital Newspapers, https://newspapers.lib.utah.edu.

"At the Hotels," *Laramie Republican*, (Semi-Weekly ed.), (February 26, 1921), Courtesy of Wyoming Newspapers, Wyoming State Library, http://newspapers.wyo.gov.

"At the Hotels," *Los Angeles Daily Herald*, (February 25, 1909), Courtesy of Genealogy Bank, https://www.genealogybank.com/doc/newspapers.

"At the Oil Wells," *Casper Press*, (June 17, 1910), Courtesy of Wyoming Newspapers, Wyoming State Library, http://newspapers.wyo.gov.

"Atlas Resuming Drilling," *Wyoming Tribune*, (Cheyenne: November 19, 1917), Courtesy of Wyoming Newspapers, Wyoming State Library, http://newspapers.wyo.gov.

"Auction Sales," *Jersey Journal*, (Jersey City: March 31, 1922), Courtesy of Genealogy Bank, https://www.genealogybank.com/doc/newspapers.

"Auto Club Shows Membership Over 300 in Statement," *Casper Herald*, (September 11, 1920), Courtesy of Wyoming Newspapers, Wyoming State Library, http://newspapers.wyo.gov.

"Automobile News," *Casper Herald*, (October 15, 1922), Courtesy of Wyoming Newspapers, Wyoming State Library, http://newspapers.wyo.gov.

"Automobiles–Motorists You Know," *Wind River Mountaineer*, (Lander: August 18, 1916), Courtesy of Wyoming Newspapers, Wyoming State Library, http://newspapers.wyo.gov.

"Bates Hole and Alcova," *Wyoming Semi-Weekly Tribune*, (Cheyenne: June 9, 1905), Courtesy of Wyoming Newspapers, Wyoming State Library, http://newspapers.wyo.gov.

"Bates Hole Spindle Top Dome Leased for Test," *Laramie Daily Boomerang*, (April 26, 1919), Courtesy of Wyoming Newspapers, Wyoming State Library, http://newspapers.wyo.gov.

"Bates' Park," *Natrona County Tribune*, (Casper: December 7, 1905), Courtesy of Wyoming Newspapers, Wyoming State Library, http://newspapers.wyo.gov.

"Bates' Park Items," *Natrona County Tribune*, (Casper: November 9, 1905), Courtesy of Wyoming Newspapers, Wyoming State Library, http://newspapers.wyo.gov.

"Bates Park Telephone," *Natrona County Tribune*, (Casper: May 29, 1902), Courtesy of Wyoming Newspapers, Wyoming State Library, http://newspapers.wyo.gov.

"Big Carbon County Deal is Pending," *Rawlins Republican*, (April 24, 1919), Courtesy of Wyoming Newspapers, Wyoming State Library, http://newspapers.wyo.gov.

"The Big Industrial Convention is Now On," *Natrona County Tribune*, (Casper: September 22, 1904), Courtesy of Wyoming Newspapers, Wyoming State Library, http://newspapers.wyo.gov.

"The Big Parade," *Natrona County Tribune*, (Casper: June 22, 1905), Courtesy of Wyoming Newspapers, Wyoming State Library, http://newspapers.wyo.gov.

"Big Wool Sales," *Wyoming Tribune*, (Cheyenne: July 6, 1906), Courtesy of Wyoming Newspapers, Wyoming State Library, http://newspapers.wyo.gov.

"The Bittner Theater Company," *Wyoming Derrick*, (Casper: February 2, 1899), Courtesy of Wyoming Newspapers, Wyoming State Library, http://newspapers.wyo.gov.

"Black Hills Items," *Sundance Gazette*, (December 1, 1893), Courtesy of Wyoming Newspapers, Wyoming State Library, http://newspapers.wyo.gov.

"Blackmore and Details," *Casper Daily Tribune*, (November 4, 1921), Courtesy of Wyoming Newspapers, Wyoming State Library, http://newspapers.wyo.gov.

"Blackmore & Gue Co. Sold," *Natrona County Tribune*, (Casper: May 19, 1909), Courtesy of Wyoming Newspapers, Wyoming State Library, http://newspapers.wyo.gov.

"Blackmore Company Gets Gusher," *Natrona County Tribune*, (Casper: March 20, 1913), Courtesy of Wyoming Newspapers, Wyoming State Library, http://news papers.wyo.gov.

"Blackmore Elected Mayor," *Casper Daily Tribune*, (November 9, 1921), Courtesy of Wyoming Newspapers, Wyoming State Library, http://newspapers.wyo.gov.

"Blackmore in Race With Time to Attend Brother's Burial in Cal.," *Casper Herald*, (June 8, 1920), Courtesy of Wyoming Newspapers, Wyoming State Library, http:// newspapers.wyo.gov.

"Blackmore is Back," *Casper Press*, (April 1, 1910), Courtesy of Wyoming Newspapers, Wyoming State Library, http://newspapers.wyo.gov.

"Blackmore Oil Company Strikes Big Gusher," *Casper Record* (March 18, 1913), Courtesy of Wyoming Newspapers, Wyoming State Library, http://newspapers.wyo.gov.

"Blackmore Oil Co. Makes Big Deal," *Casper Record*, (May 22, 1917), Courtesy of Wyoming Newspapers, Wyoming State Library, http://newspapers.wyo.gov.

"Blackmore Oil Slices Melon," *Cheyenne State Leader*, (June 15, 1917), Courtesy of Wyoming Newspapers, Wyoming State Library, http://newspapers.wyo.gov.

"Blackmore Rig at Well No. 2 Burned Down," *Natrona County Tribune*, (Casper: June 5, 1913), Courtesy of Wyoming Newspapers, Wyoming State Library, http://news papers.wyo.gov.

"Blackmore Wins Early Return as Member of Crack Company in the Anti-Aircraft Service," *Casper Daily Tribune*, (January 30, 1919), (Casper: June 5, 1913), Courtesy of Wyoming Newspapers, Wyoming State Library, http://newspapers.wyo.gov.

"Blackmore's Market," *Natrona County Tribune*, (Casper: December 19, 1906), Courtesy of Wyoming Newspapers, Wyoming State Library, http://newspapers.wyo.gov.

"Bolton Creek Land Leased," *Casper Daily Tribune*, (February 27, 1920), Courtesy of Wyoming Newspapers, Wyoming State Library, http://newspapers.wyo.gov.

"Bolton Field Scene of New Lease Deals," *Casper Herald*, (February 26, 1920), Courtesy of Wyoming Newspapers, Wyoming State Library, http://newspapers.wyo.gov.

"Bond Forfeiture Set Aside," *Natrona County Tribune*, (Casper: August 11, 1909), Courtesy of Wyoming Newspapers, Wyoming State Library, http://newspapers.wyo.gov.

"Boone Dome Drilling to be Resumed," *Casper Daily Tribune*, (December 22, 1921), Courtesy of Wyoming Newspapers, Wyoming State Library, http://newspapers .wyo.gov.

"Bought a Bates Hole Ranch," *Natrona County Tribune*, (Casper: December 8, 1909), Courtesy of Wyoming Newspapers, Wyoming State Library, http://newspapers .wyo.gov.

"Bought Pool Hall," *Basin Republican*, (September 15, 1916), Courtesy of Wyoming Newspapers, Wyoming State Library, http://newspapers.wyo.gov.

"Broncho Buster Badly Frozen," *Casper Daily Press*, (December 17, 1914), Courtesy of Wyoming Newspapers, Wyoming State Library, http://newspapers.wyo.gov.

"Brooks: His Life and His Labors," *Natrona County Tribune*, (Casper: August 25, 1904), Courtesy of Wyoming Newspapers, Wyoming State Library, http://newspapers .wyo.gov.

"A Brutal Murder," *Cheyenne Weekly Leader*, (October 19, 1882), Courtesy of Wyoming Newspapers, Wyoming State Library, http://newspapers.wyo.gov.

"Bucks For Sale," *Natrona County Tribune*, (Casper: September 15, 1909), Courtesy of Wyoming Newspapers, Wyoming State Library, http://newspapers.wyo.gov.

"Bucks For Sale," *Natrona County Tribune*, (Casper: November 16, 1910), Courtesy of Wyoming Newspapers, Wyoming State Library, http://newspapers.wyo.gov.

"Buick," *Salt Creek Journal*, (May 10, 1923), Courtesy of Wyoming Newspapers, Wyoming State Library, http://newspapers.wyo.gov.

"Buick Agency Changes Hands, New Home Here," *Casper Daily Tribune*, (June 14, 1922), Courtesy of Wyoming Newspapers, Wyoming State Library, http://news papers.wyo.gov.

"Buick Into New Branson Edifice," *Casper Herald*, (November 19, 1922), Courtesy of Wyoming Newspapers, Wyoming State Library, http://newspapers.wyo.gov.

"Building Contracts, Jersey City," *Jersey Journal*, (Jersey City: May 11, 1906), Courtesy of Genealogy Bank, https://www.genealogybank.com/doc/newspapers.

"The Burlington Machine Shops," *Natrona County Tribune*, (Casper: December 8, 1909), Courtesy of Wyoming Newspapers, Wyoming State Library, http://news papers.wyo.gov.

"Campaign Expenses," *Natrona County Tribune*, (Casper: September 25, 1912), Courtesy of Wyoming Newspapers, Wyoming State Library, http://newspapers.wyo.gov.

"Captured Two Safe Blowers," *Natrona County Tribune*, (Casper: March 20, 1913), Courtesy of Wyoming Newspapers, Wyoming State Library, http://newspapers .wyo.gov.

"Card of Thanks," *Jersey Journal*, (Jersey City: June 6, 1918), Courtesy of Genealogy Bank, https://www.genealogybank.com/doc/newspapers.

"Case against Gothberg Dismissed," *Natrona County Tribune*, (Casper: February 2, 1905), Courtesy of Wyoming Newspapers, Wyoming State Library, http://news papers.wyo.gov.

"Cashed Forged Check," *Natrona County Tribune*, (Casper: August 16, 1911), Courtesy of Wyoming Newspapers, Wyoming State Library, http://newspapers.wyo.gov.

"Casper Brewery Opens Monday," *Casper daily Press*, (July 24, 1915), Courtesy of Wyoming Newspapers, Wyoming State Library, http://newspapers.wyo.gov.

"Casper Brewing Co. Formally Organized," *Casper Press*, (February 27, 1914), Courtesy of Wyoming Newspapers, Wyoming State Library, http://newspapers.wyo.gov.

"Casper Cowboys," *Sheridan Post*, (June 17, 1897), Courtesy of Wyoming Newspapers, Wyoming State Library, http://newspapers.wyo.gov.

"Casper Has Spent Limit for Lighting," *Daily Boomerang*, (Laramie: April 20, 1922), Courtesy of Wyoming Newspapers, Wyoming State Library, http://newspapers .wyo.gov.

"Casper Locals," *Casper Herald*, (January 1, 1920), Courtesy of Wyoming Newspapers, Wyoming State Library, http://newspapers.wyo.gov.

"Casper Mayor Killed; Train Strikes Auto," *Buffalo Bulletin*, (April 26, 1923), Courtesy of Wyoming Newspapers, Wyoming State Library, http://newspapers.wyo.gov.

"Casper Petroleum Co.," *Wyoming Tribune*, (Cheyenne: April 25, 1917), Courtesy of Wyoming Newspapers, Wyoming State Library, http://newspapers.wyo.gov.

"Casper Ranger Has Good Well," *Wyoming Oil World*, (Casper: August 30, 1919), Courtesy of Wyoming Newspapers, Wyoming State Library, http://newspapers.wyo.gov.

"Casper Ranger in List Big Earning Concerns," *Casper Herald*, (January 18, 1920), Courtesy of Wyoming Newspapers, Wyoming State Library, http://newspapers .wyo.gov.

"Casper Ranger Rig to be Rebuilt Soon Texas," *Casper Herald*, (December 18, 1919), Courtesy of Wyoming Newspapers, Wyoming State Library, http://newspapers .wyo.gov.

"Casper Ranger Will Finish Well in July," *Laramie Daily Boomerang*, (July 18, 1919), Courtesy of Wyoming Newspapers, Wyoming State Library, http://newspapers .wyo.gov.

"Casper Ten Years Ago," *Casper Herald*, (March 5, 1922), Courtesy of Wyoming Newspapers, Wyoming State Library, http://newspapers.wyo.gov.

"Casper Wool Pool to Sell Wool at Auction with an Expert Present," *Laramie Republican*, (June 10, 1922), Courtesy of Wyoming Newspapers, Wyoming State Library, http://newspapers.wyo.gov.

"Casper Young Man Distinguishing Himself," *Laramie Republican*, (March 18, 1918), Courtesy of Wyoming Newspapers, Wyoming State Library, http://newspapers .wyo.gov.

"Cattle Cars Ordered," *Democratic Leader*, (Cheyenne: September 1, 1885), Courtesy of Wyoming Newspapers, Wyoming State Library, http://newspapers.wyo.gov.

"Cattle Notes," *Cheyenne Daily Leader*, (September 15, 1877), Courtesy of Wyoming Newspapers, Wyoming State Library, http://newspapers.wyo.gov.

"Cattle Notes," *Cheyenne Daily Sun*, (August 3, 1879), Courtesy of Wyoming Newspapers, Wyoming State Library, http://newspapers.wyo.gov.

"Cattle Notes," *Daily Boomerang*, (Laramie: July, 16, 1885), Courtesy of Wyoming Newspapers, Wyoming State Library, http://newspapers.wyo.gov.

"Cattle Notes," *Democratic Leader*, (Cheyenne: November 20, 1885), Courtesy of Wyoming Newspapers, Wyoming State Library, http://newspapers.wyo.gov.

"Caught in the Snow Storm," *Natrona County Tribune*, (Casper: May 15, 1907), Courtesy of Wyoming Newspapers, Wyoming State Library, http://newspapers.wyo.gov.

"A Central Wyoming Celebrity," *Bill Barlow's Budget*, (Douglas: April 5, 1893), Courtesy of Wyoming Newspapers, Wyoming State Library, http://newspapers.wyo.gov.

"Charged with Stealing Sheep at Casper," *Laramie Republican*, (July 3, 1908), Courtesy of Wyoming Newspapers, Wyoming State Library, http://newspapers.wyo.gov.

"Chief Wolf Be Major Issue in Fall Municipal Election," *Casper Daily Press*, (October 13, 1918), Courtesy of Wyoming Newspapers, Wyoming State Library, http:// newspapers.wyo.gov.

"Children Must Stay Away from Stock Yards," *Natrona County Tribune*, (Casper: September 24, 1903), Courtesy of Wyoming Newspapers, Wyoming State Library, http://newspapers.wyo.gov.

"Children Not Wanted at the Stock Yards," *Natrona County Tribune*, (Casper: September 1, 1904), Courtesy of Wyoming Newspapers, Wyoming State Library, http://newspapers.wyo.gov.

"Cited for Contempt," *Natrona County Tribune*, (Casper: July 27, 1910), Courtesy of Wyoming Newspapers, Wyoming State Library, http://newspapers.wyo.gov.

"City and County News," *Natrona County Tribune*, (Casper: July 1, 1897), Courtesy of Wyoming Newspapers, Wyoming State Library, http://newspapers.wyo.gov.

"City and County News," *Natrona County Tribune*, (Casper: August 26, 1897), Courtesy of Wyoming Newspapers, Wyoming State Library, http://newspapers.wyo.gov.

"City and County News," *Natrona County Tribune*, (Casper: September 9, 1897), Courtesy of Wyoming Newspapers, Wyoming State Library, http://newspapers.wyo.gov.

"City Briefs," *Casper Daily Press*, (September 4, 1918), Courtesy of Wyoming Newspapers, Wyoming State Library, http://newspapers.wyo.gov.

"City Briefs," *Casper Daily Tribune*, (December 22, 1921), Courtesy of Wyoming Newspapers, Wyoming State Library, http://newspapers.wyo.gov.

"City Briefs," *Casper Daily Tribune*, (March 18, 1922), Courtesy of Wyoming Newspapers, Wyoming State Library, http://newspapers.wyo.gov.

"City Briefs and Personals," *Casper Record*, (January 1, 1918), Courtesy of Wyoming Newspapers, Wyoming State Library, http://newspapers.wyo.gov.

"City News," *Casper Daily Tribune*, (May 15, 1917), Courtesy of Wyoming Newspapers, Wyoming State Library, http://newspapers.wyo.gov.

"City News," *Casper Daily Tribune*, (September 3, 1918), Courtesy of Wyoming Newspapers, Wyoming State Library, http://newspapers.wyo.gov.

"City News," *Casper Daily Tribune*, (November 18, 1918), Courtesy of Wyoming Newspapers, Wyoming State Library, http://newspapers.wyo.gov.

"City News," *Casper Daily Tribune*, (March 3, 1919), Courtesy of Wyoming Newspapers, Wyoming State Library, http://newspapers.wyo.gov.

"City News," *Casper Daily Tribune*, (March 15, 1919), Courtesy of Wyoming Newspapers, Wyoming State Library, http://newspapers.wyo.gov.

"City News," *Casper Daily Tribune*, (March 27, 1919), Courtesy of Wyoming Newspapers, Wyoming State Library, http://newspapers.wyo.gov.

"City News," *Casper Daily Tribune*, (April 8, 1919), Courtesy of Wyoming Newspapers, Wyoming State Library, http://newspapers.wyo.gov.

"City News," *Casper Daily Tribune*, (September 4, 1919), Courtesy of Wyoming Newspapers, Wyoming State Library, http://newspapers.wyo.gov.

"City News," *Casper Daily Tribune*, (September 5, 1919), Courtesy of Wyoming Newspapers, Wyoming State Library, http://newspapers.wyo.gov.

"City News," *Natrona County Tribune*, (Casper: March 1, 1917), Courtesy of Wyoming Newspapers, Wyoming State Library, http://newspapers.wyo.gov.

"City News Notes," *Jersey City News*, (August 9, 1893), Courtesy of Genealogy Bank, https://www.genealogybank.com/doc/newspapers.

"The 'Club' Cup," *Cheyenne Daily Sun*, (September 6, 1887), Courtesy of Wyoming Newspapers, Wyoming State Library, http://newspapers.wyo.gov.

"Commissioners' Proceedings," *Laramie Republican*, (February 22, 1922), Courtesy of Wyoming Newspapers, Wyoming State Library, http://newspapers.wyo.gov.

"Commissioner's Proceedings," *Buffalo Bulletin*, (October 13, 1910), Courtesy of Wyoming Newspapers, Wyoming State Library, http://newspapers.wyo.gov.

"Commissioner's Proceedings," *Buffalo Bulletin*, (January 5, 1911), Courtesy of Wyoming Newspapers, Wyoming State Library, http://newspapers.wyo.gov.

"Commissioner's Proceedings," *Buffalo Bulletin*, (February 16, 1911), Courtesy of Wyoming Newspapers, Wyoming State Library, http://newspapers.wyo.gov.

"Commissioner's Proceedings," *Buffalo Voice*, (October 14, 1910), Courtesy of Wyoming Newspapers, Wyoming State Library, http://newspapers.wyo.gov.

"Commissioner's Proceedings," *Casper Press*, (July 12, 1912), Courtesy of Wyoming Newspapers, Wyoming State Library, http://newspapers.wyo.gov.

"Commissioner's Proceedings," *Natrona County Tribune*, (Casper: December 19, 1906), Courtesy of Wyoming Newspapers, Wyoming State Library, http://newspapers.wyo.gov.

"Commissioner's Proceedings," *Natrona County Tribune*, (Casper: July 10, 1912), Courtesy of Wyoming Newspapers, Wyoming State Library, http://newspapers.wyo.gov.

"Commissioner's Proceedings," *Wyoming Derrick*, (Casper: April 13, 1905), Courtesy of Wyoming Newspapers, Wyoming State Library, http://newspapers.wyo.gov.

"Commissioner's Proceedings," *Wyoming State Journal*, (Lander: September 23, 1910), Courtesy of Wyoming Newspapers, Wyoming State Library, http://newspapers.wyo.gov.

"Commissioner's Proceedings," *Wyoming State Journal*, (Lander: October 14, 1910), Courtesy of Wyoming Newspapers, Wyoming State Library, http://newspapers.wyo.gov.

"Commissioner's Proceedings," *Wyoming State Journal*, (Lander: December 16, 1910), Courtesy of Wyoming Newspapers, Wyoming State Library, http://newspapers.wyo.gov.

"Commissioner's Proceedings," *Wyoming State Journal*, (Lander: January 6, 1911), Courtesy of Wyoming Newspapers, Wyoming State Library, http://newspapers.wyo.gov.

"Complimenting Bride-Elect," *Casper Herald*, (January 23, 1921), Courtesy of Wyoming Newspapers, Wyoming State Library, http://newspapers.wyo.gov.

"Confidence Repaid When Oil Gushes Forth Liquid Wealth 'Grease' Breaks Bolton Dyke," *Casper Herald*, (September 4, 1920), Courtesy of Wyoming Newspapers, Wyoming State Library, http://newspapers.wyo.gov.

"Contest Notice," *Natrona County Tribune*, (Casper: April 4, 1910), Courtesy of Wyoming Newspapers, Wyoming State Library, http://newspapers.wyo.gov.

"Convention Closed Last Friday afternoon," *Douglas Enterprise*, (January 15, 1918), Courtesy of Wyoming Newspapers, Wyoming State Library, http://newspapers.wyo.gov.

"Conveyances," *Jersey Journal*, (Jersey City: April 23, 1906), Courtesy of Genealogy Bank, https://www.genealogybank.com/doc/newspapers.

"Conveyances–Jersey City," *Jersey Journal*, (Jersey City: April 4, 1906), Courtesy of Genealogy Bank, https://www.genealogybank.com/doc/newspapers.

"Conveyances–Jersey City," *Jersey Journal*, (Jersey City: May 8, 1906), Courtesy of Genealogy Bank, https://www.genealogybank.com/doc/newspapers.

"Council Proceedings," *Casper Daily Press*, (October 12, 1918), Courtesy of Wyoming Newspapers, Wyoming State Library, http://newspapers.wyo.gov.

"Council Proceedings," *Casper Daily Tribune*, (April 25, 1922), Courtesy of Wyoming Newspapers, Wyoming State Library, http://newspapers.wyo.gov.

"County Completes Half of Quota," *Casper Daily Press*, (October 8, 1918), Courtesy of Wyoming Newspapers, Wyoming State Library, http://newspapers.wyo.gov.

"County Notes," *Saratoga Sun*, (December 3, 1891), Courtesy of Wyoming Newspapers, Wyoming State Library, http://newspapers.wyo.gov.

"Court in Session," *Wyoming Derrick*, (Casper: December 4, 1902), Courtesy of Wyoming Newspapers, Wyoming State Library, http://newspapers.wyo.gov.

"Court is in Recess," *Natrona County Tribune*, (Casper: August 3, 1910), Courtesy of Wyoming Newspapers, Wyoming State Library, http://newspapers.wyo.gov.

"The Court is Working Fast," *Bill Barlow's Budget*, (Douglas: September 13, 1911), Courtesy of Wyoming Newspapers, Wyoming State Library, http://newspapers.wyo.gov.

"Dain not Guilty: Verdict Formed in Short Order," *Wyoming Tribune*, (Cheyenne: July 21, 1911), Courtesy of Wyoming Newspapers, Wyoming State Library, http://newspapers.wyo.gov.

"Dam at Alcova–Government Reservoir Will Probably be Built at Grand Canyon–Sheep to be Dipped," *Wyoming Derrick*, (Casper: August 20, 1903), Courtesy of Wyoming Newspapers, Wyoming State Library, http://newspapers.wyo.gov.

"Dance Enjoyed at Ranch Home," *Casper Daily Tribune*, (December 27, 1921), Courtesy of Wyoming Newspapers, Wyoming State Library, http://newspapers.wyo.gov.

"Death of John Landon," *Wyoming Derrick*, (Casper: August 20, 1903), Courtesy of Wyoming Newspapers, Wyoming State Library, http://newspapers.wyo.gov.

"Deaths," *New York Daily Tribune*, (August 28, 1918), Courtesy of Genealogy Bank, https://www.genealogybank.com/doc/newspapers.

"Dedication of Camp Rotary is Scheduled for Coming Sunday," *Casper Daily Tribune*, (December 7, 1921), Courtesy of Wyoming Newspapers, Wyoming State Library, http://newspapers.wyo.gov.

"Democratic Commissioners," *Casper Daily Press*, (November 3, 1918), Courtesy of Wyoming Newspapers, Wyoming State Library, http://newspapers.wyo.gov.

"Democratic Convention," *Wyoming Derrick*, (Casper: September 22, 1898), Courtesy of Wyoming Newspapers, Wyoming State Library, http://newspapers.wyo.gov.

"The Democratic County Convention," *Natrona County Tribune*, (Casper: September 22, 1898), Courtesy of Wyoming Newspapers, Wyoming State Library, http://newspapers.wyo.gov.

"Democrats Nominate a Winning Ticket," *Cheyenne Daily Leader*, (May 14, 1908), Courtesy of Wyoming Newspapers, Wyoming State Library, http://newspapers.wyo.gov.

"Denied $1,400 Salary Claim," *Jersey Journal*, (Jersey City: December 19, 1922), Courtesy of Genealogy Bank, https://www.genealogybank.com/doc/newspapers.

"Denver Livestock," *Denver Rocky Mountain News*, (November 29, 1919), Courtesy of Genealogy Bank, https://www.genealogybank.com/doc/newspapers.

"Department of Interior," *Casper Herald*, (August 28, 1920), Courtesy of Wyoming Newspapers, Wyoming State Library, http://newspapers.wyo.gov.

"Department of Interior," *Casper Herald*, (September 1, 1920), Courtesy of Wyoming Newspapers, Wyoming State Library, http://newspapers.wyo.gov.

"Department of Interior," *Casper Herald*, (September 2, 1920), Courtesy of Wyoming Newspapers, Wyoming State Library, http://newspapers.wyo.gov.

"Department of the Interior," *Casper Herald*, (September 4, 1920), Courtesy of Wyoming Newspapers, Wyoming State Library, http://newspapers.wyo.gov.

"Department of the Interior," *Natrona County Tribune*, (Casper: August 5, 1908), Courtesy of Wyoming Newspapers, Wyoming State Library, http://newspapers.wyo.gov.

"Department of the Interior," *Wyoming Oil World*, (Casper: August 28, 1920), Courtesy of Wyoming Newspapers, Wyoming State Library, http://newspapers.wyo.gov.

"Derrick Darts," *Wyoming Derrick*, (Casper: December 10, 1891), Courtesy of Wyoming Newspapers, Wyoming State Library, http://newspapers.wyo.gov.

"Derrick Darts," *Wyoming Derrick*, (Casper: January 28, 1892), Courtesy of Wyoming Newspapers, Wyoming State Library, http://newspapers.wyo.gov.

"A Devoted Daughter," *Democratic Leader*, (Cheyenne: March 13, 1884), Courtesy of Wyoming Newspapers, Wyoming State Library, http://newspapers.wyo.gov.

"Died," *Jersey Journal*, (Jersey City: August 31, 1897), Courtesy of Genealogy Bank, https://www.genealogybank.com/doc/newspapers.

"Died," *Jersey Journal*, (Jersey City: June 3, 1918), Courtesy of Genealogy Bank, https://www.genealogybank.com/doc/newspapers.

"Dinner in Honor of Mrs. M. J. Gothberg," *Casper Daily Tribune*, (January 2, 1920), Courtesy of Wyoming Newspapers, Wyoming State Library, http://newspapers.wyo.gov.

"Dinner Party Given at Henning Hotel," *Casper Record*, (January 29, 1918), Courtesy of Wyoming Newspapers, Wyoming State Library, http://newspapers.wyo.gov.

"Dinner Served at Gothberg Ranch," *Casper Daily Tribune*, (December 29, 1921), Courtesy of Wyoming Newspapers, Wyoming State Library, http://newspapers.wyo.gov.

"Directors Elected for Two Hundred," *Natrona County Tribune*, (Casper: March 1, 1917), Courtesy of Wyoming Newspapers, Wyoming State Library, http://newspapers.wyo.gov.

"District Court," *Natrona County Tribune*, (Casper: January 18, 1906), Courtesy of Wyoming Newspapers, Wyoming State Library, http://newspapers.wyo.gov.

"District Court," *Natrona County Tribune*, (Casper: February 27, 1907), Courtesy of Wyoming Newspapers, Wyoming State Library, http://newspapers.wyo.gov.

"District Court," *Natrona County Tribune*, (Casper: January 26, 1910), Courtesy of Wyoming Newspapers, Wyoming State Library, http://newspapers.wyo.gov.

"District Court Convenes Today," *Natrona County Tribune*, (Casper: January 16, 1913), Courtesy of Wyoming Newspapers, Wyoming State Library, http://newspapers.wyo.gov.

"District Court Doings," *Natrona County Tribune*, (Casper: July 19, 1911), Courtesy of Wyoming Newspapers, Wyoming State Library, http://newspapers.wyo.gov.

"District Court in Session," *Wyoming Derrick*, (Casper: July 16, 1903), Courtesy of Wyoming Newspapers, Wyoming State Library, http://newspapers.wyo.gov.

"District Court News," *Natrona County Tribune*, (Casper: July 21, 1905), Courtesy of Wyoming Newspapers, Wyoming State Library, http://newspapers.wyo.gov.

"District No. 4 of Casper Gives McGraugh Majority ...," *Casper Daily Tribune*, (November 7, 1918), Courtesy of Wyoming Newspapers, Wyoming State Library, http://newspapers.wyo.gov.

"Dr. Finn and E. Gothberg Better To-Day," *Jersey Journal*, (Jersey City: August 22, 1911), Courtesy of Genealogy Bank, https://www.genealogybank.com/doc /newspapers.

"Dr. Leeper is Casper Mayor," *Wyoming Tribune*, (Cheyenne: November 7, 1917), Courtesy of Wyoming Newspapers, Wyoming State Library, http://newspapers.wyo.gov.

"Doings of the District Court Today," *Casper Daily Press*, (October 7, 1914), Courtesy of Wyoming Newspapers, Wyoming State Library, http://newspapers.wyo.gov.

"Doug and Mary to be Acting in Wyoming Scenes Soon," *Wyoming State Tribune*, (Casper: August 25, 1921), Courtesy of Wyoming Newspapers, Wyoming State Library, http://newspapers.wyo.gov.

"Douglas Items," *Northwestern Live Stock Journal*, (Cheyenne: July 22, 1887), Courtesy of Wyoming Newspapers, Wyoming State Library, http://newspapers.wyo.gov.

"Drilling Company Files its Papers," *Laramie Republican*, (July 13, 1916), Courtesy of Wyoming Newspapers, Wyoming State Library, http://newspapers.wyo.gov.

"Drilling Goes Slowly," *Wyoming State Tribune*, (Cheyenne: February 11, 1920), Courtesy of Wyoming Newspapers, Wyoming State Library, http://newspapers.wyo.gov.

"Drilling is Resumed on Atlas Well in West Salt Creek," *Casper Record*, (November 20, 1917), Courtesy of Wyoming Newspapers, Wyoming State Library, http://news papers.wyo.gov.

"Drought Effect Worse in Wyoming Than '34," *Riverside Daily Press*, (August 4, 1936), Courtesy of Genealogy Bank, https://www.genealogybank.com/doc/newspapers.

"Dutton Moving Rig," *Natrona County Tribune*, (Casper: February 8, 1917), Courtesy of Wyoming Newspapers, Wyoming State Library, http://newspapers.wyo.gov.

"E. Gothberg, Hurt in Auto Crash, Dead," *Jersey Journal*, (Jersey City: September 12, 1911), Courtesy of Genealogy Bank, https://www.genealogybank.com/doc /newspapers.

"E. Gothberg's Employees' Dance," *Jersey City News*, (August 21, 1893), Courtesy of Genealogy Bank, https://www.genealogybank.com/doc/newspapers.

"E. T. Williams Company Designates Itself as Publicity Agent for State," *Casper Daily Press*, (December 7, 1918), Courtesy of Wyoming Newspapers, Wyoming State Library, http://newspapers.wyo.gov.

"Ed Lee's Partner Caught," *Natrona County Tribune*, (Casper: September 27, 1906), Courtesy of Wyoming Newspapers, Wyoming State Library, http://newspapers .wyo.gov.

"Elaborate Arrangements for Military Ball Friday," *Casper Daily Tribune*, (May 6, 1919), Courtesy of Wyoming Newspapers, Wyoming State Library, http://newspapers .wyo.gov.

"Elizabeth Robinson Case Reversed," *Natrona County Tribune*, (Casper: January 12, 1910), Courtesy of Wyoming Newspapers, Wyoming State Library, http://news papers.wyo.gov.

"Elizabeth Robinson Convicted," *Natrona County Tribune*, (Casper: February 10, 1909), Courtesy of Wyoming Newspapers, Wyoming State Library, http://newspapers .wyo.gov.

"Encouraging News From Ranger Field," *Wyoming Oil World*, (Casper: January 10, 1920), Courtesy of Wyoming Newspapers, Wyoming State Library, http://news papers.wyo.gov.

"Entertained at Gothberg Ranch," *Casper Daily Tribune*, (October 18, 1921), Courtesy of Wyoming Newspapers, Wyoming State Library, http://newspapers.wyo.gov.

"The Evidence," *Wyoming Derrick*, (Casper: August 6, 1903), Courtesy of Wyoming Newspapers, Wyoming State Library, http://newspapers.wyo.gov.

"Examiner Looking Over Claims," *Wyoming Oil World*, (Casper: October 1, 1921), Courtesy of Wyoming Newspapers, Wyoming State Library, http://newspapers .wyo.gov.

"Exciting Times on Salt Creek," *Casper Press*, (June 3, 1910), Courtesy of Wyoming Newspapers, Wyoming State Library, http://newspapers.wyo.gov.

"Expense Is Without Limitations When Capitalists Seek Choice Holdings In Powder River Field," *Casper Daily Tribune*, (January 5, 1917), Courtesy of Wyoming News- papers, Wyoming State Library, http://newspapers.wyo.gov.

"F. J. Koezley's Will," *New York Tribune*, (October 6, 1896), Courtesy of Genealogy Bank, https://www.genealogybank.com/doc/newspapers.

"The Fattening Herds," *Cheyenne Daily Sun*, (May 21, 1885), Courtesy of Wyoming Newspapers, Wyoming State Library, http://newspapers.wyo.gov.

"The Fetterman Tragedy," *Cheyenne Daily Leader*, (October 20, 1882), Courtesy of Wyo- ming Newspapers, Wyoming State Library, http://newspapers.wyo.gov.

"Field Notes," *Wyoming Oil World*, (Casper: May 7, 1921), Courtesy of Wyoming News- papers, Wyoming State Library, http://newspapers.wyo.gov.

"Field Report of New York Oil Company," *Wyoming Oil World*, (Casper: August 6, 1921), Courtesy of Wyoming Newspapers, Wyoming State Library, http://news papers.wyo.gov.

"Field Supt. Resigns," *Rawlins Republican*, (December 11, 1919), Courtesy of Wyoming Newspapers, Wyoming State Library, http://newspapers.wyo.gov.

"Field Work," *Cheyenne State Leader*, (August 12, 1920), Courtesy of Wyoming Newspa- pers, Wyoming State Library, http://newspapers.wyo.gov.

"Fight With Train Robbers—Robbers Still at Large in Powder River—Passed through Casper Sunday Morning," *Natrona County Tribune*, (Casper: June 8, 1899), Cour- tesy of Wyoming Newspapers, Wyoming State Library, http://newspapers.wyo.gov.

"First Cases Set for Trail by Court Today," *Casper Daily Tribune*, (March 1, 1921), Cour- tesy of Wyoming Newspapers, Wyoming State Library, http://newspapers .wyo.gov.

"1st Primary Election," *Casper Press*, (August 23, 1912), Courtesy of Wyoming Newspa- pers, Wyoming State Library, http://newspapers.wyo.gov.

"Floyd Blackmore on Transport Arriving at Jersey Yesterday," *Casper Daily Tribune*, (December 19, 1918), Courtesy of Wyoming Newspapers, Wyoming State Library, http://newspapers.wyo.gov.

"Fords in Big Demand," *Casper Record*, (March 13, 1917), Courtesy of Wyoming Newspapers, Wyoming State Library, http://newspapers.wyo.gov.

"Forger Escapes," *Cheyenne State Leader*, (August 19, 1911), Courtesy of Wyoming Newspapers, Wyoming State Library, http://newspapers.wyo.gov.

"Found Lee's Saddle," *Natrona County Tribune*, (Casper: June 15, 1905), Courtesy of Wyoming Newspapers, Wyoming State Library, http://newspapers.wyo.gov.

"Freeland Notes," *Natrona County Tribune*, (Casper: February 21, 1901), Courtesy of Wyoming Newspapers, Wyoming State Library, http://newspapers.wyo.gov.

"Freeland Telephone Line Completed," *Natrona County Tribune*, (Casper: December 25, 1902), Courtesy of Wyoming Newspapers, Wyoming State Library, http://newspapers.wyo.gov.

"Friday Night Dancing Club to Start Dance Series," *Casper Daily Tribune*, (April 11, 1919), Courtesy of Wyoming Newspapers, Wyoming State Library, http://newspapers.wyo.gov.

"Friday, Nov. 28," *Rocky Mountain News*, (Denver: December 4, 1919), Courtesy of Genealogy Bank, https://www.genealogybank.com/doc/newspapers.

"Fugitives Returning," *Natrona County Tribune*, (Casper: September 30, 1908), Courtesy of Wyoming Newspapers, Wyoming State Library, http://newspapers.wyo.gov.

"Funeral of Ernest Gothberg," *Jersey Journal*, (Jersey City: September 15, 1911), Courtesy of Genealogy Bank, https://www.genealogybank.com/doc/newspapers.

"G. A. Searight," *Cheyenne Weekly Leader*, (January 16, 1879), Courtesy of Wyoming Newspapers, Wyoming State Library, http://newspapers.wyo.gov.

"The Game for L. H. S.," *Laramie Republican*, (March 23, 1918), Courtesy of Wyoming Newspapers, Wyoming State Library, http://newspapers.wyo.gov.

"Glenrock Items," *Natrona County Tribune*, (Casper: October 7, 1897), Courtesy of Wyoming Newspapers, Wyoming State Library, http://newspapers.wyo.gov.

"Glenrock News," *Bill Barlow's Budget*, (Douglas: November 20, 1901), Courtesy of Wyoming Newspapers, Wyoming State Library, http://newspapers.wyo.gov.

"Is Going Just Fine," *Laramie Republican*, (March 22, 1918), Courtesy of Wyoming Newspapers, Wyoming State Library, http://newspapers.wyo.gov.

"Golf Picnic at Gothberg Park," *Casper Herald*, (July 19, 1921), Courtesy of Wyoming Newspapers, Wyoming State Library, http://newspapers.wyo.gov.

"Got Sixty Days," *Casper Press*, (August 5, 1910), Courtesy of Wyoming Newspapers, Wyoming State Library, http://newspapers.wyo.gov.

"Gothberg Dismissed on Perjury Charge," *Cheyenne Daily Leader*, (February 4, 1905), Courtesy of Wyoming Newspapers, Wyoming State Library, http://newspapers.wyo.gov.

"Gothberg Party Return Home," *Casper Herald*, (August 16, 1921), Courtesy of Wyoming Newspapers, Wyoming State Library, http://newspapers.wyo.gov.

"Gothberg Plant Sold Second Time," *Jersey Journal*, (Jersey City: March 30, 1922), Courtesy of Genealogy Bank, https://www.genealogybank.com/doc/newspapers.

"Gothberg Ranch Is Sold To Former Newspaperman," *Casper Tribune-Herald & Star*, (December 31, 1961), Courtesy of Casper College Western History Center.

"Gothberg Reunion," *Casper Herald*, (December 25, 1919), Courtesy of Wyoming Newspapers, Wyoming State Library, http://newspapers.wyo.gov.

"Gothberg, Long Resident Here, Taken by Death–Pioneer Rancher and Businessman Came Here Five Years Before Casper Founded," *Casper Tribune-Herald*, (October 22, 1947). Courtesy of Casper College Western History Center.

"Gothberg-Lewis," *Casper Herald*, (October 22, 1919), Courtesy of Wyoming Newspapers, Wyoming State Library, http://newspapers.wyo.gov.

"Gothberg-Lewis Marriage," *Casper Daily Tribune*, (October 22, 1919), Courtesy of Wyoming Newspapers, Wyoming State Library, http://newspapers.wyo.gov.

"Gothmore Lots Sell Like Bargain Offer," *Casper Daily Tribune*, (July 14, 1919), Courtesy of Wyoming Newspapers, Wyoming State Library, http://newspapers.wyo.gov.

"Gothmore Park is Resort for Casper People," *Casper Daily Tribune*, (July 11, 1919), Courtesy of Wyoming Newspapers, Wyoming State Library, http://newspapers.wyo.gov.

"Gothmore Park Popular With Casper People," *Casper Daily Tribune*, (July 22, 1920), Courtesy of Wyoming Newspapers, Wyoming State Library, http://newspapers.wyo.gov.

"Graduation Exercises," *Casper Press*, (May 10, 1912), Courtesy of Wyoming Newspapers, Wyoming State Library, http://newspapers.wyo.gov.

"Greenville Gossip," *Jersey City News*, (January 2, 1894), Courtesy of Genealogy Bank, https://www.genealogybank.com/doc/newspapers.

"Greenville Gossip," *Jersey City News*, (February 21, 1894), Courtesy of Genealogy Bank, https://www.genealogybank.com/doc/newspapers.

"Greenville Gossip," *Jersey City News*, (April 23, 1895), Courtesy of Genealogy Bank, https://www.genealogybank.com/doc/newspapers.

"Greenville Motorists' Trip," *Jersey Journal*, (Jersey City: July 7, 1903), Courtesy of Genealogy Bank, https://www.genealogybank.com/doc/newspapers.

"Greenville Snowed In," *Jersey Journal*, (Jersey City: February 13, 1899), Courtesy of Genealogy Bank, https://www.genealogybank.com/doc/newspapers.

"Guests at the Connor Hotel," *Laramie Republican*, (September 21, 1920), Courtesy of Wyoming Newspapers, Wyoming State Library, http://newspapers.wyo.gov.

"Guy Holt the High Man," *Wyoming Tribune*, (Cheyenne: September 5, 1905), Courtesy of Wyoming Newspapers, Wyoming State Library, http://newspapers.wyo.gov.

"Happy Party at High School," *Natrona County Tribune*, (Casper: March 1, 1917), Courtesy of Wyoming Newspapers, Wyoming State Library, http://newspapers.wyo.gov.

"Hardendorf Back from South," *Casper Daily Tribune*, (December 15, 1920), Courtesy of Wyoming Newspapers, Wyoming State Library, http://newspapers.wyo.gov.

"Hardendorf–Cox," *Big Horn County Rustler*, (Basin: March 9, 1917), Courtesy of Wyoming Newspapers, Wyoming State Library, http://newspapers.wyo.gov.

"Hardendorf Goes Into Field on Inspections," *Casper Herald*, (January 12, 1921), Courtesy of Wyoming Newspapers, Wyoming State Library, http://newspapers.wyo.gov.

"Headed For Hole-In-Wall," *Cheyenne Daily Leader*, (May 16, 1905), Courtesy of Wyoming Newspapers, Wyoming State Library, http://newspapers.wyo.gov.

"A Health Resort," *Wyoming Derrick*, (Casper: September 3, 1903), Courtesy of Wyoming Newspapers, Wyoming State Library, http://newspapers.wyo.gov.

"Help Wanted–Male," *Jersey Journal*, (Jersey City: August 12, 1914), Courtesy of Genealogy Bank, https://www.genealogybank.com/doc/newspapers.

"The Henderson Oil Wells," *Laramie Republican*, (August 13, 1907), Courtesy of Wyoming Newspapers, Wyoming State Library, http://newspapers.wyo.gov.

"Herder Killed by Stroke of Lightning," *Laramie Republican*, (August 25, 1911), Courtesy of Wyoming Newspapers, Wyoming State Library, http://newspapers.wyo.gov.

"High School Notes," *Casper Daily Press*, (November 10, 1915), Courtesy of Wyoming Newspapers, Wyoming State Library, http://newspapers.wyo.gov.

"High School Notes," *Casper Record*, (March 23, 1915), Courtesy of Wyoming Newspapers, Wyoming State Library, http://newspapers.wyo.gov.

"Hines–Jackson," *Wind River Mountaineer*, (Lander: January 21, 1921), Courtesy of Wyoming Newspapers, Wyoming State Library, http://newspapers.wyo.gov.

"His Automobile Went on Rampage," *Jersey Journal*, (Jersey City: March 20, 1903), Courtesy of Genealogy Bank, https://www.genealogybank.com/doc/newspapers.

"Home Guest is Honoree," *Casper Daily Tribune*, (August 25, 1921), Courtesy of Wyoming Newspapers, Wyoming State Library, http://newspapers.wyo.gov.

"Home Happenings," *Carbon County Journal*, (Rawlins: October 22, 1887), Courtesy of Wyoming Newspapers, Wyoming State Library, http://newspapers.wyo.gov.

"Hotel Arrivals," *Cheyenne State Leader*, (May 15, 1912), Courtesy of Wyoming Newspapers, Wyoming State Library, http://newspapers.wyo.gov.

"Hotel Arrivals," *Cheyenne State Leader*, (June 21, 1913), Courtesy of Wyoming Newspapers, Wyoming State Library, http://newspapers.wyo.gov.

"Hotel Arrivals," *Cheyenne State Leader*, (June 27, 1913), Courtesy of Wyoming Newspapers, Wyoming State Library, http://newspapers.wyo.gov.

"Hotel Arrivals," *Salt Lake Herald-Republican*, (Salt Lake City: January 17, 1901), Courtesy of Utah Digital Newspapers, https://newspapers.lib.utah.edu.

"House Bandits Made Hauls in Two Cities," *Casper Herald*, (November 14, 1922), Courtesy of Wyoming Newspapers, Wyoming State Library, http://newspapers.wyo.gov.

"Hung Jury," *Wyoming Tribune*, (Cheyenne, August 4, 1903), Courtesy of Wyoming Newspapers, Wyoming State Library, http://newspapers.wyo.gov.

"Important Decision," *Natrona County Tribune*, (Casper: October 12, 1910), Courtesy of Wyoming Newspapers, Wyoming State Library, http://newspapers.wyo.gov.

"Improvements at Alcova," *Wyoming Derrick*, (Casper: November 19, 1903), Courtesy of Wyoming Newspapers, Wyoming State Library, http://newspapers.wyo.gov.

"In Chancery of New Jersey," *Jersey Journal*, (Jersey City: June 25, 1912), Courtesy of Genealogy Bank, https://www.genealogybank.com/doc/newspapers.

"In Greenville," *Jersey Journal*, (Jersey City: August 16, 1894), Courtesy of Genealogy Bank, https://www.genealogybank.com/doc/newspapers.

"In Realms of Society," *Natrona County Tribune*, (Casper: December 11, 1902), Courtesy of Wyoming Newspapers, Wyoming State Library, http://newspapers.wyo.gov.

"In the Circuit Court of the United States within and For the District of Wyoming," *Natrona County Tribune*, (Casper: June 10, 1910), Courtesy of Wyoming Newspapers, Wyoming State Library, http://newspapers.wyo.gov.

"Incorporated Yesterday," *Cheyenne State Leader*, (April 6, 1917), Courtesy of Wyoming Newspapers, Wyoming State Library, http://newspapers.wyo.gov.

"Iowa-Wyoming Elects New Officers Here," *Casper Daily Tribune*, (June 29, 1922), Courtesy of Wyoming Newspapers, Wyoming State Library, http://newspapers .wyo.gov.

"Iowa-Wyoming Oil Company to Take Over Syndicates," *Casper Herald*, (June 12, 1920), Courtesy of Wyoming Newspapers, Wyoming State Library, http://news papers.wyo.gov.

"It Was Only the Watchman," *Jersey Journal*, (Jersey City: April 6, 1887), Courtesy of Genealogy Bank, https://genealogybank.com/doc/newspapers.

"Jerky Bill is Promoting," *Wyoming Tribune*, (Cheyenne: July 25, 1905), Courtesy of Wyoming Newspapers, Wyoming State Library, http://newspapers.wyo.gov.

"Jersey City Mortgages," *Jersey Journal*, (Jersey City: July 14, 1896), Courtesy of Genealogy Bank, https://www.genealogybank.com/doc/newspapers.

"John Landon Dead," *Wyoming Tribune*, (Cheyenne: August 21, 1903), Courtesy of Wyoming Newspapers, Wyoming State Library, http://newspapers.wyo.gov.

"A Journal 'Fake' Nailed," *Jersey City News*, (August 5, 1893), Courtesy of Genealogy Bank, https://www.genealogybank.com/doc/newspapers.

"Judge Carpenter Dies," *Casper Record*, (December 31, 1912), Courtesy of Wyoming Newspapers, Wyoming State Library, http://newspapers.wyo.gov.

"Kenneth McRae's Trial," *Natrona County Tribune*, (Casper: November 18, 1897), Courtesy of Wyoming Newspapers, Wyoming State Library, http://newspapers .wyo.gov.

"Killed Diseased Sheep, State Veterinarian Slaughters Bunch of Sheep With Incurable Disease," *Natrona County Tribune*, (Casper: May 13, 1908), Courtesy of Wyoming Newspapers, Wyoming State Library, http://newspapers.wyo.gov.

"La Grippe," *Natrona County Tribune*, (Casper: January 31, 1901), Courtesy of Wyoming Newspapers, Wyoming State Library, http://newspapers.wyo.gov.

"Lady Defendant," *Wyoming Tribune*, (Cheyenne: November 17, 1909), Courtesy of Wyoming Newspapers, Wyoming State Library, http://newspapers.wyo.gov.

"Land Lease Hearing," *Wyoming Derrick*, (Casper: August 5, 1897), Courtesy of Wyoming Newspapers, Wyoming State Library, http://newspapers.wyo.gov.

"Lander for Casper," *Wyoming Derrick*, (Casper: March 10, 1904), Courtesy of Wyoming Newspapers, Wyoming State Library, http://newspapers.wyo.gov.

"Lander's Leading Local Items of Interest to All," *Wyoming State Journal*, (Lander: September 10, 1909), Courtesy of Wyoming Newspapers, Wyoming State Library, http://newspapers.wyo.gov.

"Last of Blackmore Family Leaves for Duty with Nation," *Casper Daily Press*, (October 27, 1918), Courtesy of Wyoming Newspapers, Wyoming State Library, http://news papers.wyo.gov.

"Lee Brought Back," *Natrona County Tribune*, (Casper: February 9, 1910), Courtesy of Wyoming Newspapers, Wyoming State Library, http://newspapers.wyo.gov.

"Legal Notice," *Natrona County Tribune*, (Casper: March 11, 1908), Courtesy of Wyoming Newspapers, Wyoming State Library, http://newspapers.wyo.gov.

"Leone Blackmore Ill at N. M. Army Hospital," *Casper Daily Tribune*, (April 25, 1919), Courtesy of Wyoming Newspapers, Wyoming State Library, http://newspapers .wyo.gov.

"Leone Blackmore Makes Good in Sanitary Corps," *Casper Daily Tribune*, (December 11, 1918), Courtesy of Wyoming Newspapers, Wyoming State Library, http://newspapers.wyo.gov.

"Leone Blackmore off for Hospital Activity," *Casper Daily Press*, (November 9, 1918), Courtesy of Wyoming Newspapers, Wyoming State Library, http://newspapers.wyo.gov.

"Letter List," *Casper Weekly Mail*, (February 8, 1889), Courtesy of Wyoming Newspapers, Wyoming State Library, http://newspapers.wyo.gov.

"Lightning Kills Herder," *Bill Barlow's Budget*, (Douglas: August 23, 1911), Courtesy of Wyoming Newspapers, Wyoming State Library, http://newspapers.wyo.gov.

"Lightning Shocks Many People," *Natrona County Tribune*, (Casper: June 15, 1910), Courtesy of Wyoming Newspapers, Wyoming State Library, http://newspapers.wyo.gov.

"Little Locals," *Natrona County Tribune*, (Casper: June 23, 1898), Courtesy of Wyoming Newspapers, Wyoming State Library, http://newspapers.wyo.gov.

"Little Locals," *Natrona County Tribune*, (Casper: July 7, 1898), Courtesy of Wyoming Newspapers, Wyoming State Library, http://newspapers.wyo.gov.

"Little Locals," *Natrona County Tribune*, (Casper: October 5, 1899), Courtesy of Wyoming Newspapers, Wyoming State Library, http://newspapers.wyo.gov.

"Little Locals," *Natrona County Tribune*, (Casper: January 25, 1900), Courtesy of Wyoming Newspapers, Wyoming State Library, http://newspapers.wyo.gov.

"Little Locals," *Natrona County Tribune*, (Casper: June 7, 1900), Courtesy of Wyoming Newspapers, Wyoming State Library, http://newspapers.wyo.gov.

"Load of Logs Rolled Over Him," *Natrona County Tribune*, (Casper: August 31, 1905), Courtesy of Wyoming Newspapers, Wyoming State Library, http://newspapers.wyo.gov.

"Local and Personal," *Casper Daily Press*, (September 2, 1914), Courtesy of Wyoming Newspapers, Wyoming State Library, http://newspapers.wyo.gov.

"Local and Personal," *Casper Daily Press*, (April 15, 1915), Courtesy of Wyoming Newspapers, Wyoming State Library, http://newspapers.wyo.gov.

"Local and Personal," *Casper Daily Press*, (August 13, 1915), Courtesy of Wyoming Newspapers, Wyoming State Library, http://newspapers.wyo.gov.

"Local and Personal," *Casper Daily Press*, (November 20, 1915), Courtesy of Wyoming Newspapers, Wyoming State Library, http://newspapers.wyo.gov.

"Local and Personal," *Casper Press*, (August 7, 1908), Courtesy of Wyoming Newspapers, Wyoming State Library, http://newspapers.wyo.gov.

"Local and Personal," *Casper Press*, (May 21, 1909), Courtesy of Wyoming Newspapers, Wyoming State Library, http://newspapers.wyo.gov.

"Local and Personal," *Casper Press*, (June 18, 1909), Courtesy of Wyoming Newspapers, Wyoming State Library, http://newspapers.wyo.gov.

"Local and Personal," *Casper Press*, (June 25, 1909), Courtesy of Wyoming Newspapers, Wyoming State Library, http://newspapers.wyo.gov.

"Local and Personal," *Casper Press*, (August 20, 1909), Courtesy of Wyoming Newspapers, Wyoming State Library, http://newspapers.wyo.gov.

"Local and Personal," *Casper Press*, (September 3, 1909), Courtesy of Wyoming Newspapers, Wyoming State Library, http://newspapers.wyo.gov.

"Local and Personal," *Casper Press*, (January 14, 1910), Courtesy of Wyoming Newspapers, Wyoming State Library, http://newspapers.wyo.gov.

"Local and Personal," *Casper Weekly Press*, (June 25, 1915), Courtesy of Wyoming Newspapers, Wyoming State Library, http://newspapers.wyo.gov.

"Local and Personal," *Douglas Budget*, (March 8, 1917), Courtesy of Wyoming Newspapers, Wyoming State Library, http://newspapers.wyo.gov.

"Local and Personal," *Douglas Budget*, (March 15, 1917), Courtesy of Wyoming Newspapers, Wyoming State Library, http://newspapers.wyo.gov.

"Local and Personal," *Douglas Budget*, (July 13, 1922), Courtesy of Wyoming Newspapers, Wyoming State Library, http://newspapers.wyo.gov.

"Local Brevities," *Laramie Boomerang*, (May 18, 1904), Courtesy of Wyoming Newspapers, Wyoming State Library, http://newspapers.wyo.gov.

"Local Events," *Natrona County Tribune*, (Casper: April 13, 1910), Courtesy of Wyoming Newspapers, Wyoming State Library, http://newspapers.wyo.gov.

"Local Happenings," *Casper Press*, (June 17, 1910), Courtesy of Wyoming Newspapers, Wyoming State Library, http://newspapers.wyo.gov.

"Local Happenings," *Casper Press*, (December 16, 1910), Courtesy of Wyoming Newspapers, Wyoming State Library, http://newspapers.wyo.gov.

"Local Happenings," *Casper Press*, (March 17, 1911), Courtesy of Wyoming Newspapers, Wyoming State Library, http://newspapers.wyo.gov.

"Local Happenings," *Natrona Tribune*, (Casper: October 4, 1894), Courtesy of Wyoming Newspapers, Wyoming State Library, http://newspapers.wyo.gov.

"Local Happenings," *Natrona Tribune*, (Casper: February 28, 1895), Courtesy of Wyoming Newspapers, Wyoming State Library, http://newspapers.wyo.gov.

"Local Happenings," *Thermopolis Independent*, (September 3, 1915), Courtesy of Wyoming Newspapers, Wyoming State Library, http://newspapers.wyo.gov.

"Local Happenings," *Thermopolis Independent*, (September 24, 1915), Courtesy of Wyoming Newspapers, Wyoming State Library, http://newspapers.wyo.gov.

"Local Happenings," *Wyoming Derrick*, (Casper: December 28, 1905), Courtesy of Wyoming Newspapers, Wyoming State Library, http://newspapers.wyo.gov.

"Local Lines," *Sundance Gazette*, (August 8, 1885), Courtesy of Wyoming Newspapers, Wyoming State Library, http://newspapers.wyo.gov.

"Local Mention," *News Journal*, (Newcastle: February 7, 1908), Courtesy of Wyoming Newspapers, Wyoming State Library, http://newspapers.wyo.gov.

"Local Mention," *News-Journal*, (Newcastle: September 17, 1909), Courtesy of Wyoming Newspapers, Wyoming State Library, http://newspapers.wyo.gov.

"Local News," *Basin Republican*, (October 29, 1915), Courtesy of Wyoming Newspapers, Wyoming State Library, http://newspapers.wyo.gov.

"Local News," *Big Horn County Rustler*, (Basin: April 19, 1918), Courtesy of Wyoming Newspapers, Wyoming State Library, http://newspapers.wyo.gov.

"Local News," *Casper Record*, (November 14, 1911), Courtesy of Wyoming Newspapers, Wyoming State Library, http://newspapers.wyo.gov.

"Local News," *Graphic*, (Douglas: July 11, 1891), Courtesy of Wyoming Newspapers, Wyoming State Library, http://newspapers.wyo.gov.

"Local News," *Natrona County Tribune*, (Casper: March 22, 1900), Courtesy of Wyoming Newspapers, Wyoming State Library, http://newspapers.wyo.gov.

"Local News," *Natrona County Tribune*, (Casper: July 5, 1900), Courtesy of Wyoming Newspapers, Wyoming State Library, http://newspapers.wyo.gov.

"Local News," *Natrona County Tribune*, (Casper: August 23, 1900), Courtesy of Wyoming Newspapers, Wyoming State Library, http://newspapers.wyo.gov.

"Local News," *Natrona County Tribune*, (Casper: October 18, 1900), Courtesy of Wyoming Newspapers, Wyoming State Library, http://newspapers.wyo.gov.

"Local News," *Natrona County Tribune*, (Casper: January 31, 1901), Courtesy of Wyoming Newspapers, Wyoming State Library, http://newspapers.wyo.gov.

"Local News," *Natrona County Tribune*, (Casper: August 19, 1908), Courtesy of Wyoming Newspapers, Wyoming State Library, http://newspapers.wyo.gov.

"Local News," *Natrona County Tribune*, (Casper: May 15, 1912), Courtesy of Wyoming Newspapers, Wyoming State Library, http://newspapers.wyo.gov.

"Local News and Personal Items," *Natrona County Tribune*, (Casper: September 24, 1914), Courtesy of Wyoming Newspapers, Wyoming State Library, http://newspapers.wyo.gov.

"Local News and Personal Items," *Natrona County Tribune*, (Casper: October 1, 1914), Courtesy of Wyoming Newspapers, Wyoming State Library, http://newspapers.wyo.gov.

"Local News Notes," *Natrona County Tribune*, (Casper: March 12, 1914), Courtesy of Wyoming Newspapers, Wyoming State Library, http://newspapers.wyo.gov.

"Local Notes," *Casper Weekly Mail*, (February 1, 1889), Courtesy of Wyoming Newspapers, Wyoming State Library, http://newspapers.wyo.gov.

"Local Notes," *Natrona Tribune*, (Casper: August 5, 1891), Courtesy of Wyoming Newspapers, Wyoming State Library, http://newspapers.wyo.gov.

"Local Notes," *Natrona Tribune*, (Casper: September 16, 1891), Courtesy of Wyoming Newspapers, Wyoming State Library, http://newspapers.wyo.gov.

"Local Notes," *Natrona Tribune*, (Casper: November 11, 1891), Courtesy of Wyoming Newspapers, Wyoming State Library, http://newspapers.wyo.gov.

"Local Notes," *Natrona Tribune*, Casper: December 9, 1891), Courtesy of Wyoming Newspapers, Wyoming State Library, http://newspapers.wyo.gov.

"Local Notes," *Natrona Tribune*, (Casper: December 16, 1891), Courtesy of Wyoming Newspapers, Wyoming State Library, http://newspapers.wyo.gov.

"Local Notes," *Natrona Tribune*, (Casper: February 17, 1892), Courtesy of Wyoming Newspapers, Wyoming State Library, http://newspapers.wyo.gov.

"Local Notes," *Natrona Tribune*, (Casper: May 25, 1892), Courtesy of Wyoming Newspapers, Wyoming State Library, http://newspapers.wyo.gov.

"Local Notes," *Rawlins Republican*, (January 23, 1919), Courtesy of Wyoming Newspapers, Wyoming State Library, http://newspapers.wyo.gov.

"Local Notes," *Rawlins Republican*, (August 11, 1921), Courtesy of Wyoming Newspapers, Wyoming State Library, http://newspapers.wyo.gov.

"Local Picnic Grounds," *Jersey City News*, (May 17, 1889), Courtesy of Genealogy Bank, https://www.genealogybank.com/doc/newspapers.

"Local Telephone Lines," *Wyoming Derrick*, (Casper: August 7, 1902), Courtesy of Wyoming Newspapers, Wyoming State Library, http://newspapers.wyo.gov.

"Lonabaugh a Lucky Cuss," *Big Horn County Rustler*, (Basin: April 8, 1921), Courtesy of Wyoming Newspapers, Wyoming State Library, http://newspapers.wyo.gov.

"Lost in a Snowstorm," *Semi-Weekly Boomerang*, (Laramie: December 16, 1895), Courtesy of Wyoming Newspapers, Wyoming State Library, http://newspapers.wyo.gov.

"Lost on Prairie," *Wyoming Tribune*, (Cheyenne: March 14, 1906), Courtesy of Wyoming Newspapers, Wyoming State Library, http://newspapers.wyo.gov.

"Lots in Addition to Gothmore Park Selling," *Casper Daily Tribune*, (July 22, 1920), Courtesy of Wyoming Newspapers, Wyoming State Library, http://newspapers.wyo.gov.

"Lusk Local News," *Lusk Herald*, (May 10, 1917), Courtesy of Wyoming Newspapers, Wyoming State Library, http://newspapers.wyo.gov.

"Lusk Local News," *Lusk Herald*, (January 10, 1918), Courtesy of Wyoming Newspapers, Wyoming State Library, http://newspapers.wyo.gov.

"Lusk Local News," *Lusk Herald*, (June 6, 1918), Courtesy of Wyoming Newspapers, Wyoming State Library, http://newspapers.wyo.gov.

"Lusk Local News," *Lusk Herald*, (November 14, 1918), Courtesy of Wyoming Newspapers, Wyoming State Library, http://newspapers.wyo.gov.

"Many Bidders in Casper for Big Wool Sale," *Casper Daily Tribune*, (June 15, 1922), Courtesy of Wyoming Newspapers, Wyoming State Library, http://newspapers.wyo.gov.

"Many Companies in Field," *Casper Daily Tribune*, (April 2, 1921), Courtesy of Wyoming Newspapers, Wyoming State Library, http://newspapers.wyo.gov.

"Market Gossip and Field News," *Casper Daily Tribune*, (September 28, 1921), Courtesy of Wyoming Newspapers, Wyoming State Library, http://newspapers.wyo.gov.

"Market Gossip and Field News–Casper is interested in Utah," *Casper Daily Tribune*, (March 15, 1921), Courtesy of Wyoming Newspapers, Wyoming State Library, http://newspapers.wyo.gov.

"Market Gossip and Field News–Storm Slows up Well Drilling," *Casper Daily Tribune*, (December 22, 1921), Courtesy of Wyoming Newspapers, Wyoming State Library, http://newspapers.wyo.gov.

"Martin Trout Caught at San Francisco," *Cheyenne Daily Leader*, (December 24, 1905), Courtesy of Wyoming Newspapers, Wyoming State Library, http://newspapers.wyo.gov.

"Mayor Returns," *Casper Daily Tribune*, (February 20, 1922), Courtesy of Wyoming Newspapers, Wyoming State Library, http://newspapers.wyo.gov.

"McRae Held for Murder," *Natrona County Tribune*, (Casper: June 10, 1897), Courtesy of Wyoming Newspapers, Wyoming State Library, http://newspapers.wyo.gov.

"Meeting of Women's Club," *Casper Daily Press*, (December 7, 1918), Courtesy of Wyoming Newspapers, Wyoming State Library, http://newspapers.wyo.gov.

"Memorial Day–Casper People Observe it for the First Time," *Natrona County Tribune,* (June 3, 1897: Casper), Courtesy of Wyoming Newspapers, Wyoming State Library, http://newspapers.wyo.gov.

"Merry Party Friday at Jourgensen Home," *Casper Daily Tribune*, (January 8, 1917), Courtesy of Wyoming Newspapers, Wyoming State Library, http://newspapers.wyo.gov.

"Midwest Will Buy Hjorth Oil Company's Product," *Casper Daily Press*, (July 17, 1914), Courtesy of Wyoming Newspapers, Wyoming State Library, http://newspapers.wyo.gov.

"Military Ball Tomorrow Night," *Casper Daily Tribun*e, (May 8, 1919), Courtesy of Wyoming Newspapers, Wyoming State Library, http://newspapers.wyo.gov.

"Miller Wakes Up," *Wyoming Tribune*, (Cheyenne: August 21, 1905), Courtesy of Wyoming Newspapers, Wyoming State Library, http://newspapers.wyo.gov.

"Mineral Land Contest," *Wyoming Derrick*, (Casper: April 5, 1900), Courtesy of Wyoming Newspapers, Wyoming State Library, http://newspapers.wyo.gov.

"Mining Notes," *Rawlins Semi-Weekly Republican*, (September 20, 1899), Courtesy of Wyoming Newspapers, Wyoming State Library, http://newspapers.wyo.gov.

"Minor Mention," *Weekly Boomerang*, (Laramie: July 12, 1883), Courtesy of Wyoming Newspapers, Wyoming State Library, http://newspapers.wyo.gov.

"Miss Blackmore Enter Upon Duties in School of Vocational Training," *Casper Daily Tribune*, (November 29, 1918), Courtesy of Wyoming Newspapers, Wyoming State Library, http://newspapers.wyo.gov.

"Miss Blackmore Improving," *Casper Daily Tribune*, (May 3, 1919), Courtesy of Wyoming Newspapers, Wyoming State Library, http://newspapers.wyo.gov.

"Miss Blackmore, Reconstruction Aide, to Recuperate Here," *Casper Daily Tribune*, (May 23, 1919), Courtesy of Wyoming Newspapers, Wyoming State Library, http://newspapers.wyo.gov.

"Mrs. Louise Foster Entertains at Dinner," *Natrona County Tribune*, (Casper: April 11, 1918), Courtesy of Wyoming Newspapers, Wyoming State Library, http://news papers.wyo.gov.

"Mrs. Sam Service to Head Red Cross Drive Starting Sunday," *Casper Daily Tribune*, (November 1, 1919, Courtesy of Wyoming Newspapers, Wyoming State Library, http://newspapers.wyo.gov.

"Mrs. Story Entertains at Informal Dinner," *Casper Daily Tribune*, (March 4, 1919), Courtesy of Wyoming Newspapers, Wyoming State Library, http://newspapers. wyo.gov.

"Missou Hines May Enter Movies," *Casper Daily Tribune*, (April 25, 1921), Courtesy of Wyoming Newspapers, Wyoming State Library, http://newspapers.wyo.gov.

"Missou Hines Now a Benedict," *Douglas Budget*, (January 20, 1921), Courtesy of Wyoming Newspapers, Wyoming State Library, http://newspapers.wyo.gov.

"Missou Hines Passes Fifty-Sixth Stepping Stone and Celebrates," *Casper Record*, (July 17, 1918), Courtesy of Wyoming Newspapers, Wyoming State Library, http:// newspapers.wyo.gov.

"Missou Hines Returns from Ranger Field," *Casper Daily Tribune*, (February 22, 1919), Courtesy of Wyoming Newspapers, Wyoming State Library, http://newspapers .wyo.gov.

"Missou Hines Selling Stock for a Casper Asbestos Mine," *Casper Press*, (June 25, 1909), Courtesy of Wyoming Newspapers, Wyoming State Library, http://news papers.wyo.gov.

"Missou is Selling Asbestos," *Wyoming Semi-Weekly Tribune*, (Cheyenne: January 28, 1910), Courtesy of Wyoming Newspapers, Wyoming State Library, http://news papers.wyo.gov.

"Missou's New Position," *Riverton Republican*, (December 14, 1907), Courtesy of Wyoming Newspapers, Wyoming State Library, http://newspapers.wyo.gov.

"Mr. and Mrs. Sam Service Will Entertain," *Casper Herald*, (January 1, 1920), Courtesy of Wyoming Newspapers, Wyoming State Library, http://newspapers.wyo.gov.

"Mr. R. Davis Carey," *Cheyenne Daily Sun*, (July 24, 1877), Courtesy of Wyoming Newspapers, Wyoming State Library, http://newspapers.wyo.gov.

"'Molly' Wolf Married," *Natrona County Tribune*, (Casper: July 14, 1904), Courtesy of Wyoming Newspapers, Wyoming State Library, http://newspapers.wyo.gov.

"More About Capp," *Cheyenne Weekly Leader*, (October 19, 1882), Courtesy of Wyoming Newspapers, Wyoming State Library, http://newspapers.wyo.gov.

"More Local," *Casper Press*, (December 17, 1909), Courtesy of Wyoming Newspapers, Wyoming State Library, http://newspapers.wyo.gov.

"More War on Salt Creek," *Casper Press*, (July 22, 1910), Courtesy of Wyoming Newspapers, Wyoming State Library, http://newspapers.wyo.gov.

"Mortgages–Bayonne," *Jersey Journal*, (Jersey City: June 27, 1910), Courtesy of Genealogy Bank, https://www.genealogybank.com/doc/newspapers.

"Mortgages–Jersey City," *Jersey Journal*, (Jersey City: February 1, 1913), Courtesy of Genealogy Bank, https://www.genealogybank.com/doc/newspapers.

"Mortuary Notice," *New York Herald*, (June 1, 1890), Courtesy of Genealogy Bank, https://www.genealogybank.com/doc/newspapers.

"Motor Pool Highlites," *The Slip Stream*, (Casper: December 23, 1942), Courtesy of Wyoming Newspapers, Wyoming State Library, http://newspapers.wyo.gov.

"Mountain Cabin Proves Cache for 95 Gallons Hootch," *Wyoming State Tribune*, (Cheyenne: December 12, 1921), Courtesy of Wyoming Newspapers, Wyoming State Library, http://newspapers.wyo.gov.

"Murphy Murder Trial," *Natrona County Tribune*, (Casper: July 30, 1903), Courtesy of Wyoming Newspapers, Wyoming State Library, http://newspapers.wyo.gov.

"Murphy's Trial," *Wyoming Derrick*, (Casper: July 30, 1903), Courtesy of Wyoming Newspapers, Wyoming State Library, http://newspapers.wyo.gov.

"My Mountain Cabin," *Casper Daily Tribune*, (April 28, 1922), Courtesy of Wyoming Newspapers, Wyoming State Library, http://newspapers.wyo.gov.

"Narrow Escape from Lightning," *Casper Press*, (June 17, 1910), Courtesy of Wyoming Newspapers, Wyoming State Library, http://newspapers.wyo.gov.

"Natrona County Must Furnish Red Cross with 1,960 Pieces of Linen for Hospital Supply," *Casper Daily Tribune*, (September 28, 1918), Courtesy of Wyoming Newspapers, Wyoming State Library, http://newspapers.wyo.gov.

"Natrona Delphian Chapter Organized," *Casper Daily Tribune*, (July 29, 1918), Courtesy of Wyoming Newspapers, Wyoming State Library, http://newspapers.wyo.gov.

"Natrona Short $600 in Drive for Near East," *Casper Daily Tribune*, (January 20, 1919), Courtesy of Wyoming Newspapers, Wyoming State Library, http://newspapers.wyo.gov.

"Natrona's Legislative Candidates," *Natrona County Tribune*, (Casper: July 24, 1912), Courtesy of Wyoming Newspapers, Wyoming State Library, http://newspapers.wyo.gov.

"Nearly Freezes to Death," *Douglas Enterprise*, (December 22, 1914), Courtesy of Wyoming Newspapers, Wyoming State Library, http://newspapers.wyo.gov.

"New Blackmore Apartment Ready by Thanksgiving," *Casper Herald*, (October 5, 1919), Courtesy of Wyoming Newspapers, Wyoming State Library, http://news papers.wyo.gov.

"New Corporations," *Wyoming Tribune*, (Cheyenne: July 31, 1903), Courtesy of Wyoming Newspapers, Wyoming State Library, http://newspapers.wyo.gov.

"New Dancing Club Makes Debut Friday," *Casper Daily Tribune*, (April 8, 1919), Courtesy of Wyoming Newspapers, Wyoming State Library, http://newspapers.wyo.gov.

"New Exhibits at Arkeon to Charm Second Nighters," *Casper Herald*, (October 25, 1922), Courtesy of Wyoming Newspapers, Wyoming State Library, http://news papers.wyo.gov.

"New Field Manager," *Wyoming State Tribune*, (Cheyenne: March 10, 1920), Courtesy of Genealogy Bank, https://www.genealogybank.com/doc/newspapers.

"New Law is a Freak," *Natrona County Tribune*, (Casper: March 17, 1909), Courtesy of Wyoming Newspapers, Wyoming State Library, http://newspapers.wyo.gov.

"New Oil Company Formed to Drill Carbon County," *Casper Daily Tribune*, (November 28, 1919), Courtesy of Wyoming Newspapers, Wyoming State Library, http://newspapers.wyo.gov.

"New Pool Hall," *Basin Republican*, (April 21, 1916), Courtesy of Wyoming Newspapers, Wyoming State Library, http://newspapers.wyo.gov.

"New Refinery Site Purchased, Location East of City, Report," *Casper Daily Tribune*, (November 29, 1921), Courtesy of Wyoming Newspapers, Wyoming State Library, http://newspapers.wyo.gov.

"New Refinery With 20,000 bbls. Crude Capacity for Casper," *Wyoming Oil World*, (Casper: November 12, 1921), Courtesy of Wyoming Newspapers, Wyoming State Library, http://newspapers.wyo.gov.

"New York Oil," *Wyoming Oil World*, (Casper: September 24, 1921), Courtesy of Wyoming Newspapers, Wyoming State Library, http://newspapers.wyo.gov.

"New York Oil Company," *Wyoming Oil World*, (Casper: September 4, 1920), Courtesy of Wyoming Newspapers, Wyoming State Library, http://newspapers.wyo.gov.

"New York Oil Operations," *Casper Daily Tribune*, (June 30, 1922), Courtesy of Wyoming Newspapers, Wyoming State Library, http://newspapers.wyo.gov.

"New York Oil Operations," *Casper Daily Tribune*, (August 24, 1922), Courtesy of Wyoming Newspapers, Wyoming State Library, http://newspapers.wyo.gov.

"New York Oil to Pipe Gas," *Wyoming Oil World*, (Casper: January 10, 1920), Courtesy of Wyoming Newspapers, Wyoming State Library, http://newspapers.wyo.gov.

"New York Strikes Oil in Test Well in Spindle Top District," *Casper Daily Tribune*, (July 11, 1922), Courtesy of Wyoming Newspapers, Wyoming State Library, http://newspapers.wyo.gov.

"Newcastle," *Sheridan Post*, (September 17, 1909), Courtesy of Wyoming Newspapers, Wyoming State Library, http://newspapers.wyo.gov.

"News in Brief," *Wyoming State Tribune*, (Cheyenne: August 10, 1921), Courtesy of Wyoming Newspapers, Wyoming State Library, http://newspapers.wyo.gov.

"News of the West–Wyoming," *Salt Lake Herald-Republican*, (Salt Lake City: March, 24, 1898), Courtesy of Utah Digital Newspapers, https://newspapers.lib.utah.edu.

"Nicknames Labeled Rough and Tough Rugged Men of '86: Early Days of Cowpunching are Told by "Molly" Wolfe," *Douglas Enterprise*, (June 23, 1936), Courtesy of Wyoming Newspapers, Wyoming State Library, http://newspapers.wyo.gov.

"Nine Candidates Representing Four Political Parties take the Field for Municipal Election," *Casper Daily Tribune*, (October 12, 1918), Courtesy of Wyoming Newspapers, Wyoming State Library, http://newspapers.wyo.gov.

"Nine Casper Men Will Do Jury Service," *Casper Herald*, (October 19, 1922), Courtesy of Wyoming Newspapers, Wyoming State Library, http://newspapers.wyo.gov.

"No Isle of Pines for Them," *Casper Press*, (July 9, 1909), Courtesy of Wyoming Newspapers, Wyoming State Library, http://newspapers.wyo.gov.

"Non-Partisan Ticket Named at Casper," *Laramie Republican*, (October 30, 1917), Courtesy of Wyoming Newspapers, Wyoming State Library, http://newspapers.wyo.gov.

"Northwest Oil Co. Brings in its First Well in Big Muddy," *Casper Daily Tribune*, (January 20, 1917), Courtesy of Wyoming Newspapers, Wyoming State Library, http://newspapers.wyo.gov.

"Northwestern Lays Off Two Good Men," *Wyoming State Journal & Lander Clipper*, (November 22, 1907), Courtesy of Wyoming Newspapers, Wyoming State Library, http://newspapers.wyo.gov.

"Northwestern Officials," *Wind River Mountaineer*, (Lander: June 14, 1907), Courtesy of Wyoming Newspapers, Wyoming State Library, http://newspapers.wyo.gov.

"Northwestern Surveyors Working Towards Pinedale," *Pinedale Roundup*, (September 18, 1907), Courtesy of Wyoming Newspapers, Wyoming State Library, http://newspapers.wyo.gov.

"Not in Contempt," *Natrona County Tribune*, (Casper: August 3, 1910), Courtesy of Wyoming Newspapers, Wyoming State Library, http://newspapers.wyo.gov.

"Notable Improvements Show Growth of City," *Casper Daily Press*, (October 9, 1915), Courtesy of Wyoming Newspapers, Wyoming State Library, http://newspapers.wyo.gov.

"Notes From the Osage Field," *Wyoming Oil World*, (December 20, 1919), Courtesy of Wyoming Newspapers, Wyoming State Library, http://newspapers.wyo.gov.

"Notes From the Southern Fields," *Wyoming Oil World*, (Casper: December 27, 1919), Courtesy of Wyoming Newspapers, Wyoming State Library, http://newspapers.wyo.gov.

"Notice," *Natrona County Tribune*, (Casper: April 3, 1907), Courtesy of Wyoming Newspapers, Wyoming State Library, http://newspapers.wyo.gov.

"Notice," *Natrona County Tribune*, (Casper: July 22, 1908), Courtesy of Wyoming Newspapers, Wyoming State Library, http://newspapers.wyo.gov.

"Notice for Publication," *Casper Daily Tribune*, (October 23, 1922), Courtesy of Wyoming Newspapers, Wyoming State Library, http://newspapers.wyo.gov.

"Notice for Publication," *Natrona Tribune*, (Casper: July 22, 1891), Courtesy of Wyoming Newspapers, Wyoming State Library, http://newspapers.wyo.gov.

"Notice of Annual Stock Holders' Meeting," *Rawlins Republican*, (November 25, 1920), Courtesy of Wyoming Newspapers, Wyoming State Library, http://newspapers.wyo.gov.

"Notice of Appropriations of Water," *Natrona County Tribune*, (Casper: October 20, 1909), Courtesy of Wyoming Newspapers, Wyoming State Library, http://news papers.wyo.gov.

"Notice of Change of Capital Stock," *Casper Daily Tribune*, (February 28, 1919), Courtesy of Wyoming Newspapers, Wyoming State Library, http://newspapers.wyo.gov.

"Notice of Dissolution," *Casper Daily Tribune*, (November 6, 1918), Courtesy of Wyoming Newspapers, Wyoming State Library, http://newspapers.wyo.gov.

"Notice of Dissolution," *Casper Daily Tribune*, (May 19, 1919), Courtesy of Wyoming Newspapers, Wyoming State Library, http://newspapers.wyo.gov.

"Notice of Dissolution," *Casper Daily Tribune*, (June 16, 1919), Courtesy of Wyoming Newspapers, Wyoming State Library, http://newspapers.wyo.gov.

"Notice of Foreclosure of Chattel Mortgage," *Natrona County Tribune*, (Casper: July 3, 1913), Courtesy of Wyoming Newspapers, Wyoming State Library, http://news papers.wyo.gov.

"Notice of Incorporation," *Casper Daily Tribune*, (May 16, 1922), Courtesy of Wyoming Newspapers, Wyoming State Library, http://newspapers.wyo.gov.

"Notice of Incorporation," *Casper Daily Tribune*, (November 23, 1922), Courtesy of Wyoming Newspapers, Wyoming State Library, http://newspapers.wyo.gov.

"Notice of Incorporation," *Casper Herald*, (June 27, 1922), Courtesy of Wyoming Newspapers, Wyoming State Library, http://newspapers.wyo.gov.

"Notice of Incorporation," *Casper Press*, (December 13, 1912), Courtesy of Wyoming Newspapers, Wyoming State Library, http://newspapers.wyo.gov.

"Notice of Incorporation," *Casper Record*, (November 14, 1916), Courtesy of Wyoming Newspapers, Wyoming State Library, http://newspapers.wyo.gov.

"Notice of Incorporation," *Casper Record*, (December 19, 1916), Courtesy of Wyoming Newspapers, Wyoming State Library, http://newspapers.wyo.gov.

"Notice of Incorporation," *Casper Record*, (March 6, 1917), Courtesy of Wyoming Newspapers, Wyoming State Library, http://newspapers.wyo.gov.

"Notice of Incorporation," *Casper Record*, (May 15, 1917), Courtesy of Wyoming Newspapers, Wyoming State Library, http://newspapers.wyo.gov.

"Notice of Incorporation," *Casper Weekly Press*, (August 4, 1916), Courtesy of Wyoming Newspapers, Wyoming State Library, http://newspapers.wyo.gov.

"Notice of Incorporation," *Natrona County Tribune*, (Casper: October 31, 1906), Courtesy of Wyoming Newspapers, Wyoming State Library, http://newspapers.wyo.gov.

"Notice of Incorporation," *Natrona County Tribune*, (Casper: February 19, 1908), Courtesy of Wyoming Newspapers, Wyoming State Library, http://newspapers.wyo.gov.

"Notice of Incorporation," *Natrona County Tribune*, (Casper: December 18, 1913), Courtesy of Wyoming Newspapers, Wyoming State Library, http://newspapers .wyo.gov.

"Notice of Lands to be Leased," *Saratoga Sun*, (March 12, 1908), Courtesy of Wyoming Newspapers, Wyoming State Library, http://newspapers.wyo.gov.

"Notice of Publication," *Natrona County Tribune*, (Casper: September 14, 1910), Courtesy of Wyoming Newspapers, Wyoming State Library, http://newspapers.wyo.gov.

"Notice of Quarantine," *Natrona County Tribune*, (Casper: February 12, 1908), Courtesy of Wyoming Newspapers, Wyoming State Library, http://newspapers.wyo.gov.

"Notice of Special Meeting of the Stockholders of the Casper Ranger Oil Company," *Casper Daily Tribune*, (October 22, 1919), Courtesy of Wyoming Newspapers, Wyoming State Library, http://newspapers.wyo.gov.

"Notice to Appropriators of Water," *Natrona County Tribune*, (Casper: November 4, 1908), Courtesy of Wyoming Newspapers, Wyoming State Library, http://news papers.wyo.gov.

"O'Day Gets Six Years," *Natrona County Tribune*, (Casper: March 3, 1904), Courtesy of Wyoming Newspapers, Wyoming State Library, http://newspapers.wyo.gov.

"O'Day's Third Trial," *Natrona County Tribune*, (Casper: February 25, 1904), Courtesy of Wyoming Newspapers, Wyoming State Library, http://newspapers.wyo.gov.

"October Oddities," *Cheyenne Daily Sun*, (October 23, 1885), Courtesy of Wyoming Newspapers, Wyoming State Library, http://newspapers.wyo.gov.

"Offered a Reward," *Wyoming Tribune*, (Cheyenne: February 11, 1910), Courtesy of Wyoming Newspapers, Wyoming State Library, http://newspapers.wyo.gov.

"Official Returns," *Natrona County Tribune*, (Casper: November 17, 1898), Courtesy of Wyoming Newspapers, Wyoming State Library, http://newspapers.wyo.gov.

"Oil and Gas Permits," *Douglas Enterprise*, (July 26, 1921), Courtesy of Wyoming Newspapers, Wyoming State Library, http://newspapers.wyo.gov.

"The Oil Case Quiet," *Natrona County Tribune*, (Casper: June 15, 1910), Courtesy of Wyoming Newspapers, Wyoming State Library, http://newspapers.wyo.gov.

"Oil Land Compromise," *Natrona County Tribune*, (Casper: November 2, 1910), Courtesy of Wyoming Newspapers, Wyoming State Library, http://newspapers.wyo.gov.

"Oil Machinery Arrives," *Casper Press*, (February 18, 1910), Courtesy of Wyoming Newspapers, Wyoming State Library, http://newspapers.wyo.gov.

"Oil Men Meet," *Wyoming Derrick*, (Casper: January 8, 1903), Courtesy of Wyoming Newspapers, Wyoming State Library, http://newspapers.wyo.gov.

"Oil News," *Laramie Boomerang*, (August 24, 1918), Courtesy of Wyoming Newspapers, Wyoming State Library, http://newspapers.wyo.gov.

"Oil News of the Week," *Basin Republican*, (February 23, 1917), Courtesy of Wyoming Newspapers, Wyoming State Library, http://newspapers.wyo.gov.

"Oil Notes," *Buffalo Bulletin*, (August 30, 1917), Courtesy of Wyoming Newspapers, Wyoming State Library, http://newspapers.wyo.gov.

"Oil Notes," *Laramie Daily Boomerang*, (July 23, 1920), Courtesy of Wyoming Newspapers, Wyoming State Library, http://newspapers.wyo.gov.

"Oil Prospecting in Southern Utah," *Salt Lake Telegram*, (Salt Lake City: November 29, 1920), Courtesy of Utah Digital Newspapers, https://newspapers.lib.utah.edu.

"Omaha Paper Writes Up Hon. Missou Hines," *Thermopolis Independent*, (March 8, 1918), Courtesy of Wyoming Newspapers, Wyoming State Library, http://news papers.wyo.gov.

"One Man Convicted, Another Acquitted," *Natrona County Tribune*, (Casper: February 6, 1913), Courtesy of Wyoming Newspapers, Wyoming State Library, http://news papers.wyo.gov.

"Operation Fatal To Mrs. Brandt," *Casper Herald*, (November 20, 1922), Courtesy of Wyoming Newspapers, Wyoming State Library, http://newspapers.wyo.gov.

"Operation on Mr. Gothberg," *Jersey City News*, (October 23, 1902), Courtesy of Genealogy Bank, https://www.genealogybank.com/doc/newspapers.

"Order," *Natrona County Tribune*, (Casper: June 21, 1911), Courtesy of Wyoming Newspapers, Wyoming State Library, http://newspapers.wyo.gov.

"Our Eastern Neighbors," *Salt Lake Herald-Republican*, (Salt Lake City: April, 22, 1895), Courtesy of Utah Digital Newspapers, https://newspapers.lib.utah.edu.

"Pal of Ed Lee Located in Kansas," *Cheyenne Daily Leader*, (September 29, 1906), Courtesy of Wyoming Newspapers, Wyoming State Library, http://newspapers .wyo.gov.

"Party at Gothberg Home," *Casper Herald*, (November 22 1921), Courtesy of Wyoming Newspapers, Wyoming State Library, http://newspapers.wyo.gov.

"Party Leave for Yellowstone," *Casper Daily Tribune*, (August 10, 1920), Courtesy of Wyoming Newspapers, Wyoming State Library, http://newspapers.wyo.gov.

"Party Recognizes Birth Anniversary," *Casper Daily Tribune*, (March 21, 1922), Courtesy of Wyoming Newspapers, Wyoming State Library, http://newspapers.wyo.gov.

"Performed Two Delicate Surgeries," Douglas *Enterprise*, (December 29, 1914), Courtesy of Wyoming Newspapers, Wyoming State Library, http://newspapers.wyo.gov.

"Personal," *Cheyenne Daily Sun*, (March 12, 1892), Courtesy of Wyoming Newspapers, Wyoming State Library, http://newspapers.wyo.gov.

"Personal and Local News," *Converse County Herald*, (Lusk: October 27, 1898), Courtesy of Wyoming Newspapers, Wyoming State Library, http://newspapers.wyo.gov.

"Personal and Local News," *Lusk Herald*, (November 24, 1892), Courtesy of Wyoming Newspapers, Wyoming State Library, http://newspapers.wyo.gov.

"Personal Intelligence," *Bill Barlow's Budget*, (Douglas: December 1, 1886), Courtesy of Wyoming Newspapers, Wyoming State Library, http://newspapers.wyo.gov.

"Personal Mention," *Daily Boomerang*, (Laramie: June 06, 1898), Courtesy of Wyoming Newspapers, Wyoming State Library, http://newspapers.wyo.gov.

"Personal Paragraphs," *Casper Record*, (January 2, 1912), Courtesy of Wyoming Newspapers, Wyoming State Library, http://newspapers.wyo.gov.

"Personal Paragraphs," *Laramie Republican*, (May 17, 1904), Courtesy of Wyoming Newspapers, Wyoming State Library, http://newspapers.wyo.gov.

"Personal Points," *Cheyenne Daily Leader*, (August 5, 1879), Courtesy of Wyoming Newspapers, Wyoming State Library, http://newspapers.wyo.gov.

"Personal Taxrears, 1921," *Jersey Journal*, (Jersey City: March 30, 1922), Courtesy of Genealogy Bank, https://www.genealogybank.com/doc/newspapers.

"Personals," *Casper Daily Press*, (January 12, 1916), Courtesy of Wyoming Newspapers, Wyoming State Library, http://newspapers.wyo.gov.

"Personals," *Casper Daily Press*, (January 25, 1916), Courtesy of Wyoming Newspapers, Wyoming State Library, http://newspapers.wyo.gov.

"Personals," *Casper Daily Tribune*, (December 12, 1919), Courtesy of Wyoming Newspapers, Wyoming State Library, http://newspapers.wyo.gov.

"Personals," *Casper Daily Tribune*, (March 13, 1920), Courtesy of Wyoming Newspapers, Wyoming State Library, http://newspapers.wyo.gov.

"Personals," *Casper Daily Tribune*, (May 17, 1920), Courtesy of Wyoming Newspapers, Wyoming State Library, http://newspapers.wyo.gov.

"Personals," *Casper Daily Tribune*, (May 20, 1920), Courtesy of Wyoming Newspapers, Wyoming State Library, http://newspapers.wyo.gov.

"Personals," *Casper Daily Tribune*, (June 24, 1920), Courtesy of Wyoming Newspapers, Wyoming State Library, http://newspapers.wyo.gov.

"Personals," *Casper Daily Tribune*, (January 28, 1921), Courtesy of Wyoming Newspapers, Wyoming State Library, http://newspapers.wyo.gov.

"Personals," *Casper Daily Tribune*, (March 3, 1921), Courtesy of Wyoming Newspapers, Wyoming State Library, http://newspapers.wyo.gov.

"Personals," *Casper Daily Tribune*, (March 28, 1921), Courtesy of Wyoming Newspapers, Wyoming State Library, http://newspapers.wyo.gov.

"Personals," *Casper Daily Tribune*, (May 10, 1921), Courtesy of Wyoming Newspapers, Wyoming State Library, http://newspapers.wyo.gov.

"Personals," *Casper Daily Tribune*, (July 14, 1921), Courtesy of Wyoming Newspapers, Wyoming State Library, http://newspapers.wyo.gov.

"Personals," *Casper Daily Tribune*, (August 27, 1921), Courtesy of Wyoming Newspapers, Wyoming State Library, http://newspapers.wyo.gov.

"Personals," *Casper Daily Tribune*, (September 2, 1921), Courtesy of Wyoming Newspapers, Wyoming State Library, http://newspapers.wyo.gov.

"Personals," *Casper Daily Tribune*, (September 22, 1921), Courtesy of Wyoming Newspapers, Wyoming State Library, http://newspapers.wyo.gov.

"Personals," *Casper Daily Tribune*, (September 29, 1921), Courtesy of Wyoming Newspapers, Wyoming State Library, http://newspapers.wyo.gov.

"Personals," *Casper Daily Tribune*, (October 21, 1921), Courtesy of Wyoming Newspapers, Wyoming State Library, http://newspapers.wyo.gov.

"Personals," *Casper Daily Tribune*, (December 13, 1921), Courtesy of Wyoming Newspapers, Wyoming State Library, http://newspapers.wyo.gov.

"Personals," *Casper Daily Tribune*, (March 30, 1922), Courtesy of Wyoming Newspapers, Wyoming State Library, http://newspapers.wyo.gov.

"Personals," *Casper Daily Tribune*, (April 29, 1922), Courtesy of Wyoming Newspapers, Wyoming State Library, http://newspapers.wyo.gov.

"Personals," *Northwestern Live Stock Journal*, (Cheyenne: June 27, 1884), Courtesy of Wyoming Newspapers, Wyoming State Library, http://newspapers.wyo.gov.

"Petroleum Notes," *Salt Lake Mining Review*, (Salt Lake City: March 30, 1921), Courtesy of Utah Digital Newspapers, https://newspapers.lib.utah.edu.

"Petroleum Notes," *Salt Lake Mining Review*, (Salt Lake City: April 15, 1921), Courtesy of Utah Digital Newspapers, https://newspapers.lib.utah.edu.

"Pipeline From Bolton Field Held Assured," *Casper Daily Tribune*, (June 20, 1922), Courtesy of Wyoming Newspapers, Wyoming State Library, http://newspapers.wyo.gov.

"Please Settle Your Accounts," *Natrona County Tribune*, (Casper: May 19, 1909), Courtesy of Wyoming Newspapers, Wyoming State Library, http://newspapers.wyo.gov.

"Prairie Queen," *Chanute Times*, (June 16, 1911), Courtesy of Genealogy Bank, https://www.genealogybank.com/doc/newspapers.

"Prairie Queen," *Chanute Times*, (July 7, 1911), Courtesy of Genealogy Bank, https://www.genealogybank.com/doc/newspapers.

"Preparing for Operations," *Natrona County Tribune*, (Casper: June 18, 1917), Courtesy of Wyoming Newspapers, Wyoming State Library, http://newspapers.wyo.gov.

"Prisoners Escape," *Wyoming Derrick*, (Casper: May 18, 1905), Courtesy of Wyoming Newspapers, Wyoming State Library, http://newspapers.wyo.gov.

"Prisoners Break Jail," *Natrona County Tribune*, (Casper: May 18, 1905), Courtesy of Wyoming Newspapers, Wyoming State Library, http://newspapers.wyo.gov.

"Proclaims Quarantine," *Semi-Weekly Enterprise*, (Sheridan: April 3, 1908), Courtesy of Wyoming Newspapers, Wyoming State Library, http://newspapers.wyo.gov.

"Progress in Oil Development is Rapid," *Salt Lake Telegram*, (Salt Lake City: May 15, 1921), Courtesy of Utah Digital Newspapers, https://newspapers.lib.utah.edu.

"Prominent New York Matron Visits Relatives," *Casper Herald*, (April 15, 1921), Courtesy of Wyoming Newspapers, Wyoming State Library, http://newspapers.wyo.gov.

"Proposals for Bids," *Natrona County Tribune*, (Casper: October 5, 1905), Courtesy of Wyoming Newspapers, Wyoming State Library, http://newspapers.wyo.gov.

"Prospects Good," *Wyoming Tribune*, (Cheyenne: January 25, 1904), Courtesy of Wyoming Newspapers, Wyoming State Library, http://newspapers.wyo.gov.

"Quarantine Notice," *Natrona County Tribune*, (Casper: January 20, 1909), Courtesy of Wyoming Newspapers, Wyoming State Library, http://newspapers.wyo.gov.

"Quarter of a Century Ago," *Douglas Budget*, (April 5, 1917), Courtesy of Wyoming Newspapers, Wyoming State Library, http://newspapers.wyo.gov.

"Quarter of a Century Ago," *Douglas Budget*, (May 30, 1918), Courtesy of Wyoming Newspapers, Wyoming State Library, http://newspapers.wyo.gov.

"Quarter of a Century Ago," *Douglas Budget*, (July 29, 1920), Courtesy of Wyoming Newspapers, Wyoming State Library, http://newspapers.wyo.gov.

"The Railroad is Getting Interested," *Natrona County Tribune*, (Casper: June 16, 1904), Courtesy of Wyoming Newspapers, Wyoming State Library, http://newspapers.wyo.gov.

"Railroad News Notes," *Natrona County Tribune*, (Casper: May 10, 1906), Courtesy of Wyoming Newspapers, Wyoming State Library, http://newspapers.wyo.gov.

"Ranchmen Will Exhibition," *Wyoming Derrick*, (Casper: September 8, 1904), Courtesy of Wyoming Newspapers, Wyoming State Library, http://newspapers.wyo.gov.

"Rawlins Paper Gives Details of Late Death," *Casper Daily Tribune*, (February 26, 1919), Courtesy of Wyoming Newspapers, Wyoming State Library, http://newspapers.wyo.gov.

"Real Estate Transfers," *Casper Daily Tribune*, (September 16, 1919), Courtesy of Wyoming Newspapers, Wyoming State Library, http://newspapers.wyo.gov.

"Real Estate Transfers–Jersey City," *Jersey Journal*, (Jersey City: July 25, 1884), Courtesy of Genealogy Bank, https://www.genealogybank.com/doc/newspapers.

"Real Estate Transfers Still Lively," *Casper Daily Tribune*, (August 4, 1919), Courtesy of Wyoming Newspapers, Wyoming State Library, http://newspapers.wyo.gov.

"Real Estate Works," *Jersey Journal*, (Jersey City: July 14, 1896), Courtesy of Genealogy Bank, https://www.genealogybank.com/doc/newspapers.

"Realty Transfers," *Casper Daily Tribune*, (April 17, 1920), Courtesy of Wyoming Newspapers, Wyoming State Library, http://newspapers.wyo.gov.

"Receiver Sale," *Jersey Journal*, (Jersey City: February 15, 1922), Courtesy of Genealogy Bank, https://www.genealogybank.com/doc/newspapers.

"Recent Wells Are Close to Mike Henry," *Douglas Enterprise*, (September 7, 1920), Courtesy of Wyoming Newspapers, Wyoming State Library, http://newspapers .wyo.gov.

"Reception to Be Followed by Novel Entertainment," *Casper Daily Tribune*, (January 5, 1922), Courtesy of Wyoming Newspapers, Wyoming State Library, http://news papers.wyo.gov.

"Report of New York Oil Operations," *Wyoming Oil World*, (Casper: January 3, 1920), Courtesy of Wyoming Newspapers, Wyoming State Library, http://newspapers .wyo.gov.

"Resolution," *Natrona County Tribune*, (Casper: July 15, 1908), Courtesy of Wyoming Newspapers, Wyoming State Library, http://newspapers.wyo.gov.

"Return from Delightful Shopping Trip," *Casper Herald*, (January 6, 1920), Courtesy of Wyoming Newspapers, Wyoming State Library, http://newspapers.wyo.gov.

"Return from Delightful Trip," *Casper Herald*, (January 14, 1920), Courtesy of Wyoming Newspapers, Wyoming State Library, http://newspapers.wyo.gov.

"Returning From Western Coast," *Casper Herald*, (March 9, 1920), Courtesy of Wyoming Newspapers, Wyoming State Library, http://newspapers.wyo.gov.

"Robbery and Murder! Bold Bandits Flag and Rob the Union Pacific Flyer," *Bill Barlow's Budget*, (Douglas: June 7, 1899), Courtesy of Wyoming Newspapers, Wyoming State Library, http://newspapers.wyo.gov.

"Rotary Club Receives Congratulations on 'Back to School' Aid," *Casper Daily Tribune*, (January 17, 1922), Courtesy of Wyoming Newspapers, Wyoming State Library, http://newspapers.wyo.gov.

"Round Up Racket," *Cheyenne Weekly Leader*, (June 12, 1879), Courtesy of Wyoming Newspapers, Wyoming State Library, http://newspapers.wyo.gov.

"Round Ups, Wyoming Stock Growers Association, 1883," *Cheyenne Weekly Leader*, (April 19, 1883), Courtesy of Wyoming Newspapers, Wyoming State Library, http://newspapers.wyo.gov.

"Roundup Racket," *Bill Barlow's Budget*, (Douglas: June 15, 1887), Courtesy of Wyoming Newspapers, Wyoming State Library, http://newspapers.wyo.gov.

"St. Mark's Scene of Impressive Wedding," *Casper Herald*, (October 13, 1920), Courtesy of Wyoming Newspapers, Wyoming State Library, http://newspapers.wyo.gov.

"San Juan Company Strikes Big Gusher in Bolton Creek Field," *Casper Herald*, (June 06, 1922), Courtesy of Wyoming Newspapers, Wyoming State Library, http:// newspapers.wyo.gov.

"San Juan Petroleum Co.," *Casper Herald*, (August 5, 1920), Courtesy of Wyoming Newspapers, Wyoming State Library, http://newspapers.wyo.gov.

"San Juan Petroleum Company Strikes Oil," *Rawlins Republican*, (August 4, 1921), Courtesy of Wyoming Newspapers, Wyoming State Library, http://newspapers .wyo.gov.

"Sanders-Brandt," *Laramie Weekly Boomerang*, (January 7, 1886), Courtesy of Wyoming Newspapers, Wyoming State Library, http://newspapers.wyo.gov.

"Says East is Busy With War Orders," *Casper Record*, (November 9, 1915), Courtesy of Wyoming Newspapers, Wyoming State Library, http://newspapers.wyo.gov.

359

"Says Sale Was Frame-Up," *Jersey Journal*, (Jersey City: February 21, 1922), Courtesy of Genealogy Bank, https://www.genealogybank.com/doc/newspapers.

"School 20 in Flames," *Jersey Journal*, (Jersey City: February 13, 1899), Courtesy of Genealogy Bank, https://www.genealogybank.com/doc/newspapers.

"Scouts Perfect Organization," *Natrona County Tribune*, (Casper: April 4, 1918), Courtesy of Wyoming Newspapers, Wyoming State Library, http://newspapers.wyo.gov.

"Selling Oil Lands," *Rawlins Republican*, (October 22, 1902), Courtesy of Wyoming Newspapers, Wyoming State Library, http://newspapers.wyo.gov.

"Secure Leases in Bates Hole," *Rock River Review*, (March 5, 1920), Courtesy of Wyoming Newspapers, Wyoming State Library, http://newspapers.wyo.gov.

"Settle Affairs of Gothberg Co.," *Jersey Journal*, (Jersey City: July 24, 1923), Courtesy of Genealogy Bank, https://www.genealogybank.com/doc/newspapers.

"Sheep and Sheep Men," *Bill Barlow's Budget*, (Douglas: May 2, 1900), Courtesy of Wyoming Newspapers, Wyoming State Library, http://newspapers.wyo.gov.

"Sheepmen Attention," *Natrona County Tribune*, (Casper: May 26, 1909), Courtesy of Wyoming Newspapers, Wyoming State Library, http://newspapers.wyo.gov.

"Sheepmen Attention," *Natrona County Tribune*, (Casper: July 7, 1909), Courtesy of Wyoming Newspapers, Wyoming State Library, http://newspapers.wyo.gov.

"Sheepmen Attention," *Natrona County Tribune*, (Casper: July 28, 1909), Courtesy of Wyoming Newspapers, Wyoming State Library, http://newspapers.wyo.gov.

"Sheepmen Attention," *Natrona County Tribune*, (Casper: August 18, 1909), Courtesy of Wyoming Newspapers, Wyoming State Library, http://newspapers.wyo.gov.

"Sheepmen's Meeting," *Natrona County Tribune*, (Casper: February 17, 1909), Courtesy of Wyoming Newspapers, Wyoming State Library, http://newspapers.wyo.gov.

"Sheriff Webb Returns," *Natrona County Tribune*, (Casper: March 1, 1906), Courtesy of Wyoming Newspapers, Wyoming State Library, http://newspapers.wyo.gov.

"Short Court Session," *Casper Press*, (July 16, 1909), Courtesy of Wyoming Newspapers, Wyoming State Library, http://newspapers.wyo.gov.

"Short Stops," *Bill Barlow's Budget*, (Douglas: February 24, 1892), Courtesy of Wyoming Newspapers, Wyoming State Library, http://newspapers.wyo.gov.

"Short Stops," *Bill Barlow's Budget*, (Douglas: November 23, 1892), Courtesy of Wyoming Newspapers, Wyoming State Library, http://newspapers.wyo.gov.

"Short Stops," *Natrona Tribune*, (Casper: July 11, 1895), Courtesy of Wyoming Newspapers, Wyoming State Library, http://newspapers.wyo.gov.

"Short Stories," *Cheyenne Daily Sun*, (October 8, 1892), Courtesy of Wyoming Newspapers, Wyoming State Library, http://newspapers.wyo.gov.

"Shot to Death," *Natrona County Tribune*, (Casper: June 3, 1897), Courtesy of Wyoming Newspapers, Wyoming State Library, http://newspapers.wyo.gov.

"Shriners Were Much Delighted," *Riverside Daily Press*, (May 9, 1906), Courtesy of Genealogy Bank, https://www.genealogybank.com/doc/newspapers.

"Society," *Casper Daily Tribune*, (May 4, 1917), Courtesy of Wyoming Newspapers, Wyoming State Library, http://newspapers.wyo.gov.

"Society," *Casper Daily Tribune*, (June 8, 1917), Courtesy of Wyoming Newspapers, Wyoming State Library, http://newspapers.wyo.gov.

"Society," *Casper Daily Tribune*, (August 6, 1918), Courtesy of Wyoming Newspapers, Wyoming State Library, http://newspapers.wyo.gov.

"Society," *Casper Daily Tribune*, (February 3, 1919), Courtesy of Wyoming Newspapers, Wyoming State Library, http://newspapers.wyo.gov.

"Society," *Casper Daily Tribune*, (June 8, 1921), Courtesy of Wyoming Newspapers, Wyoming State Library, http://newspapers.wyo.gov.

"Society," *Casper Daily Tribune*, (August 16, 1921), Courtesy of Wyoming Newspapers, Wyoming State Library, http://newspapers.wyo.gov.

"Society," *Casper Daily Tribune*, (August 30, 1921), Courtesy of Wyoming Newspapers, Wyoming State Library, http://newspapers.wyo.gov.

"Society," *Casper Herald*, (October 1, 1920), Courtesy of Wyoming Newspapers, Wyoming State Library, http://newspapers.wyo.gov.

"Society," *Casper Herald*, (December 11, 1920), Courtesy of Wyoming Newspapers, Wyoming State Library, http://newspapers.wyo.gov.

"Society," *Casper Herald*, (February 19, 1921), Courtesy of Wyoming Newspapers, Wyoming State Library, http://newspapers.wyo.gov.

"Society," *Natrona County Tribune*, (Casper: February 4, 1904), Courtesy of Wyoming Newspapers, Wyoming State Library, http://newspapers.wyo.gov.

"Society," *Wyoming Derrick*, (Casper: January 8, 1903), Courtesy of Wyoming Newspapers, Wyoming State Library, http://newspapers.wyo.gov.

"Society Events," *Casper Daily Tribune*, (December 24, 1918), Courtesy of Wyoming Newspapers, Wyoming State Library, http://newspapers.wyo.gov.

"Society Events," *Casper Daily Tribune*, (May 6, 1919), Courtesy of Wyoming Newspapers, Wyoming State Library, http://newspapers.wyo.gov.

"Society Events," *Casper Daily Tribune*, (May 22, 1919), Courtesy of Wyoming Newspapers, Wyoming State Library, http://newspapers.wyo.gov.

"Society Events," *Casper Daily Tribune*, (February 2, 1920), Courtesy of Wyoming Newspapers, Wyoming State Library, http://newspapers.wyo.gov.

"Society Notes," *Jersey Journal*, (Jersey City: May 1, 1891), Courtesy of Genealogy Bank, https://www.genealogybank.com/doc/newspapers.

"Society Notes," *Jersey Journal*, (Jersey City: July 8, 1895), Courtesy of Genealogy Bank, https://www.genealogybank.com/doc/newspapers.

"Society Notes," *Jersey Journal*, (Jersey City: July 15, 1901), Courtesy of Genealogy Bank, https://www.genealogybank.com/doc/newspapers.

"Society Notes-Bergen," *Jersey Journal*, (Jersey City: July 3, 1905), Courtesy of Genealogy Bank, https://www.genealogybank.com/doc/newspapers.

"Society Notes–Greenville," *Jersey Journal*, (Jersey City: October 17, 1903), Courtesy of Genealogy Bank, https://www.genealogybank.com/doc/newspapers.

"Society Notes–Greenville," *Jersey Journal*, (Jersey City: January 13, 1905), Courtesy of Genealogy Bank, https://www.genealogybank.com/doc/newspapers.

"Society Notes–Lower Jersey City," *Jersey Journal*, (Jersey City: June 27, 1904), Courtesy of Genealogy Bank, https://www.genealogybank.com/doc/newspapers.

"Society Organized Here for Protection and Help Little French Children ...," *Casper Daily Press*, (December 1, 1918), Courtesy of Wyoming Newspapers, Wyoming State Library, http://newspapers.wyo.gov.

"Soldiers and Sailors Club Ready to Open," *Casper Daily Tribune*, (February 25, 1919), Courtesy of Wyoming Newspapers, Wyoming State Library, http://newspapers.wyo.gov.

"Spindle Top Field Added Proven Class by New York Oil Company," *Casper Herald*, (November 22, 1919), Courtesy of Wyoming Newspapers, Wyoming State Library, http://newspapers.wyo.gov.

"Spindle Top Oil Well Holds Good Promise," *Casper Daily Tribune*, (July 12, 1922), Courtesy of Wyoming Newspapers, Wyoming State Library, http://newspapers.wyo.gov.

"Spindle Top Test Contracted," *Casper Daily Tribune*, (September 3, 1921), Courtesy of Wyoming Newspapers, Wyoming State Library, http://newspapers.wyo.gov.

"Spray of the Oil Area," *Casper Record*, (October 13, 1914), Courtesy of Wyoming Newspapers, Wyoming State Library, http://newspapers.wyo.gov.

"Spray of the Oil Area," *Casper Record*, (March 23, 1915), Courtesy of Wyoming Newspapers, Wyoming State Library, http://newspapers.wyo.gov.

"Spray of the Oil Area," *Casper Record*, (April 27, 1915), Courtesy of Wyoming Newspapers, Wyoming State Library, http://newspapers.wyo.gov.

"Spray of the Oil Area," *Casper Record*, (June 08, 1915), Courtesy of Wyoming Newspapers, Wyoming State Library, http://newspapers.wyo.gov.

"Spray of the Oil Area," *Casper Record*, (April 18, 1916), Courtesy of Wyoming Newspapers, Wyoming State Library, http://newspapers.wyo.gov.

"Spray of the Oil Area," *Casper Record*, (March 13, 1917), Courtesy of Wyoming Newspapers, Wyoming State Library, http://newspapers.wyo.gov.

"State Topics," *Bill Barlow's Budget*, (Douglas: March 16, 1892), Courtesy of Wyoming Newspapers, Wyoming State Library, http://newspapers.wyo.gov.

"Stock & Range," *Wyoming Derrick*, (Casper: May 5, 1904), Courtesy of Wyoming Newspapers, Wyoming State Library, http://newspapers.wyo.gov.

"Stock Cars Ordered," *Daily Boomerang*, (Laramie: August 11, 1884), Courtesy of Wyoming Newspapers, Wyoming State Library, http://newspapers.wyo.gov.

"Stock Cars Ordered," *Daily Boomerang*, (Laramie: October 14, 1884), Courtesy of Wyoming Newspapers, Wyoming State Library, http://newspapers.wyo.gov.

"Stock Cars Ordered," *Democratic Leader*, (Cheyenne: October 9, 1885), Courtesy of Wyoming Newspapers, Wyoming State Library, http://newspapers.wyo.gov.

"Stock Movements," *Wyoming Derrick*, (Casper: September 16, 1897), Courtesy of Wyoming Newspapers, Wyoming State Library, http://newspapers.wyo.gov.

"Stock Notes," *Cheyenne Daily Leader*, (November 29, 1878), Courtesy of Wyoming Newspapers, Wyoming State Library, http://newspapers.wyo.gov.

"Stock Shipments," *Natrona County Tribune*, (Casper: October 2, 1902), Courtesy of Wyoming Newspapers, Wyoming State Library, http://newspapers.wyo.gov.

"Stock Shipments," *Natrona County Tribune*, (Casper: September 24, 1903), Courtesy of Wyoming Newspapers, Wyoming State Library, http://newspapers.wyo.gov.

"Stock Shipments," *Natrona County Tribune*, (Casper: October 19, 1905), Courtesy of Wyoming Newspapers, Wyoming State Library, http://newspapers.wyo.gov.

"Stock Shipments," *Natrona County Tribune*, (Casper: September 23, 1908), Courtesy of Wyoming Newspapers, Wyoming State Library, http://newspapers.wyo.gov.

"Stock Shipments," *Natrona County Tribune*, (Casper: September 7, 1910), Courtesy of Wyoming Newspapers, Wyoming State Library, http://newspapers.wyo.gov.

"Stock Shipments This Week," *Natrona County Tribune*, (Casper: September 14, 1905), Courtesy of Wyoming Newspapers, Wyoming State Library, http://newspapers .wyo.gov.

"Stockmen ask to Buy Lands," *Casper Daily Tribune*, (November 8, 1921), Courtesy of Wyoming Newspapers, Wyoming State Library, http://newspapers.wyo.gov.

"Stockmen Petition US to Sell Them All Wyoming Lands," *Wyoming State Tribune*, (Cheyenne: November 8, 1921), Courtesy of Wyoming Newspapers, Wyoming State Library, http://newspapers.wyo.gov.

"Stocks and Bonds," *Jersey Journal*, (Jersey City: June 16, 1906), Courtesy of Genealogy Bank, https://www.genealogybank.com/doc/newspapers.

"Storrie-Gothberg," *Lusk Herald*, (February 21, 1918), Courtesy of Wyoming Newspapers, Wyoming State Library, http://newspapers.wyo.gov.

"Stray Horse Column," *Northwestern Live Stock Journal*, (Cheyenne: June 10, 1887), Courtesy of Wyoming Newspapers, Wyoming State Library, http://newspapers .wyo.gov.

"Struck a Gusher," *Natrona County Tribune*, (Casper: October 9, 1912), Courtesy of Wyoming Newspapers, Wyoming State Library, http://newspapers.wyo.gov.

"Students Returning From School," *Casper Herald*, (December 13, 1919), Courtesy of Wyoming Newspapers, Wyoming State Library, http://newspapers.wyo.gov.

"Summer Homes Being Built at Gothmore Park," *Casper Daily Tribune*, (June 8, 1921), Courtesy of Wyoming Newspapers, Wyoming State Library, http://newspapers .wyo.gov.

"Survey Bought," *Wyoming Derrick*, (Casper: March 23, 1905), Courtesy of Wyoming Newspapers, Wyoming State Library, http://newspapers.wyo.gov.

"Takes Body to Kansas," *Rawlins Republican*, (February 27, 1919), Courtesy of Wyoming Newspapers, Wyoming State Library, http://newspapers.wyo.gov.

"This 'Detective' Came to Grief," *Jersey Journal*, (Jersey City: April 21, 1902), Courtesy of Genealogy Bank, https://www.genealogybank.com/doc/newspapers.

"This Week Twenty Years Ago," *Natrona County Tribune*, (Casper: July 12, 1911), Courtesy of Wyoming Newspapers, Wyoming State Library, http://newspapers .wyo.gov.

"Three Alleged Crooks Caught," *Cheyenne Daily Leader*, (January 28, 1909), Courtesy of Wyoming Newspapers, Wyoming State Library, http://newspapers.wyo.gov.

"3 Corporations Filed Yesterday," *Cheyenne State Leader*, (February 3, 1917), Courtesy of Wyoming Newspapers, Wyoming State Library, http://newspapers.wyo.gov.

"Throughout Wyoming," *Daily Boomerang*, (Laramie: February 25, 1897), Courtesy of Wyoming Newspapers, Wyoming State Library, http://newspapers.wyo.gov.

"To the Creditors of H. & E. Gothberg Manufacturing co., Inc.," *Jersey Journal*, (Jersey City: January 30, 1922), Courtesy of Genealogy Bank, https://www.genealogybank .com/doc/newspapers.

"Toltec Dome to be Proven," *Wyoming Oil World*, (Casper: July 13, 1918), Courtesy of Wyoming Newspapers, Wyoming State Library, http://newspapers.wyo.gov.

"Tonight," *Casper Daily Tribune*, (October 26, 1922), Courtesy of Wyoming Newspapers, Wyoming State Library, http://newspapers.wyo.gov.

"Town Council Proceedings," *Natrona County Tribune*, (Casper: September 16, 1908), Courtesy of Wyoming Newspapers, Wyoming State Library, http://newspapers.wyo.gov.

"Town Topics," *Natrona Tribune*, (Casper: May 10, 1894), Courtesy of Wyoming Newspapers, Wyoming State Library, http://newspapers.wyo.gov.

"Town Topics," *Natrona Tribune*, (Casper: June 7, 1894), Courtesy of Wyoming Newspapers, Wyoming State Library, http://newspapers.wyo.gov.

"Town Topics," *Natrona Tribune*, (Casper: June 28, 1894), Courtesy of Wyoming Newspapers, Wyoming State Library, http://newspapers.wyo.gov.

"Town Topics," *Natrona Tribune*, (Casper: July 5, 1894), Courtesy of Wyoming Newspapers, Wyoming State Library, http://newspapers.wyo.gov.

"Town Topics," *Natrona Tribune*, (Casper: July 19, 1894), Courtesy of Wyoming Newspapers, Wyoming State Library, http://newspapers.wyo.gov.

"The Trail at Portland Will be the Best Ever," *Wyoming Tribune*, (Cheyenne: May 16, 1905), Courtesy of Wyoming Newspapers, Wyoming State Library, http://newspapers.wyo.gov.

"Transfers are Filed at Rapid Rate in County," *Casper Daily Tribune*, (July 31, 1919), Courtesy of Wyoming Newspapers, Wyoming State Library, http://newspapers.wyo.gov.

"Tribune Overlooks City Attorney Who Received Greatest Vote at Recent Election, Taken as Slight," *Casper Daily Press*, (November 21, 1918), Courtesy of Wyoming Newspapers, Wyoming State Library, http://newspapers.wyo.gov.

"Turkey Dinner at Gothberg Home," *Casper Herald*, (November 27, 1920), Courtesy of Wyoming Newspapers, Wyoming State Library, http://newspapers.wyo.gov.

"Tusler Bros. Shipped 27 Cars," *Cheyenne Daily Leader*, (September 15, 1877), Courtesy of Wyoming Newspapers, Wyoming State Library, http://newspapers.wyo.gov.

"Twelve in 1916 Graduating Class," *Casper Record*, (May 23, 1916), Courtesy of Wyoming Newspapers, Wyoming State Library, http://newspapers.wyo.gov.

"27 Cars of Sheep to Omaha," *Casper Weekly Press*, (September 4, 1914), Courtesy of Wyoming Newspapers, Wyoming State Library, http://newspapers.wyo.gov.

"Two Deaths at Pathfinder," *Natrona County Tribune*, (Casper: August 2, 1906), Courtesy of Wyoming Newspapers, Wyoming State Library, http://newspapers.wyo.gov.

"200 Club Gets Big Producer," *Casper Daily Tribune*, (March 3, 1919), Courtesy of Wyoming Newspapers, Wyoming State Library, http://newspapers.wyo.gov.

"$250.00 Reward," *Natrona County Tribune*, (Casper: June 22, 1905), Courtesy of Wyoming Newspapers, Wyoming State Library, http://newspapers.wyo.gov.

"United States Land Office," *Natrona County Tribune*, (Casper: February 4, 1904), Courtesy of Wyoming Newspapers, Wyoming State Library, http://newspapers.wyo.gov.

"Unofficial Returns," *Natrona County Tribune*, (Casper: November 06, 1912), Courtesy of Wyoming Newspapers, Wyoming State Library, http://newspapers.wyo.gov.

"Unofficial Vote of Natrona Co," *Natrona Tribune*, (Casper: November 8, 1894), Courtesy of Wyoming Newspapers, Wyoming State Library, http://newspapers.wyo.gov.

"Used Car Clearance," *Casper Daily Tribune*, (June 16, 1917), Courtesy of Wyoming Newspapers, Wyoming State Library, http://newspapers.wyo.gov.

"Utah Test Projected," *Casper Daily Tribune*, (December 27, 1919), Courtesy of Wyoming Newspapers, Wyoming State Library, http://newspapers.wyo.gov.

"Van Nostrand's Eclectic Engineering Magazine," *Boston Traveler*, (June 28, 1876), Courtesy of Genealogy Bank, https://www.genealogybank.com/doc/newspapers.

"'Virginian' Characters Get a Write-up from the Eastern Newspaper Correspondents," *Lander Eagle*, (October 20, 1911), Courtesy of Wyoming Newspapers, Wyoming State Library, http://newspapers.wyo.gov.

"A Visitor at Fetterman," *Cheyenne Weekly Leader*, (June 21, 1883), Courtesy of Wyoming Newspapers, Wyoming State Library, http://newspapers.wyo.gov.

"Vote for Decency and Municipal Economy," *Casper Daily Tribune*, (November 7, 1921), Courtesy of Wyoming Newspapers, Wyoming State Library, http://news papers.wyo.gov.

"W. A. Blackmore 9 Days Overland Casper to Coast," *Casper Herald*, (November 25, 1920), Courtesy of Wyoming Newspapers, Wyoming State Library, http://news papers.wyo.gov.

"Want Water Rights," *Wyoming Tribune*, (Casper: May 7, 1907), Courtesy of Wyoming Newspapers, Wyoming State Library, http://newspapers.wyo.gov.

"Wardlaw's Story," *Wyoming Derrick*, (Casper: May 18, 1905), Courtesy of Wyoming Newspapers, Wyoming State Library, http://newspapers.wyo.gov.

"Warranty Deeds," *Casper Herald*, (April 14, 1920), Courtesy of Wyoming Newspapers, Wyoming State Library, http://newspapers.wyo.gov.

"Warranty Deeds Recorded," *Casper Herald*, (May 29, 1920), Courtesy of Wyoming Newspapers, Wyoming State Library, http://newspapers.wyo.gov.

"Was Writing Fiction and not Geography," *Wyoming Oil World*, (Casper: May 14, 1921), Courtesy of Wyoming Newspapers, Wyoming State Library, http://newspapers .wyo.gov.

"Wedding at Freeland," *Casper Press*, (July 3, 1908), Courtesy of Wyoming Newspapers, Wyoming State Library, http://newspapers.wyo.gov.

"Wedding Bells," *Jersey Journal*, (Jersey City: May 2, 1895), Courtesy of Genealogy Bank, https://www.genealogybank.com/doc/newspapers.

"Wedding Bells," *Jersey Journal*, (Jersey City: February 8, 1896), Courtesy of Genealogy Bank, https://www.genealogybank.com/doc/newspapers.

"Wedding Bells," *Jersey Journal*, (Jersey City: February 24, 1900), 10. Courtesy of Genealogy Bank, https://www.genealogybank.com/doc/newspapers.

"Wedding Bells," *Wyoming Derrick*, (Casper: November 19, 1891), Courtesy of Wyoming Newspapers, Wyoming State Library, http://newspapers.wyo.gov.

"Weekly Roundup," *Cheyenne Daily Sun-Leader*, (April 16, 1898), Courtesy of Wyoming Newspapers, Wyoming State Library, http://newspapers.wyo.gov.

"The Week's Doings," *Casper Record*, (September 10, 1912), Courtesy of Wyoming Newspapers, Wyoming State Library, http://newspapers.wyo.gov.

"Weeks Oil News," *Basin Republican*, (September 8, 1916), Courtesy of Wyoming Newspapers, Wyoming State Library, http://newspapers.wyo.gov.

"The Western Inn," *Natrona County Tribune*, (Casper: July 22, 1908), Courtesy of Wyoming Newspapers, Wyoming State Library, http://newspapers.wyo.gov.

"Westerners in Chicago," *Salt Lake Tribune*, (Salt Lake City: December 18, 1907), Courtesy of Utah Digital Newspapers, https://newspapers.lib.utah.edu.

"What Mr. Gothberg Thinks," *Casper Daily Tribune*, (October 27, 1921), Courtesy of Utah Digital Newspapers, https://newspapers.lib.utah.edu.

"What's Doing Over the State," *Thermopolis Record*, (August 31, 1911), Courtesy of Wyoming Newspapers, Wyoming State Library, http://newspapers.wyo.gov.

"What's Doing Over the State," *Thermopolis Record*, (October 19, 1911), Courtesy of Wyoming Newspapers, Wyoming State Library, http://newspapers.wyo.gov.

"Whirled to Death," *Jersey City News*, (June 13, 1894), Courtesy of Genealogy Bank, https://www.genealogybank.com/doc/newspapers.

"Wholesale House," *Wyoming Derrick*, (Casper: April 13, 1905), Courtesy of Wyoming Newspapers, Wyoming State Library, http://newspapers.wyo.gov.

"Wholesale House," *Wyoming Derrick*, (Casper: April 20, 1905), Courtesy of Wyoming Newspapers, Wyoming State Library, http://newspapers.wyo.gov.

"Why we are for Blackmore," *Casper Daily Tribune*, (November 1, 1921), Courtesy of Wyoming Newspapers, Wyoming State Library, http://newspapers.wyo.gov.

"Wild West Shows," *Boomerang*, (Laramie: August 25, 1892), Courtesy of Wyoming Newspapers, Wyoming State Library, http://newspapers.wyo.gov.

"Will Be Well Treated," *Wyoming Tribune*, (Casper: June 27, 1905), Courtesy of Wyoming Newspapers, Wyoming State Library, http://newspapers.wyo.gov.

"Will Drill Oil Wells at Alcova," *Natrona County Tribune*, (Casper: April 16, 1903), Courtesy of Wyoming Newspapers, Wyoming State Library, http://newspapers.wyo.gov.

"Will Enforce Hide Inspection Law," *Natrona County Tribune*, (Casper: July 20, 1910), Courtesy of Wyoming Newspapers, Wyoming State Library, http://newspapers.wyo.gov.

"Will Enjoy Southern California During the Winter," *Casper Herald*, (December 13, 1919), Courtesy of Wyoming Newspapers, Wyoming State Library, http://newspapers.wyo.gov.

"William Clayton," *Bill Barlow's Budget*, (Douglas: August 9, 1905), Courtesy of Wyoming Newspapers, Wyoming State Library, http://newspapers.wyo.gov.

"William Clayton Frozen," *Douglas Budget*, (December 17, 1914), Courtesy of Wyoming Newspapers, Wyoming State Library, http://newspapers.wyo.gov.

"William Clayton is Dead," *Douglas Budget*, (December 31, 1914), Courtesy of Wyoming Newspapers, Wyoming State Library, http://newspapers.wyo.gov.

"William Clayton Will Recover," *Douglas Budget*, (December 24, 1914), Courtesy of Wyoming Newspapers, Wyoming State Library, http://newspapers.wyo.gov.

"Win Their Point," *Casper Press*, (May 21, 1909), Courtesy of Wyoming Newspapers, Wyoming State Library, http://newspapers.wyo.gov.

"With the Motorists," *Natrona County Tribune*, (Casper: July 2, 1914), Courtesy of Wyoming Newspapers, Wyoming State Library, http://newspapers.wyo.gov.

"Wool Men in Large Meeting," *Sheridan Post*, (August 3, 1922), Courtesy of Wyoming Newspapers, Wyoming State Library, http://newspapers.wyo.gov.

"Wool Sale is Failure Here," *Casper Daily Tribune*, (June 16, 1922), Courtesy of Wyoming Newspapers, Wyoming State Library, http://newspapers.wyo.gov.

"Woolgrowers Meet," *Natrona County Tribune*, (Casper: December 5, 1901), Courtesy of Wyoming Newspapers, Wyoming State Library, http://newspapers.wyo.gov.

"Work on Scout Cabin Making Fine Progress," *Casper Daily Tribune*, (November 22, 1921), Courtesy of Wyoming Newspapers, Wyoming State Library, http://news papers.wyo.gov.

"Wyoming," *Salt Lake Herald-Republican*, (Salt Lake City: April 19, 1898), Courtesy of Utah Digital Newspapers, https://newspapers.lib.utah.edu.

"Wyoming Highway Commission Sued," *Denver Post*, (July 15, 1928), Courtesy of Genealogy Bank, https://www.genealogybank.com/doc/newspapers.

"Wyoming Men Given Denver Licenses," *Laramie Republican*, (February 5, 1918), Courtesy of Wyoming Newspapers, Wyoming State Library, http://newspapers .wyo.gov.

"Wyoming Oil News," *Wyoming State Tribune*, (Cheyenne: July 31, 1922), Courtesy of Wyoming Newspapers, Wyoming State Library, http://newspapers.wyo.gov.

"Wyoming Pioneer Gone," *Natrona County Tribune*, (Casper: Sep. 25, 1907), Courtesy of Wyoming Newspapers, Wyoming State Library, http://newspapers.wyo.gov.

"Wyoming Refining Co. Calls in Stock, Will Liquidate all Claims," *Casper Daily Tribune*, (July 15, 1922), Courtesy of Wyoming Newspapers, Wyoming State Library, http://newspapers.wyo.gov.

"Wyoming State Fair," *Bill Barlow's Budget*, (Douglas: July 9, 1902), Courtesy of Wyoming Newspapers, Wyoming State Library, http://newspapers.wyo.gov.

"Wyoming State News," *Guernsey Gazette*, (March 2, 1917), Courtesy of Wyoming Newspapers, Wyoming State Library, http://newspapers.wyo.gov.

"Wyoming State News," *Manville News*, (February 5, 1920), Courtesy of Wyoming Newspapers, Wyoming State Library, http://newspapers.wyo.gov.

"Wyoming Wisps," *Salt Lake Tribune*, (Salt Lake City: May 6, 1895), Courtesy of Utah Digital Newspapers, https://newspapers.lib.utah.edu.

"Young Fish from the Laramie Hatchery," *Laramie Republican*, (July 24, 1908), Courtesy of Wyoming Newspapers, Wyoming State Library, http://newspapers.wyo.gov.

Unpublished and Informally Published Material:

_____, *Mrs. Blackmore Looks Back*, unpublished manuscript, (Douglas: circa 1951), Wyoming Pioneer Memorial Museum.

Blackmore, Robert Bruce, *Letter to Wyoming Pioneer Association Museum, September 16, 1966*, Wyoming Pioneer Memorial Museum, Douglas, Wyoming.

Campbell, Adolphena Gothberg, *Martin J. Gothberg–Notes*, unpublished manuscript, (Casper: circa 1947), Susan Littlefield Haines Collection.

Glass, Jefferson and Haines, Susan Littlefield, *Letter to the Wyoming State Historic Preservation Office*, (Casper: February 6, 2017).

Gothberg, Martin John, *Letter to Edward T. David*, July 2, 1891, David Collection, Casper College Western History Center.

Grant, Duncan Paul, *Memoirs 1881–1975*, unpublished manuscript, (Wheatland: 1975), Robert Grant Family Collection, Grant Ranch, Richeau Creek Rd., Wheatland, Wyoming.

Haines, Susan Littlefield, *Gothberg Family Genealogy*.

Lewis, Rex G., *M. J. Gothberg, Pioneer Range Rider and Rancher*, (WPA Subject #755, June 20, 1936).

Meteorologist, University of Wyoming, Agricultural College Department, Wyoming Experiment Station, Laramie, Wyoming, Meteorology For 1895, and Notes on Climate From 1891–1896, Bulletin No. 27, (Laramie: 1896).

Roles, Karen, *Letter to Jefferson Glass, July 6, 2018*, (Cody: Buffalo Bill Center of the West).

Walker, Hilery, *A History of The Gothberg Ranch*, unpublished manuscript, (Casper: 2003), based on research by Susan Littlefield Haines.

Electronic Media:

Brown, Jim "The Wyoming North and South Railroad, 1923–1935." WyoHistory.org, 2016, accessed May 24, 2019 at https://www.wyohistory.org/encyclopedia /wyoming-north-and-south-railroad-1923-1935.

"Historical Decennial Census Population for Wyoming Counties, Cities, and Towns," http://eadiv.state.wy.us/pop/citypop.htm.

http://www.encyclopedia.chicagohistory.org/pages/11591.html.

http://www.in2013dollars.com/1885-dollars-in-2017?amount=1000000.

http://www.in2013dollars.com/1885-dollars-in-2017?amount=160000.

http://www.wyomingtalesandtrails.com/bessemer.html.

http://www.wyomingtalesandtrails.com/nplatte3.html.

https://chicagology.com/prefire/chicagoillustrated/1866jul02/.

https://en.wikipedia.org/wiki/World_War_I.

https://parasitipedia.net/index.php?option=com_content&view=article&id=2541&Ite mid=2817.

https://www.greatchicagofire.org/landmarks/briggs-house/.

Illinois, County Marriages, 1810–1940, database with images, FamilySearch (https:// familysearch.org/ark:/).

Illinois Deaths and Stillbirths, 1916–1947, database with images, FamilySearch (https:// familysearch.org/ark:/).

Kutac, C., "The Carlisle Cattle Company," (http://www.elbowcreek.com/html/).

Louisiana, New Orleans Passenger Lists, 1820–1945, database with images, FamilySearch (https://familysearch.org/ark:/).

Massachusetts Births, 1841–1915, database with images, *FamilySearch* (https://family search.org/ark:/).

Merriam-Webster.com. Merriam-Webster, n.d. Web.

New Jersey Marriages, 1670–1980, database with images, *FamilySearch* (https://family search.org/ark:/).

New Jersey Marriages, 1678–1985, database with images, *FamilySearch* (https://family search.org/ark:/).

New Jersey State Census, 1905, database with images, *FamilySearch* (https://family search.org/ark:/).

New York Passenger Lists, 1820–1891, database with images, *FamilySearch* (https://fami- lysearch.org/ark:/).

"See Ben Realty Co. v. Martin J. Gothberg, 109 P.2d 455 (Wyo. 1941), Wyoming Supreme Court," Casemine.com, accessed May 28, 2019, https://www.casemine .com/judgement/us/5914cbd4add7b049348057da.

"Trigger (horse)," *Wikipedia, the Free Encyclopedia*, accessed May 28, 2019, (https:// en.wikipedia.org/wiki/Trigger_(horse)).

United States Census, 1880, database with images, *GenealogyBank* (https://genealogy bank.com/#).

United States Census, 1900, database with images, FamilySearch (https://familysearch .org/ark:/).

United States Census, 1910, database with images, FamilySearch (https://familysearch .org/ark:/).

United States Census, 1920, database with images, GenealogyBank (https://genealogy bank.com/#).

United States Census, 1930, database with images, FamilySearch (https://www.family search.org/ark:/).

United States Census, 1930, database with images, GenealogyBank (https://genealogy bank.com/#).

United States Census, 1940, database with images, GenealogyBank (https://genealogy bank.com/#).

United States World War I Draft Registration Cards, 1917–1918, database with images, FamilySearch (https://familysearch.org/ark:/).

Government Documents:

_____, *Official Brand Book of the State of Wyoming*, (State Board of Livestock Commissioners, Cheyenne: July 1, 1919).

Census of Cheyenne, Laramie County, Wyoming, 1880.

Declaration of Intention, Laramie County District Court, Laramie County, Wyoming (Territory), 1885.

Fuller, Robert P., Commissioner of Public Lands, *Appendix to Third Annual Report*, (Cheyenne: September 30, 1910).

Gothberg, Martin J., *Homestead Proof–Testimony of Claimant*, (US Land Office, Douglas, Wyoming: September 4, 1891).

Land Patent, Beaver, Novia S.: #WYWYAA 010644, December 16, 1907.

Land Patent, Clayton, Thomas C.: #WYWYAA 009844, October 6, 1894.

Land Patent, Fuller, Clinton G.: #WYC 0037974, March 9, 1927.

Land Patent, Gothberg, Edwin G.: #WYD 0014103, April 30, 1923.

Land Patent, Gothberg, Edwin G.: #WYC 0053210, July 20, 1937.

Land Patent, Gothberg, Emma L.: #WYC 0051627, October 12, 1931.

Land Patent, Gothberg, Martin J.: #TC 0432-051, January 14, 1899.

Land Patent, Gothberg, Martin J.: #WYWYAA 012082, April 13, 1908.

Land Patent, Gothberg, Martin J.: #WYWYAA 012142, April 29, 1893.

Land Patent, Gothberg, Martin J.: #WYC 0040643, January 4, 1932.

Land Patent, Gothberg, Martin J.: #WYC 0051628, February 9, 1932.

Land Patent, Gothberg, Martin J. and Billingsly, John: #WYWYAA 012079, May 23, 1905.

Land Patent, Gothberg, Martin J. and Clark, John W.: #WYD 0008488, April 29, 1918.

Land Patent, Gothberg, Martin J. and Clarke, William: #WYD 0000337, November 27, 1914.

Land Patent, Gothberg, Martin J. and Deuel, Franklin J.: #WYWYAA 012081, May 25, 1907.

Land Patent, Gothberg, Martin J. and Dorsey, Grandeson: #WYWYAA 012084, October 22, 1908.

Land Patent, Gothberg, Martin J.; Scott, Benjamin F and Scott, John D.: #WYD 0000945 01, November 8, 1909.

Land Patent, Gothberg, Martin J. and Shelton, William: #WYWYAA 012083, September 3, 1908.

Land Patent, Gothberg, Martin J. and Silver, James M.: #WYWYAA 011715, May 25, 1907.

Land Patent, Gothberg, Martin J.; Thompson, Benjamin F.; Houck, George C. and Lake, Ira S.: #WYD 0007686, November 19, 1915.

Land Patent, Gothberg, Martin J.; Gothberg, Mary E.; Blackmore, Walter A.; Blackmore, Minnie A. Jarvis, George W.; Jarvis, O. D.; Weber, Mark U. and Weber, V. S.: #WYD 0029388, September 20, 1922.

Land Patent, Gothberg, Martin J.; Gothberg, Mary E.; Blackmore, Walter A.; Blackmore, Minnie A. Jarvis, George W.; Jarvis, O. D.; Weber, Mark U. and Weber, V. S.: #WYD 0029389, September 20, 1922.

Land Patent, Gothberg, Martin J.; Gothberg, Mary E.; Blackmore, Walter A.; Blackmore, Minnie A. Jarvis, George W.; Jarvis, O. D.; Weber, Mark U. and Weber, V. S.: #WYD 0029390, September 20, 1922.

Land Patent, Gothberg, Martin J.; Gothberg, Mary E.; Blackmore, Walter A.; Blackmore, Minnie A. Jarvis, George W.; Jarvis, O. D.; Weber, Mark U. and Weber, V. S.: #WYD 0029391, December 13, 1922.

Land Patent, Gothberg, Mary E.: #MV 0718-153, January 27, 1908.

Land Patent, Gothberg, Mary E.: #WYD 0008465, March 10, 1922.

Land Patent, Gothberg, Mary E. and Stevens, Charles: #WYWYAA 012017, January 27, 1908.

Land Patent, Gothberg, Walter A.: #WYC 0038879, January 30, 1928.

Land Patent, Harris, John: #WYWYAA 011702, October 22, 1908.

Land Patent, Hawks, Charles M.: #WYD 0004742, July 11, 1912.

Land Patent, Hench, John M.: #WYWYAA 012966, May 1, 1906.

Land Patent, Hines, William P.: #WYWYAA 011416, June 10, 1891.

Land Patent, Lindsey, Noah: #WYWYAA 012866, February 27, 1908.

Land Patent, Madison, George: #WYWYAA 012085, May 17, 1909.

Land Patent, McGraugh, Edward L.: #WYO 180.077, December 27, 1895.

Land Patent, McNelly, Jane B.: #WYWYAA 011712, December 20, 1904.

Land Patent, Ogburn, William I.: #WYWYAA 012150, April 12, 1903.

Land Patent, Parsons, Harry E.: #WYD 0001971, June 26, 1918.

Land Patent, Sanders, Frank A.: #WYWYAA 012062, December 17, 1903.

Land Patent, Spalding, Louis A.: #WYWYAA 012143, August 14, 1893.

Land Patent, Stevens, Charles: #WYWYAA 012015, April 14, 1906.

Land Patent, Stevens, Charles O.: #WYWYAA 015829, July 3, 1902.

Land Patent, Stevens, Charles O.: #WYWYAA 015830, December 1, 1905.

Land Patent, Storrie, Adolphena D.: #WYC 0055034, January 31, 1940.

Land Patent, Storrie, Walter: #WYC 0036847, January 31, 1927.

Land Patent, Storrie, Walter and Lightle, Henry: #WYD 0010437, February 1, 1918.

Land Patent, Swan, Alexander H.: #WYWYAA 007553, October 1, 1878.

Land Patent, Weston, Robert S.: #WYWYAA 012158, June 9, 1910.

Land Patent, Wolf, Marion: #WYWYAA 014500, October 1, 1903.

Natrona County Clerk Abstract Book #1 R77-82 1890-1905.

Natrona County Clerk Abstract Book #2 R77-82 1906-1917.

Sixth Biennial Report of the State Engineer to the Governor of Wyoming for the Years 1901 and 1902, (Laramie: 1902).

Wegemann, Carroll H., *The Salt Creek Oil Field, Wyoming–Bulletin 670*, (Washington: US Government Printing Office, 1918).

Index

Garbutt, A. M., 162, 171
Gardner, Gertrude, 131, 132
Garvey, O. K., 22
gentlemen's resort, grand larceny at,
 131–33
Gokel, Al, 210, 211
Gokel, Charles, 227, 230, 236
Goodnight, Charles, 319n33
Goose Egg Ranch, 5, 6, *19*, 22–24,
 289n10; roundup by, 13, 18–19; *The
 Virginian* and, 83, 229
Gordon, Robert, 59–61, 271–77
Gothberg, Adolphena Dora
 "Sis"(daughter), 61, 116, 168, 177,
 178, 180, *186*, 231–32, 246, 261,
 261; divorce of, 254; at Gothberg
 Ranch, 264–65; homestead of, 254,
 258; marriage of, 184, 186, 187, 189,
 311n30; second marriage of, 258;
 Young People's Good Time Club
 and, 198
Gothberg, Adolphena Spalding (wife),
 24–27, *28, 37*, 50; death of, 37, 39;
 illness of, 35; in New Jersey, 36–38,
 37, 40
Gothberg, Benjamin (brother), 150
Gothberg, Bernard (brother), 115, 179,
 293n18
Gothberg, Dorothy Stitt (daughter-in-
 law), 227, 235, 260–61
Gothberg, Edwin George (son), 56, 116,
 153–54, 170–71, 177, *186*, 195, 213,
 216, 218, 230–31, 242, 257, *261*,
 265; airplane and, 252; automobile
 and, 168–69, 172; marriage of, 203;
 as valedictorian of high school
 class, 172; in World War I, 184; at
 Yellowstone National Park, 173
Gothberg, Edwin Herman (father), 23, 46,
 48, 51–52, 115, 116–17, 172, 179
Gothberg, Edwin K. (grandson), 52–53,
 227, 260, 323n51
Gothberg, Ellen Corcoran (sister-in-law),
 37, 293n18

Gothberg, Emma Loretta (daughter),
 109, *186*, 198, 221, 240, 254–55,
 261, 265
Gothberg, Ernst (brother), 23, 45–46, 51,
 86, 96, 114, 115, 150; automobile
 of, 87–89, *89*, 91, 150; con man and,
 81–82; death of, 151; marriage of,
 288n7
Gothberg, Herman (brother), 65, 75,
 77–78, 96, 115, 150
Gothberg, Jennie Greville (sister-in-law),
 77–78, 96
Gothberg, Lillian (sister). *See* Childs,
 Lillian Gothberg
Gothberg, Margaret Martha Lewis
 (daughter-in-law), 203, 207–8, 209,
 211, 213, 216, 218, 227, 230–31,
 237, 242
Gothberg, Martin John, xi–xii, *1, 28*,
 74–75, 94, 141, 181, *186, 261*;
 alfalfa of, 61; arrival in America,
 1; arrival in Wyoming, 2–3;
 automobile of, 163, *163*, 178,
 216; at Blackmore, W. mayor
 victory party, 232; brands and
 earmarks of, 205, *205*; brick of,
 44; in California, 250, *250*; at
 Carey Brothers Company, 22–25,
 34; cattle of, 23, 58, 77, 86; in
 Chicago, 122–23; on city council,
 183, 192–93; cow/calf operation
 by, 52; at CY Ranch, 55–56; death
 of, xii, 263; at Democratic County
 Convention, 63–64; diphtheria
 of, 34; foreclosure by, 161; forgery
 and, 148–49; at Goose Egg Ranch,
 8–19; grand larceny at gentlemen's
 resort trial and, 131–33; on
 grasshoppers, 84–85; homestead
 of, xi, 31, 34–35, 120, 165–66, 250;
 horse-hobble by, 291n27; horse
 rustling trial and, 98–99; horses
 of, *77*; horse theft from, 157–59;
 to Hot Springs, Arkansas, 145–46;

Hot Springs, Arkansas, 145–46
Houck, Ed, 59
Houck, Georg, 171
Hudspeth, Al, 70
Humble, J. L., 223
Hunton, John, 6
Hupmobile Sales Agency, 184, 244
Huskey, A. J., 133, 147

Ideal Apartments, 162–65, 180, 309n27
Indians, 14–15, *36*
Indian Springs, 266
Industrial Club, 139
influenza, 79–80
Interstate Petroleum Company, 176–77
Iowa-Wyoming Oil Company, 212, 213,
    214–15, 222, 230, 241, 242–43, 245
irrigation, 92–94, 97, 100
Irvin, W. C., 224
Irwin, Ade, 157–59
Irwin, Dallas, 158
Irwin, Edward M., 158
Isle of Pines, 134–35

Jackson, Hugh, 19
Jackson, Mary D. (Hines), 220–21,
    224–25
jailbreak, 106–8, 278–82
Jameson, Frank, 101
Jarvis, George W., 210, 212, 223, 233, 241
Jaycox, 'Billy,' 22, 23
Jeremiah Williams Company, 244
Johnson, Frank, 109
Johnson, Henry, 159
Johnson, John, 27
Johnson, Oliver G., 129
Johnson, Sam, 24
Jones, George, 281
Jones, John A., 284–85
Joshua Stroud, 7
Jourgensen, Charlotte, 177
Jourgensen, George, 177
Jourgensen, Norma, 177, 178
Julian, Anna, 116

Julian, Frank, 93, 94, 116
Julian, Leslie, 116
Julian, Sarah C. "Kate," 101
Julian, Thomas H., 101
Julian, Wilda. *See* Wolf, Wilda Julian
Jupiter Oil Company, 173

Kearns, Tom, 112
Keith, Peter, 60, 271–73
Kelly, Hiram B. "Hi," 3, 18–19
Kennedy, A., 22
Keoughan-Hurst Drilling Company, 210
Kerbert, Coenraad, 283
Kerry, Andy, 9
Kershaw, Frank, 177
Kimball Livestock Company, 111, 114,
    118, 142
King, C. H., 97
King, James, 105
King, John, 148–49
King, Tom, 24
Kinney, Tom, 117
Kittredge, Bill, 144
Knittle, Frank Severn, 311n30
Knittle, Margaret, 178, 231
Kocher, William, 213, 235–36
Koezly, Doretta Helen, 54–55, 114, 191,
    292n35, 313n71
Koezly, Frederick J., 54
Koezly, Teresa Gothberg, 33, *37*, 47–48,
    54–55, 191, 225, 256–57, 288n3,
    292n35, 303n49
Koezly, Theodore Frederick, 33, 288n3,
    292n35
Kreinbuehl, William, 101
Kuhne, Louis, 46, 287n1

Lajeunesse, Charles "Seminoe," 9, 290n18
Lajeunesse, George, 9
Lajeunesse, Joe, 9
Lake, Ira, 171
Lamb, Tom, *8*
Landon, John F., 90, 92, 275–76
Lane, James, 9, 17, 18, 19, 31

About the Author

Jefferson Glass relocated to central Wyoming from Oregon in 1981. He was the founder and former chair of the Evansville Historical Commission, a Certified Local Government (CLG) for the town of Evansville, Wyoming. He later served on the board of directors for the Cadoma Foundation, a non-profit historic preservation organization based in Casper, Wyoming. He is a relentless researcher with specific interests in the Rocky Mountain and Northern Plains regions of the United States. He has written several articles for *Annals of Wyoming, True West Magazine,* and WyoHistory.org.